SURPRISE!

You may be reading the wrong way!

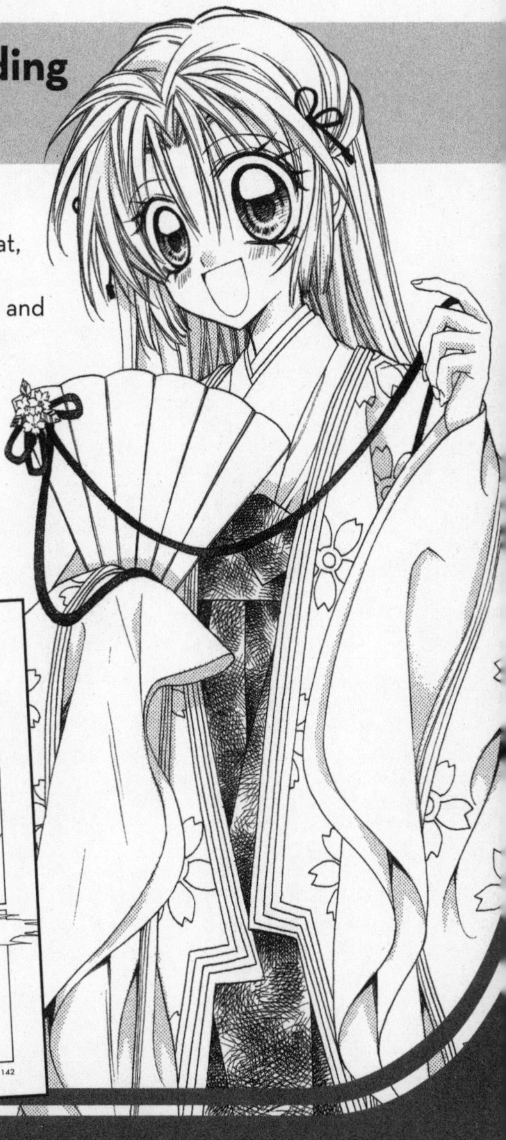

It's true: In keeping with the original Japanese comic format, this book reads from right to left—so action, sound effects, and word balloons are completely reversed. This preserves the orientation of the original artwork—plus, it's fun! Check out the diagram shown here to get the hang of things, and then turn to the other side of the book to get started!

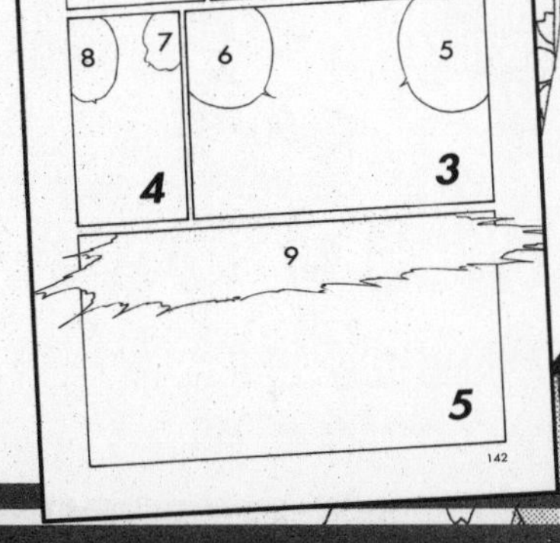
1
2
3
4
1
2
5
6
7
8
3
4
9
5
142

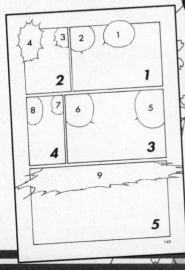

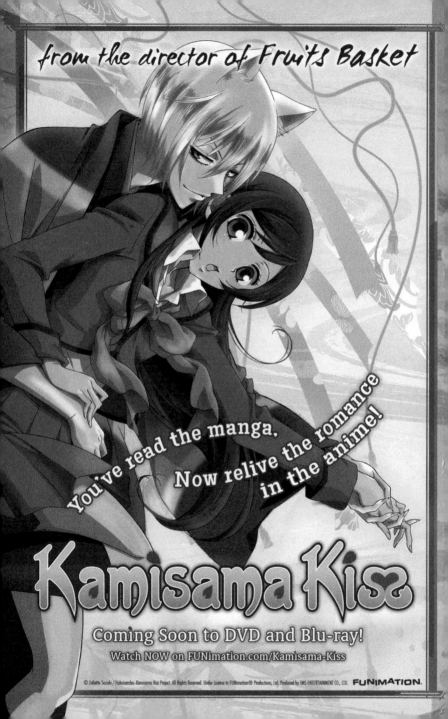

ᴠɪᴢMΛɴGΛ

Read manga anytime, anywhere!

From our newest hit series to the classics you know and love, the best manga in the world is now available digitally. Buy a volume* of digital manga for your:

- iOS device (**iPad®**, **iPhone®**, **iPod®** touch) through the **VIZ Manga app**

- Android-powered device (**phone or tablet**) with a browser by visiting **VIZManga.com**

- **Mac or PC computer** by visiting **VIZManga.com**

VIZ Digital has loads to offer:

- 500+ ready-to-read volumes
- New volumes each week
- FREE previews
- Access on multiple devices! Create a log-in through the app so you buy a book once, and read it on your device of choice!*

To learn more, visit www.viz.com/apps

* Some series may not be available for multiple devices.
Check the app on your device to find out what's available.

Aiwo Utauyori Oreni Oborero! Volume 1 © Mayu SHINJO 2010
DEATH NOTE © 2003 by Tsugumi Ohba, Takeshi Obata/SHUEISHA Inc.
NURARIHYON NO MAGO © 2008 by Hiroshi Shiibashi/SHUEISHA Inc.

viz.com/apps

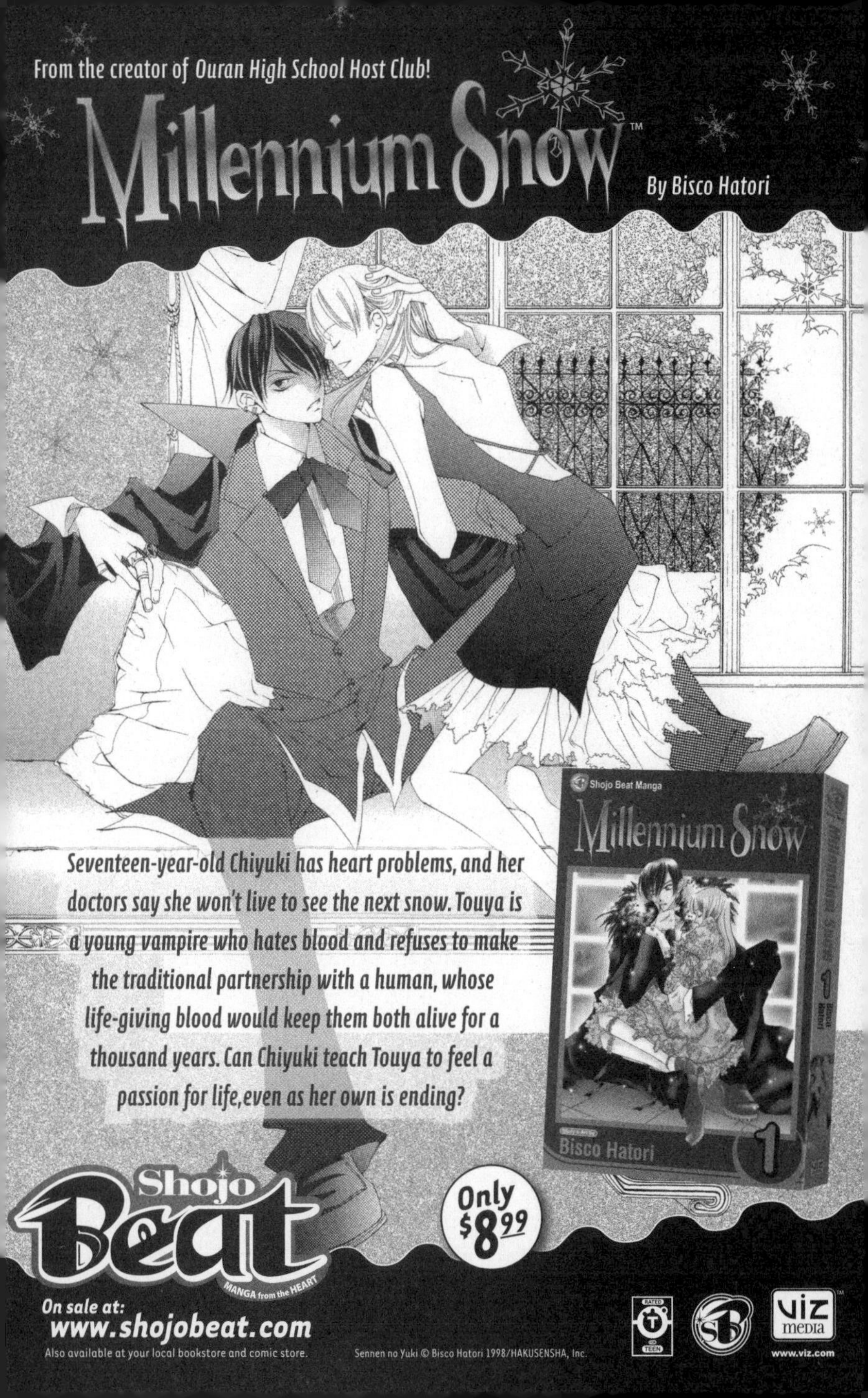
From the creator of Ouran High School Host Club!
Millennium Snow™
By Bisco Hatori
Shojo Beat Manga
Millennium Snow
Bisco Hatori
1
Seventeen-year-old Chiyuki has heart problems, and her doctors say she won't live to see the next snow. Touya is a young vampire who hates blood and refuses to make the traditional partnership with a human, whose life-giving blood would keep them both alive for a thousand years. Can Chiyuki teach Touya to feel a passion for life, even as her own is ending?
Only $8.99
Shojo Beat
MANGA from the HEART
On sale at:
www.shojobeat.com
Also available at your local bookstore and comic store.
Sennen no Yuki © Bisco Hatori 1998/HAKUSENSHA, Inc.
RATED T TEEN
viz media
www.viz.com

Sakura Hime: The Legend of Princess Sakura
Volume 10
Shojo Beat Edition

STORY AND ART BY
Arina Tanemura

Translation & Adaptation/Tetsuichiro Miyaki
Touch-up Art & Lettering/Inori Fukuda Trant
Design/Sam Elzway
Editor/Nancy Thistlethwaite

SAKURA-HIME KADEN © 2008 by Arina Tanemura
All rights reserved.
First published in Japan in 2008 by SHUEISHA Inc., Tokyo.
English translation rights arranged by SHUEISHA Inc.

Printed in the U.S.A.

Published by VIZ Media, LLC
P.O. Box 77010
San Francisco, CA 94107

10 9 8 7 6 5 4 3 2 1
First printing, June 2013

ENJU

Princess Sakura's older brother. He used to be kind, but he hates humans now and hopes to reinstate the moon kingdom.

PRINCESS YURI

The daughter of the Minister of the Right. She's accepted Fujimurasaki's marriage proposal.

MAIMAI

Enju's follower who values beauty above all else.

SAKURA HIME
The Legend of Princess Sakura

Story Thus Far

Heian era. Princess Sakura, granddaughter to Princess Kaguya, has the power to wield the mystic sword Chizakura. Under orders from the Emperor, she must hunt down youko with Aoba, her betrothed.

Enju, whom she thought dead, kidnaps her and takes her to Shura Yugenden. While under Enju's control, Sakura kills Ukyo with her sword Chizakura. Sakura also learns of Enju's plans to resurrect Princess Kaguya and decides to part ways with him. She escapes Shura Yugenden with the help of Aoba, Fujimurasaki, and her other allies who came to save her.

Sakura and Aoba return to their daily lives, but Sakura discovers that Aoba will have a life cut short, just like Asagiri. Sakura is determined to take responsibility for his fate and begins her search for Enju once again.

Hayate comes across Rurijo by chance, and after spending some time with her, he begins to grow fond of her. However, on the night with a full moon, Rurijo attacks the human Hayate with moon spring water. She claims she's following Enju's orders...?!

Sakura Hime
The Legend of Princess Sakura

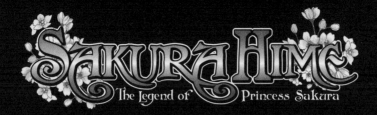

Contents

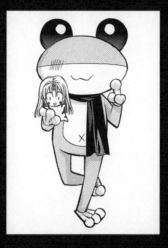

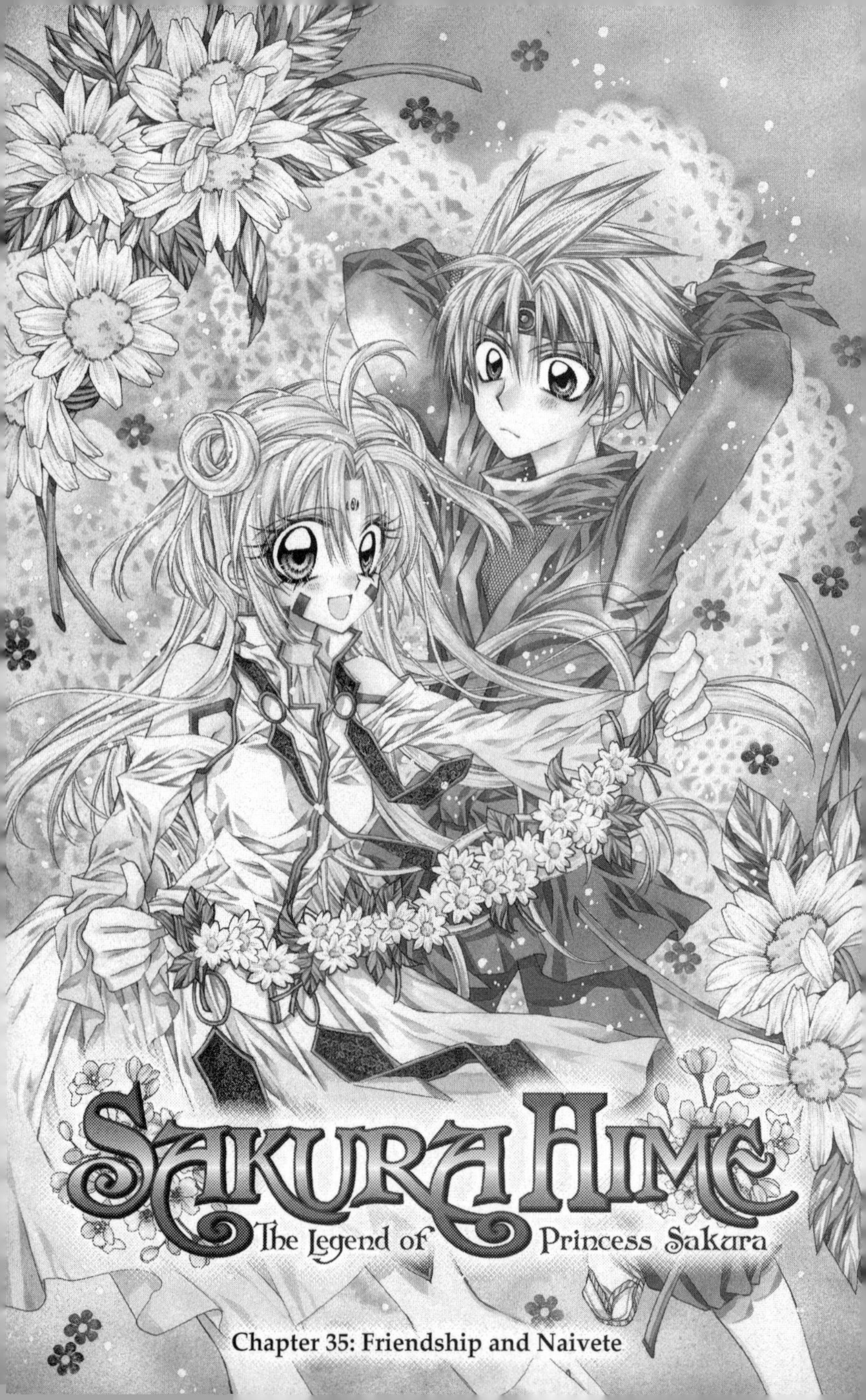
SAKURA HIME
The Legend of Princess Sakura
Chapter 35: Friendship and Naivete

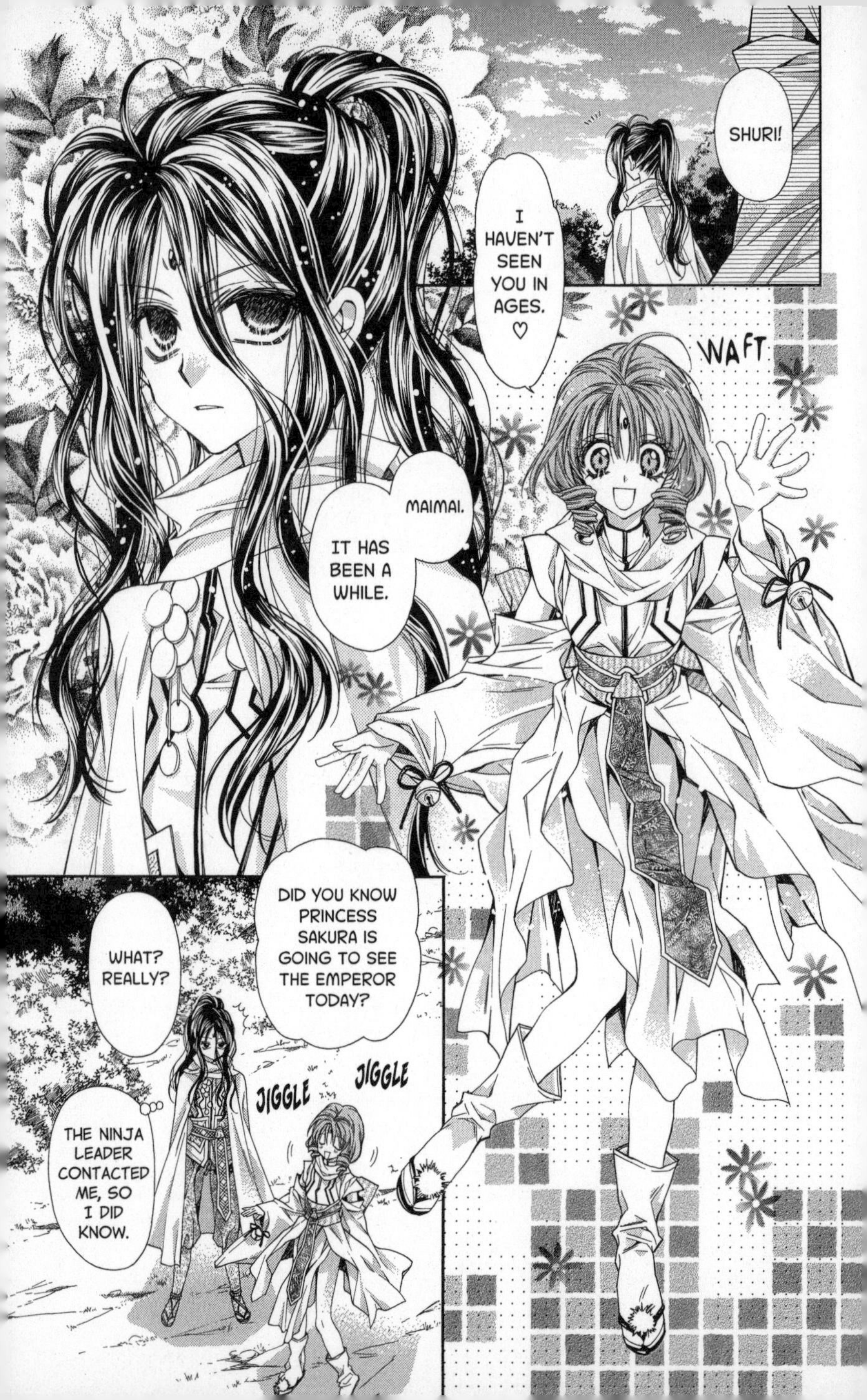
SHURI!
I HAVEN'T SEEN YOU IN AGES. ♡
WAFT
MAIMAI.
IT HAS BEEN A WHILE.
DID YOU KNOW PRINCESS SAKURA IS GOING TO SEE THE EMPEROR TODAY?
WHAT? REALLY?
JIGGLE
JIGGLE
THE NINJA LEADER CONTACTED ME, SO I DID KNOW.

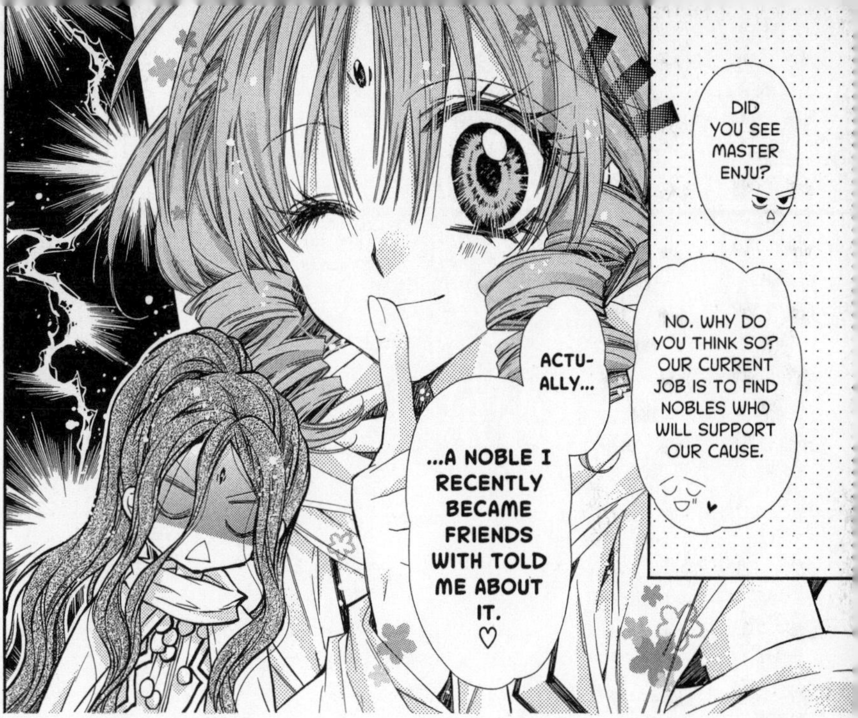
DID YOU SEE MASTER ENJU?
NO. WHY DO YOU THINK SO? OUR CURRENT JOB IS TO FIND NOBLES WHO WILL SUPPORT OUR CAUSE.
ACTU-ALLY...
...A NOBLE I RECENTLY BECAME FRIENDS WITH TOLD ME ABOUT IT. ♡

Chapter 35: Friendship and Naivete

※ I'm giving away the story.

The chapter title page illustration is of Hayate and Rurijo. Chapter 33 (in volume 9) had the frog and naked Rurijo in it, so I decided to go with the human version of Hayate and give Rurijo a new outfit for a refreshing atmosphere.♥ I am very fond of this chapter. Originally, the Hayate and Rurijo arc was meant to end in a chapter or two, but I found myself flooded with new ideas when I started working on it. That's why it has ended up being so long... It may even continue on a bit more. I received many comments from fans telling me, "We can't wait to see what happens, ;" so please look forward to it!

Now we have a string of crushes: Shuri → Kohaku → Hayate → Rurijo → Enju → Sakura (Well, "Enju → Sakura" isn't exactly a crush). As the author, I personally think that their crushes are all pretty hopeless... (KOFF KOFF) I have already thought about how everything will turn out, but I don't really know until I draw it. Why don't you try to predict it? How do you think their relationships will turn out? (^ω^)/
Personally... I'm rooting for Rurijo.

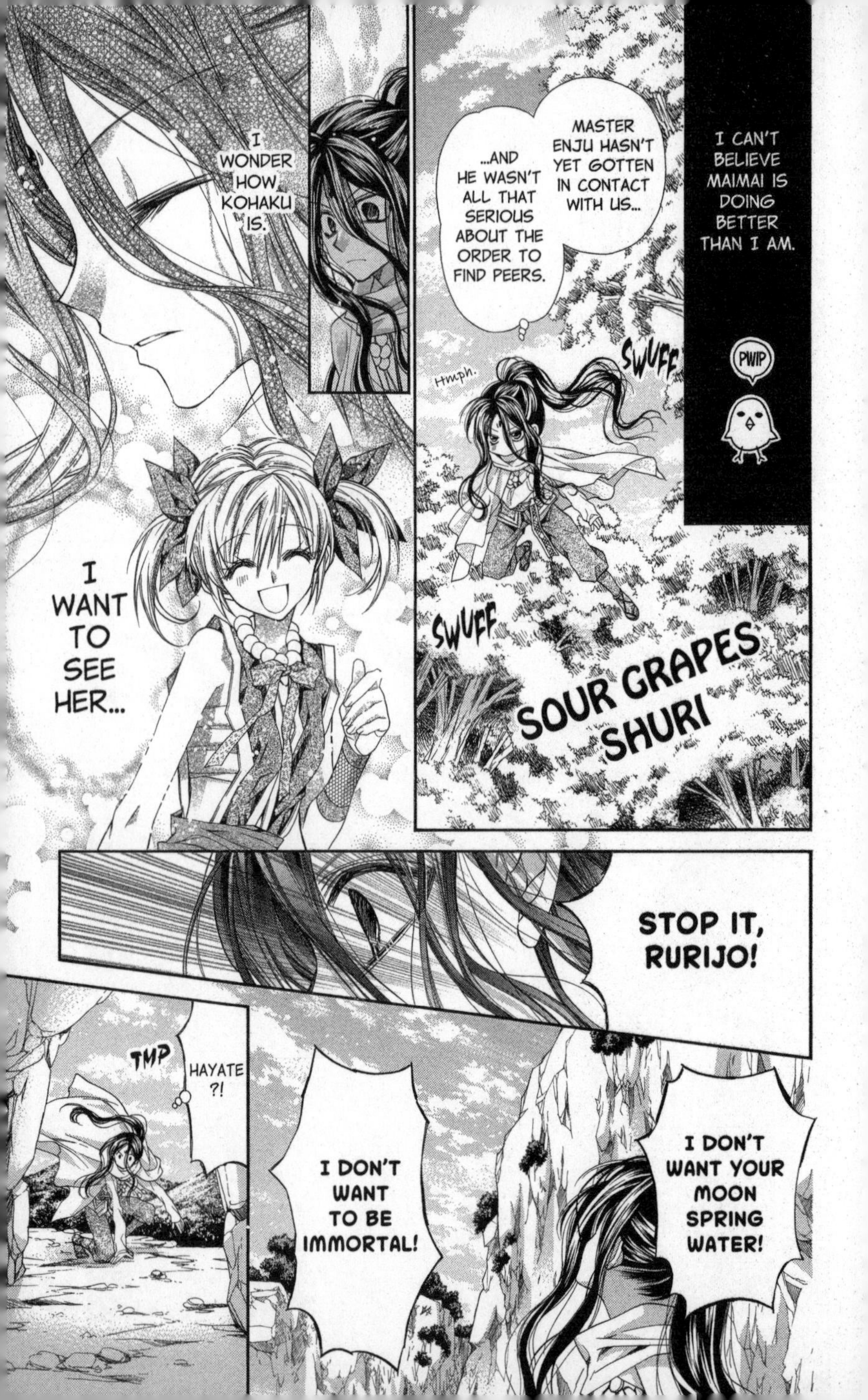
I CAN'T BELIEVE MAIMAI IS DOING BETTER THAN I AM.
PWIP
MASTER ENJU HASN'T YET GOTTEN IN CONTACT WITH US...
...AND HE WASN'T ALL THAT SERIOUS ABOUT THE ORDER TO FIND PEERS.
SWUFF
Hmph.
SWUFF
SOUR GRAPES SHURI
I WONDER HOW KOHAKU IS.
I WANT TO SEE HER...
STOP IT, RURIJO!
I DON'T WANT YOUR MOON SPRING WATER!
I DON'T WANT TO BE IMMORTAL!
TMP
HAYATE?!

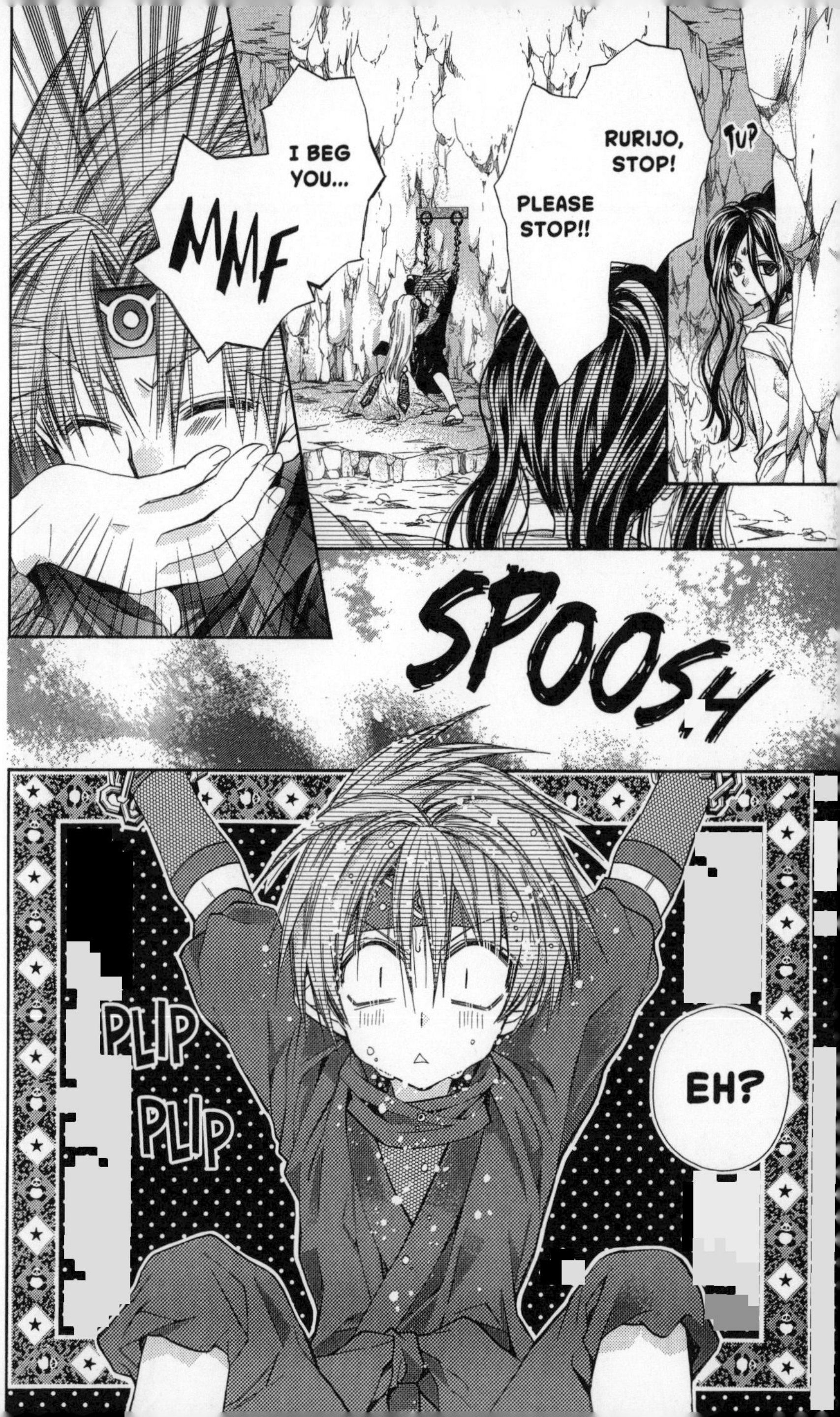
TUP
RURIJO, STOP!
PLEASE STOP!!
I BEG YOU...
MMF
SPOOSH
EH?
PLIP
PLIP

Hello, hello.

Hello. ☺ This is Arina Tanemura! I bring you volume 10 of *Sakura Hime: The Legend of Princess Sakura.* ♪ Rurijo and Hayate (frog version) are on the cover this volume. It's rare for the cover illustration of *Sakura Hime* to be a close-up.

But I love these two (this pairing?), so I'm glad I was able to do a cover illustration with them.

Well then, let's start volume 10. ♪

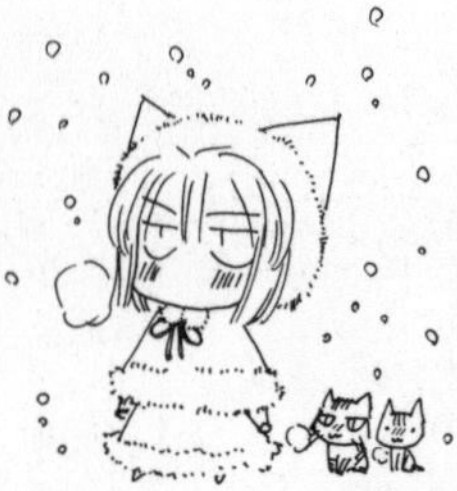

I love winter.

It's quiet...

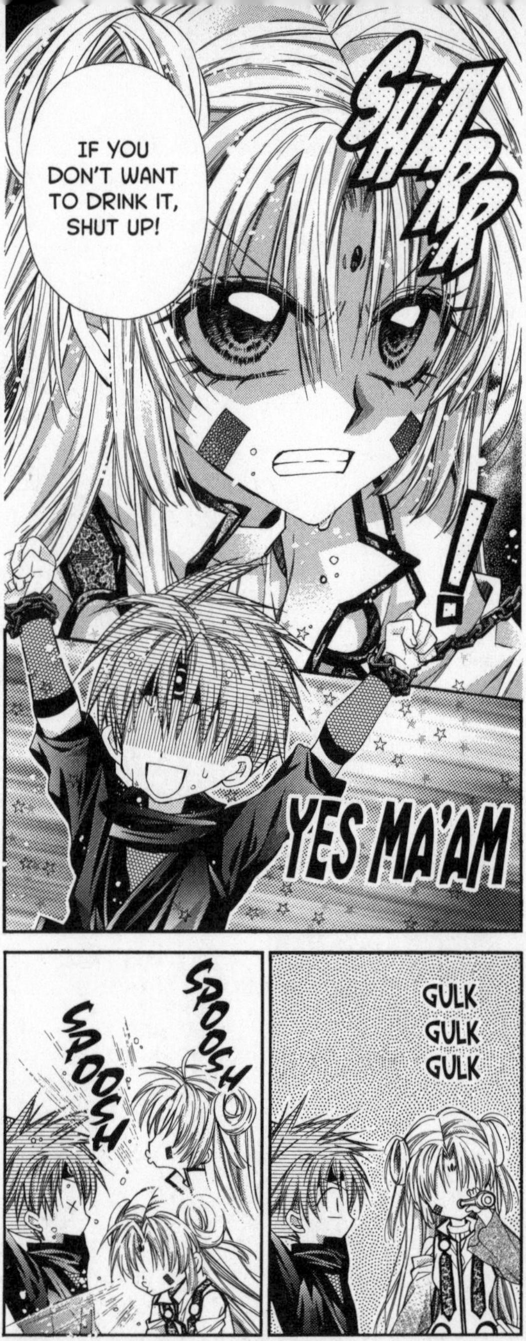
IF YOU DON'T WANT TO DRINK IT, SHUT UP!
SHARR!
YES MA'AM
GULK GULK GULK
SPOOOSH
SPOOOSH

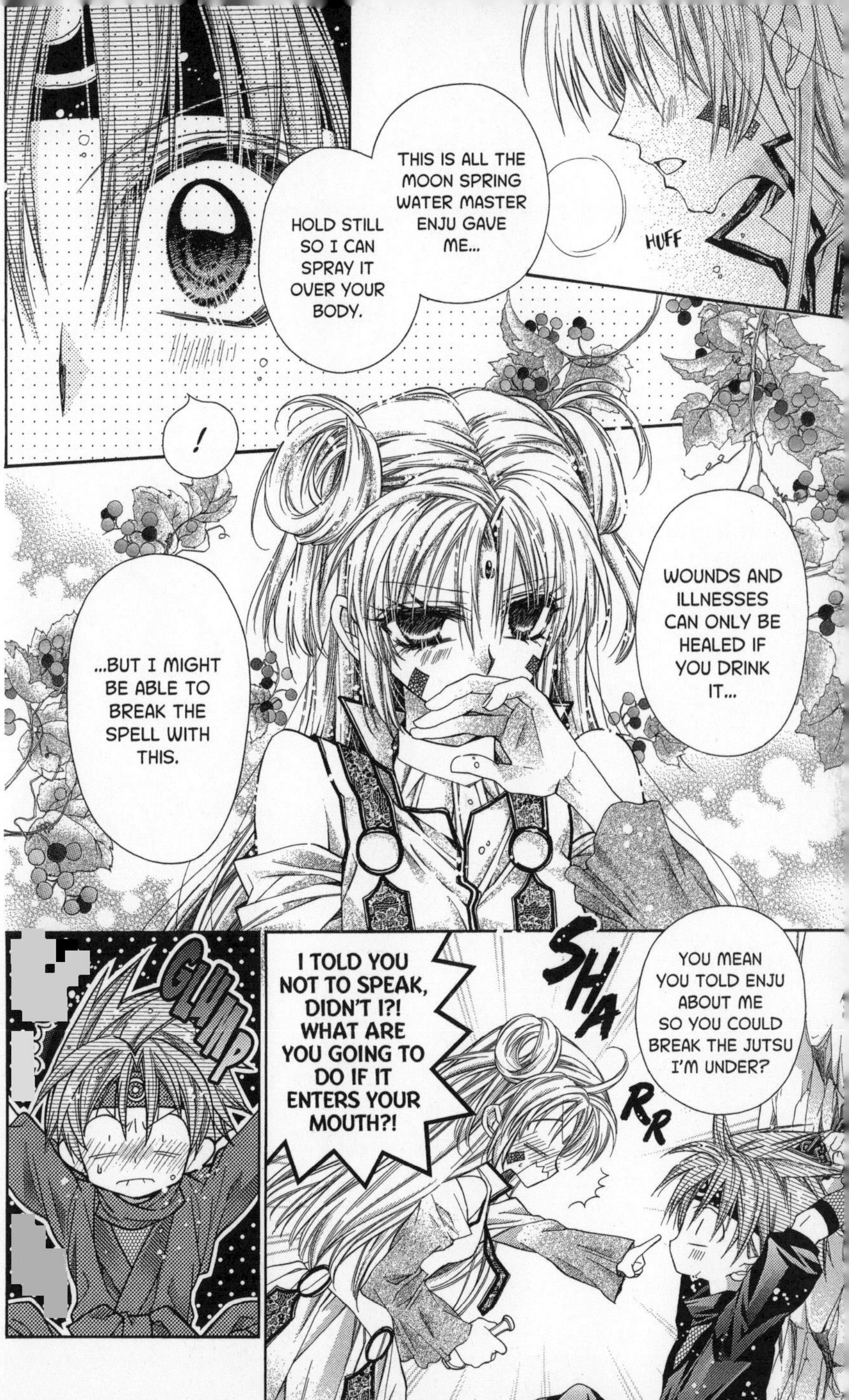
HUFF
THIS IS ALL THE MOON SPRING WATER MASTER ENJU GAVE ME...
HOLD STILL SO I CAN SPRAY IT OVER YOUR BODY.
!
WOUNDS AND ILLNESSES CAN ONLY BE HEALED IF YOU DRINK IT...
...BUT I MIGHT BE ABLE TO BREAK THE SPELL WITH THIS.
YOU MEAN YOU TOLD ENJU ABOUT ME SO YOU COULD BREAK THE JUTSU I'M UNDER?
SHARR
I TOLD YOU NOT TO SPEAK, DIDN'T I?! WHAT ARE YOU GOING TO DO IF IT ENTERS YOUR MOUTH?!
GLUMP

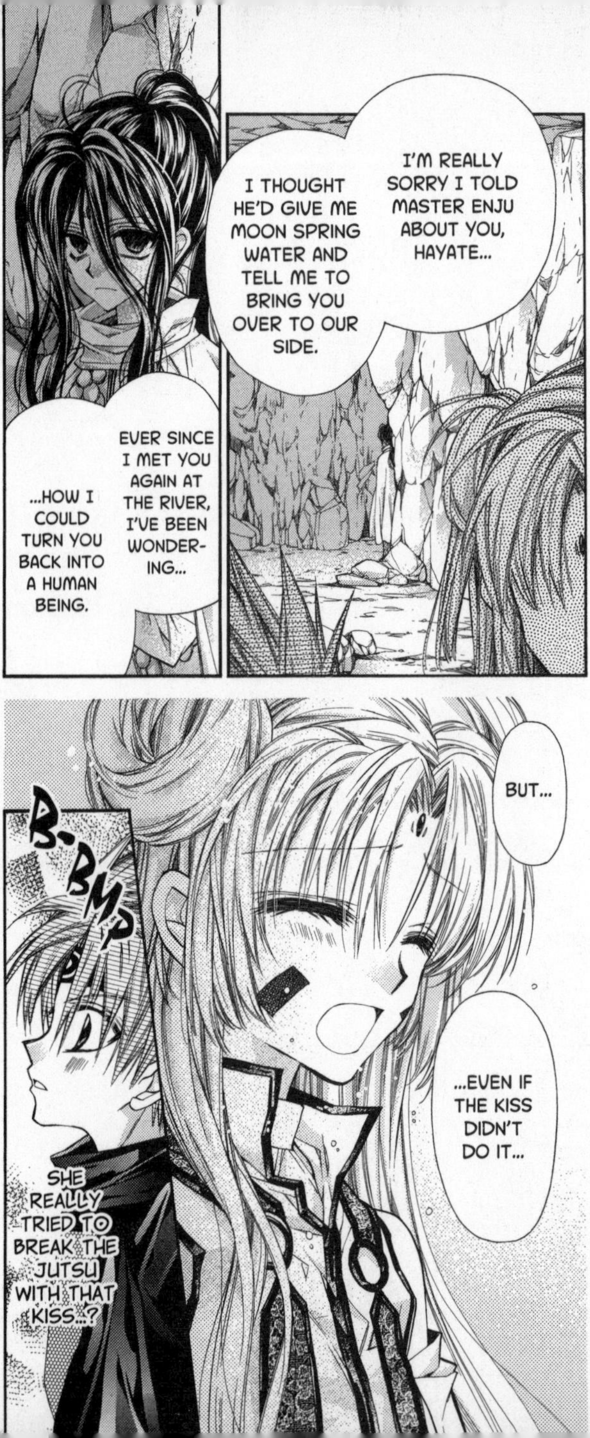
I'M REALLY SORRY I TOLD MASTER ENJU ABOUT YOU, HAYATE...
I THOUGHT HE'D GIVE ME MOON SPRING WATER AND TELL ME TO BRING YOU OVER TO OUR SIDE.
EVER SINCE I MET YOU AGAIN AT THE RIVER, I'VE BEEN WONDER-ING...
...HOW I COULD TURN YOU BACK INTO A HUMAN BEING.
BUT...
...EVEN IF THE KISS DIDN'T DO IT...
B-BMP
SHE REALLY TRIED TO BREAK THE JUTSU WITH THAT KISS...?

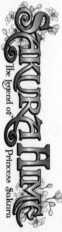

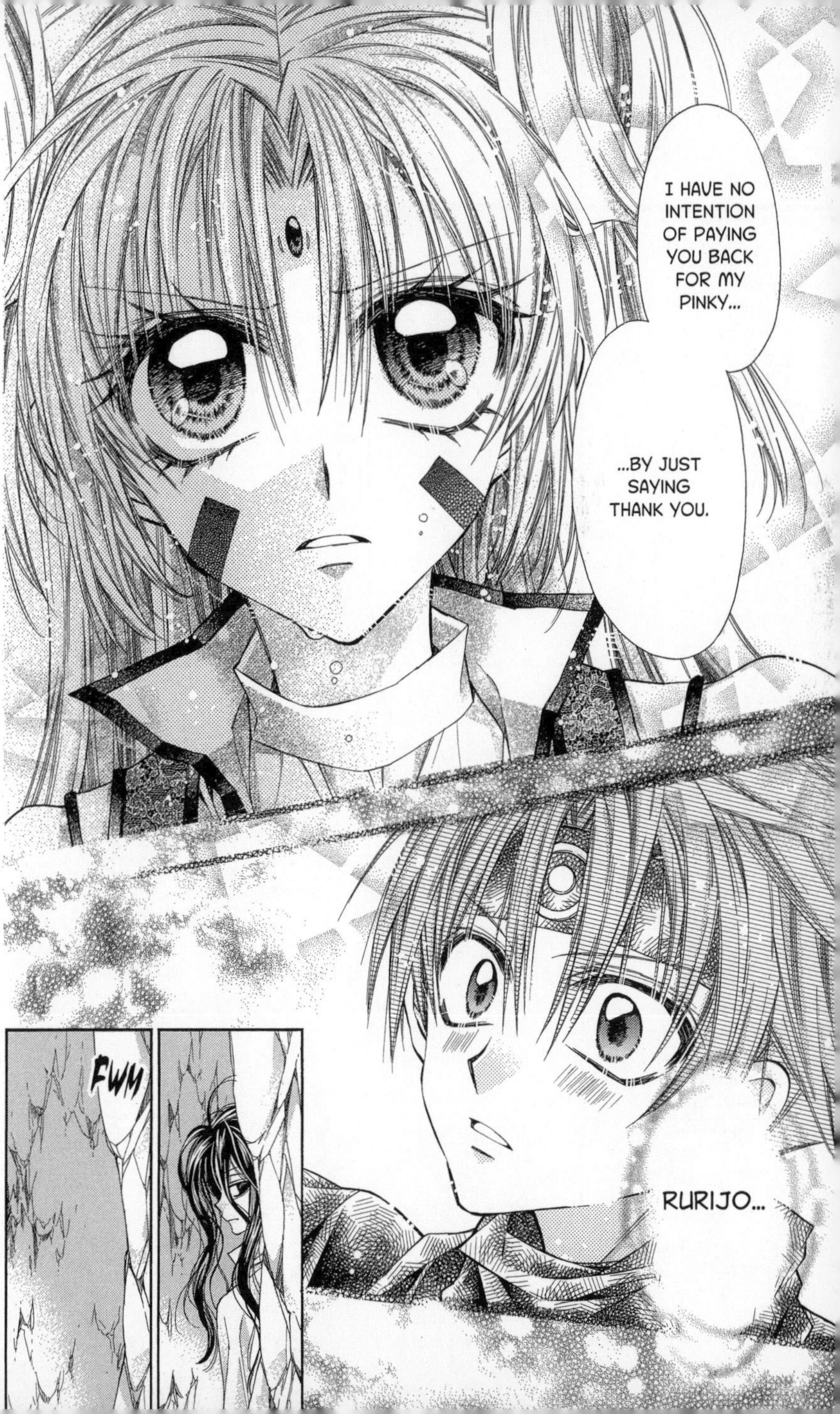
I HAVE NO INTENTION OF PAYING YOU BACK FOR MY PINKY...
...BY JUST SAYING THANK YOU.
RURIJO...
FWM

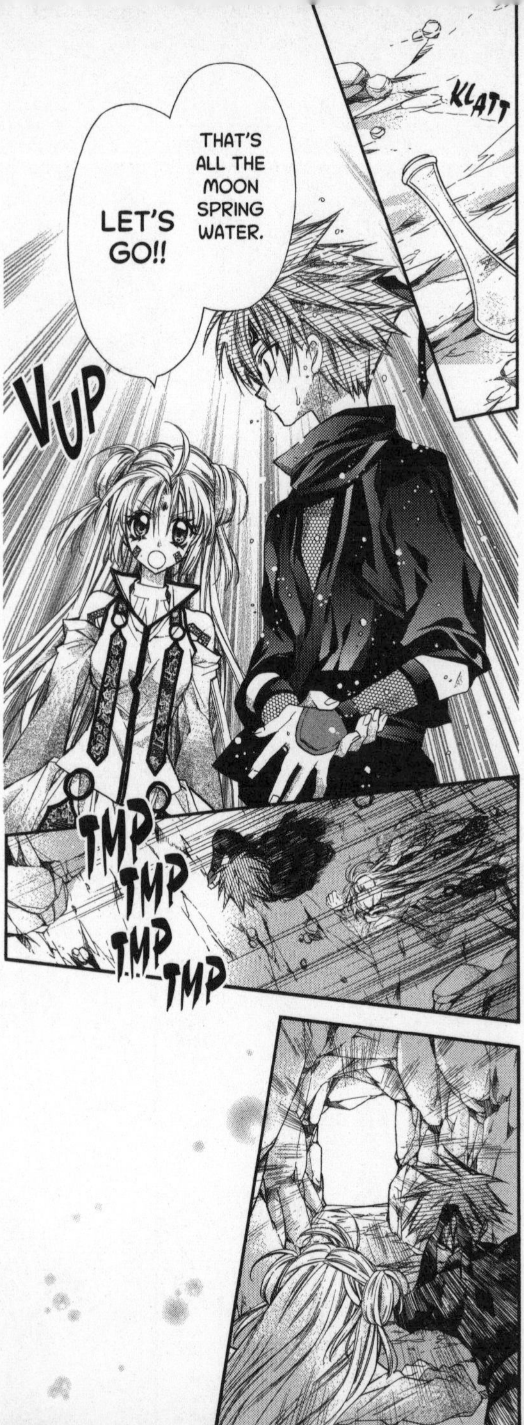
KLATT
THAT'S ALL THE MOON SPRING WATER.
LET'S GO!!
VUP
TMP TMP TMP TMP

I went to Hokkaido.

I went to Hokkaido at the end of November. ♪
This was, um, the fourth time I've been there including for work, I think? It was my second time for a personal trip. ✓
And this time! I took the deluxe suite in room 1 of the first carriage of the Cassiopeia sleeper train! I rode the Cassiopeia the last time too, but this was my first time having the suite!

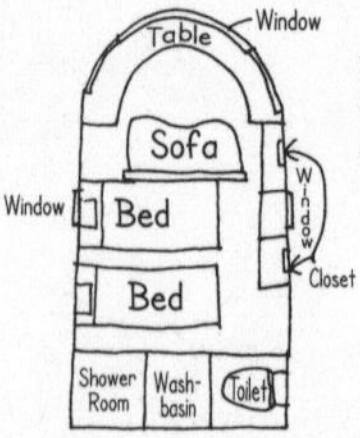
Table
Window
Sofa
Window
Window
Bed
Bed
Closet
Shower Room
Wash-basin
Toilet

This is what the room was like.

It was so pretty. ✧ It's just like an ordinary hotel! And I wanted to keep sitting on the sofa forever. As soon as the train departed, I received a drink service of whiskey, wine, sake, soft drinks, and water! But both myco-chan (whom I went with) and I could not drink alcohol, so it went to waste. (laugh) But the orange juice was good! It was said the shower would run for 18 minutes. (I think they count the time the water is running). My showers take only 7 minutes and 20 seconds, so it was a piece of cake! We departed from Ueno station and headed for Toya. We got onto the train at 4 o'clock and arrived around 7 a.m. the next day. I would like to talk about our trip next!

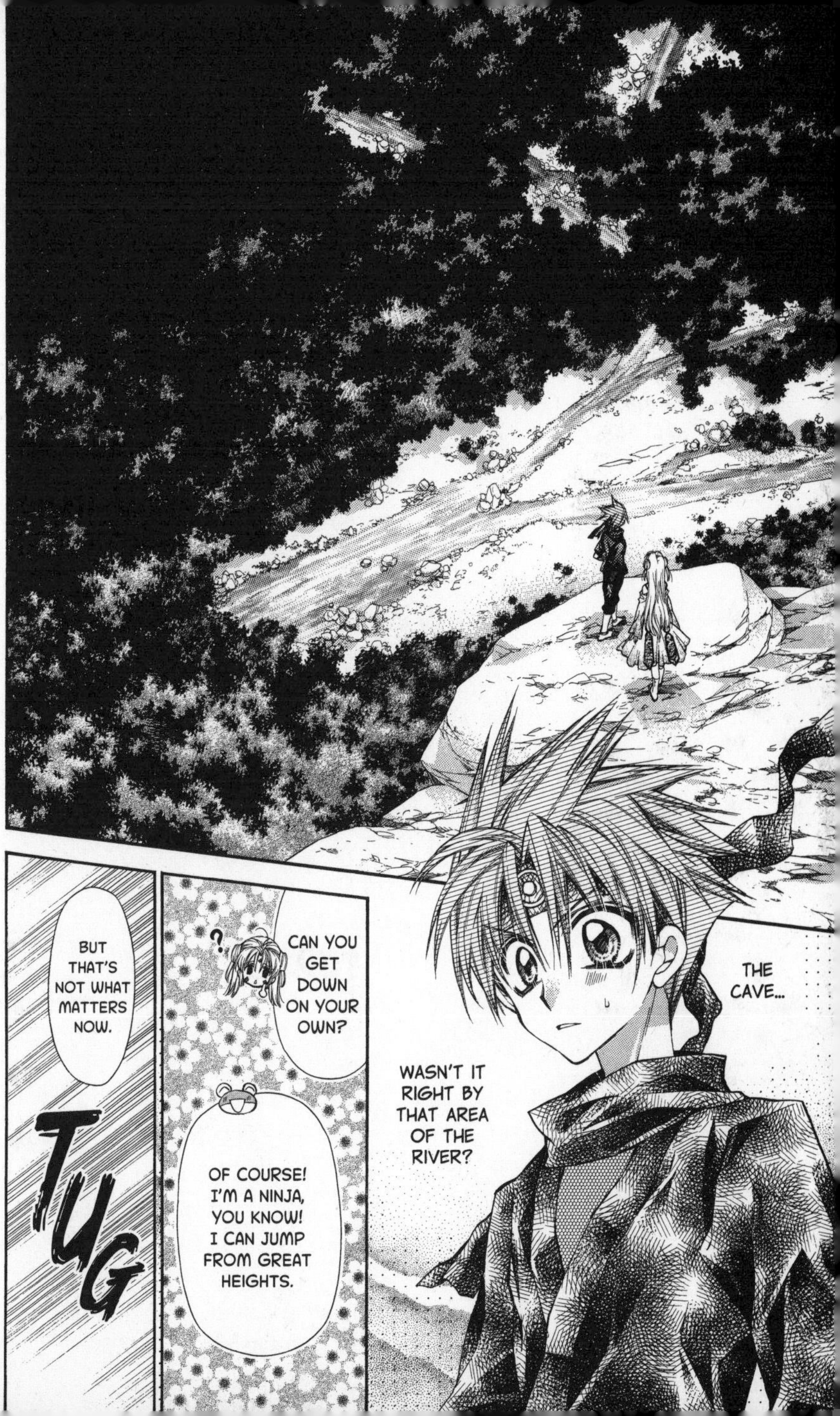
THE CAVE...
WASN'T IT RIGHT BY THAT AREA OF THE RIVER?
?
CAN YOU GET DOWN ON YOUR OWN?
OF COURSE! I'M A NINJA, YOU KNOW! I CAN JUMP FROM GREAT HEIGHTS.
BUT THAT'S NOT WHAT MATTERS NOW.
TUG

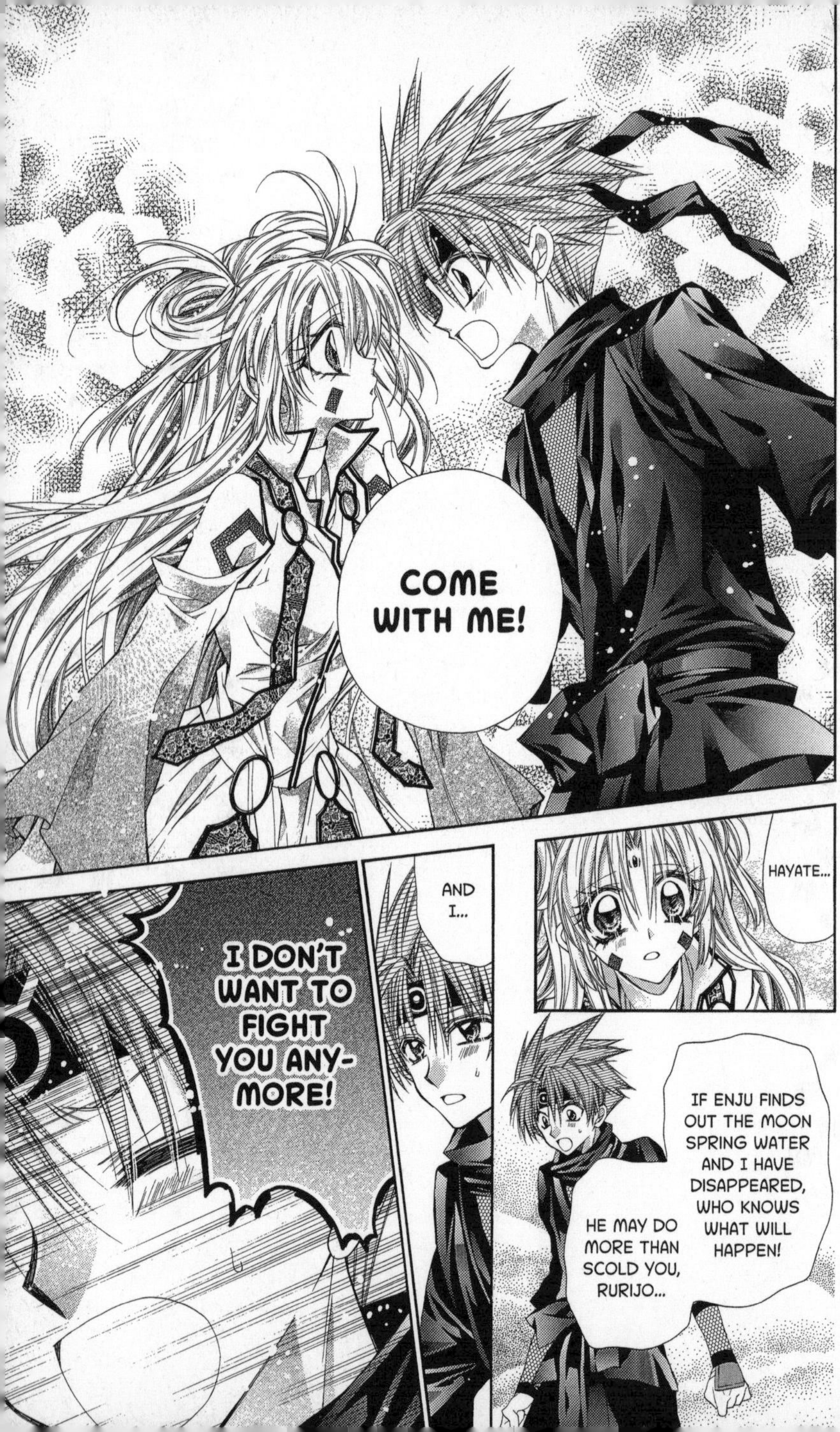
COME WITH ME!
HAYATE...
IF ENJU FINDS OUT THE MOON SPRING WATER AND I HAVE DISAPPEARED, WHO KNOWS WHAT WILL HAPPEN!
HE MAY DO MORE THAN SCOLD YOU, RURIJO...
AND I...
I DON'T WANT TO FIGHT YOU ANY-MORE!

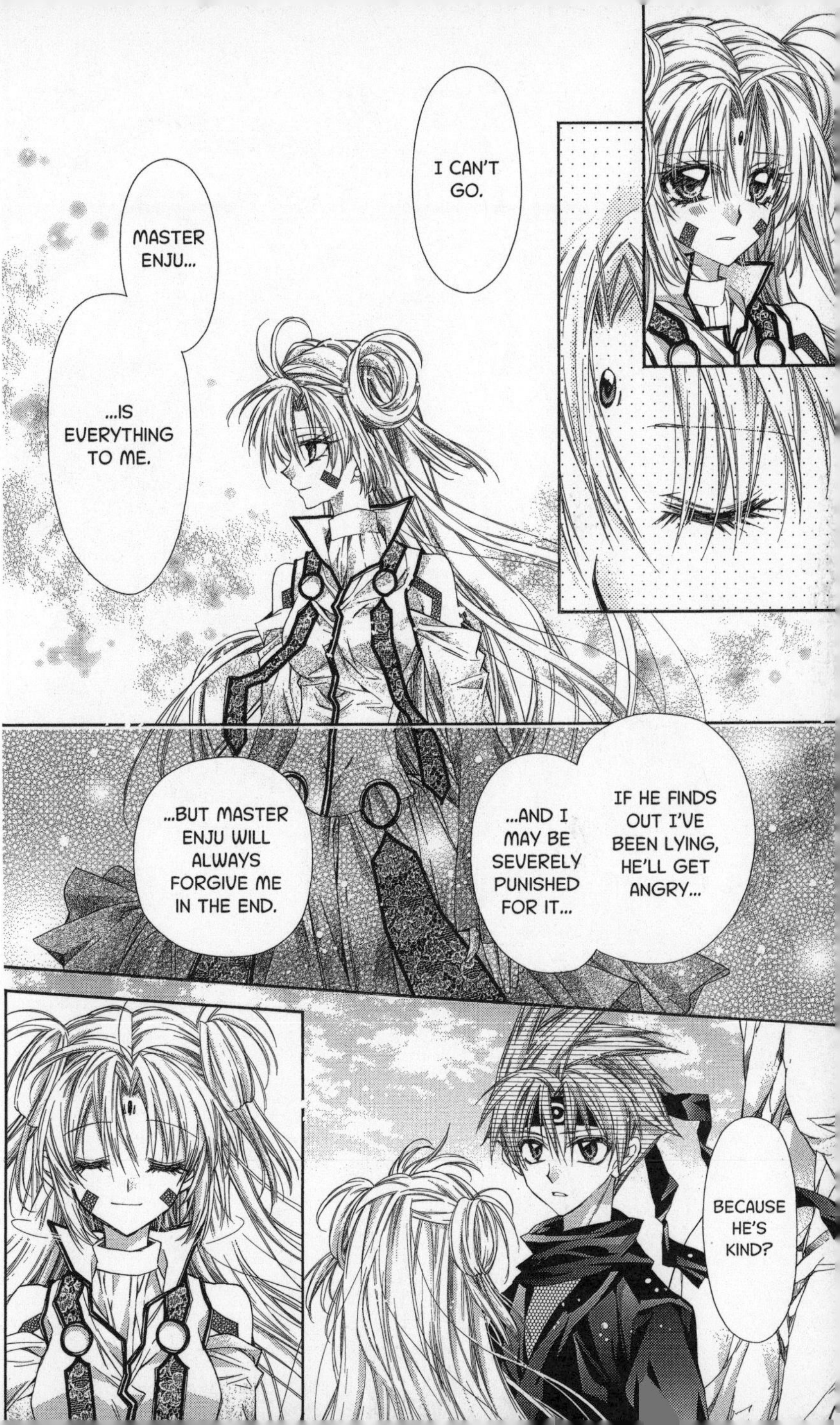
I CAN'T GO.
MASTER ENJU...
...IS EVERYTHING TO ME.
IF HE FINDS OUT I'VE BEEN LYING, HE'LL GET ANGRY...
...AND I MAY BE SEVERELY PUNISHED FOR IT...
...BUT MASTER ENJU WILL ALWAYS FORGIVE ME IN THE END.
BECAUSE HE'S KIND?

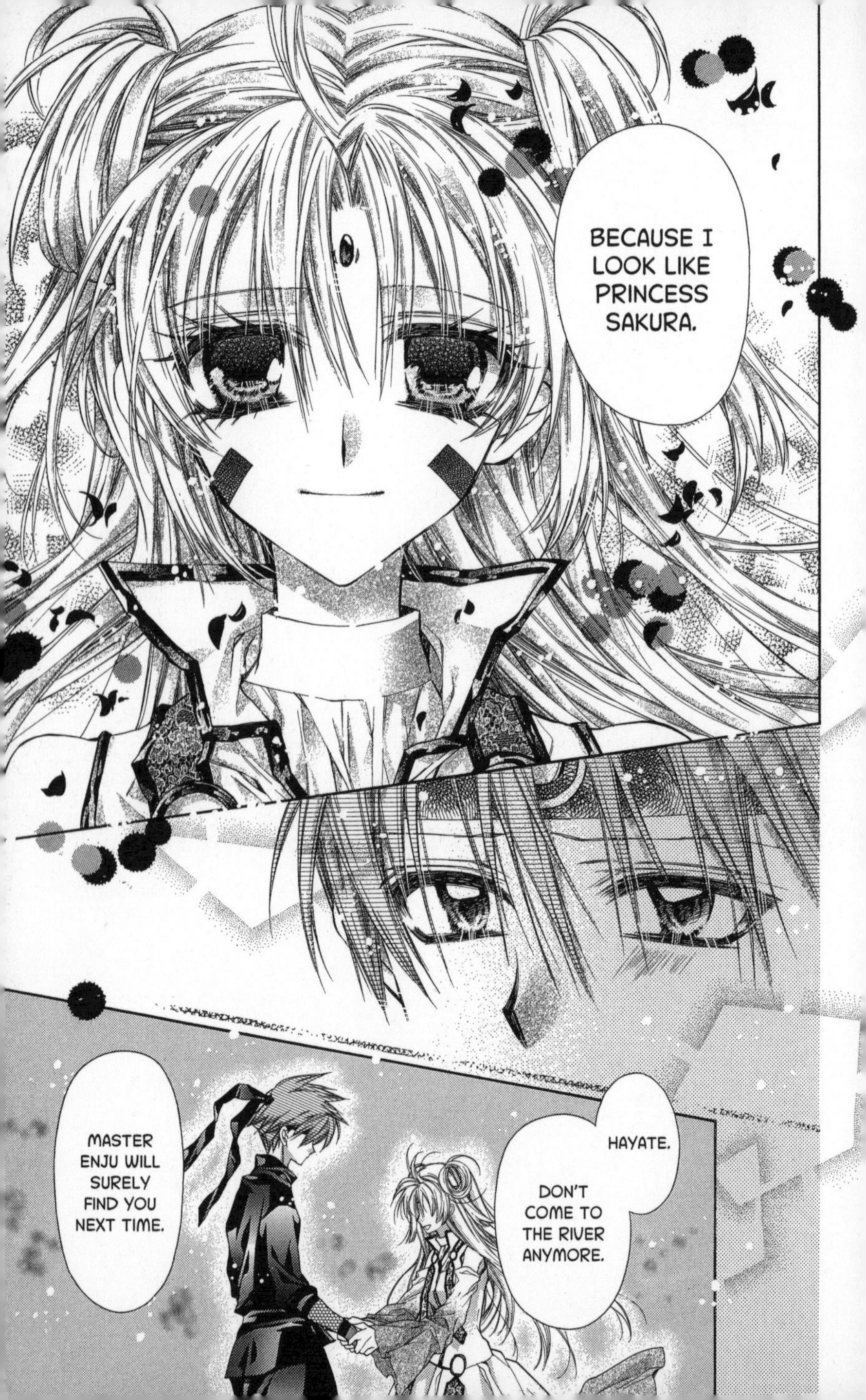
BECAUSE I LOOK LIKE PRINCESS SAKURA.
HAYATE.
DON'T COME TO THE RIVER ANYMORE.
MASTER ENJU WILL SURELY FIND YOU NEXT TIME.

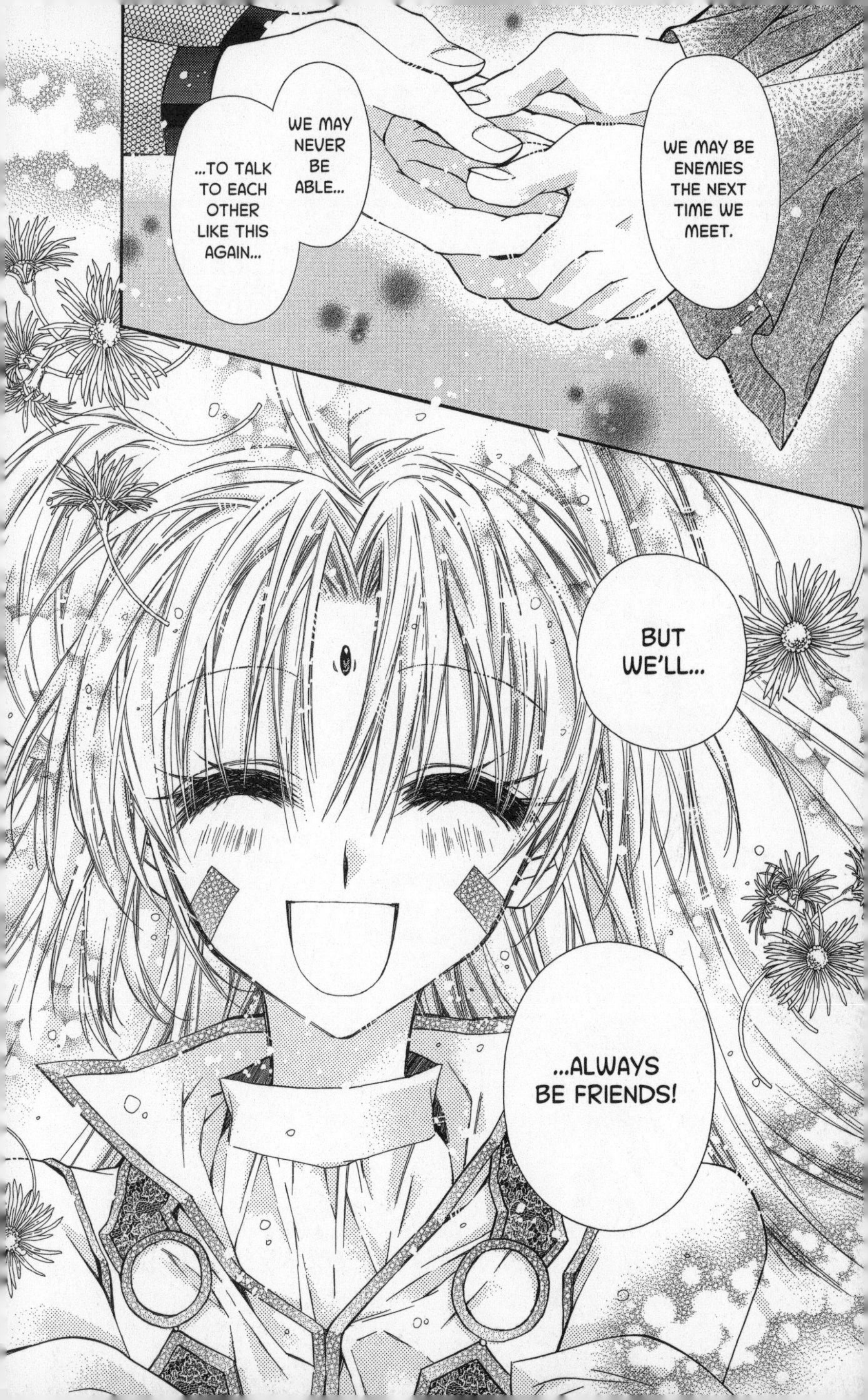
WE MAY BE ENEMIES THE NEXT TIME WE MEET.
WE MAY NEVER BE ABLE...
...TO TALK TO EACH OTHER LIKE THIS AGAIN...
BUT WE'LL...
...ALWAYS BE FRIENDS!

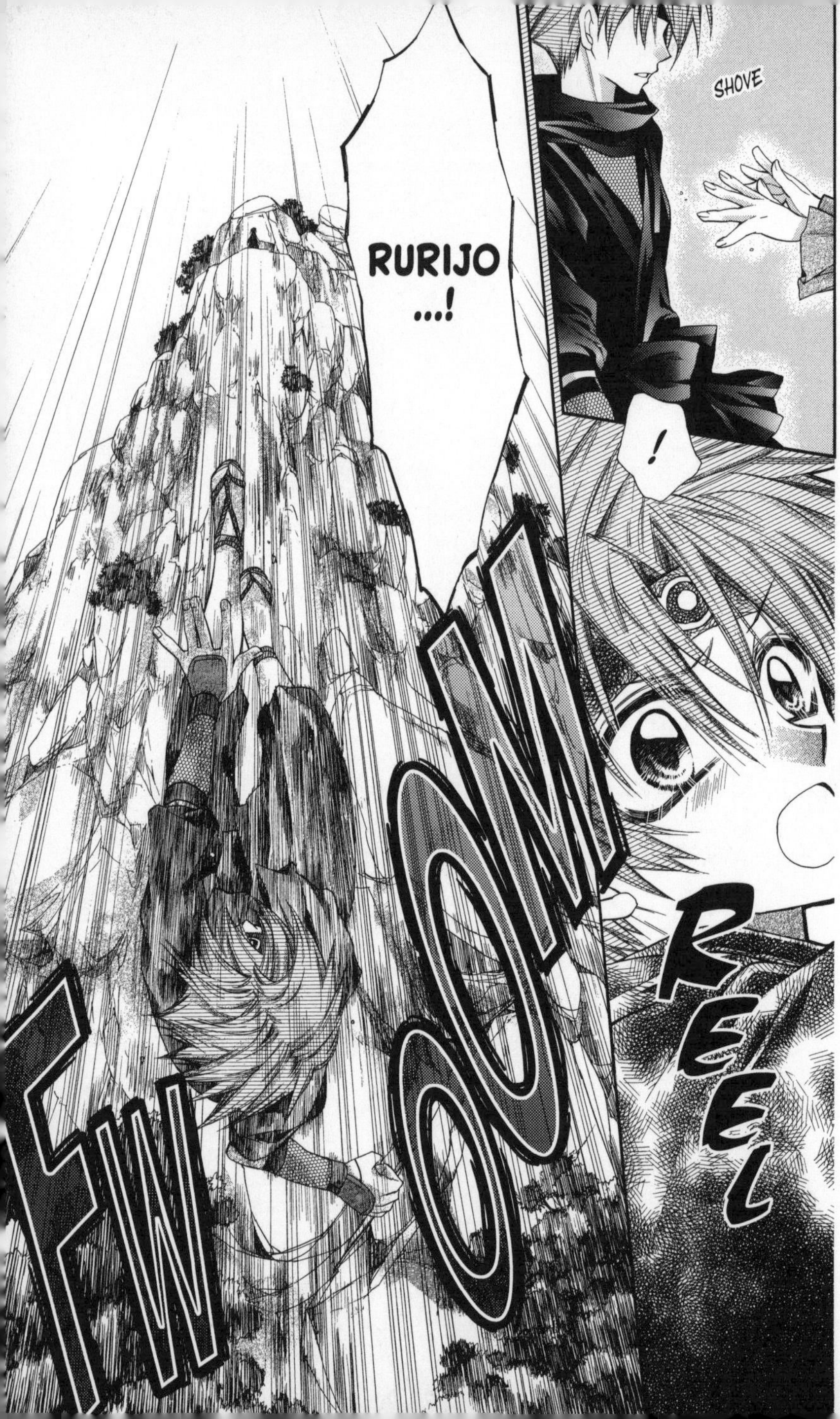
SHOVE
!
REEL
RURIJO ...!
FWOOM

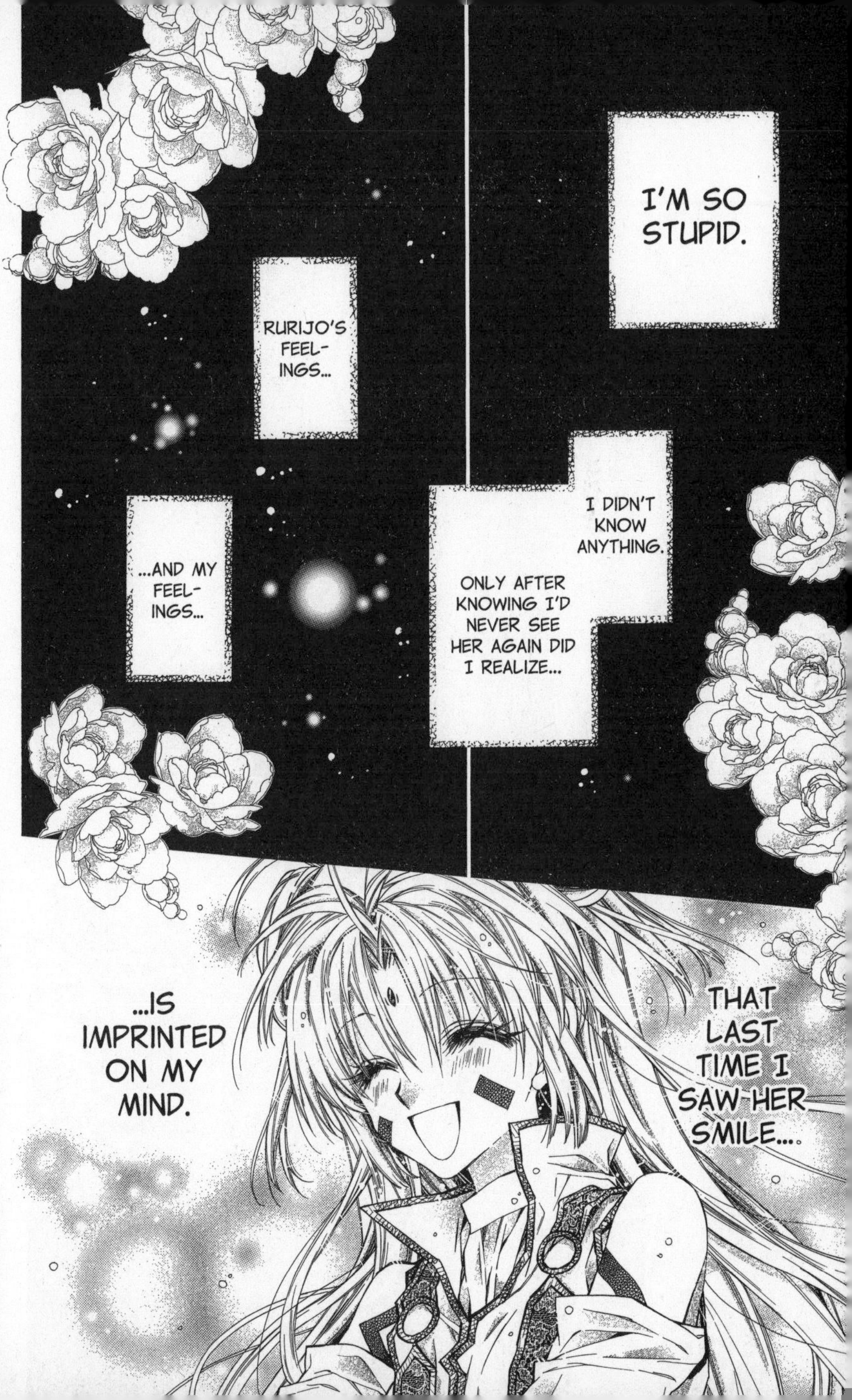
I'M SO STUPID.
I DIDN'T KNOW ANYTHING.
ONLY AFTER KNOWING I'D NEVER SEE HER AGAIN DID I REALIZE...
RURIJO'S FEEL-INGS...
...AND MY FEEL-INGS...
THAT LAST TIME I SAW HER SMILE...
...IS IMPRINTED ON MY MIND.

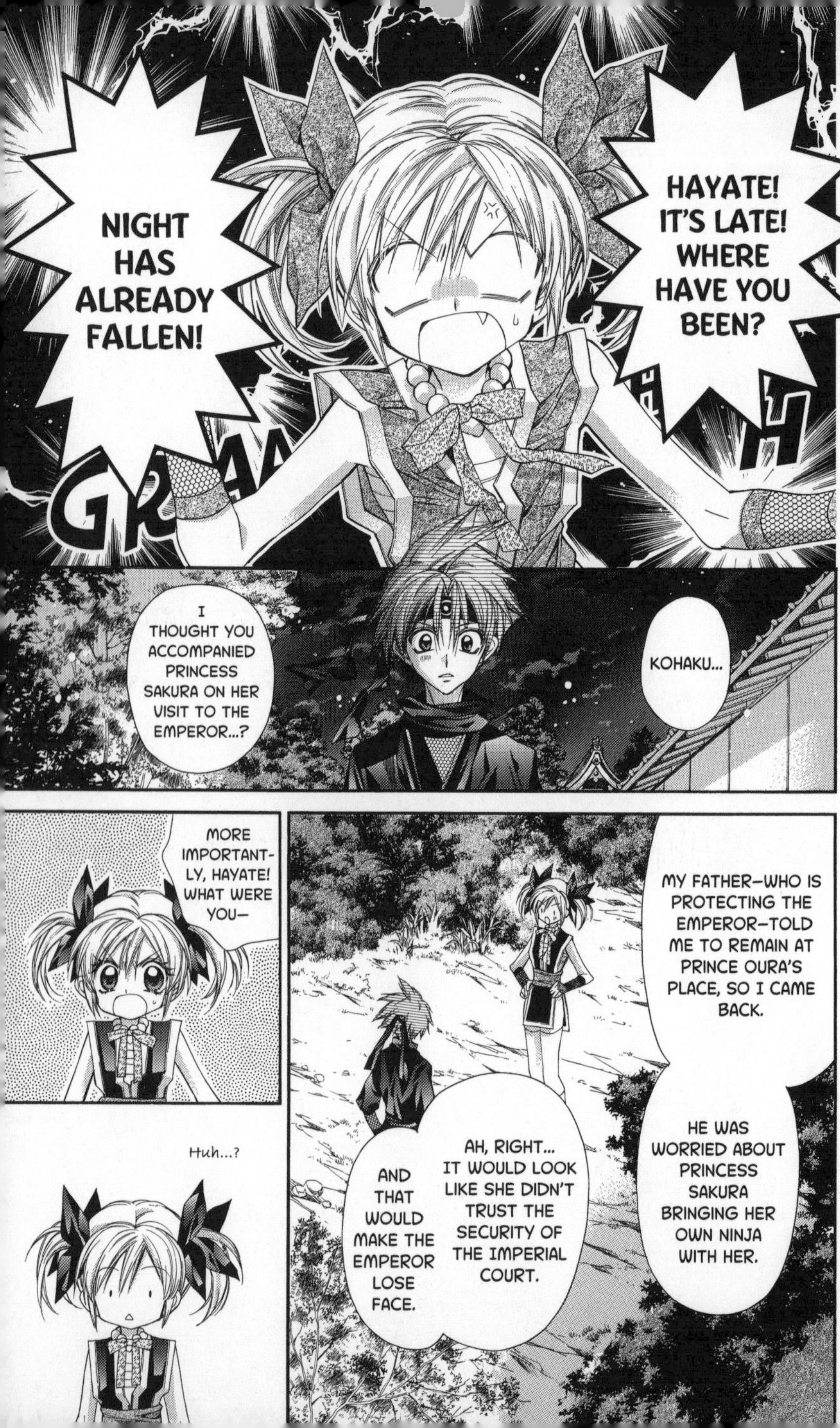
HAYATE! IT'S LATE! WHERE HAVE YOU BEEN?
NIGHT HAS ALREADY FALLEN!
KOHAKU...
I THOUGHT YOU ACCOMPANIED PRINCESS SAKURA ON HER VISIT TO THE EMPEROR...?
MY FATHER—WHO IS PROTECTING THE EMPEROR—TOLD ME TO REMAIN AT PRINCE OURA'S PLACE, SO I CAME BACK.
HE WAS WORRIED ABOUT PRINCESS SAKURA BRINGING HER OWN NINJA WITH HER.
AH, RIGHT... IT WOULD LOOK LIKE SHE DIDN'T TRUST THE SECURITY OF THE IMPERIAL COURT.
AND THAT WOULD MAKE THE EMPEROR LOSE FACE.
MORE IMPORTANT-LY, HAYATE! WHAT WERE YOU—
Huh...?

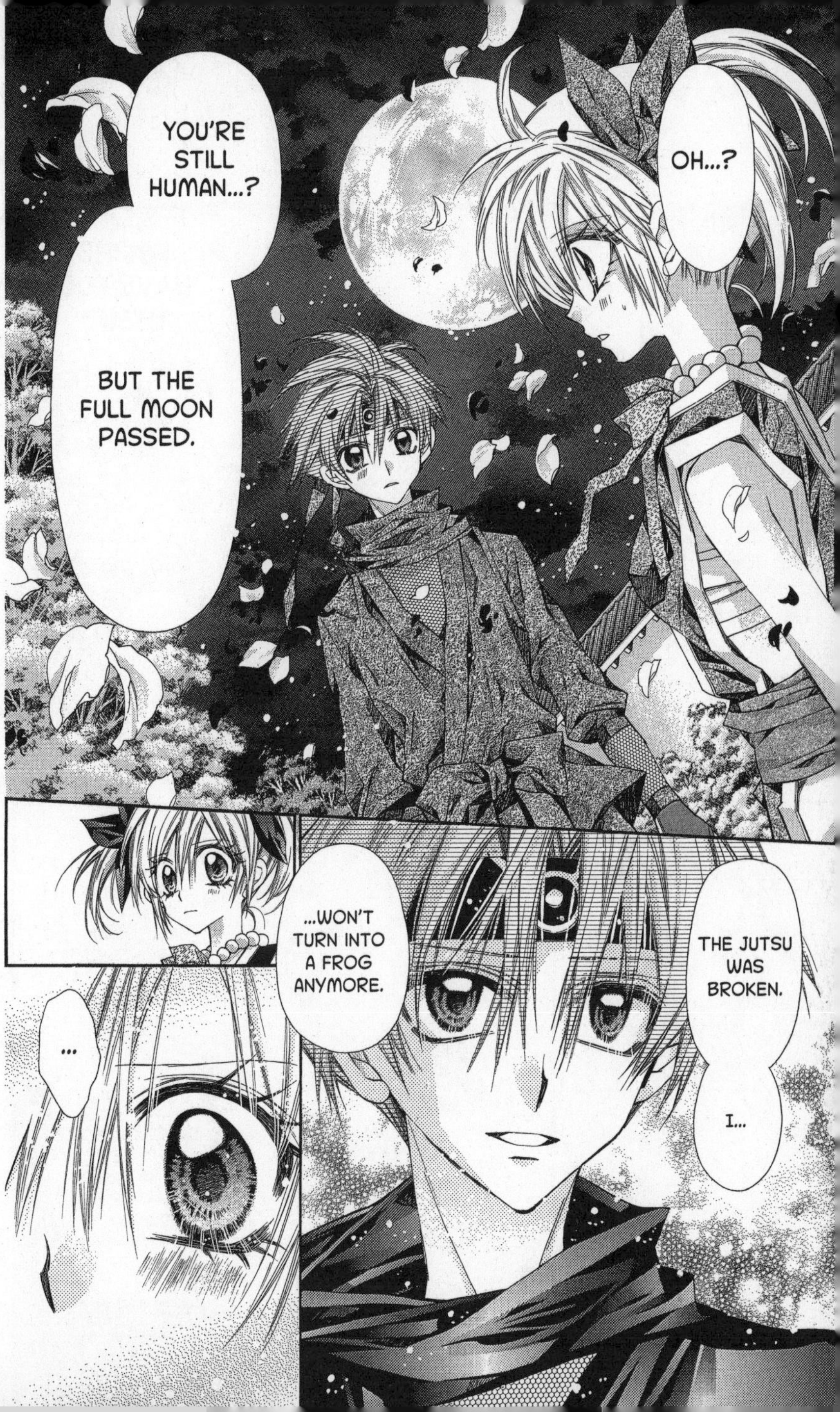
OH...?
YOU'RE STILL HUMAN...?
BUT THE FULL MOON PASSED.
THE JUTSU WAS BROKEN.
I...
...WON'T TURN INTO A FROG ANYMORE.
...

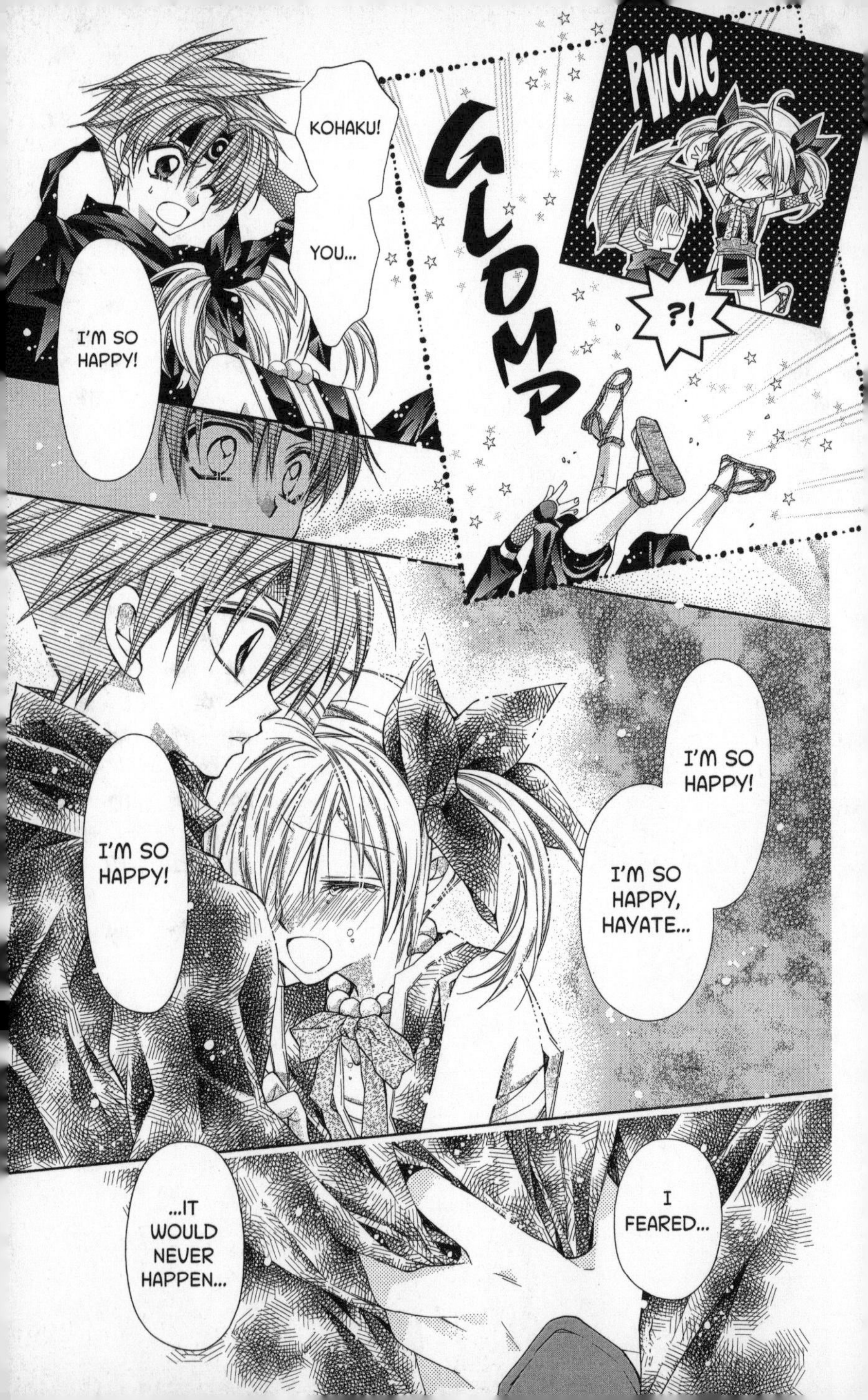
PWONG
?!
GLOMP
KOHAKU!
YOU...
I'M SO HAPPY!
I'M SO HAPPY!
I'M SO HAPPY, HAYATE...
I'M SO HAPPY!
I FEARED...
...IT WOULD NEVER HAPPEN...

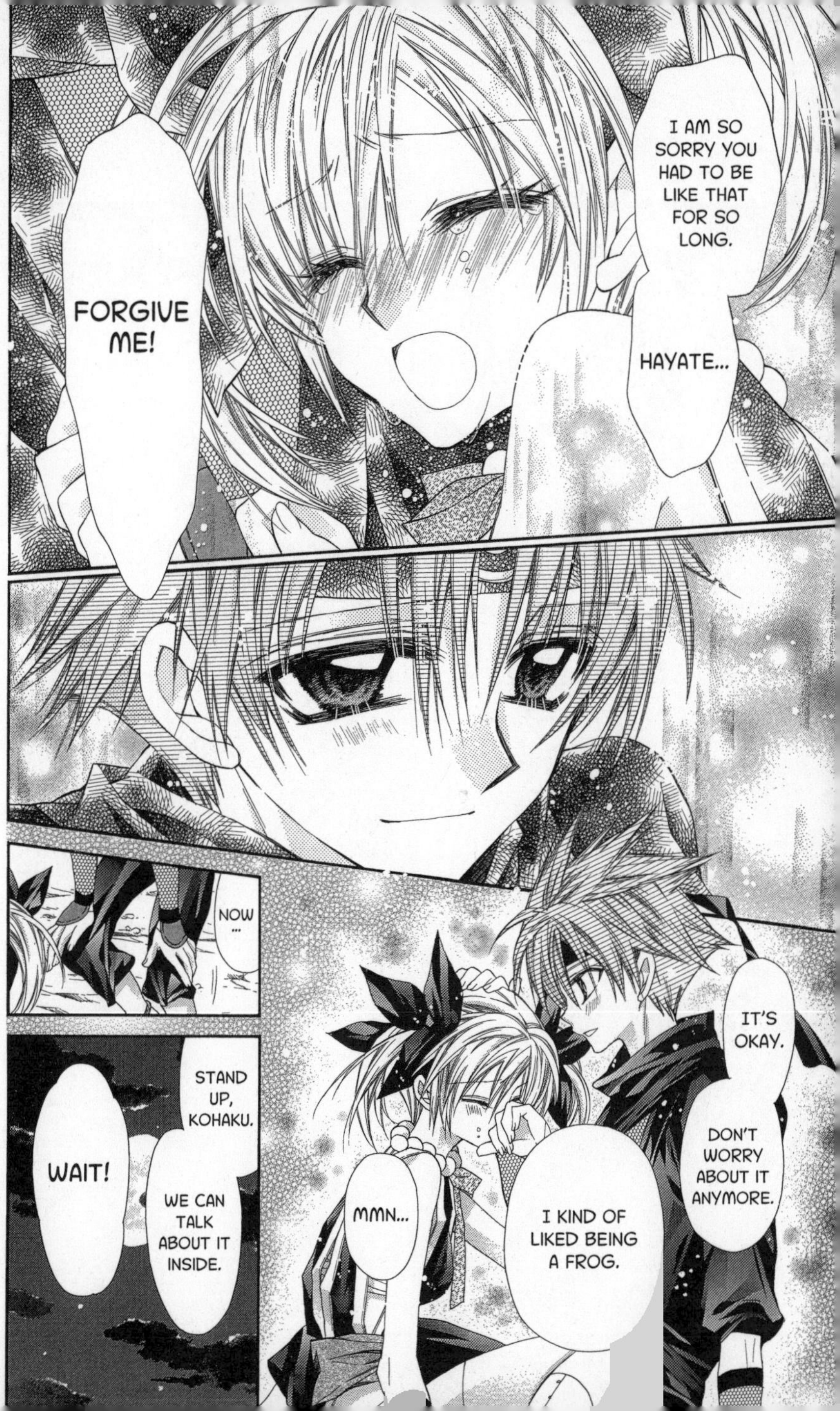
I AM SO SORRY YOU HAD TO BE LIKE THAT FOR SO LONG.
HAYATE...
FORGIVE ME!
IT'S OKAY.
DON'T WORRY ABOUT IT ANYMORE.
I KIND OF LIKED BEING A FROG.
MMN...
NOW...
STAND UP, KOHAKU.
WE CAN TALK ABOUT IT INSIDE.
WAIT!

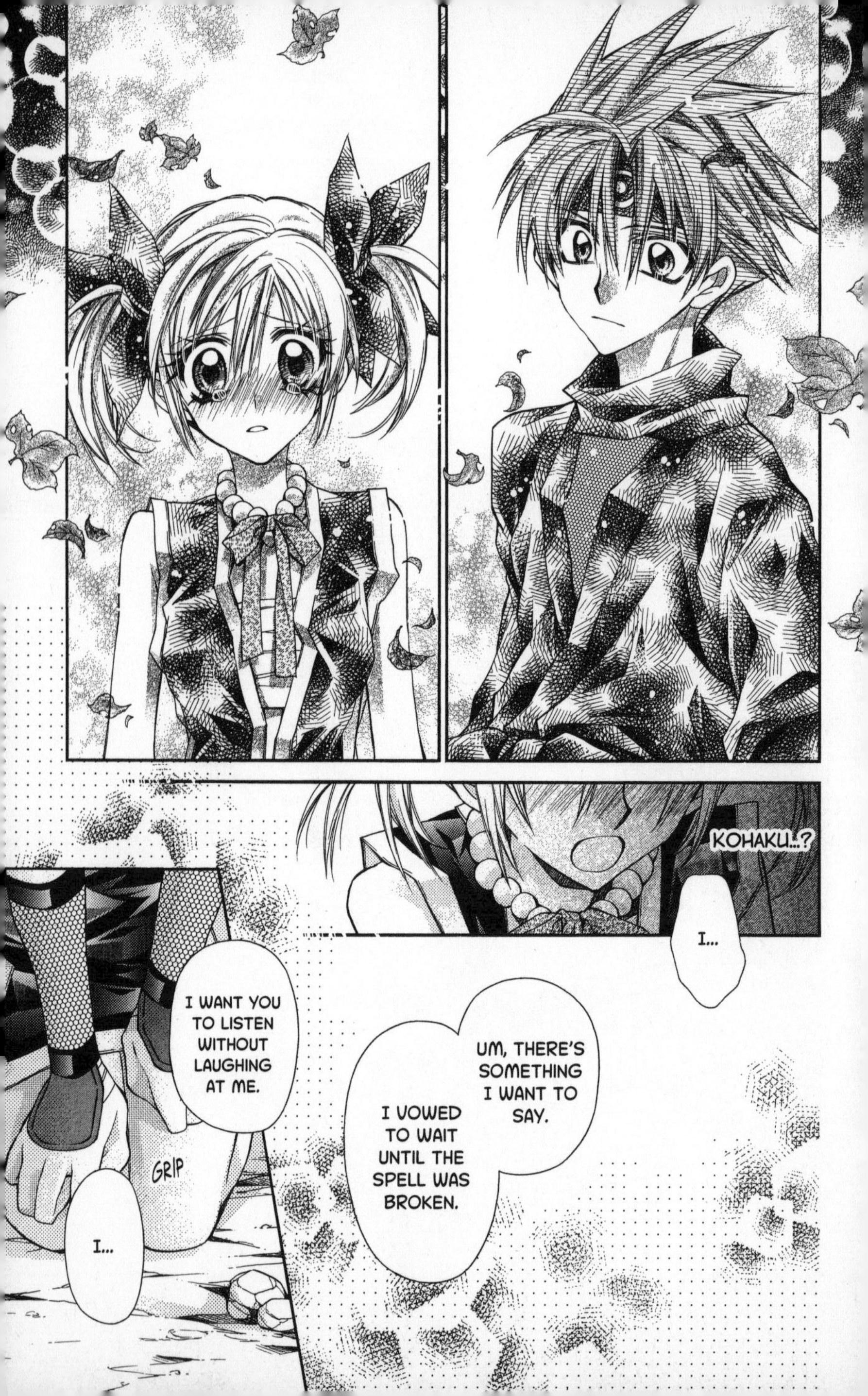
KOHAKU...?
I...
UM, THERE'S SOMETHING I WANT TO SAY.
I VOWED TO WAIT UNTIL THE SPELL WAS BROKEN.
I WANT YOU TO LISTEN WITHOUT LAUGHING AT ME.
GRIP
I...

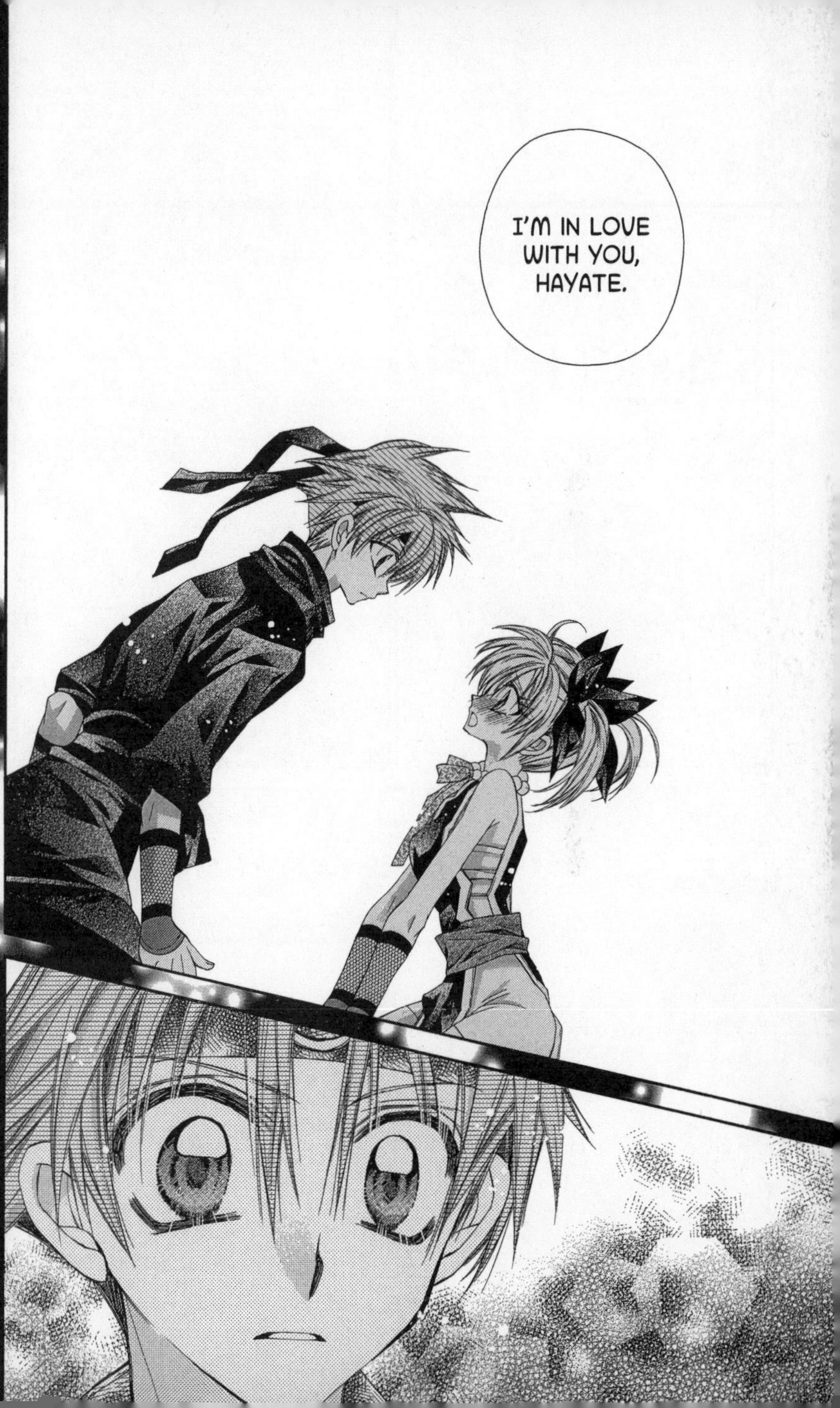
I'M IN LOVE WITH YOU, HAYATE.

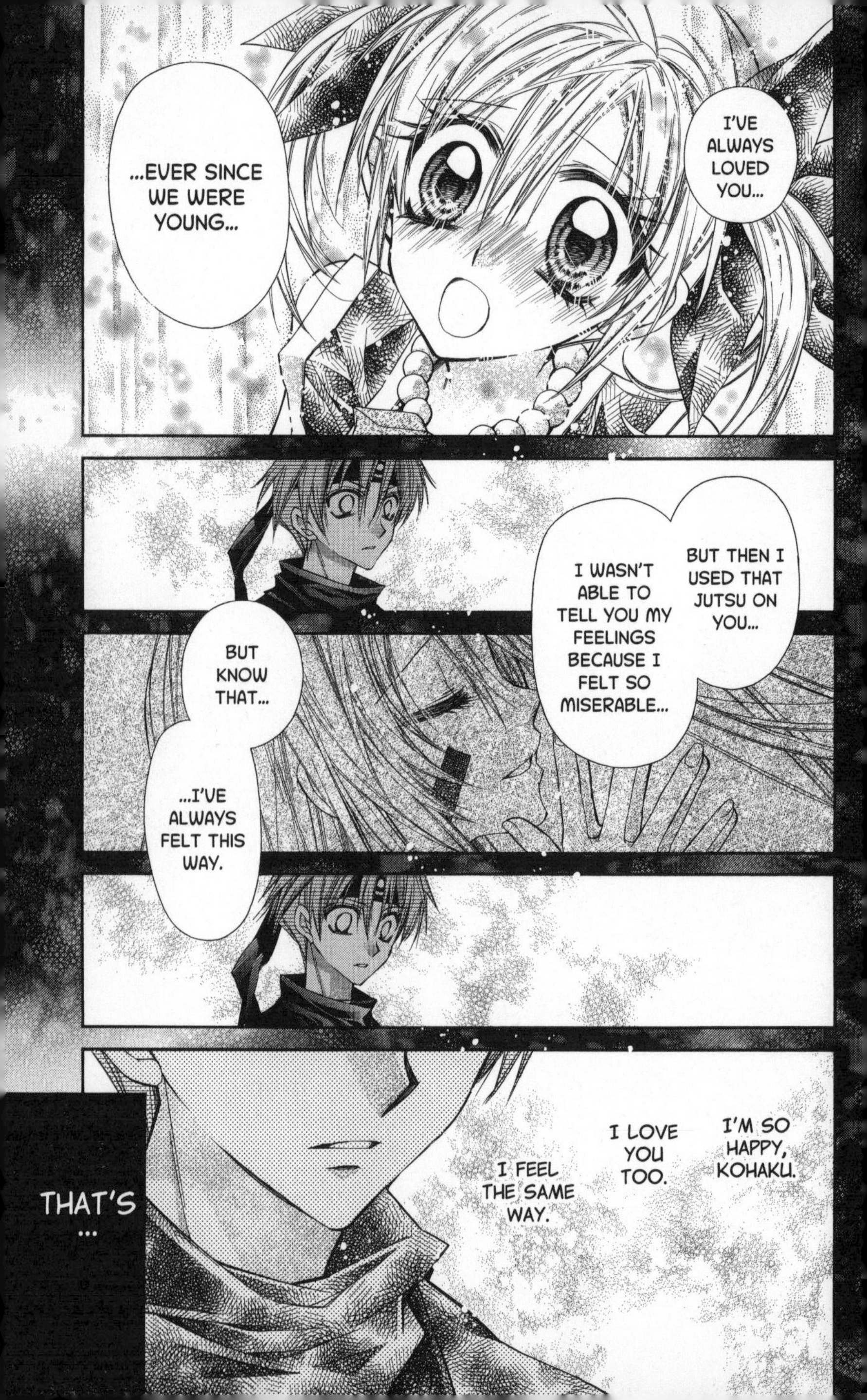
I'VE ALWAYS LOVED YOU...
...EVER SINCE WE WERE YOUNG...
BUT THEN I USED THAT JUTSU ON YOU...
I WASN'T ABLE TO TELL YOU MY FEELINGS BECAUSE I FELT SO MISERABLE...
BUT KNOW THAT...
...I'VE ALWAYS FELT THIS WAY.
I'M SO HAPPY, KOHAKU.
I LOVE YOU TOO.
I FEEL THE SAME WAY.
THAT'S ...

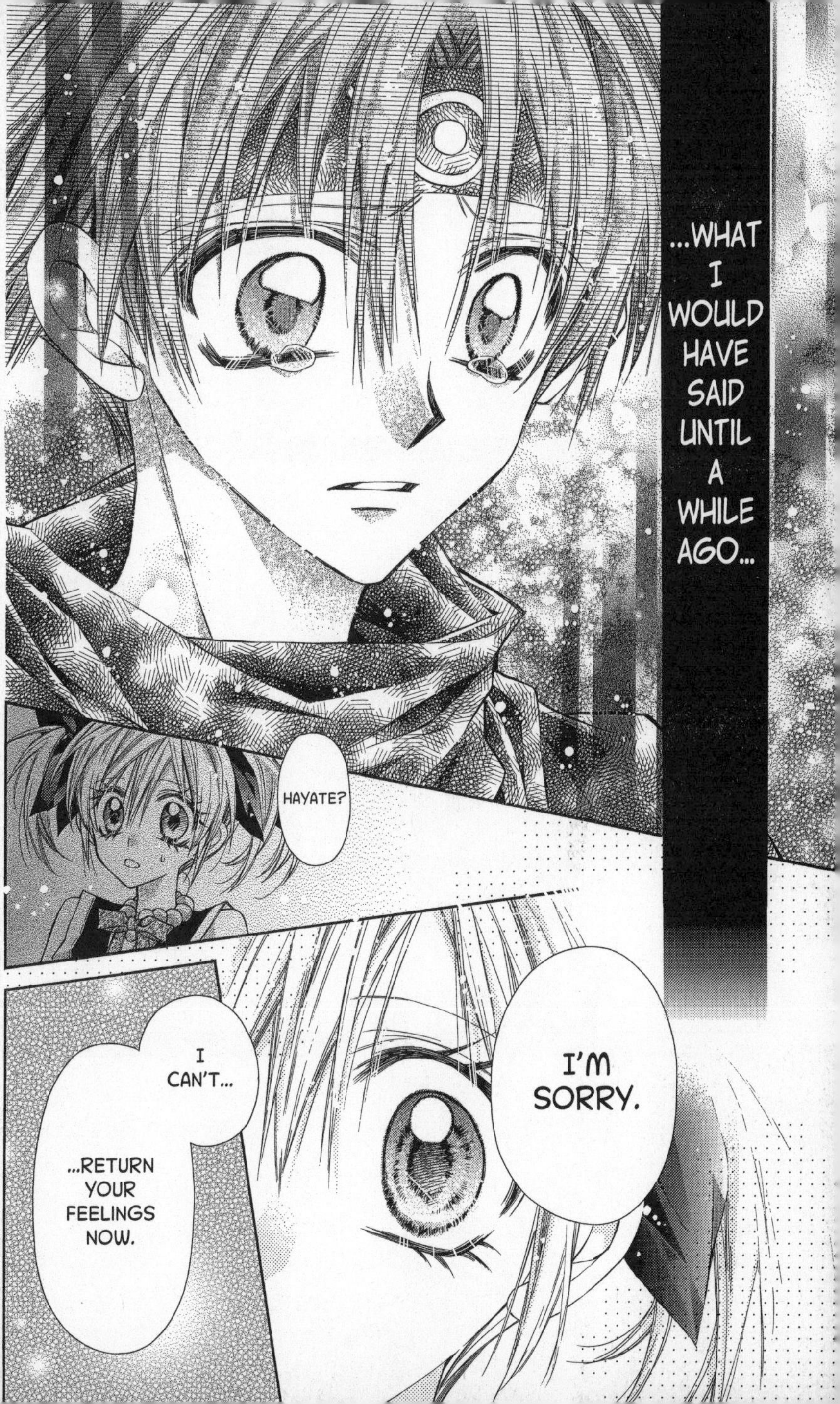
...WHAT I WOULD HAVE SAID UNTIL A WHILE AGO...
HAYATE?
I'M SORRY.
I CAN'T...
...RETURN YOUR FEELINGS NOW.

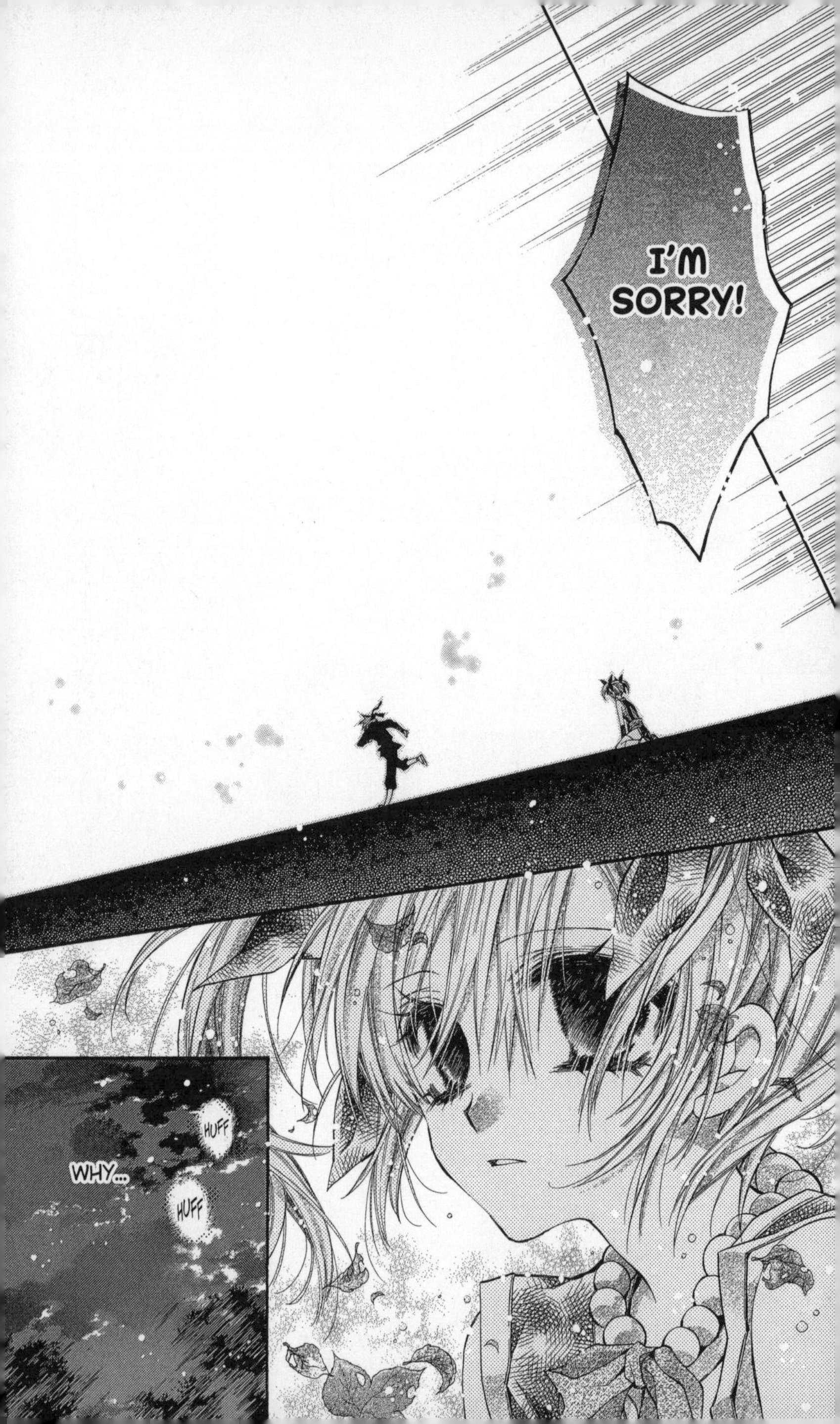
I'M SORRY!
HUFF
WHY...
HUFF

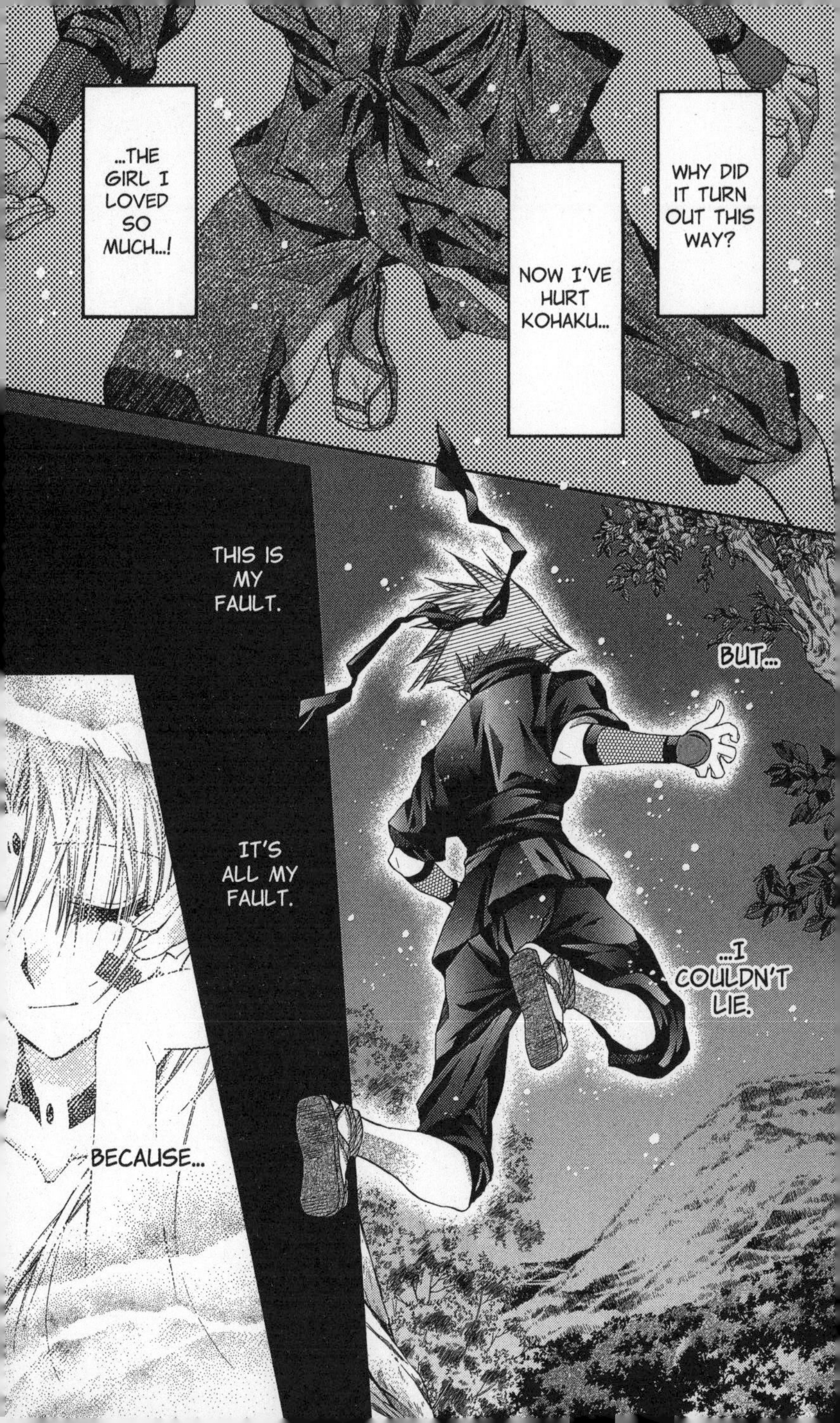
WHY DID IT TURN OUT THIS WAY?
NOW I'VE HURT KOHAKU...
...THE GIRL I LOVED SO MUCH...!
BUT...
...I COULDN'T LIE.
THIS IS MY FAULT.
IT'S ALL MY FAULT.
BECAUSE...

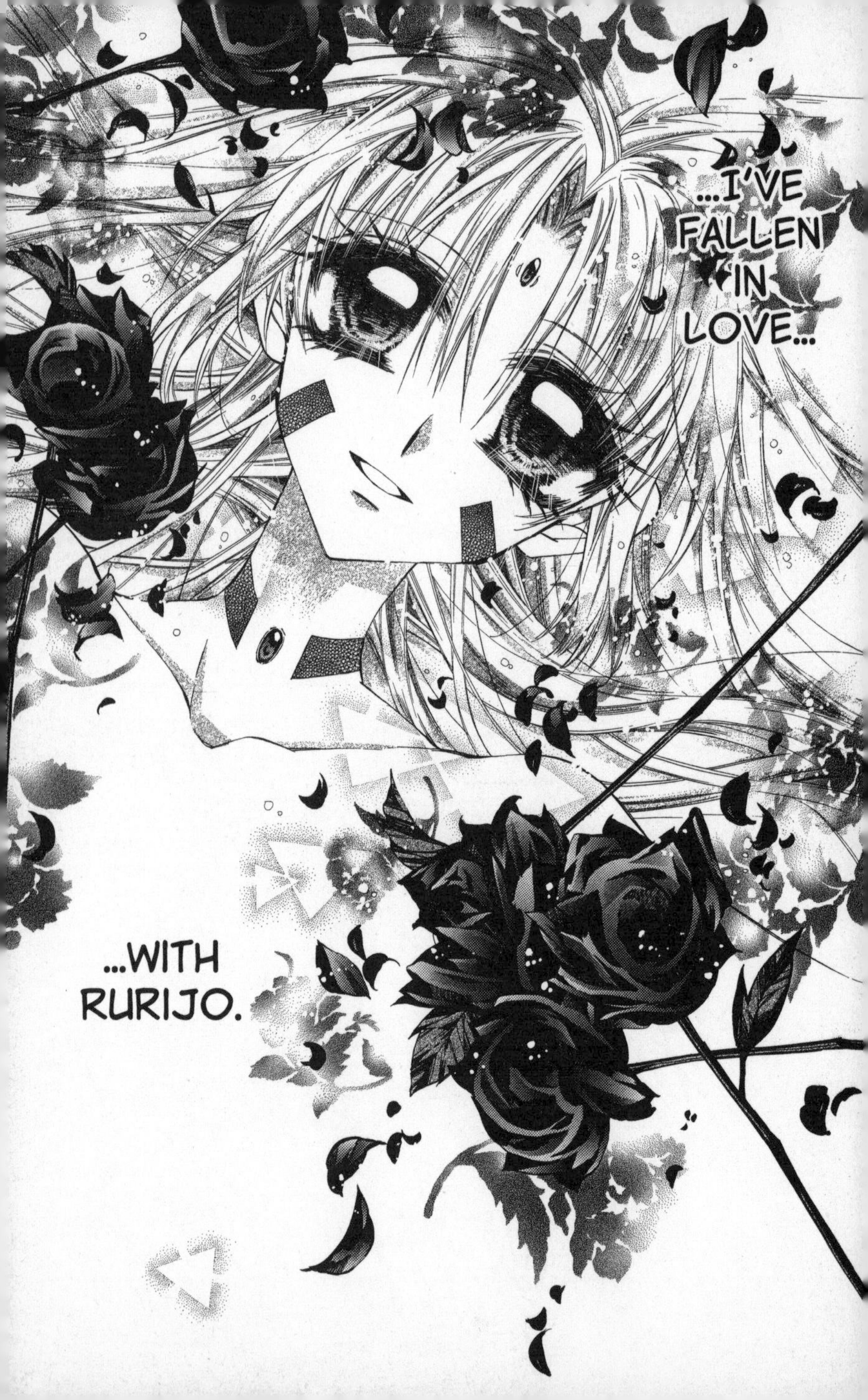
...I'VE FALLEN IN LOVE...
...WITH RURIJO.

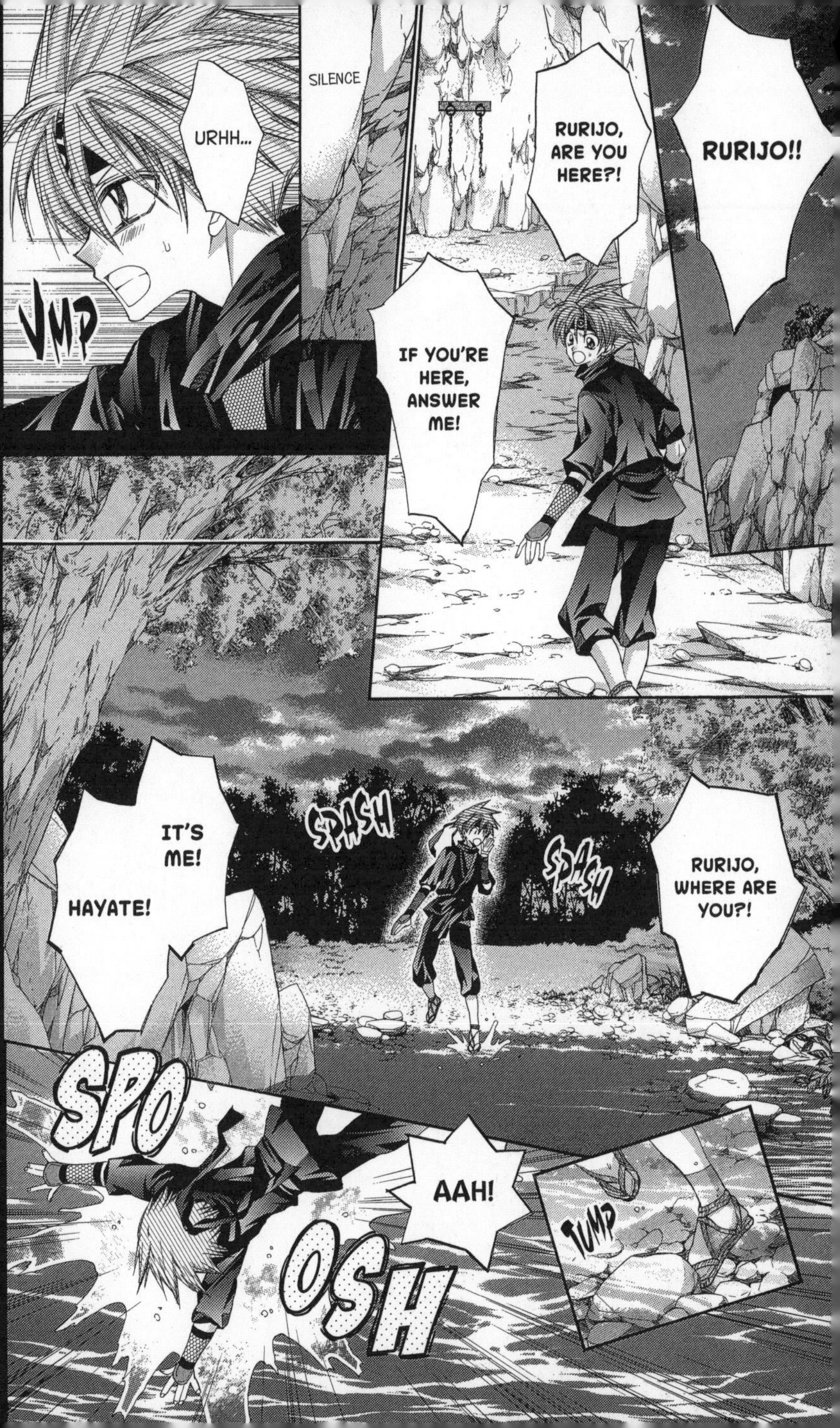
RURIJO!!
RURIJO, ARE YOU HERE?!
IF YOU'RE HERE, ANSWER ME!
SILENCE
URHH...
VMP
RURIJO, WHERE ARE YOU?!
SPASH
SPASH
IT'S ME!
HAYATE!
TUMP
AAH!
SPO
OSH

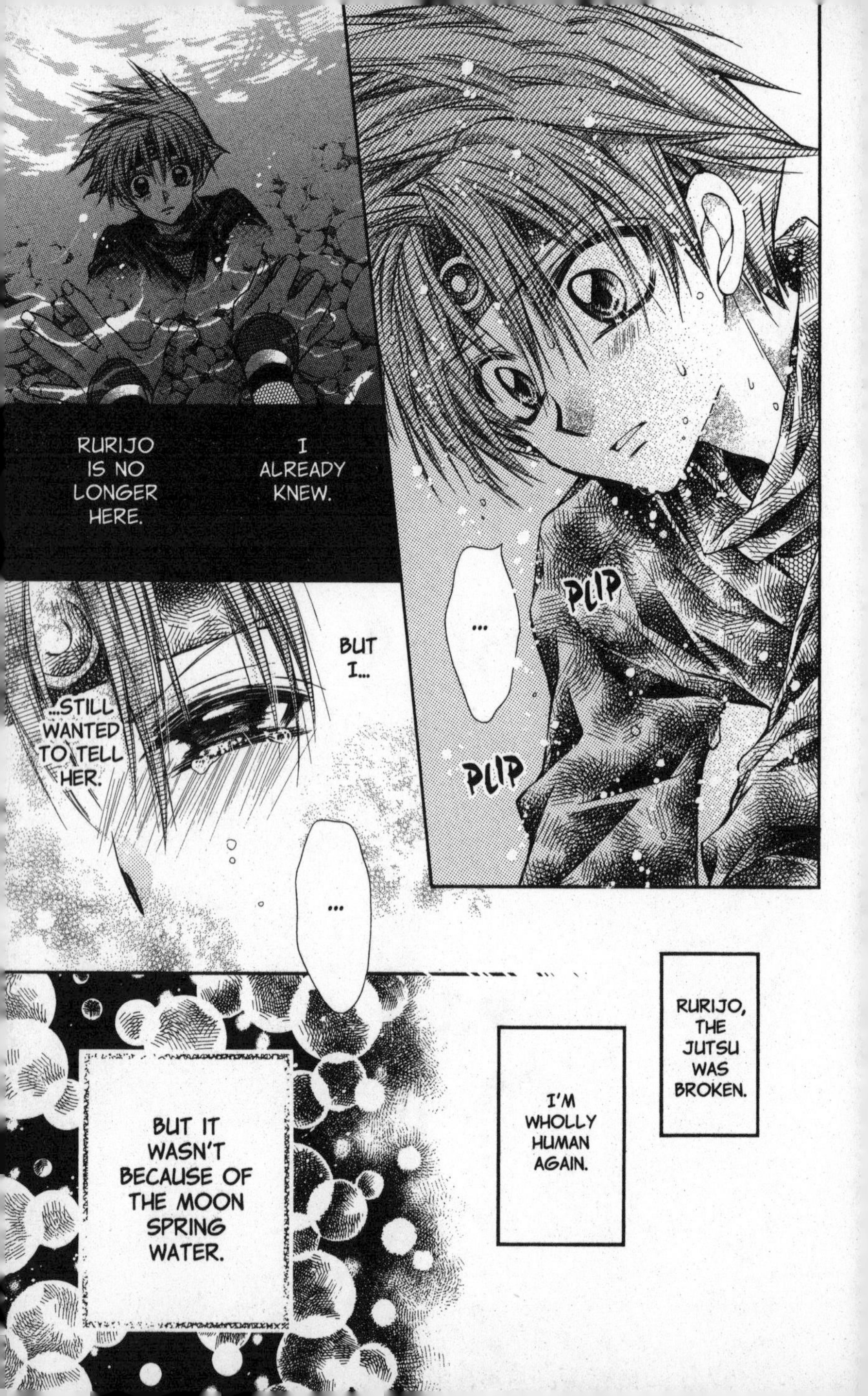
...
PLIP
PLIP
I ALREADY KNEW.
RURIJO IS NO LONGER HERE.
BUT I...
...STILL WANTED TO TELL HER.
...
RURIJO, THE JUTSU WAS BROKEN.
I'M WHOLLY HUMAN AGAIN.
BUT IT WASN'T BECAUSE OF THE MOON SPRING WATER.

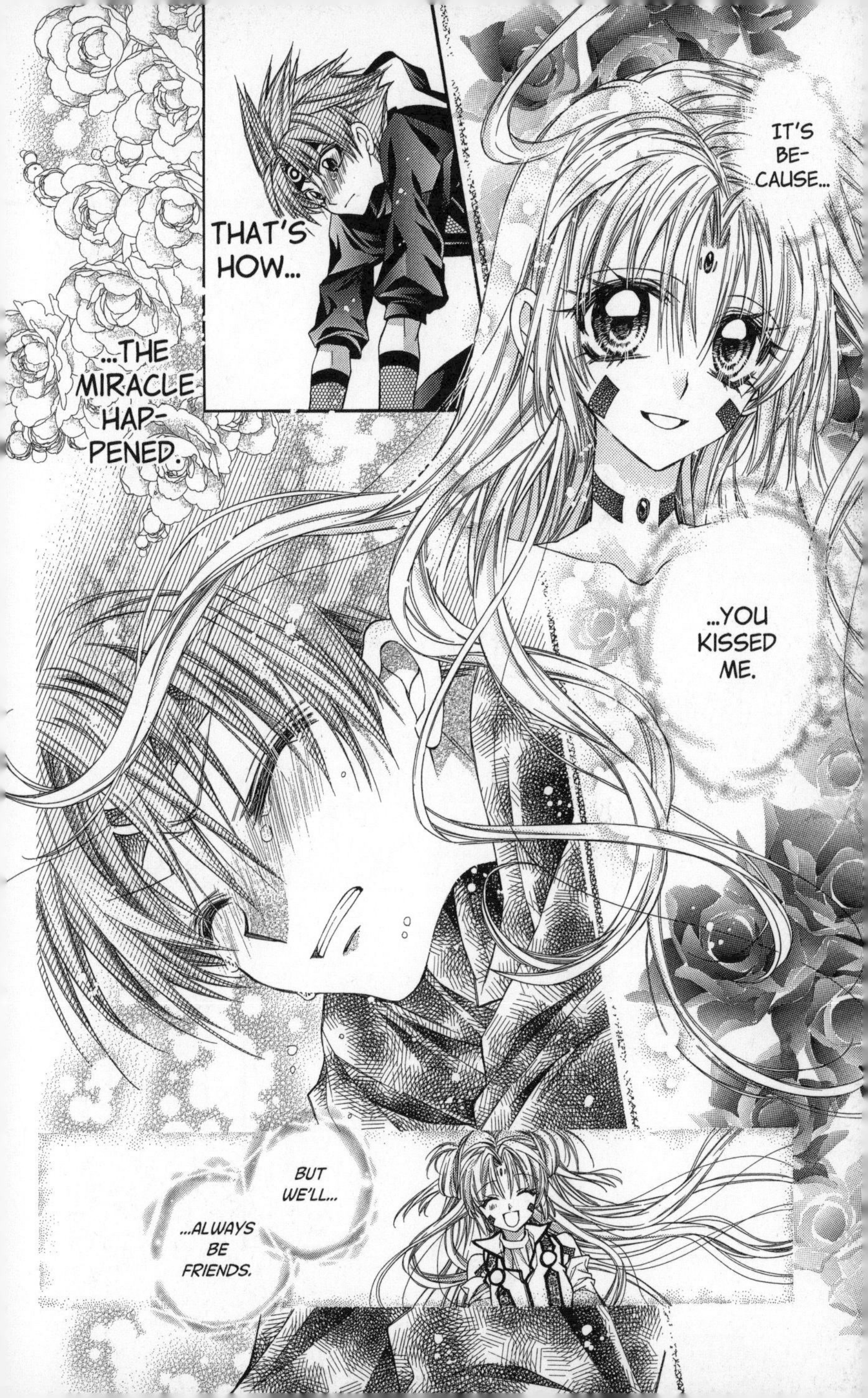
IT'S BE-CAUSE...
...YOU KISSED ME.
THAT'S HOW...
...THE MIRACLE HAP-PENED.
BUT WE'LL...
...ALWAYS BE FRIENDS.

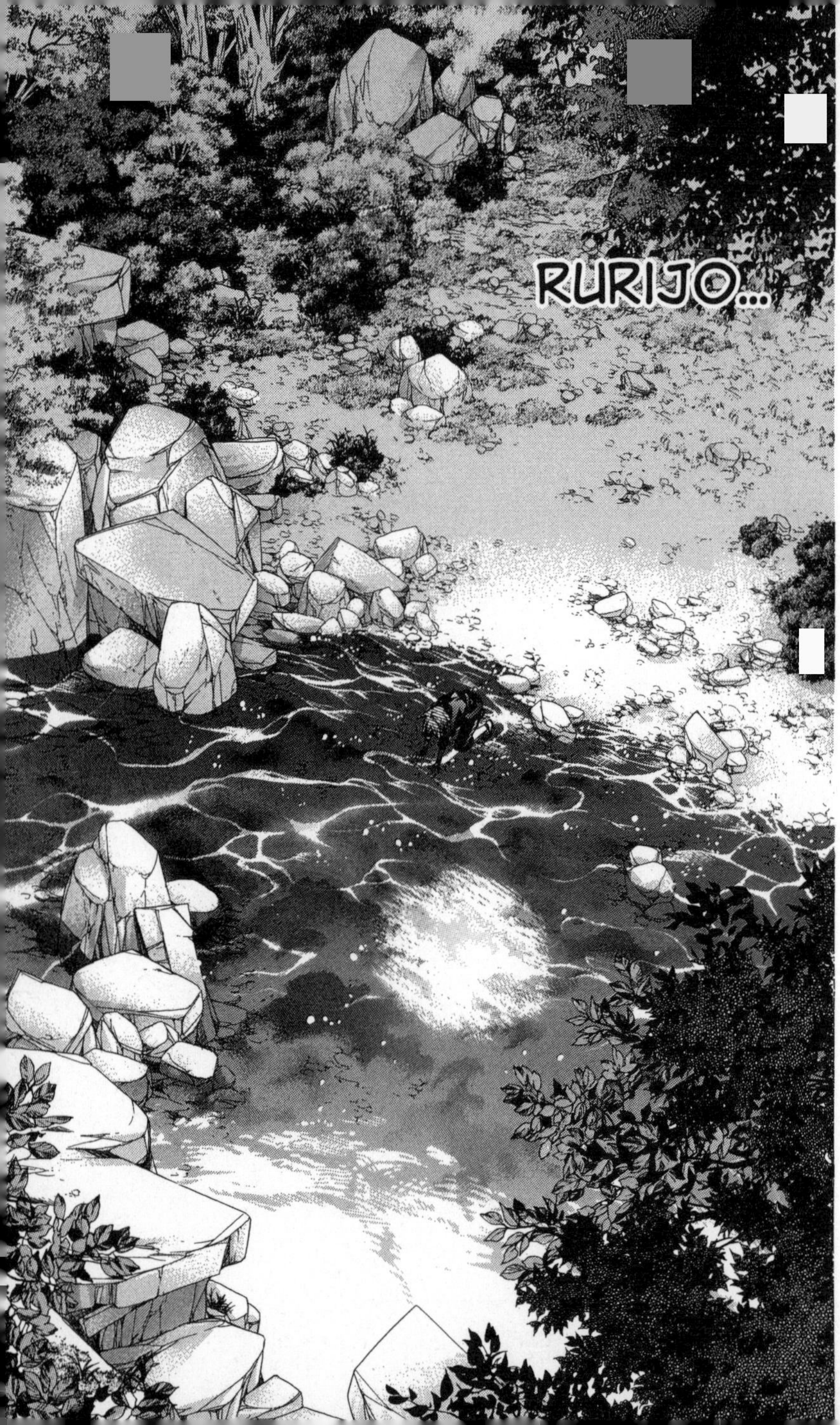
RURIJO...

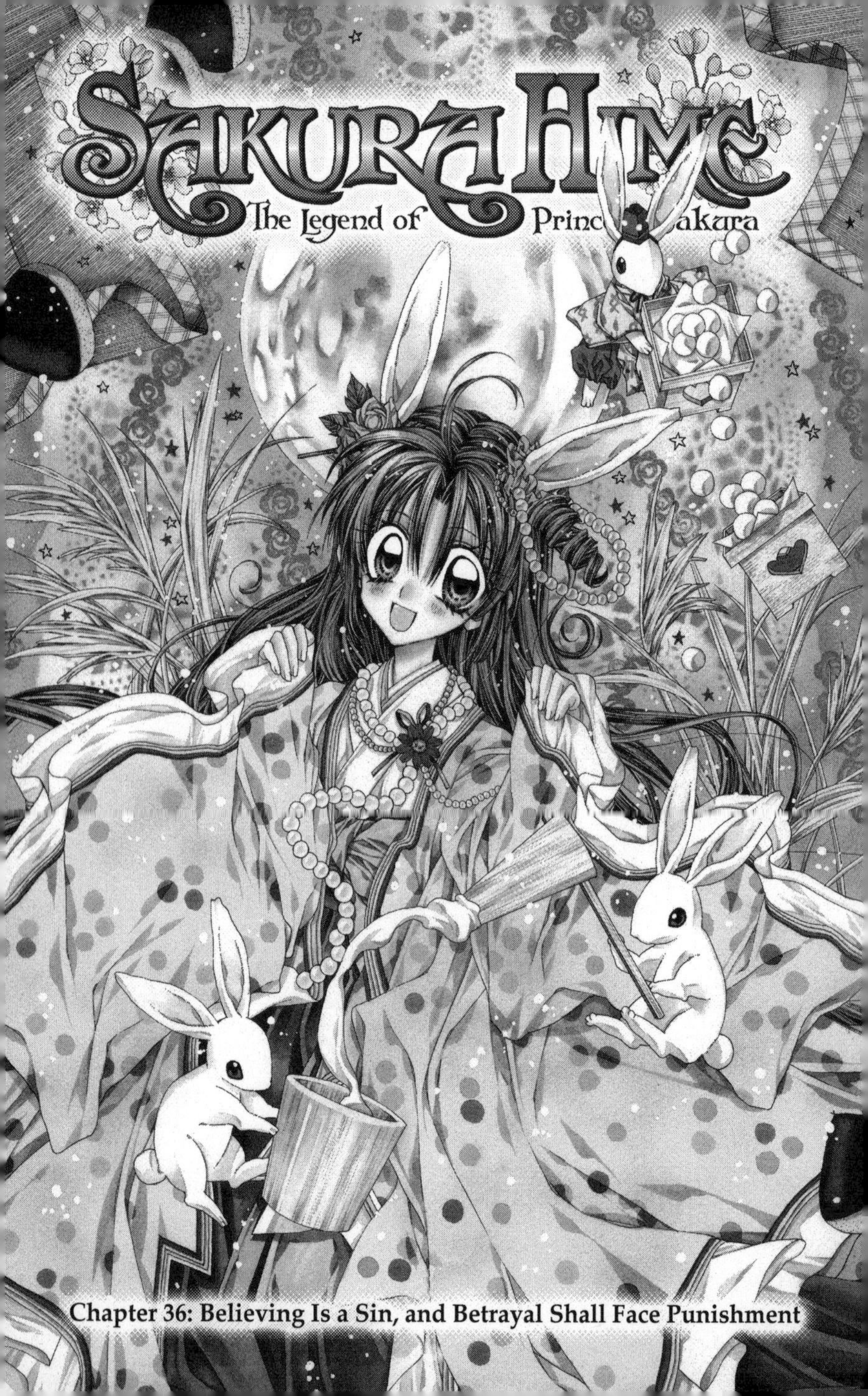
SAKURA HIME
The Legend of Princ akura

Chapter 36: Believing Is a Sin, and Betrayal Shall Face Punishment

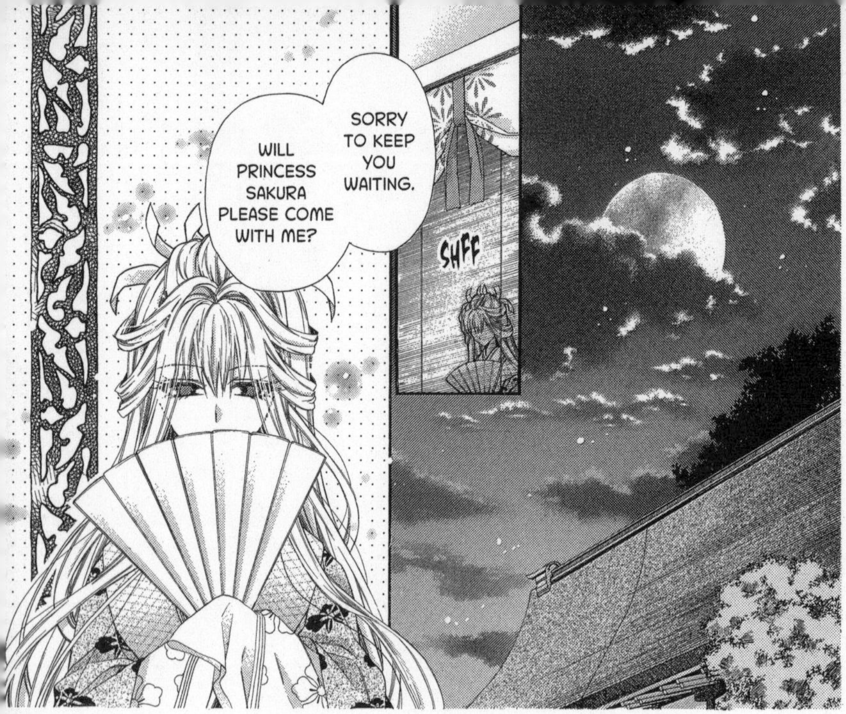
SORRY TO KEEP YOU WAITING.
WILL PRINCESS SAKURA PLEASE COME WITH ME?
SHFF

Chapter 36: Believing Is a Sin, and Betrayal Shall Face Punishment

※I'm giving away the story.

The chapter title page illustration is my concept of a moon watching festival. Pop art illustrations like this are pretty rare in this series. Well then, we finally get to see the emperor. I gave him a typical Heian-era look (the long, narrow eyes). He was really easy to draw... Even though Sakura is immortal, I'm sure it must be hard for her to be going through so much. (It's excruciating pain, after all.)

↑ (when the wounds are healing)

As for Enju, I guess he wanted to get his revenge at the place where his nightmare began. (But I think he showed himself earlier than he expected to when Sakura was thrown into the water chamber.)

The moon people are basically "beautiful," so I think Enju looks good in clothes like this too. I had a feeling the readers would figure out the outcome of this chapter, so I decided to include a surprise at the end.

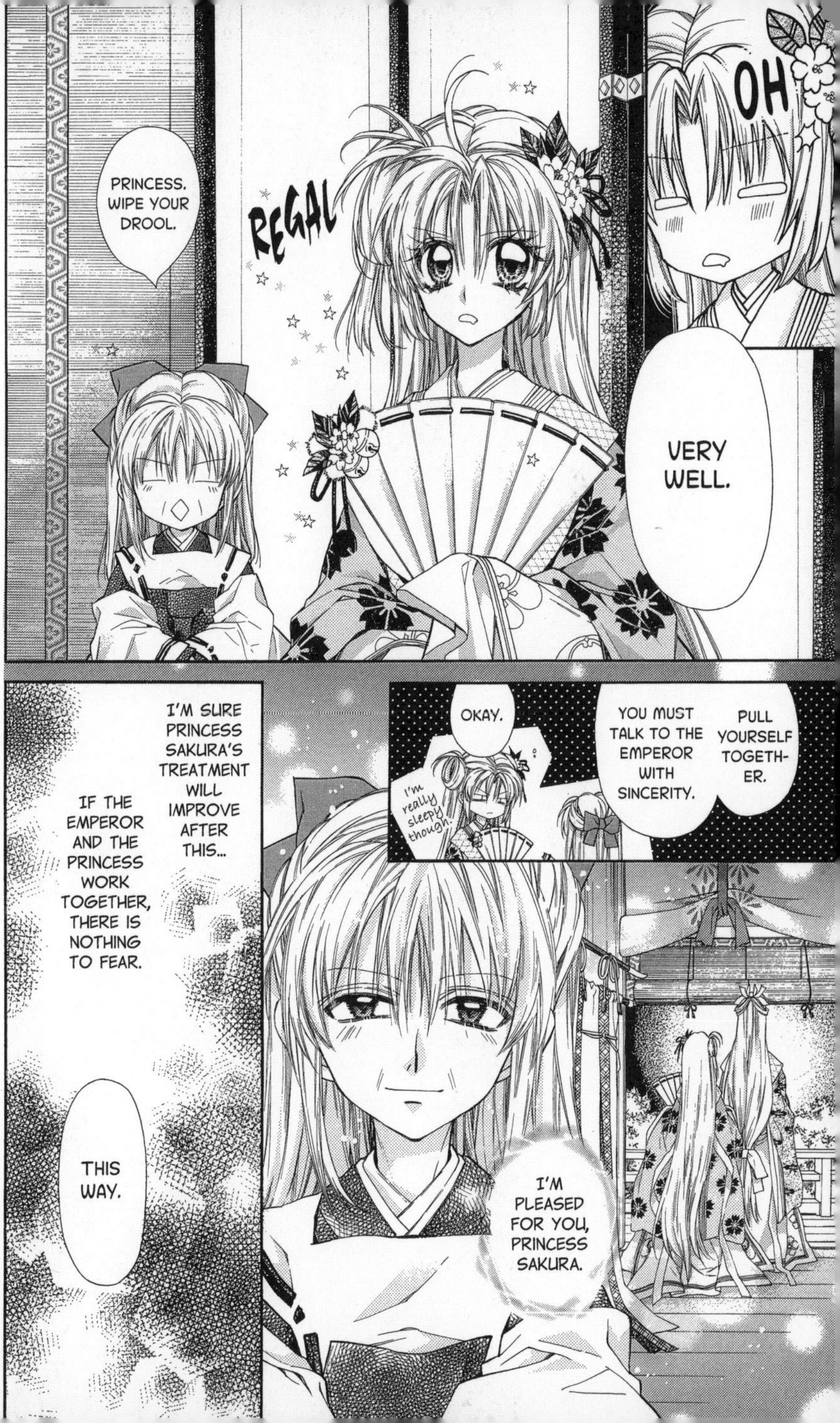
OH
VERY WELL.
REGAL
PRINCESS. WIPE YOUR DROOL.
PULL YOURSELF TOGETH-ER.
YOU MUST TALK TO THE EMPEROR WITH SINCERITY.
OKAY.
I'm really sleepy though.
I'M PLEASED FOR YOU, PRINCESS SAKURA.
I'M SURE PRINCESS SAKURA'S TREATMENT WILL IMPROVE AFTER THIS...
IF THE EMPEROR AND THE PRINCESS WORK TOGETHER, THERE IS NOTHING TO FEAR.
THIS WAY.

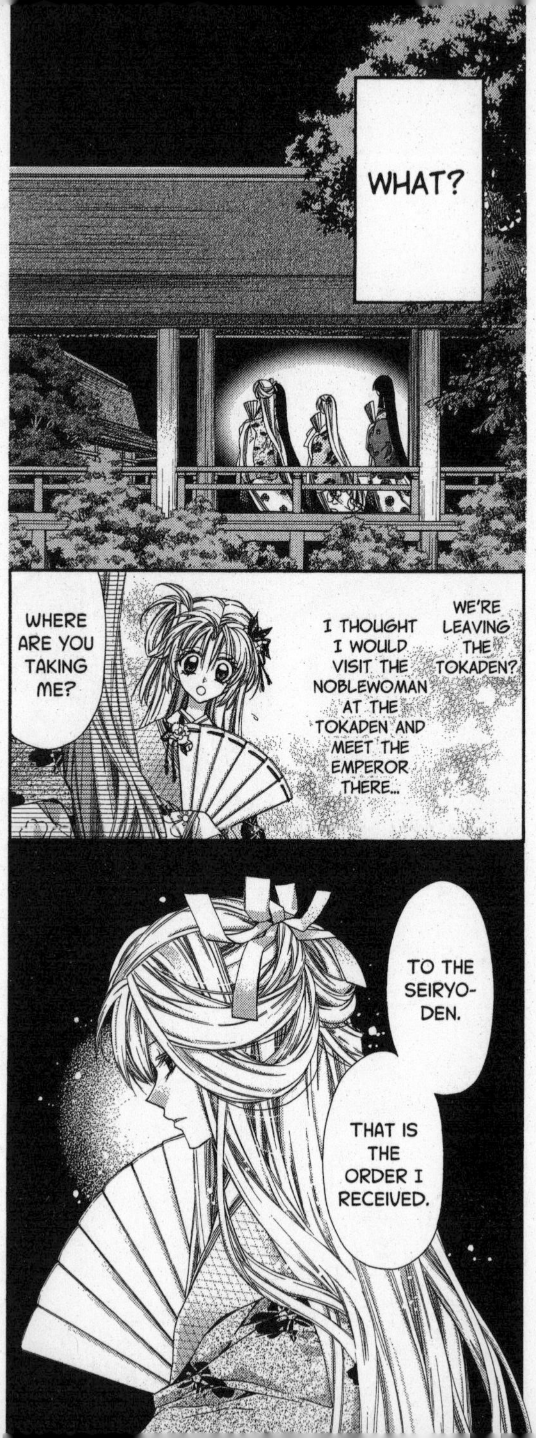
WHAT?
WE'RE LEAVING THE TOKADEN?
I THOUGHT I WOULD VISIT THE NOBLEWOMAN AT THE TOKADEN AND MEET THE EMPEROR THERE...
WHERE ARE YOU TAKING ME?
TO THE SEIRYO-DEN.
THAT IS THE ORDER I RECEIVED.

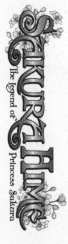

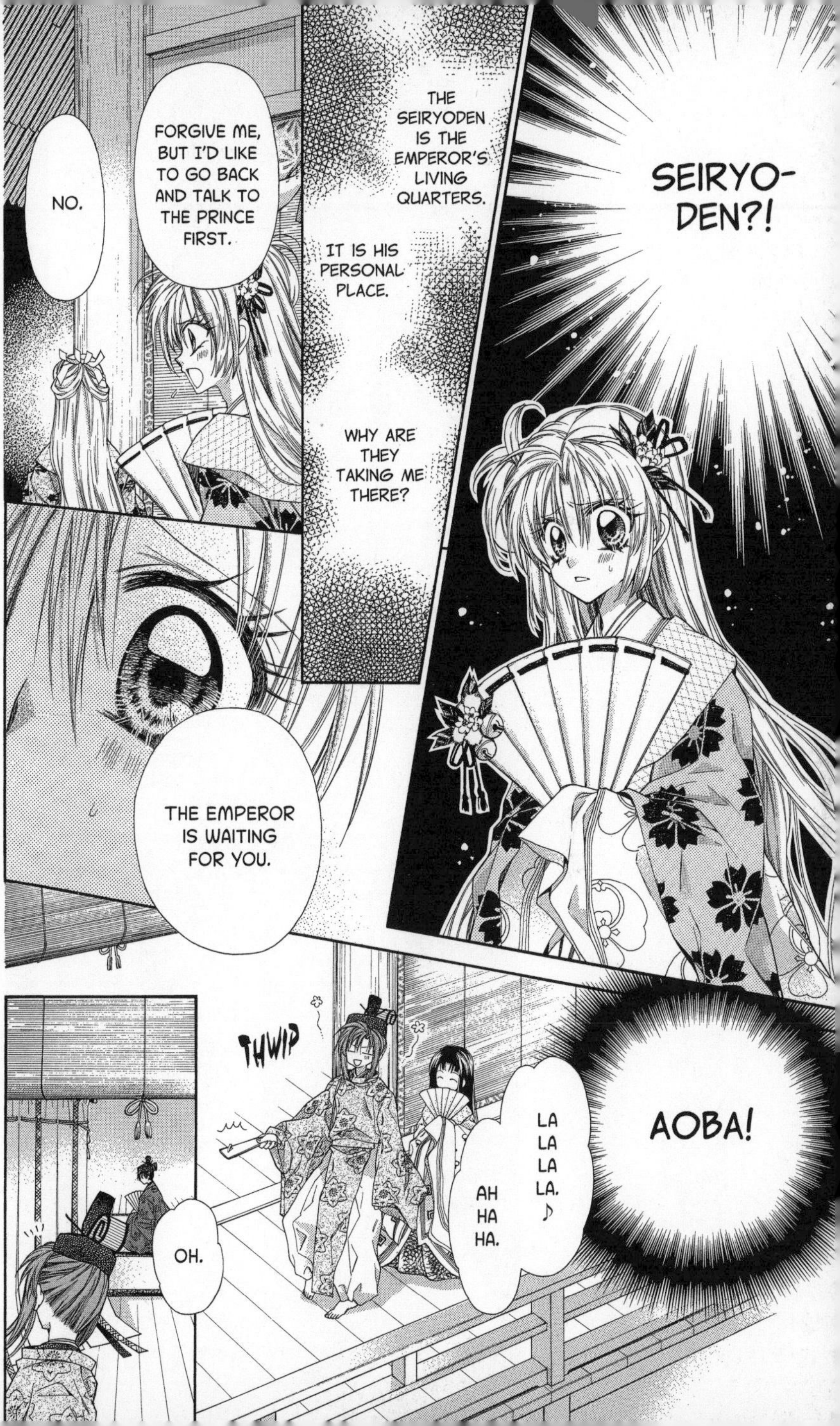
SEIRYO-DEN?!
THE SEIRYODEN IS THE EMPEROR'S LIVING QUARTERS.
IT IS HIS PERSONAL PLACE.
WHY ARE THEY TAKING ME THERE?
FORGIVE ME, BUT I'D LIKE TO GO BACK AND TALK TO THE PRINCE FIRST.
NO.
THE EMPEROR IS WAITING FOR YOU.
AOBA!
LA LA LA LA. ♪
AH HA HA.
THWIP
OH.

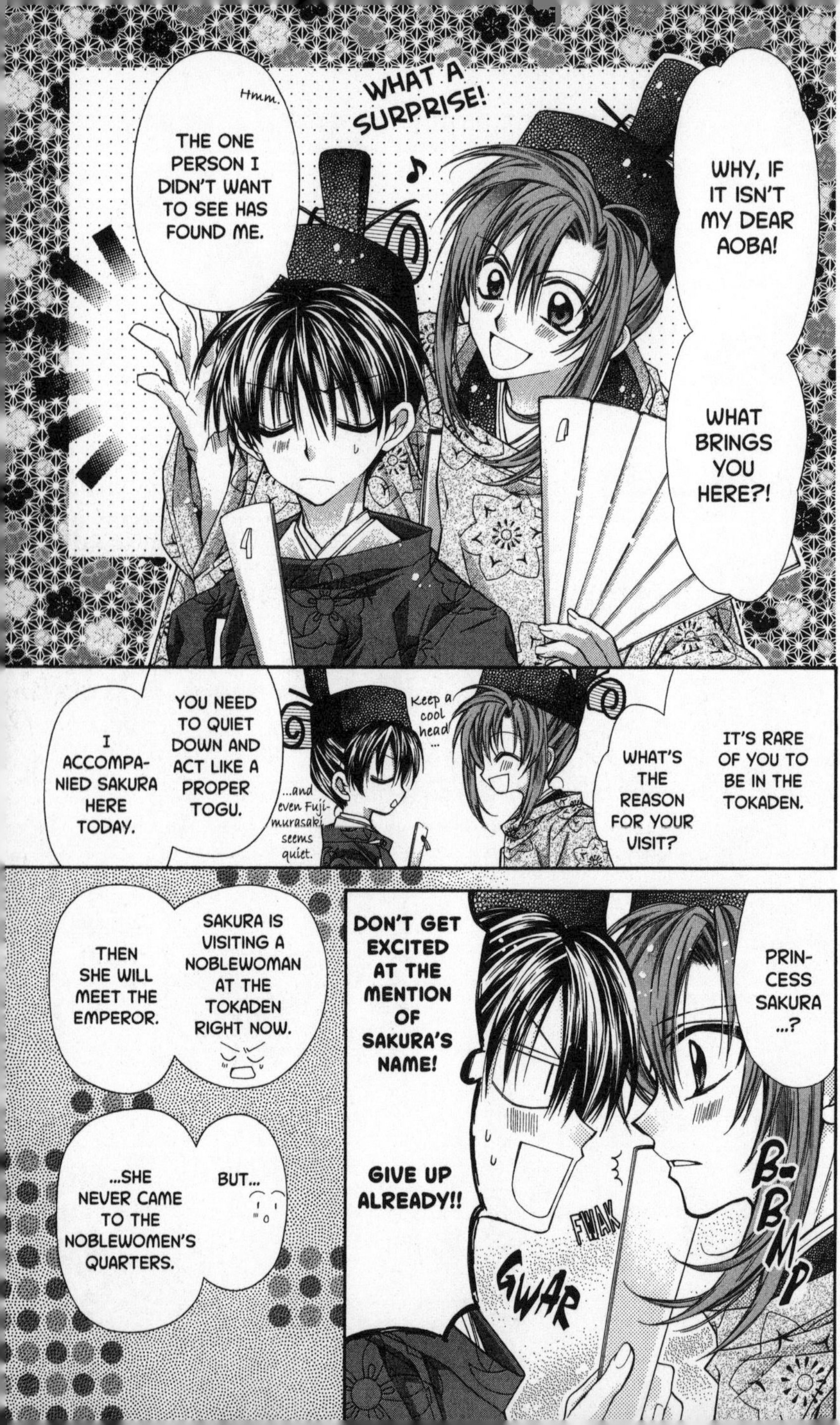
WHY, IF IT ISN'T MY DEAR AOBA!
WHAT BRINGS YOU HERE?!
WHAT A SURPRISE!
Hmm.
THE ONE PERSON I DIDN'T WANT TO SEE HAS FOUND ME.
IT'S RARE OF YOU TO BE IN THE TOKADEN.
WHAT'S THE REASON FOR YOUR VISIT?
Keep a cool head! ...
...and even Fuji-murasaki seems quiet.
YOU NEED TO QUIET DOWN AND ACT LIKE A PROPER TOGU.
I ACCOMPA-NIED SAKURA HERE TODAY.
PRIN-CESS SAKURA ...?
DON'T GET EXCITED AT THE MENTION OF SAKURA'S NAME!
GIVE UP ALREADY!!
B-BMP
FWAK
GWAR
SAKURA IS VISITING A NOBLEWOMAN AT THE TOKADEN RIGHT NOW.
THEN SHE WILL MEET THE EMPEROR.
BUT...
...SHE NEVER CAME TO THE NOBLEWOMEN'S QUARTERS.

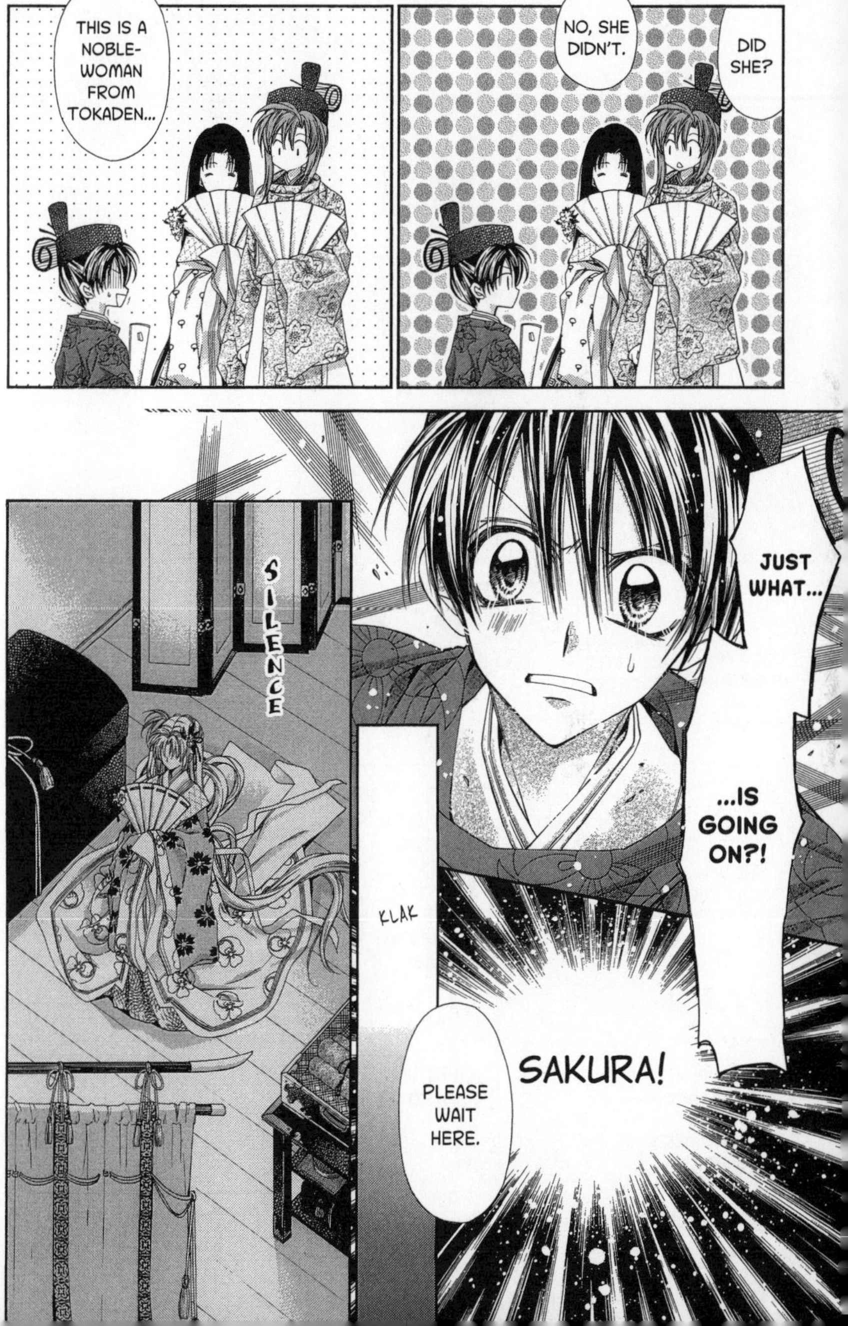
DID SHE?
NO, SHE DIDN'T.
THIS IS A NOBLE-WOMAN FROM TOKADEN...
JUST WHAT...
...IS GOING ON?!
SAKURA!
SILENCE
KLAK
PLEASE WAIT HERE.

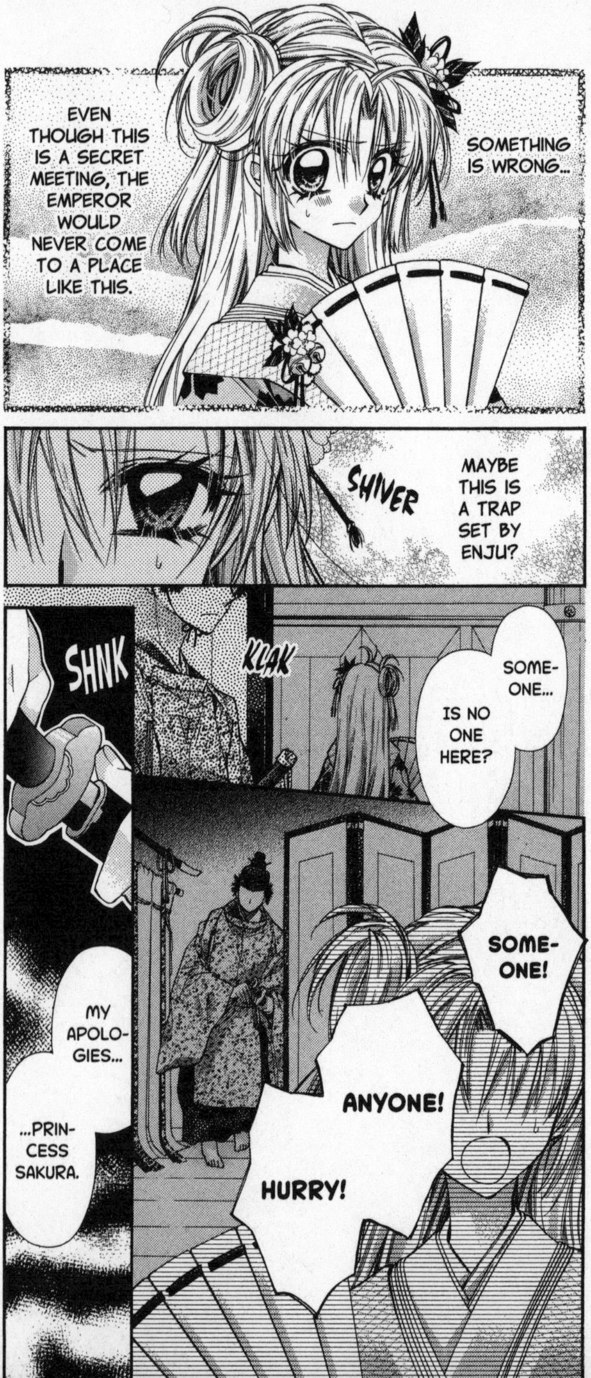
SOMETHING IS WRONG...
EVEN THOUGH THIS IS A SECRET MEETING, THE EMPEROR WOULD NEVER COME TO A PLACE LIKE THIS.
MAYBE THIS IS A TRAP SET BY ENJU?
SHIVER
SOME-ONE...
IS NO ONE HERE?
KLAK
SOME-ONE!
ANYONE!
HURRY!
SHNK
MY APOLOGIES...
...PRIN-CESS SAKURA.

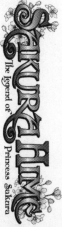

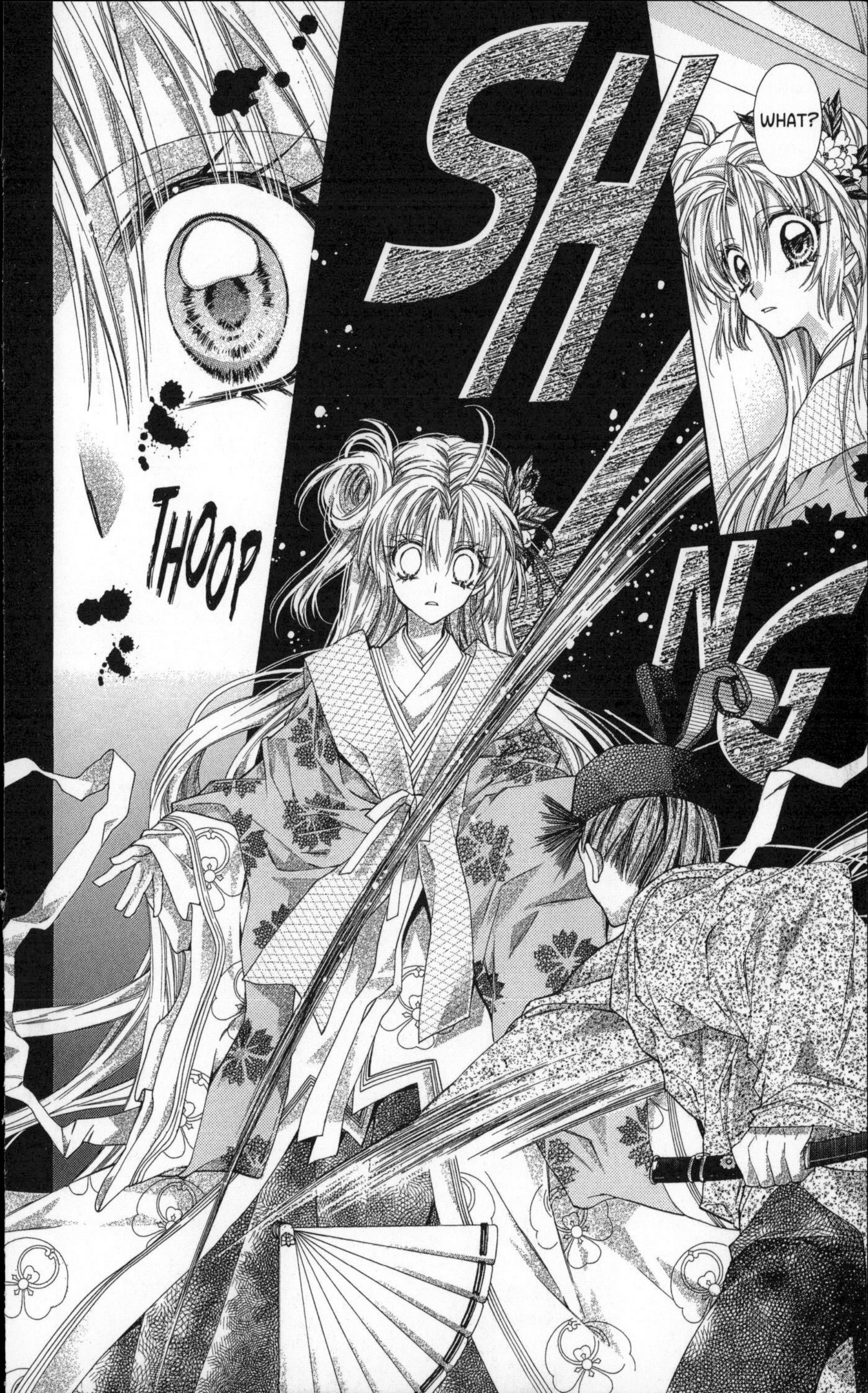
WHAT?
SHING
THOOP

Hokkaido continued →

You need to make reservations for the dinner at Cassiopeia beforehand, and you can choose the Western course or the Japanese course. I really recommend the Western course! (The last time I went, I took a bite of the Japanese course that my assistant ordered, and that was good too.) But the portions were rather small, so myco was saying that it wasn't enough... ; for her stomach. (laugh)

After going back to our room and lounging around, we reached Hachinohe in Aomori Prefecture at one o'clock! How fast! I started to have some doubts whether we could reach Toya by seven at the speed we were going, but apparently the train took about an hour and a half to add a traction unit before entering the Seikan Tunnel.

I had already fallen asleep and didn't notice, but myco heard some sound and looked out to see about fifteen workers outside. That's right! We had fallen asleep...with the curtains wide open! How embarrassing!

But those workers are used to that. They quickly turned their eyes away from us, and after that they never looked at us. And so, we went through the tunnel to Hokkaido. We woke up around six o'clock, but the shops at Toya probably don't open that early, right? We were both hungry, so we had breakfast on the Cassiopeia and decided to remain on the train for a little longer. And how did that turn out...?

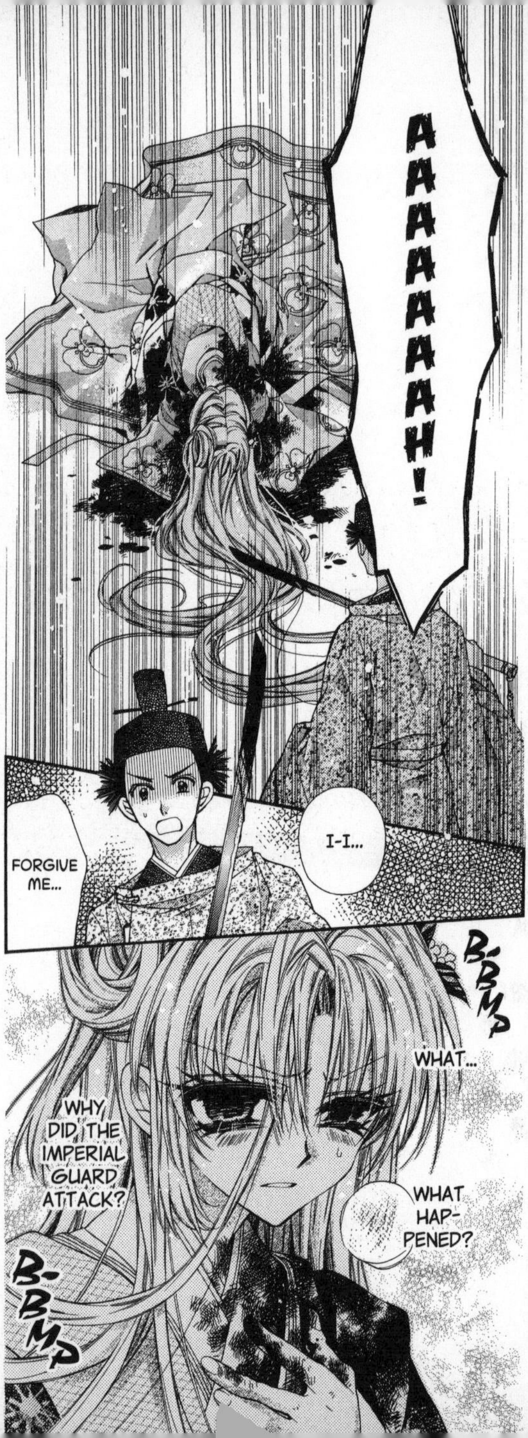

AAAAAAAAAH!
I-I...
FORGIVE ME...
B-BMP
WHAT...
WHY DID THE IMPERIAL GUARD ATTACK?
WHAT HAP-PENED?
B-BMP

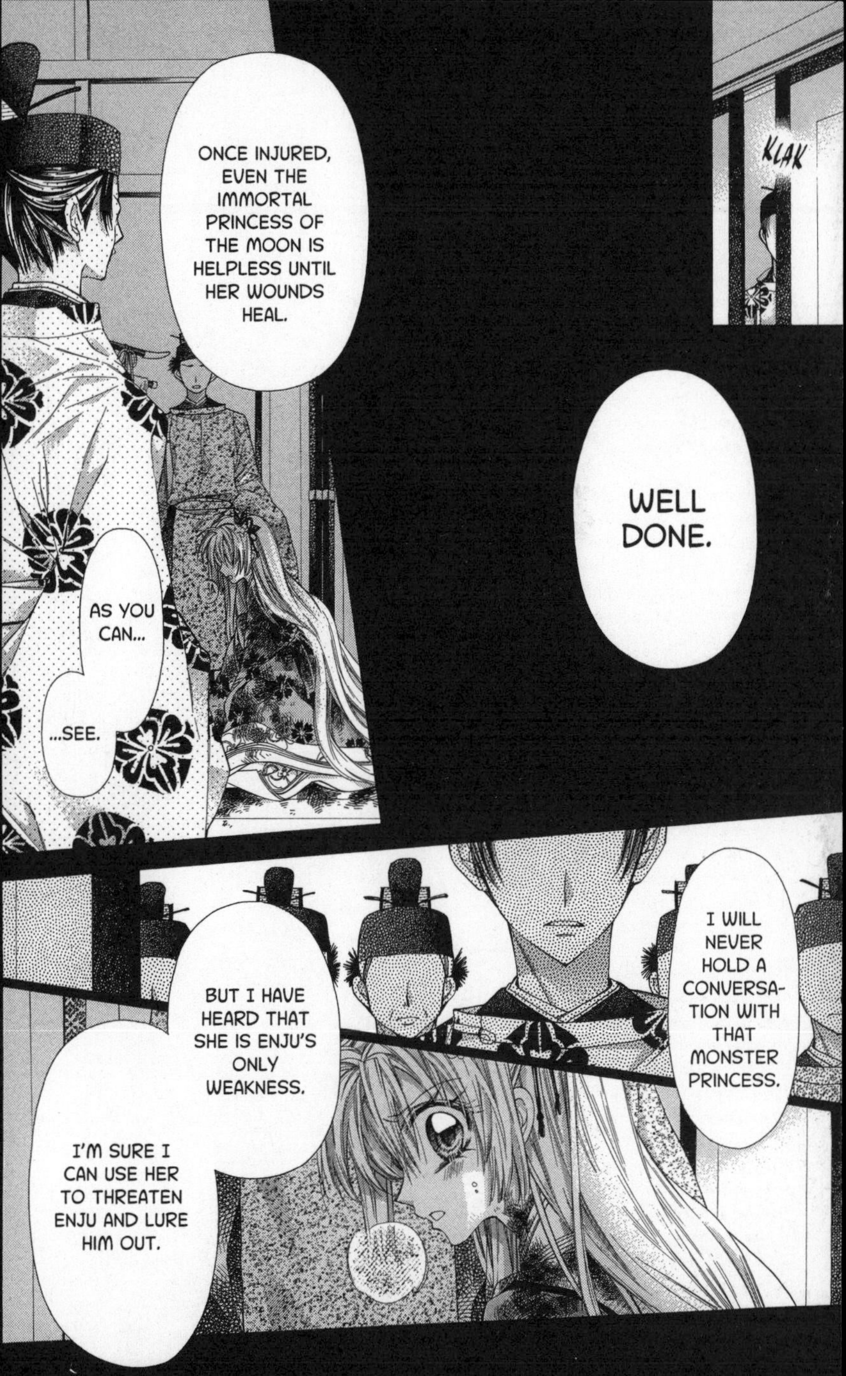
KLAK
WELL DONE.
ONCE INJURED, EVEN THE IMMORTAL PRINCESS OF THE MOON IS HELPLESS UNTIL HER WOUNDS HEAL.
AS YOU CAN...
...SEE.
I WILL NEVER HOLD A CONVERSA-TION WITH THAT MONSTER PRINCESS.
BUT I HAVE HEARD THAT SHE IS ENJU'S ONLY WEAKNESS.
I'M SURE I CAN USE HER TO THREATEN ENJU AND LURE HIM OUT.

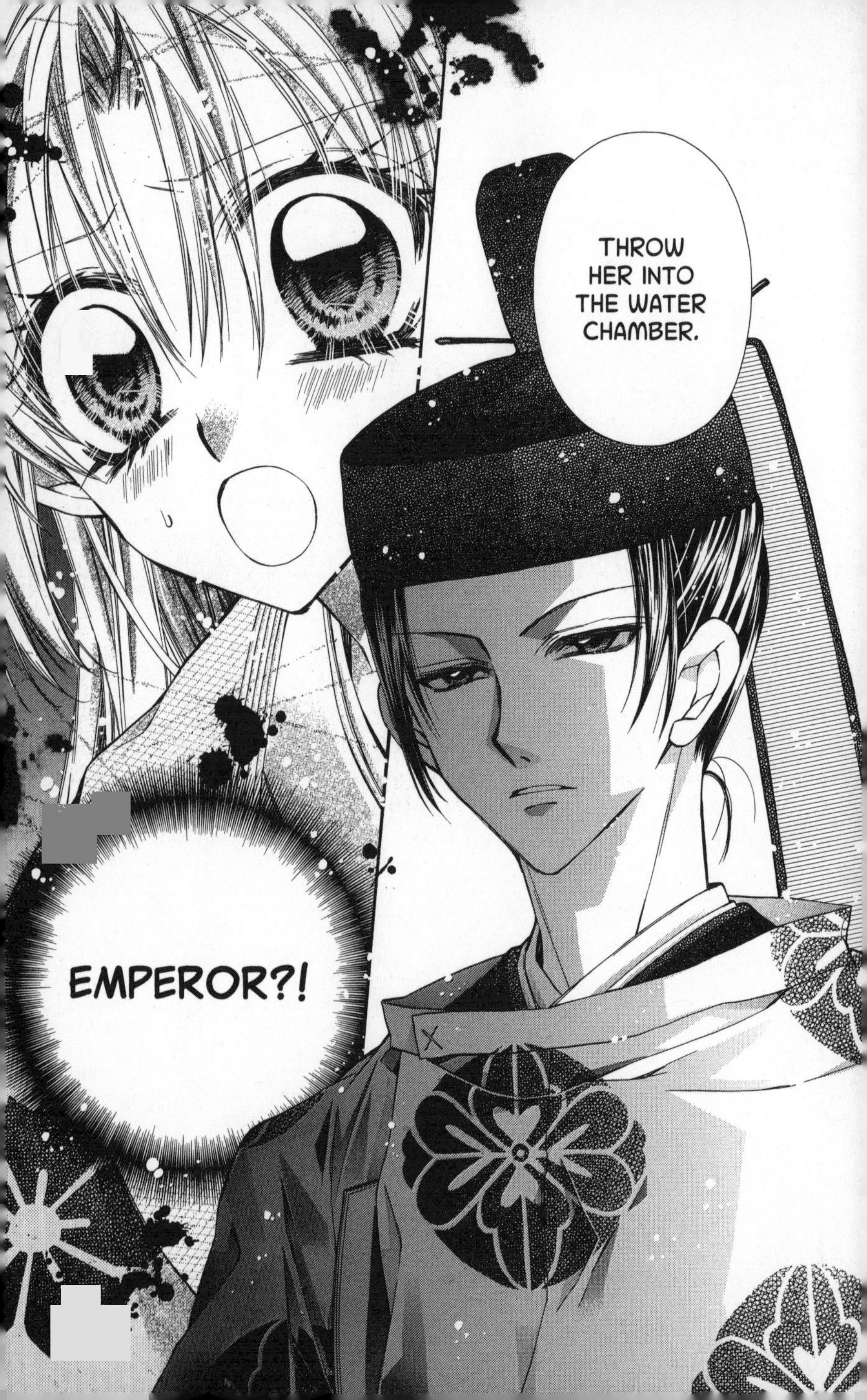
THROW HER INTO THE WATER CHAMBER.
EMPEROR?!

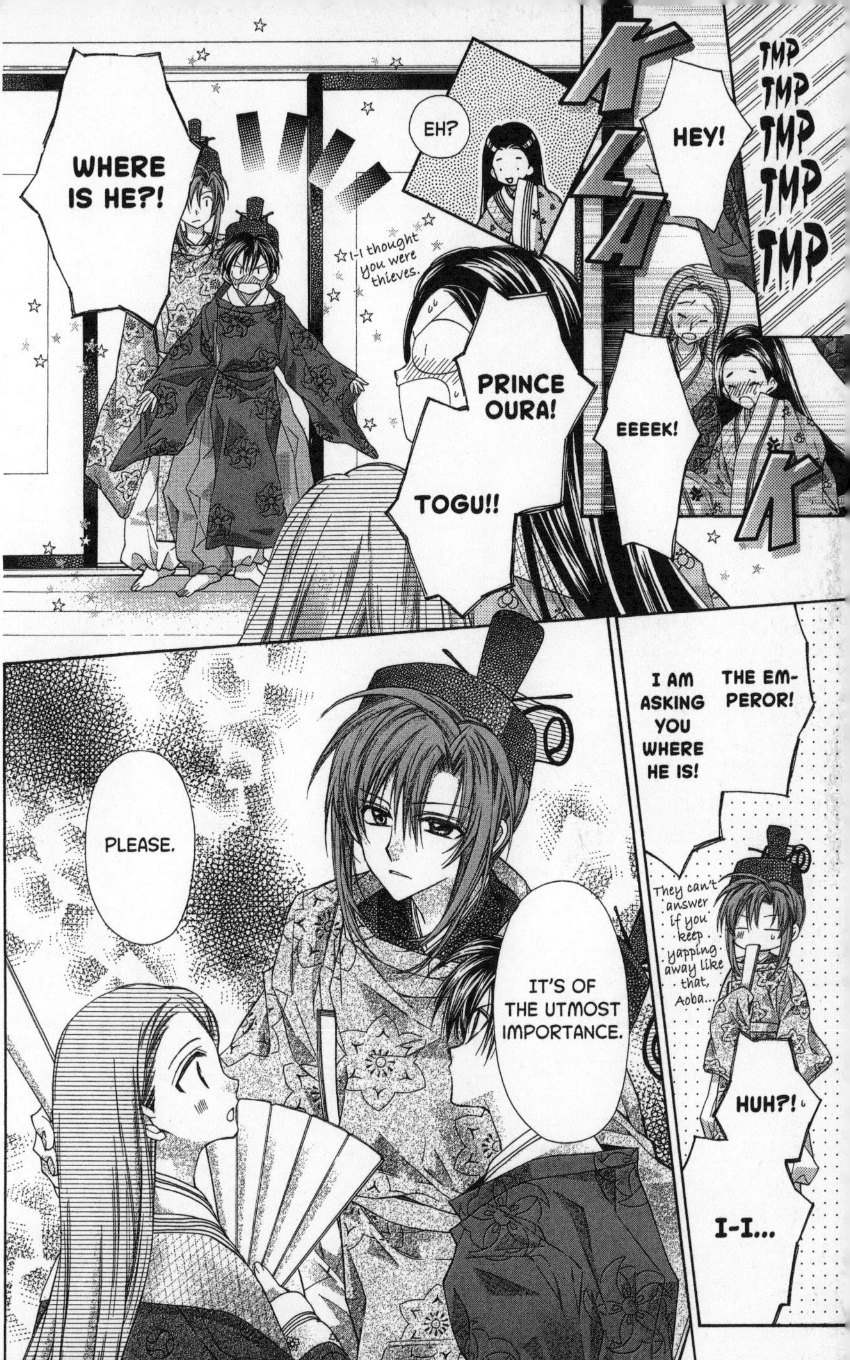
TMP TMP TMP TMP TMP
HEY!
EEEEK!
EH?
PRINCE OURA!
TOGU!!
WHERE IS HE?!
I-I thought you were thieves.
THE EM-PEROR!
I AM ASKING YOU WHERE HE IS!
They can't answer if you keep yapping away like that, Aoba...
HUH?!
I-I...
PLEASE.
IT'S OF THE UTMOST IMPORTANCE.

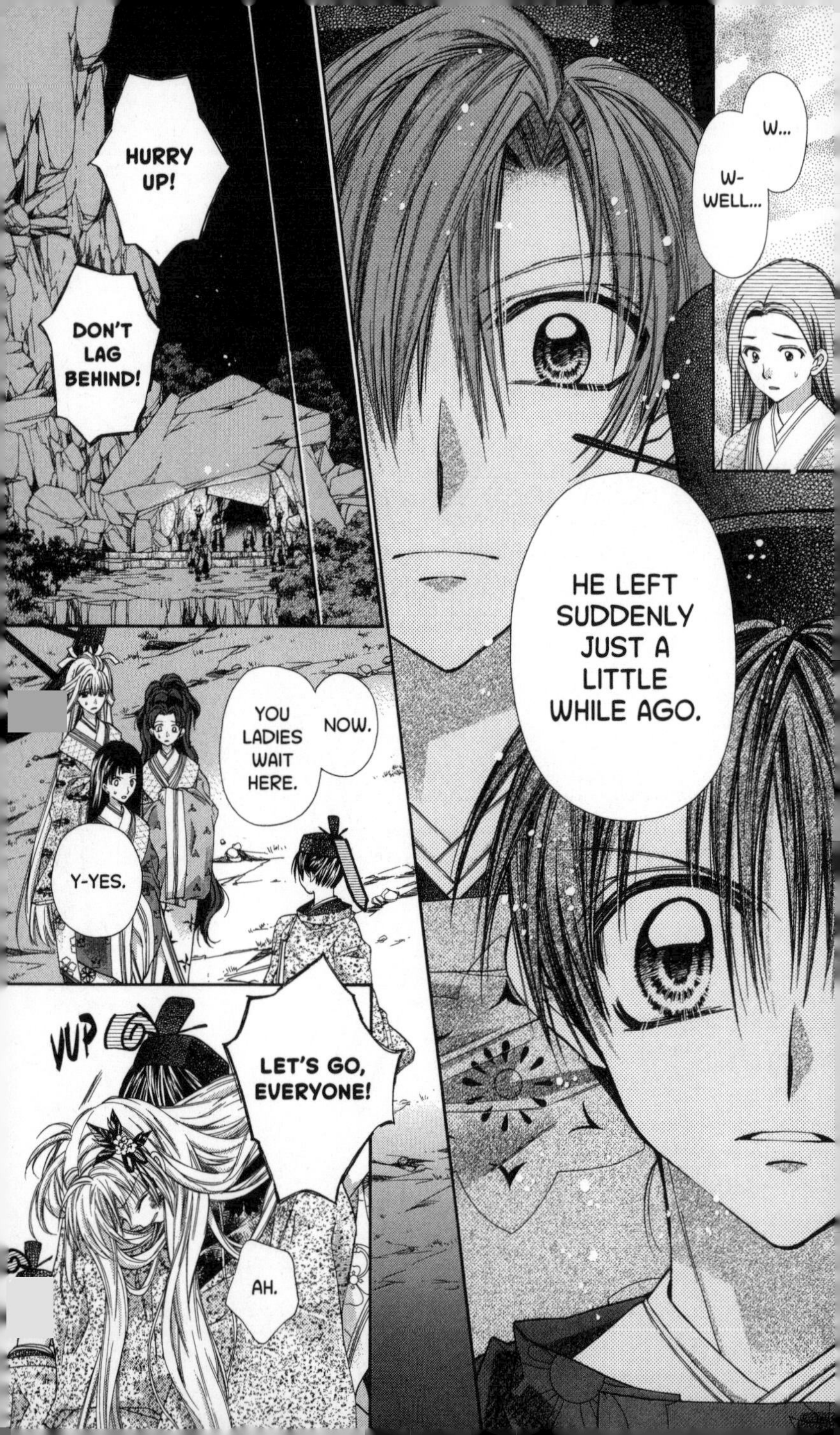

W...
W-WELL...
HE LEFT SUDDENLY JUST A LITTLE WHILE AGO.
HURRY UP!
DON'T LAG BEHIND!
YOU LADIES WAIT HERE.
NOW.
Y-YES.
VUP
LET'S GO, EVERYONE!
AH.

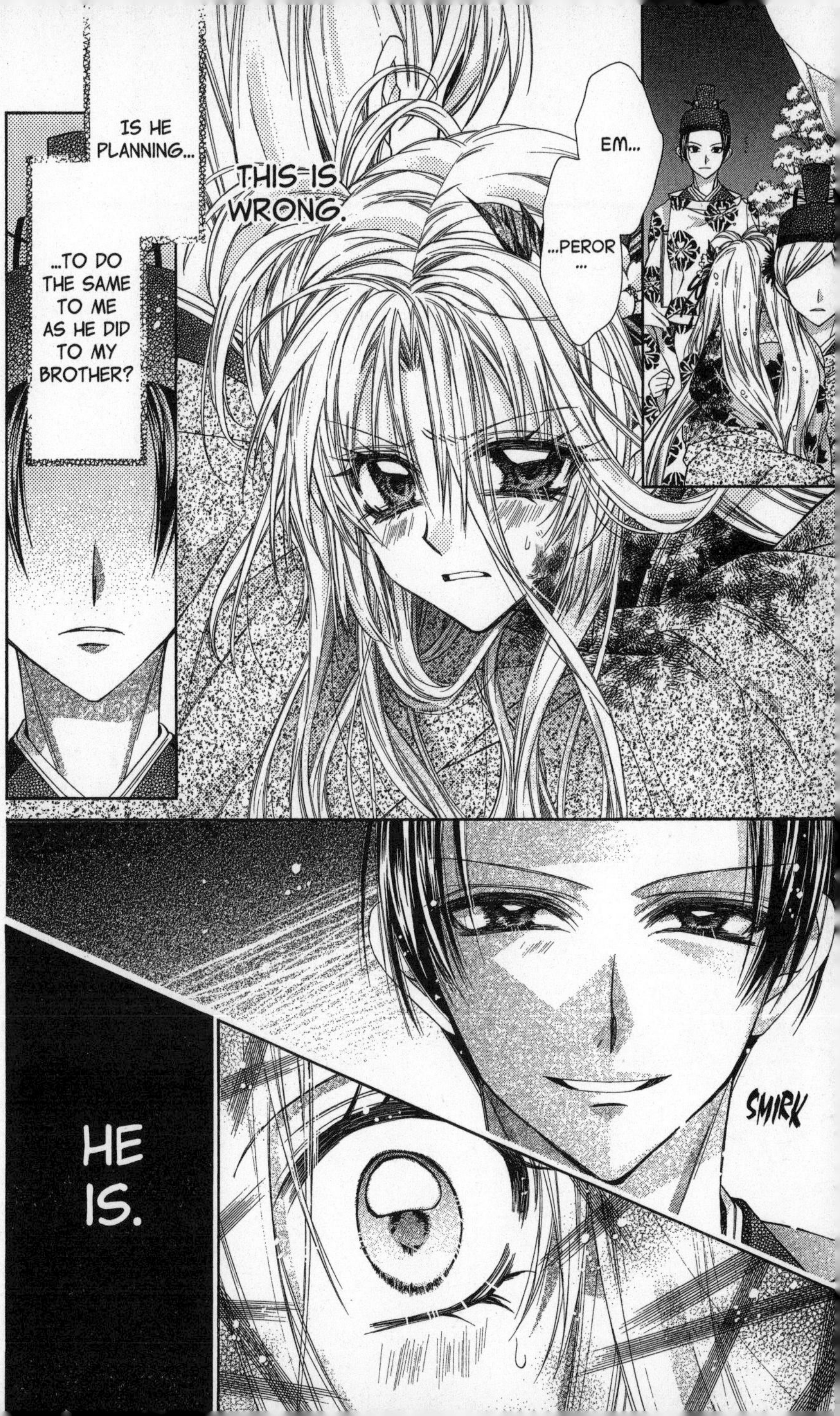
EM...
...PEROR ...
THIS IS WRONG.
IS HE PLANNING...
...TO DO THE SAME TO ME AS HE DID TO MY BROTHER?
SMIRK
HE IS.

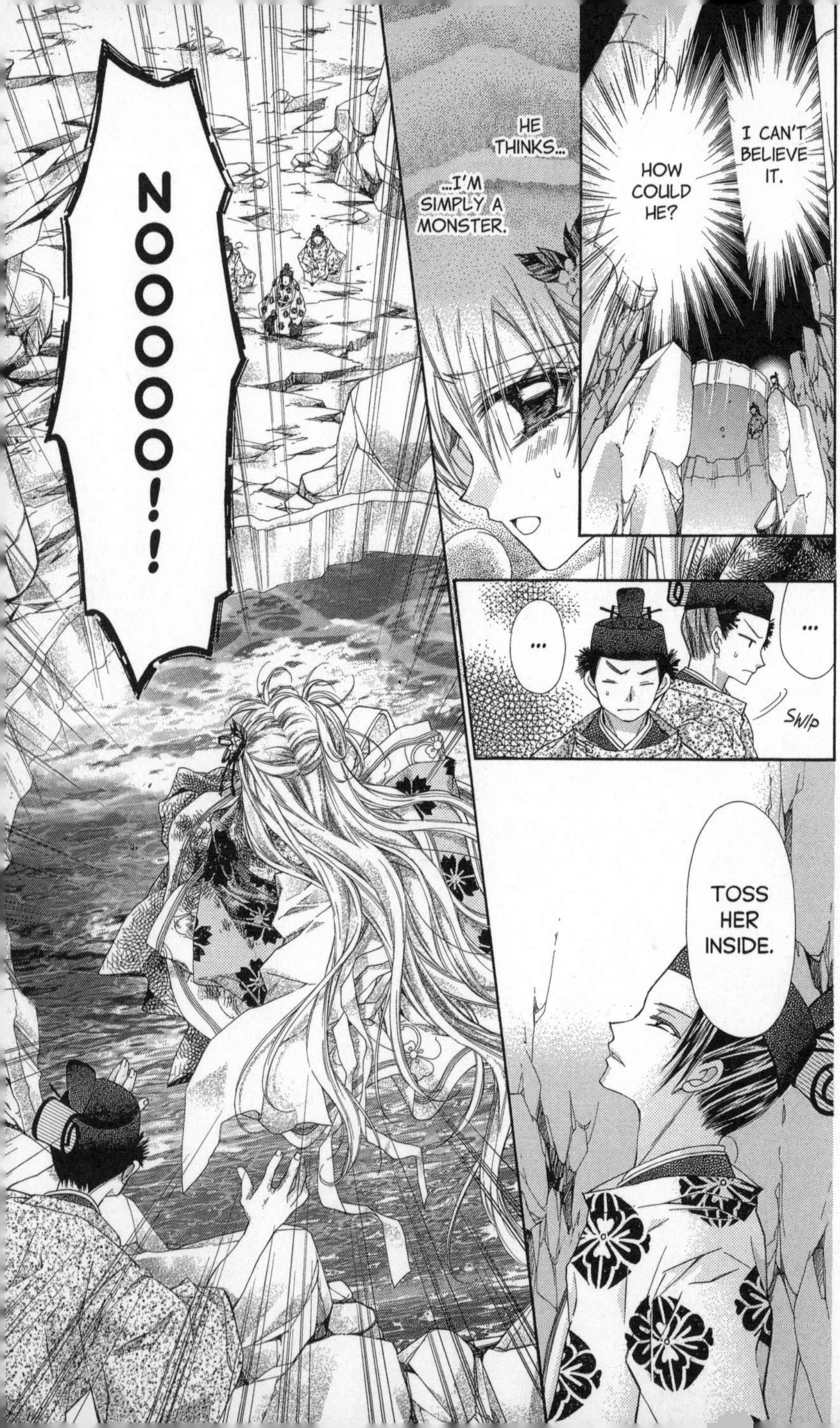
I CAN'T BELIEVE IT.
HOW COULD HE?
HE THINKS...
...I'M SIMPLY A MONSTER.
...
...
SWIP
TOSS HER INSIDE.
NOOOOO!!!

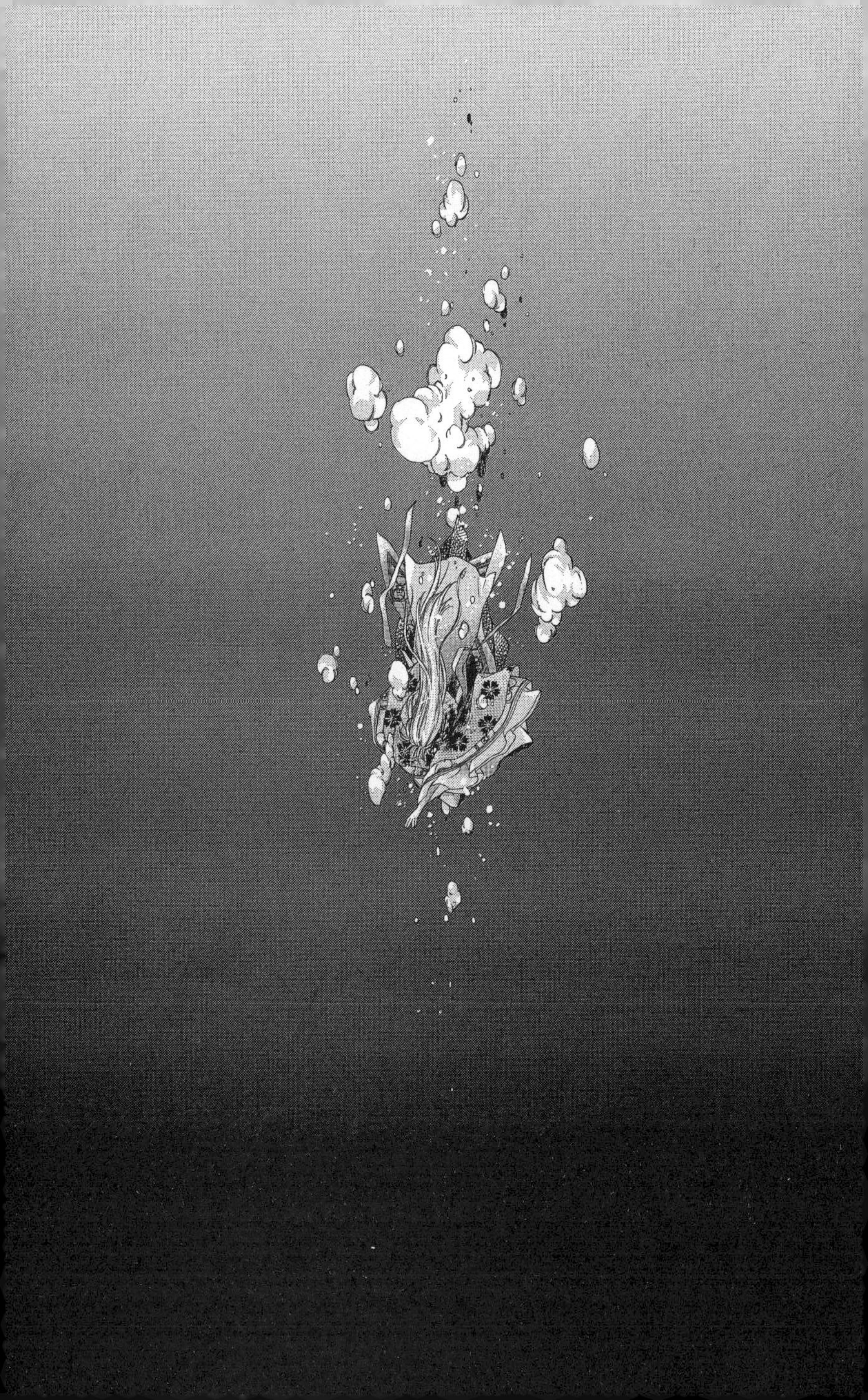

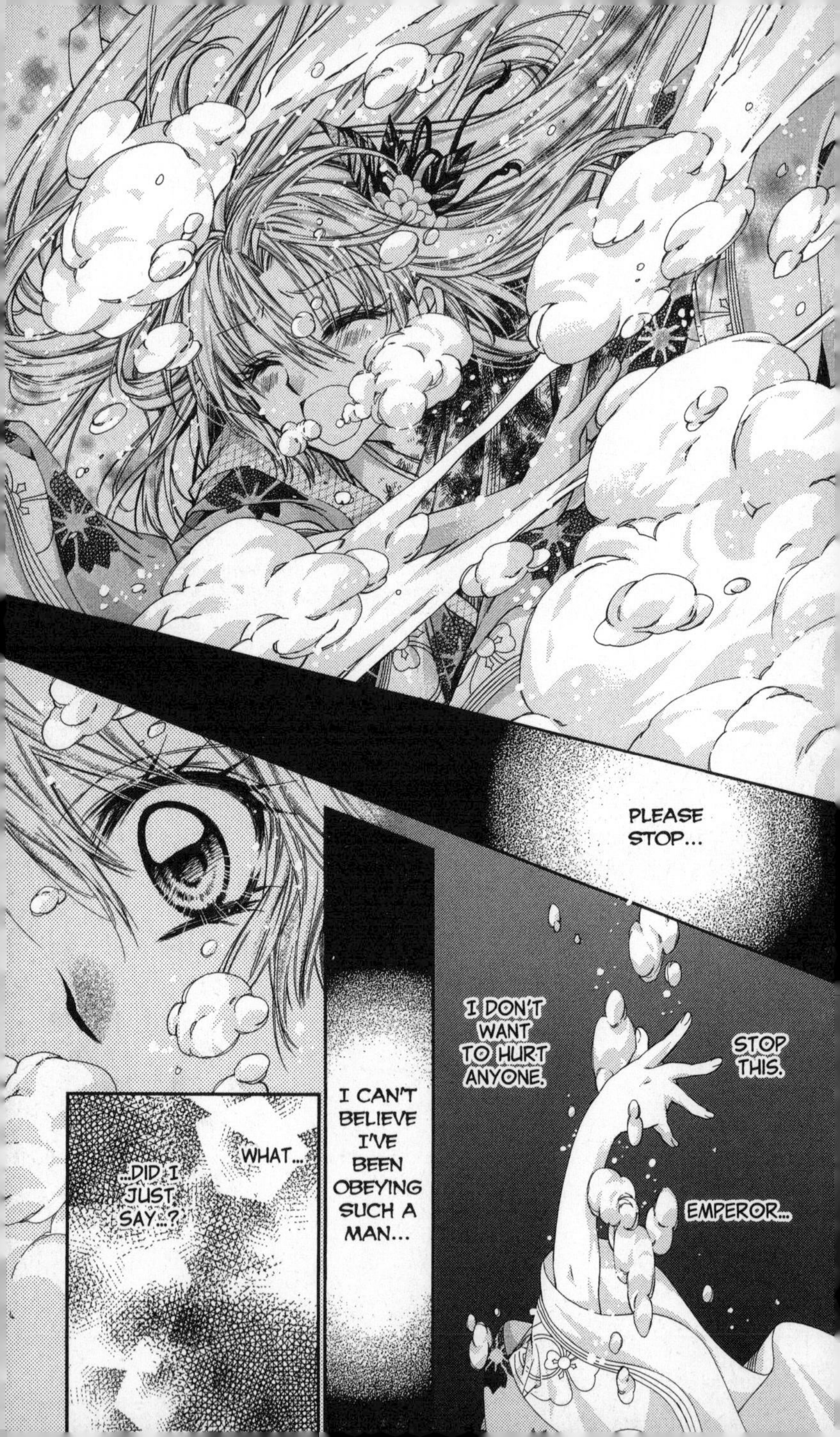
PLEASE STOP...
STOP THIS.
I DON'T WANT TO HURT ANYONE.
EMPEROR...
I CAN'T BELIEVE I'VE BEEN OBEYING SUCH A MAN...
WHAT...
...DID I JUST SAY...?

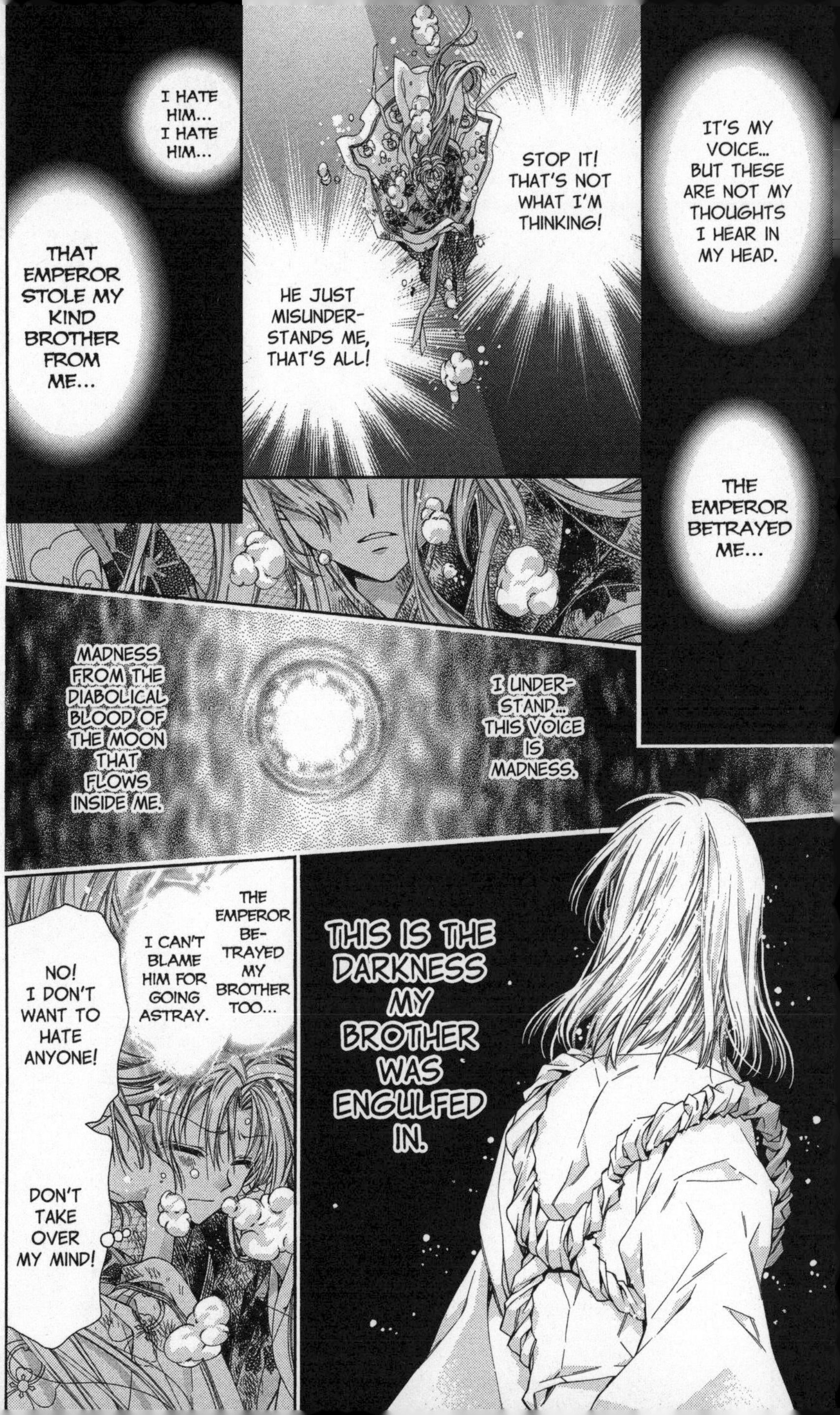

IT'S MY VOICE... BUT THESE ARE NOT MY THOUGHTS I HEAR IN MY HEAD.
THE EMPEROR BETRAYED ME...
STOP IT! THAT'S NOT WHAT I'M THINKING!
HE JUST MISUNDER-STANDS ME, THAT'S ALL!
I HATE HIM... I HATE HIM...
THAT EMPEROR STOLE MY KIND BROTHER FROM ME...
I UNDER-STAND... THIS VOICE IS MADNESS.
MADNESS FROM THE DIABOLICAL BLOOD OF THE MOON THAT FLOWS INSIDE ME.
THIS IS THE DARKNESS MY BROTHER WAS ENGULFED IN.
THE EMPEROR BE-TRAYED MY BROTHER TOO...
I CAN'T BLAME HIM FOR GOING ASTRAY.
NO! I DON'T WANT TO HATE ANYONE!
DON'T TAKE OVER MY MIND!

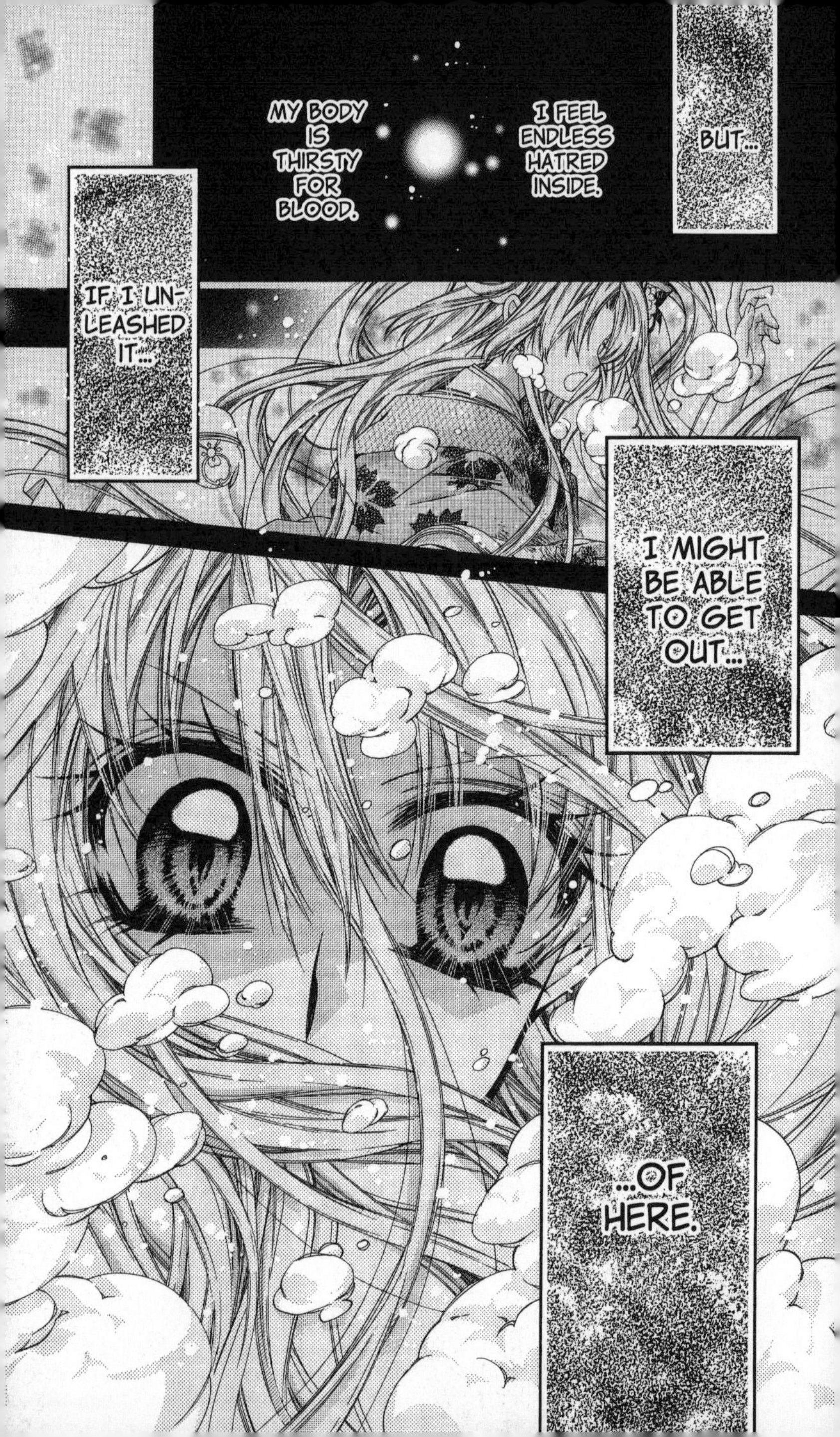
I FEEL ENDLESS HATRED INSIDE.
MY BODY IS THIRSTY FOR BLOOD.
BUT...
IF I UNLEASHED IT...
I MIGHT BE ABLE TO GET OUT...
...OF HERE.

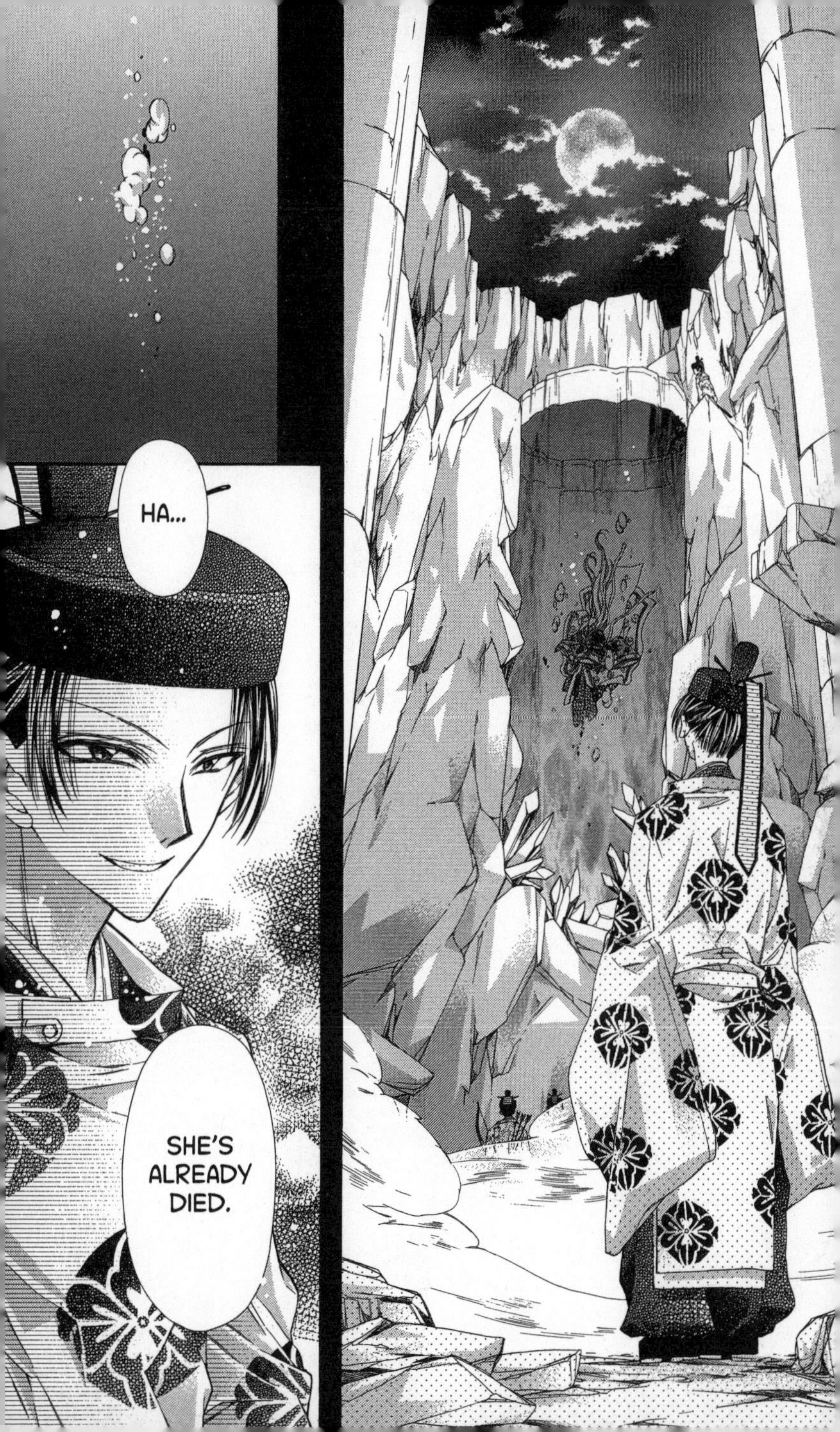
HA...
SHE'S ALREADY DIED.

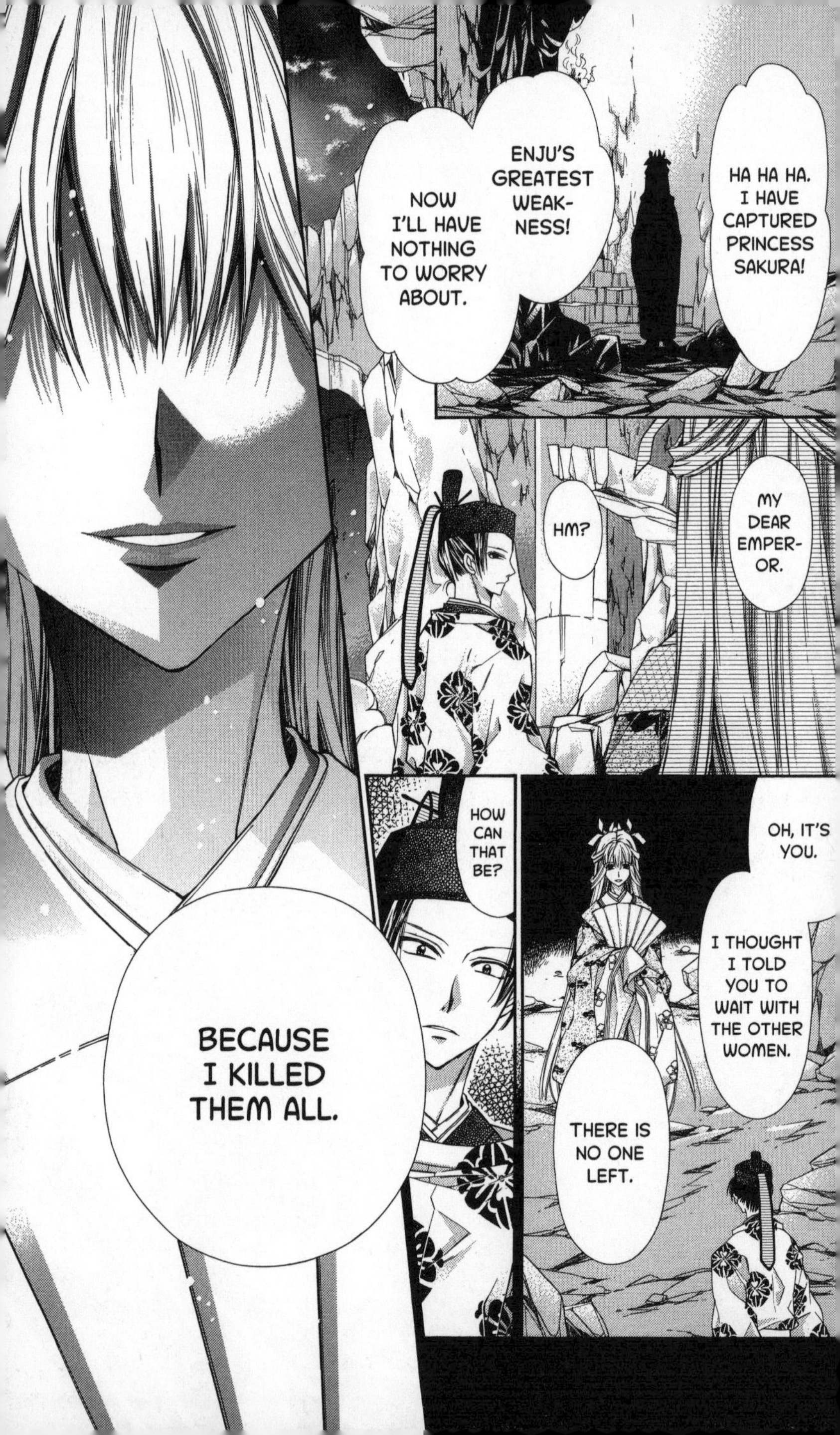
HA HA HA. I HAVE CAPTURED PRINCESS SAKURA!
ENJU'S GREATEST WEAK-NESS!
NOW I'LL HAVE NOTHING TO WORRY ABOUT.
MY DEAR EMPER-OR.
HM?
OH, IT'S YOU.
I THOUGHT I TOLD YOU TO WAIT WITH THE OTHER WOMEN.
THERE IS NO ONE LEFT.
HOW CAN THAT BE?
BECAUSE I KILLED THEM ALL.

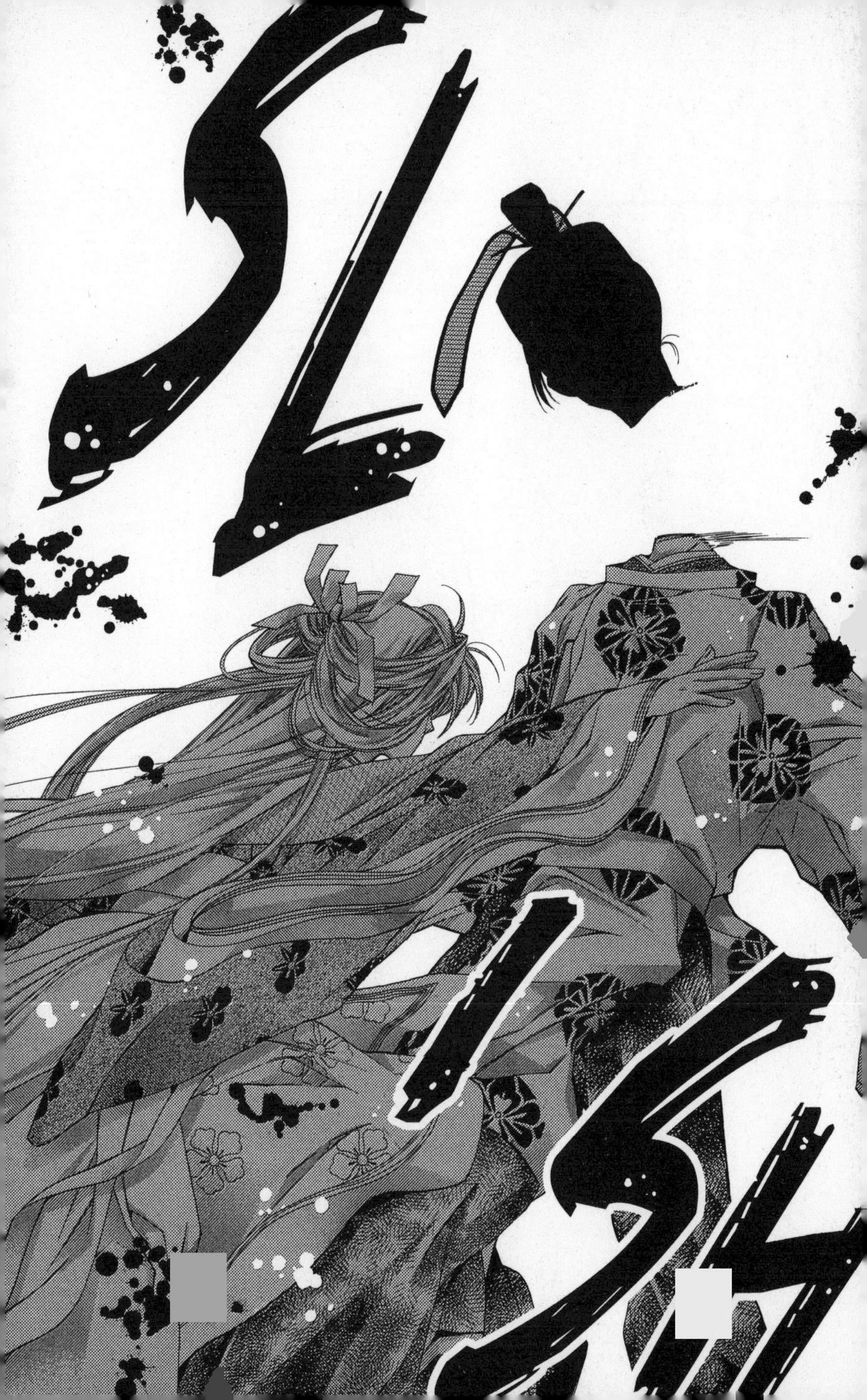

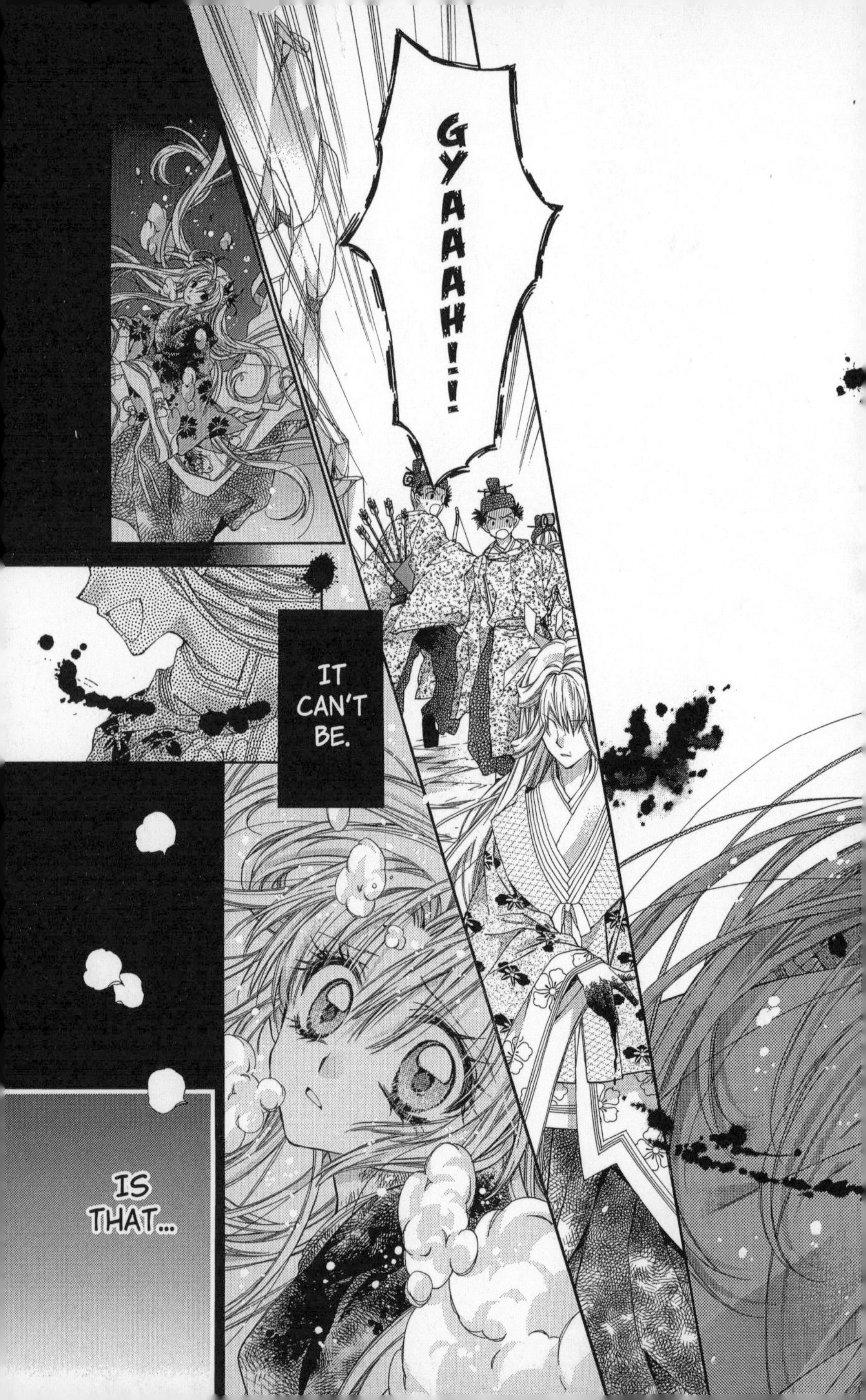
GYAAAH!!!
IT CAN'T BE.
IS THAT...

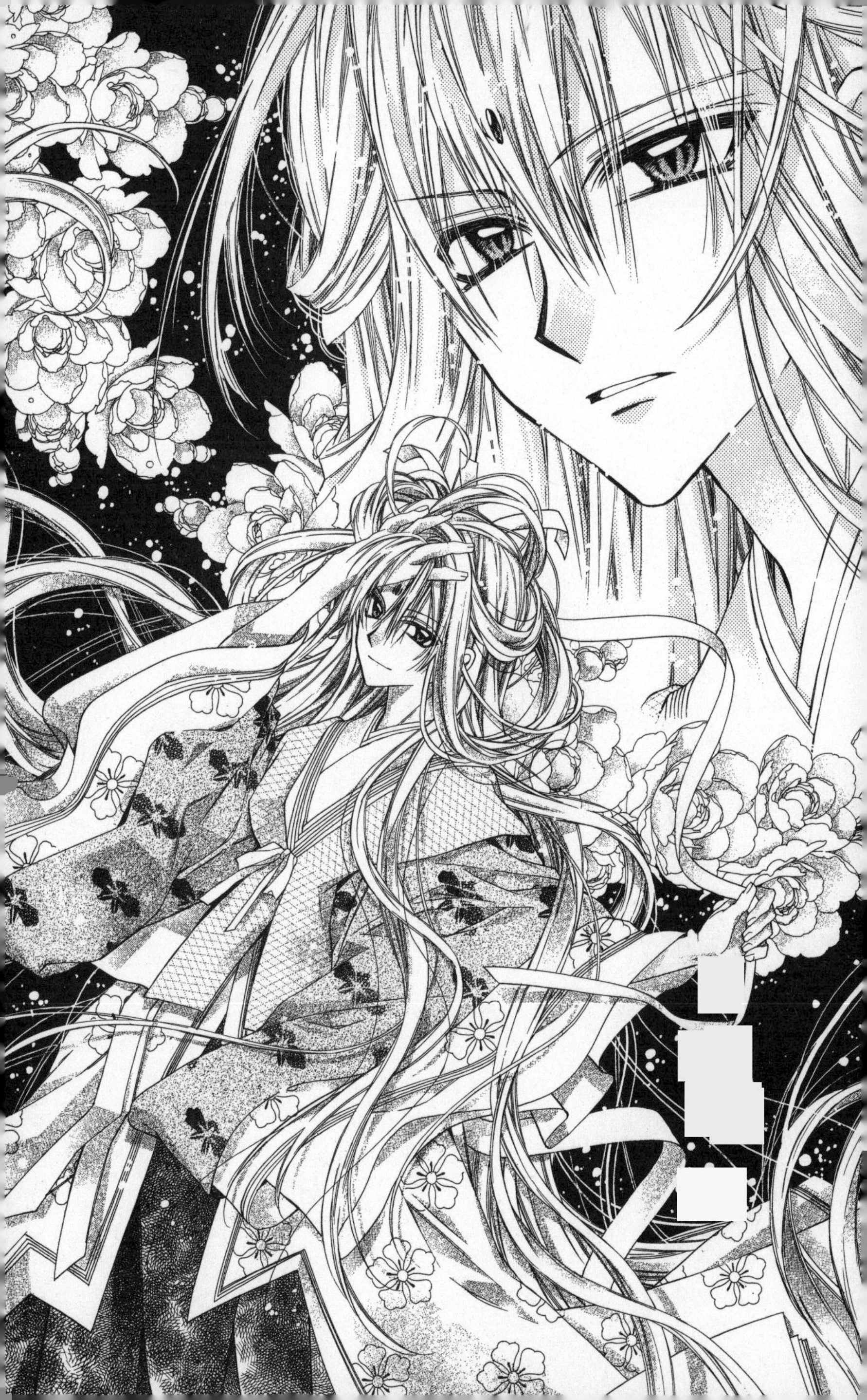

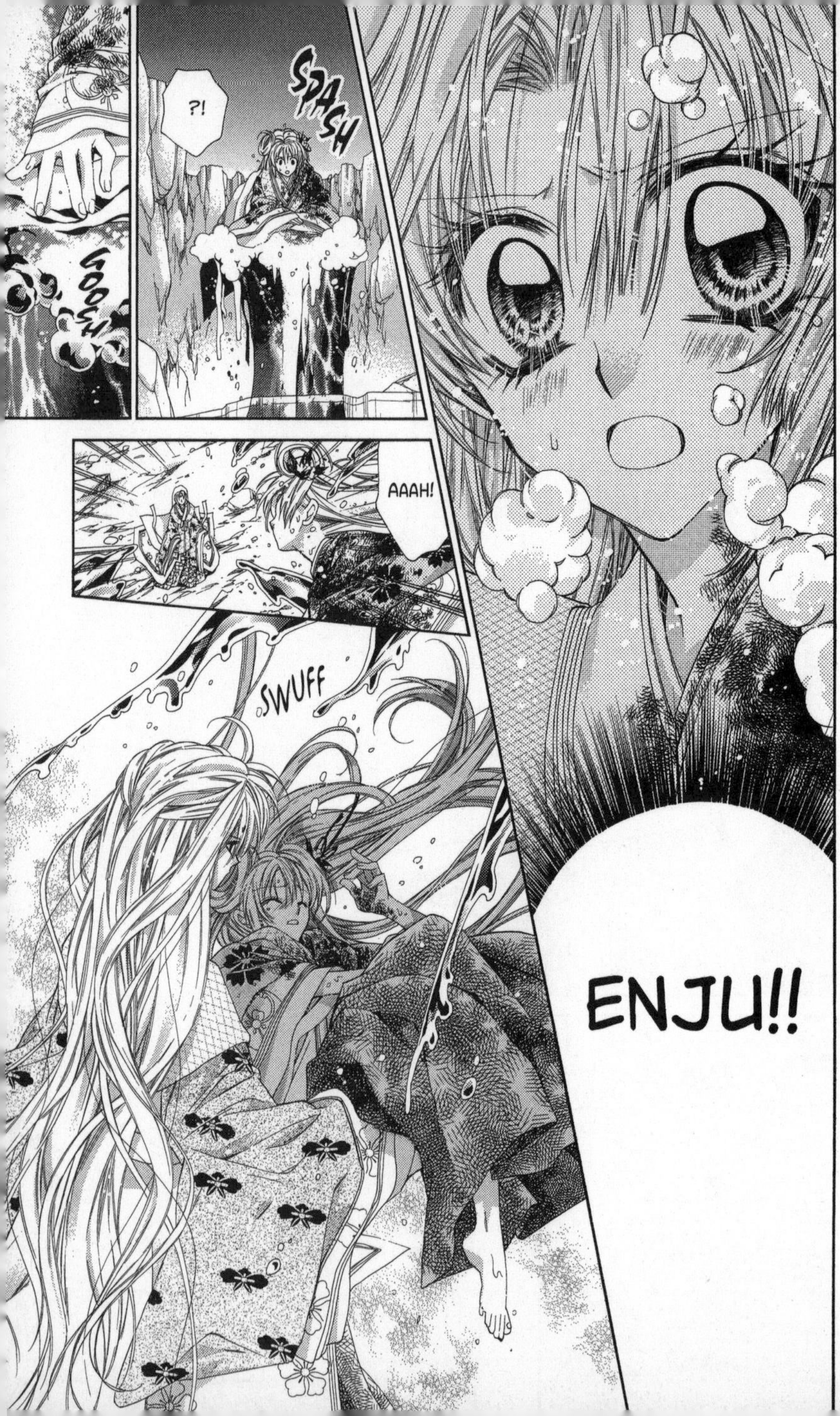
ENJU!!
SPASH
?!
GOOOSH
AAAH!
SWUFF

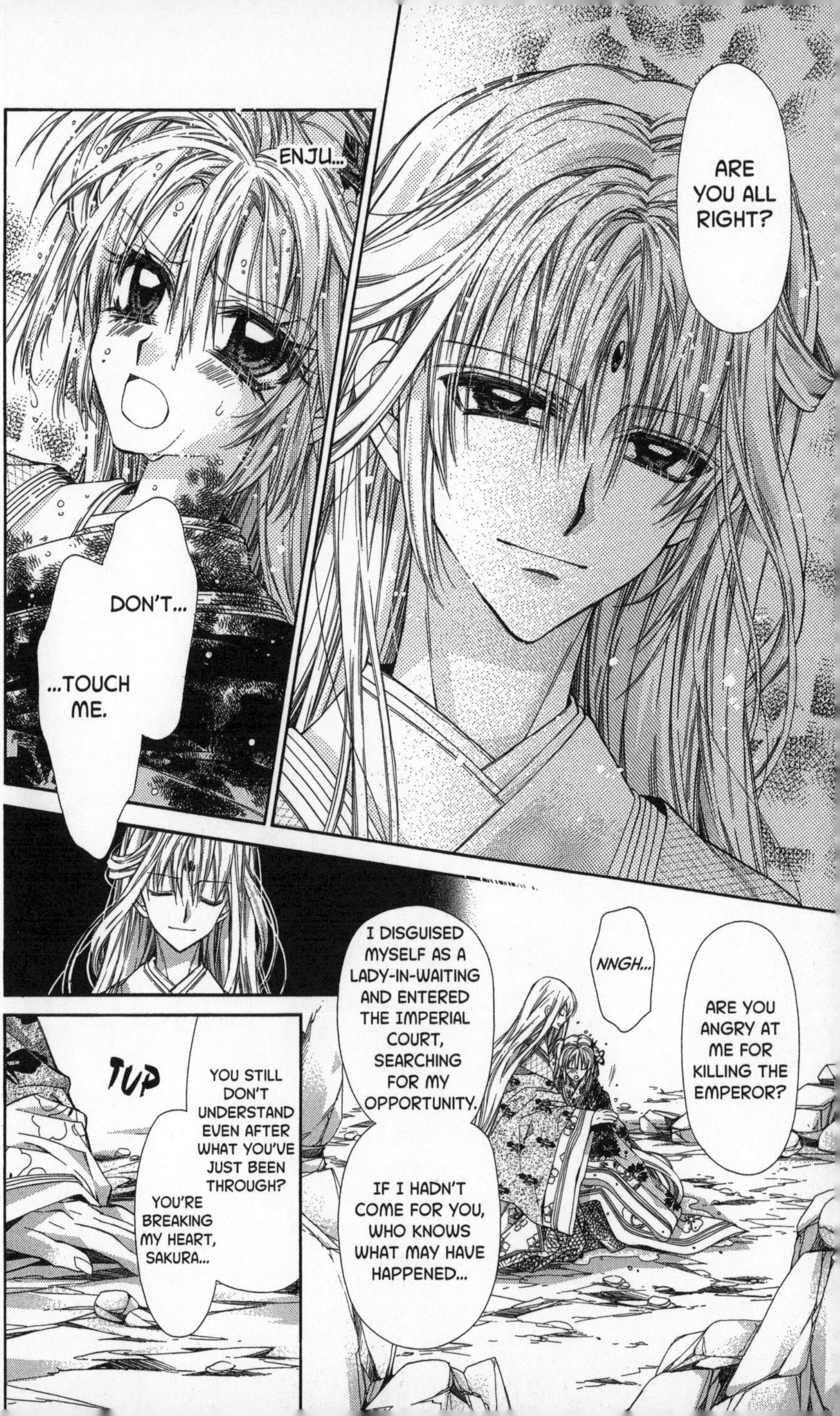
ARE YOU ALL RIGHT?
ENJU...
DON'T...
...TOUCH ME.
ARE YOU ANGRY AT ME FOR KILLING THE EMPEROR?
NNGH...
I DISGUISED MYSELF AS A LADY-IN-WAITING AND ENTERED THE IMPERIAL COURT, SEARCHING FOR MY OPPORTUNITY.
IF I HADN'T COME FOR YOU, WHO KNOWS WHAT MAY HAVE HAPPENED...
TUP
YOU STILL DON'T UNDERSTAND EVEN AFTER WHAT YOU'VE JUST BEEN THROUGH?
YOU'RE BREAKING MY HEART, SAKURA...

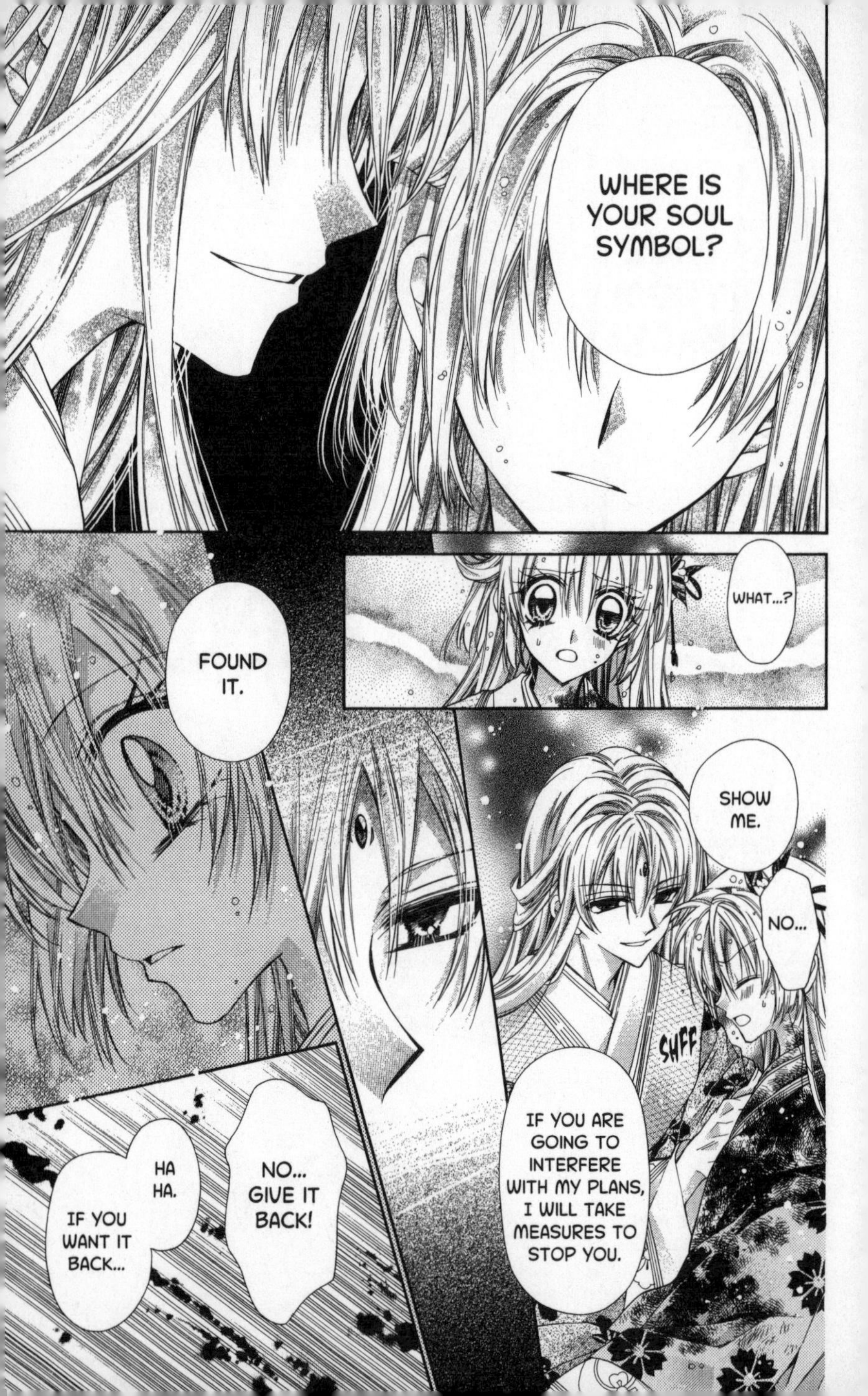
WHERE IS YOUR SOUL SYMBOL?
WHAT...?
SHOW ME.
NO...
SHFF
IF YOU ARE GOING TO INTERFERE WITH MY PLANS, I WILL TAKE MEASURES TO STOP YOU.
FOUND IT.
NO... GIVE IT BACK!
HA HA.
IF YOU WANT IT BACK...

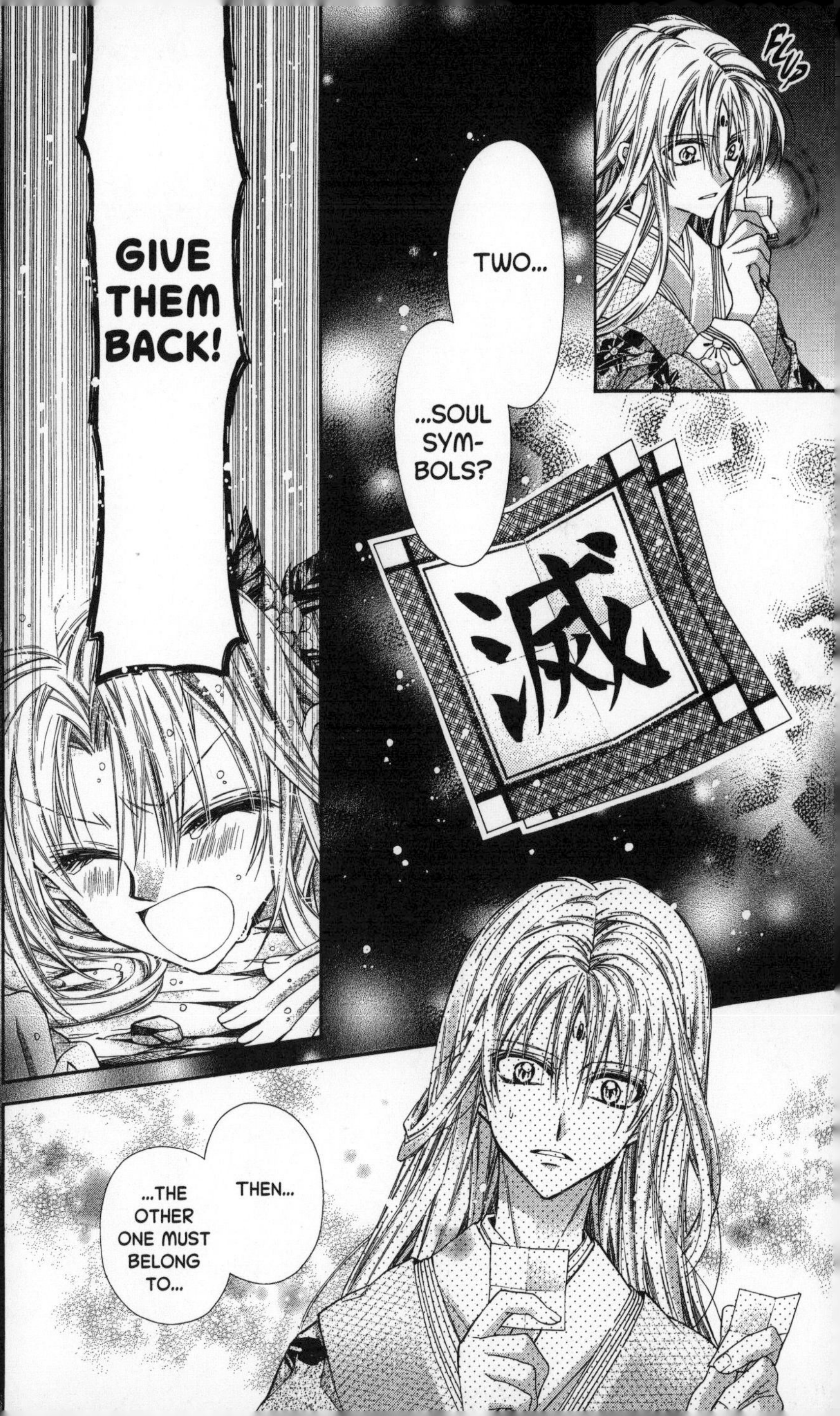
FLUP
TWO...
...SOUL SYM-BOLS?
滅
GIVE THEM BACK!
THEN...
...THE OTHER ONE MUST BELONG TO...

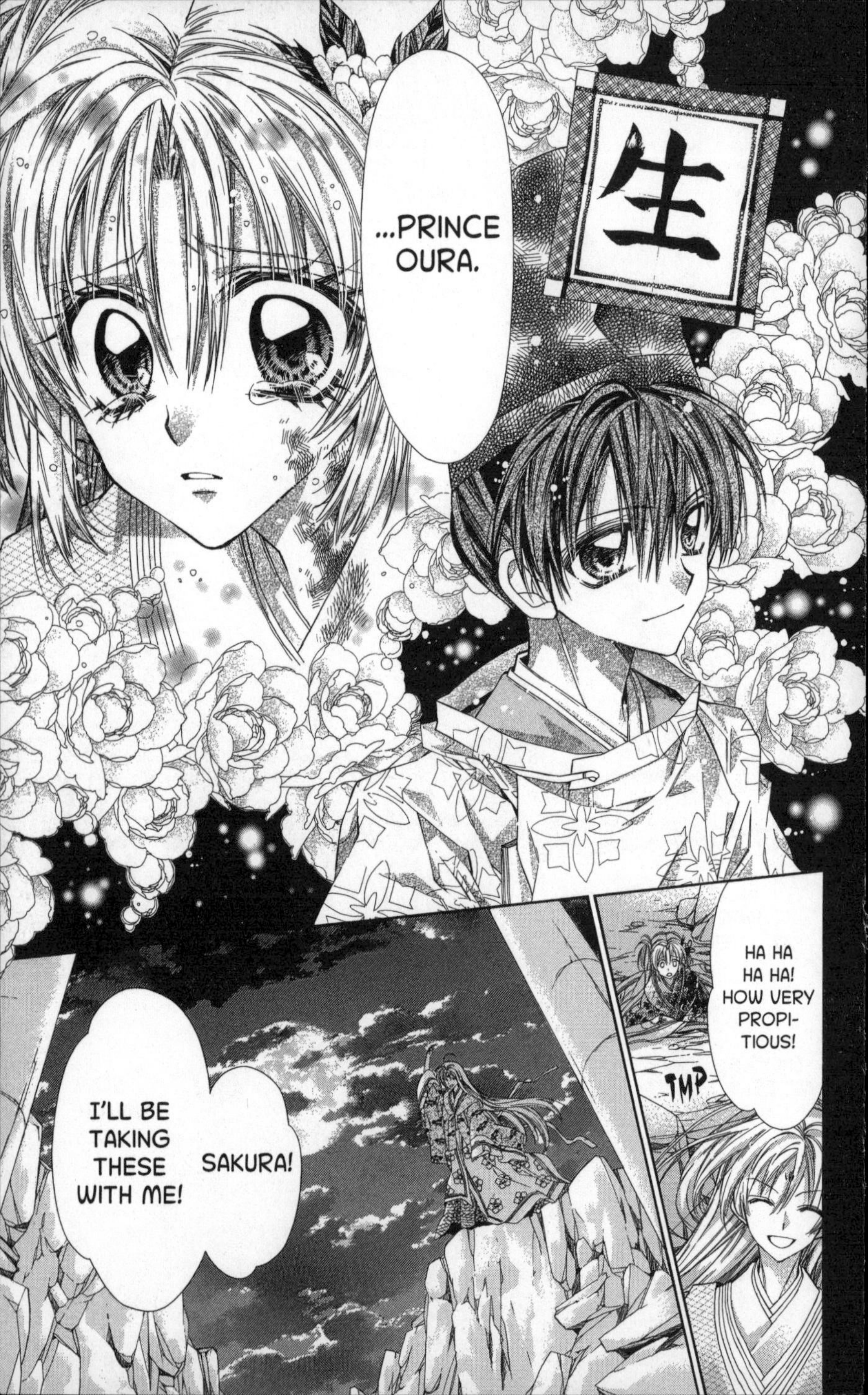
生
...PRINCE OURA.
HA HA HA HA! HOW VERY PROPI-TIOUS!
TMP
SAKURA!
I'LL BE TAKING THESE WITH ME!

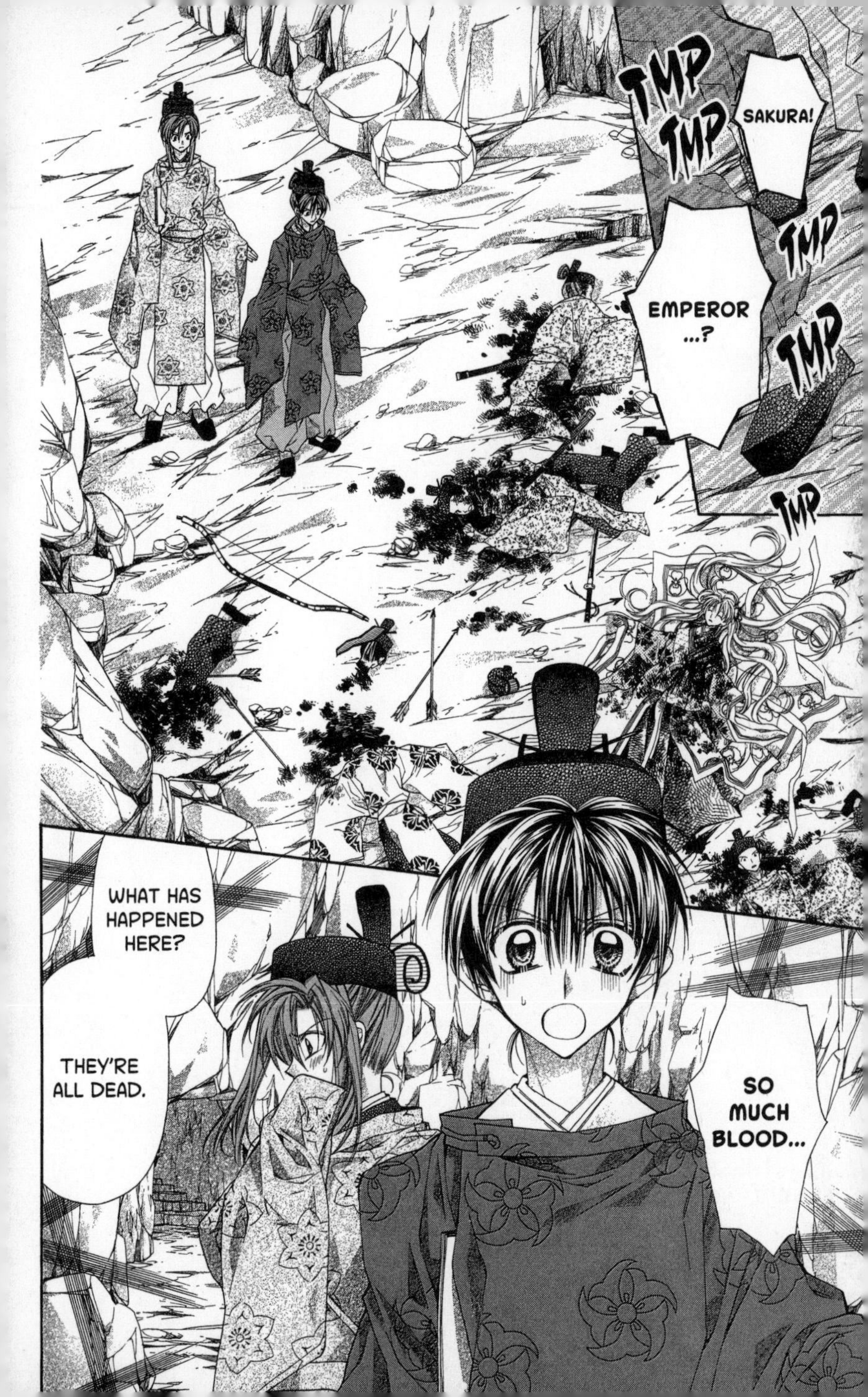
TMP TMP
SAKURA!
TMP
EMPEROR ...?
TMP
TMP
SO MUCH BLOOD...
WHAT HAS HAPPENED HERE?
THEY'RE ALL DEAD.

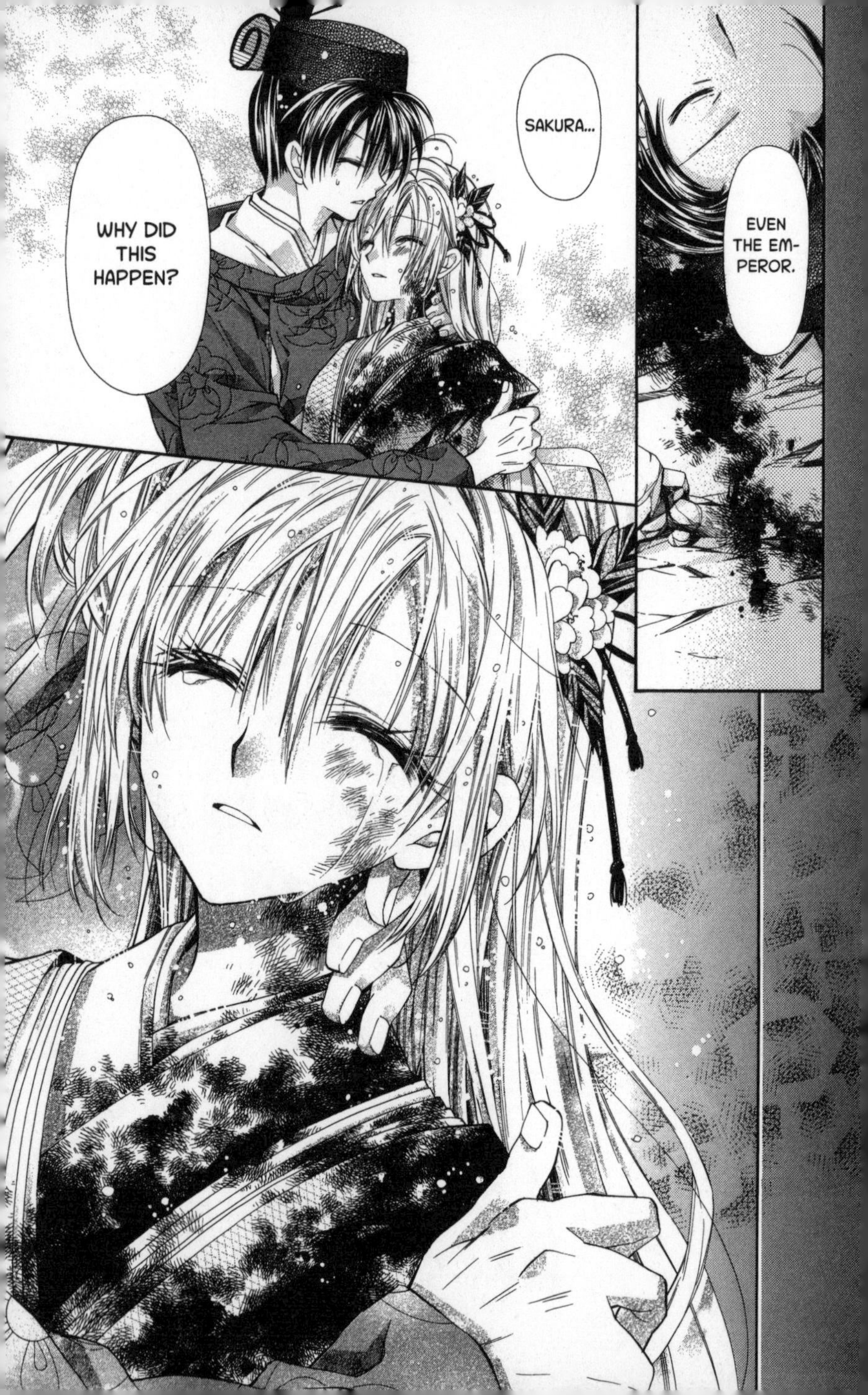
EVEN THE EM-PEROR.
SAKURA...
WHY DID THIS HAPPEN?

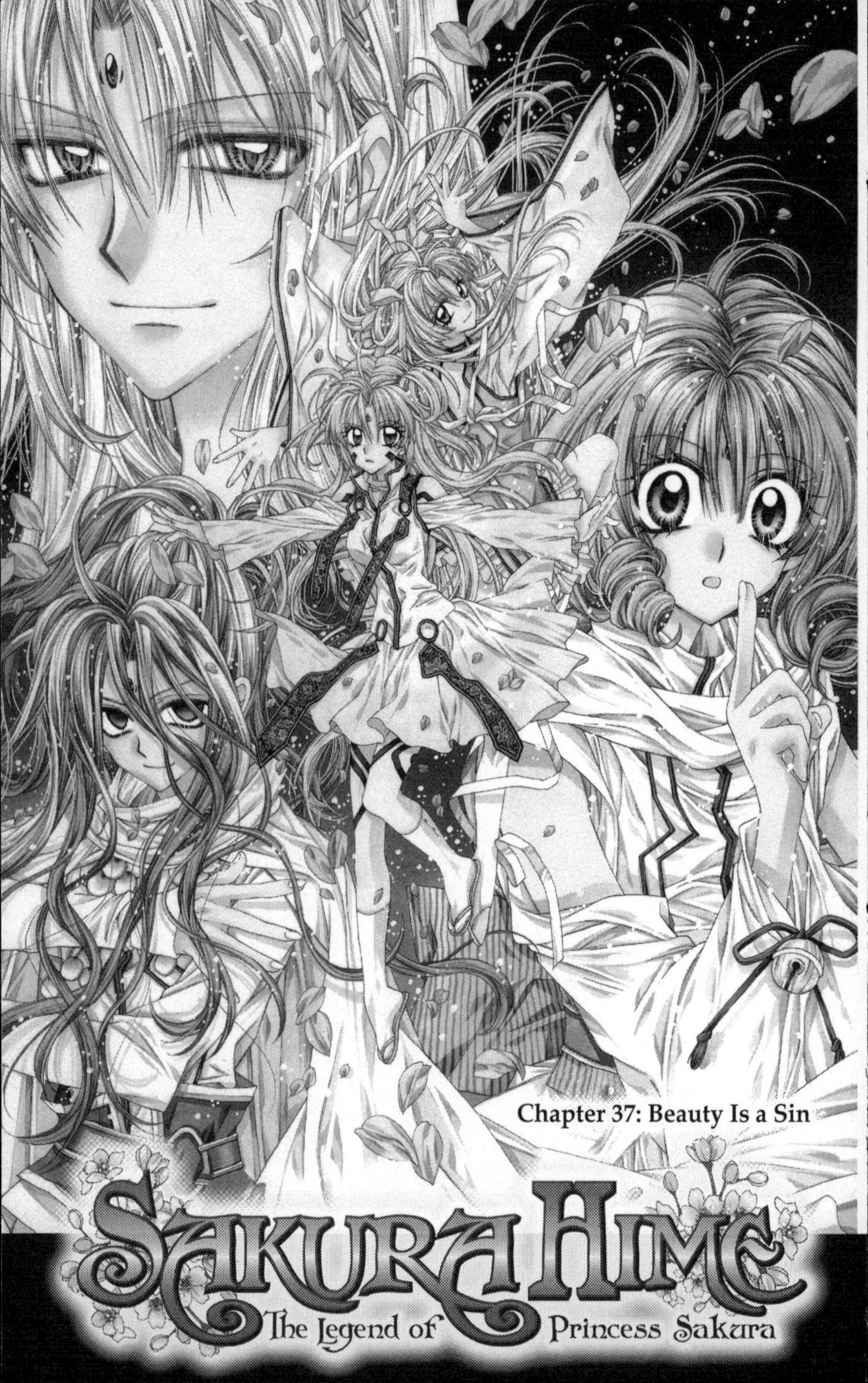
Chapter 37: Beauty Is a Sin
Sakura Hime
The Legend of Princess Sakura

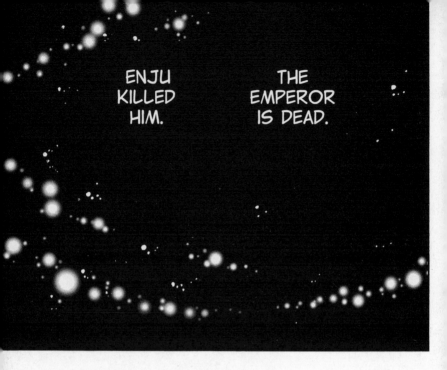

THE EMPEROR IS DEAD.
ENJU KILLED HIM.

Chapter 37: Beauty Is a Sin

※ I'm giving away the story.

The chapter title illustration is meant to be the Enju Clan! But it's rather off-balance without Ukyo. (At the start I designed them to be a group of five.) So that's why I included Sakura in it. Phew! The art is so detailed!

Anyhow, the "wild" character in the *Sakura Hime* series, Princess Yuri, makes a comeback! I have been told she is too similar to Maimai, but I daringly decided to put them together. (laugh) Princess Yuri is a very useful character because the story doesn't get too heavy when she's involved. I'm not fond of drawing large gag panels, but interestingly enough I don't have any problems drawing them when Princess Yuri is featured.

Princess Yuri represents girls to me. She is 100% girl power, which is the opposite of what I'm like. I worried whether I'd be able to draw this character, but I guess she turned out okay. It may not seem so, but Princess Yuri has opened up to Sakura. (Well, she did want to become friends with Sakura in the beginning.) I like Maimai and Princess Yuri together, but my favorite is the princess pair of Sakura and Princess Yuri. ♪

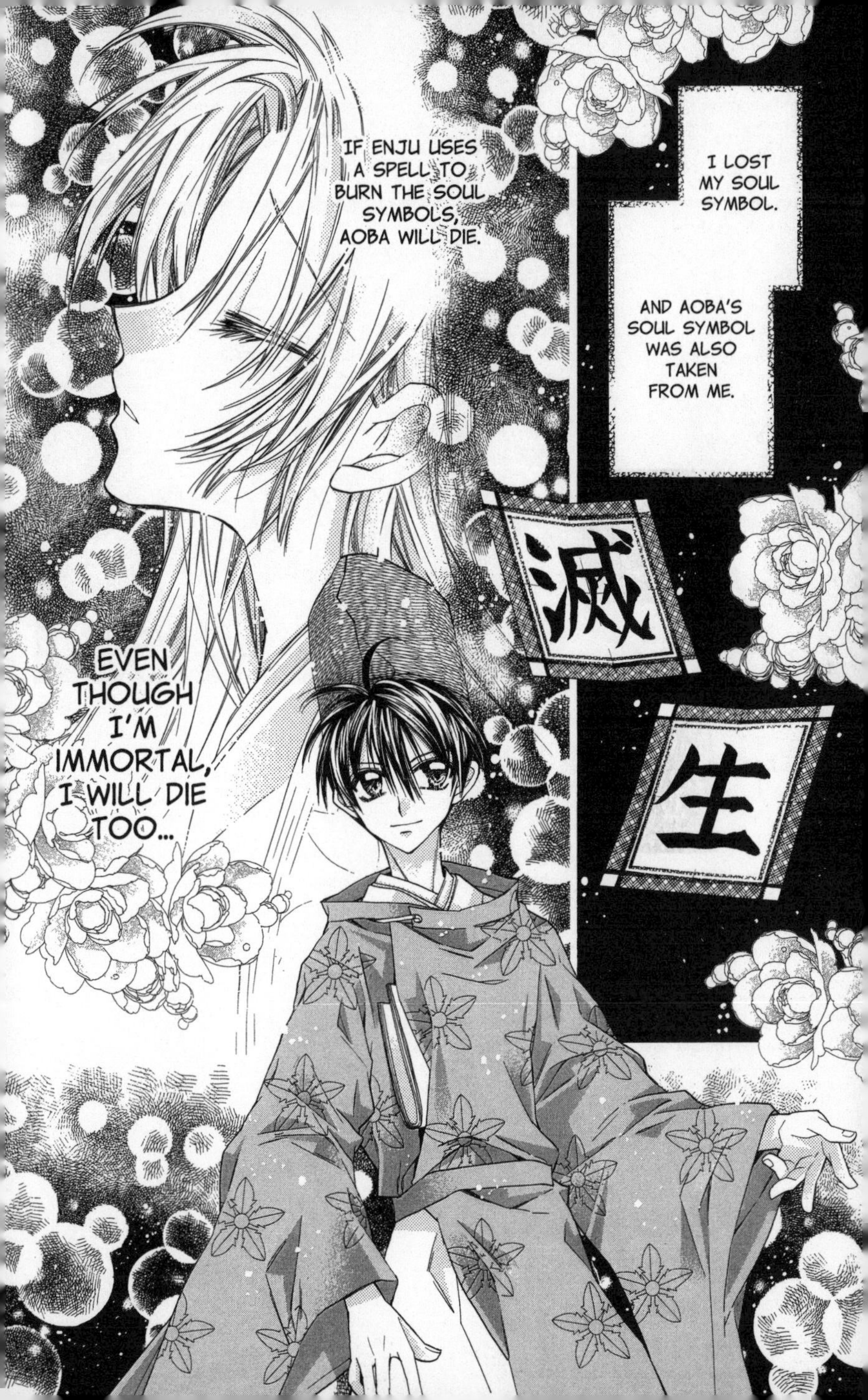
I LOST MY SOUL SYMBOL.
AND AOBA'S SOUL SYMBOL WAS ALSO TAKEN FROM ME.
IF ENJU USES A SPELL TO BURN THE SOUL SYMBOLS, AOBA WILL DIE.
滅
生
EVEN THOUGH I'M IMMORTAL, I WILL DIE TOO...

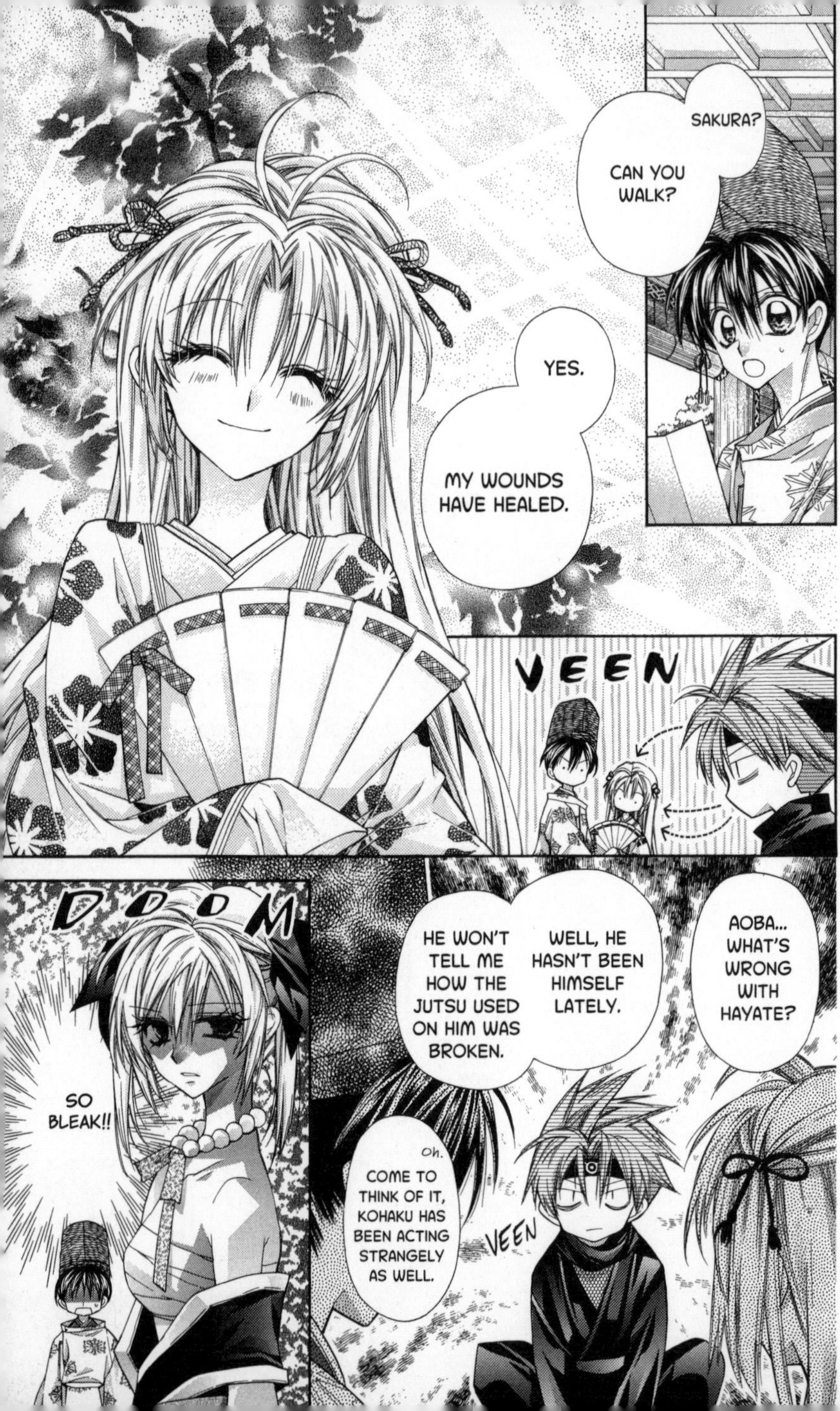
SAKURA?
CAN YOU WALK?
YES.
MY WOUNDS HAVE HEALED.
VEEN
AOBA... WHAT'S WRONG WITH HAYATE?
WELL, HE HASN'T BEEN HIMSELF LATELY.
HE WON'T TELL ME HOW THE JUTSU USED ON HIM WAS BROKEN.
VEEN
Oh.
COME TO THINK OF IT, KOHAKU HAS BEEN ACTING STRANGELY AS WELL.
DOOM
SO BLEAK!!

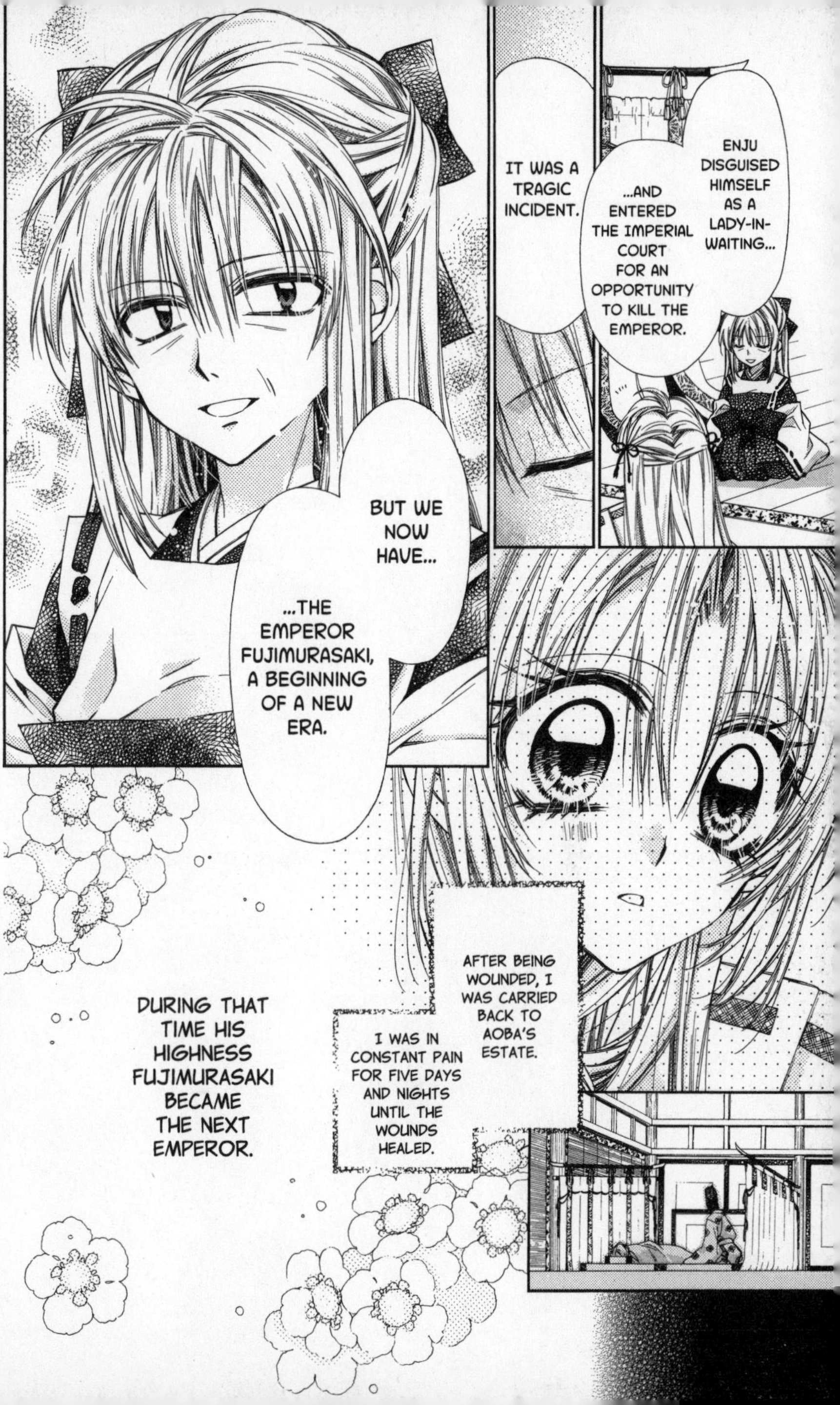
ENJU DISGUISED HIMSELF AS A LADY-IN-WAITING...
...AND ENTERED THE IMPERIAL COURT FOR AN OPPORTUNITY TO KILL THE EMPEROR.
IT WAS A TRAGIC INCIDENT.
BUT WE NOW HAVE...
...THE EMPEROR FUJIMURASAKI, A BEGINNING OF A NEW ERA.
AFTER BEING WOUNDED, I WAS CARRIED BACK TO AOBA'S ESTATE.
I WAS IN CONSTANT PAIN FOR FIVE DAYS AND NIGHTS UNTIL THE WOUNDS HEALED.
DURING THAT TIME HIS HIGHNESS FUJIMURASAKI BECAME THE NEXT EMPEROR.

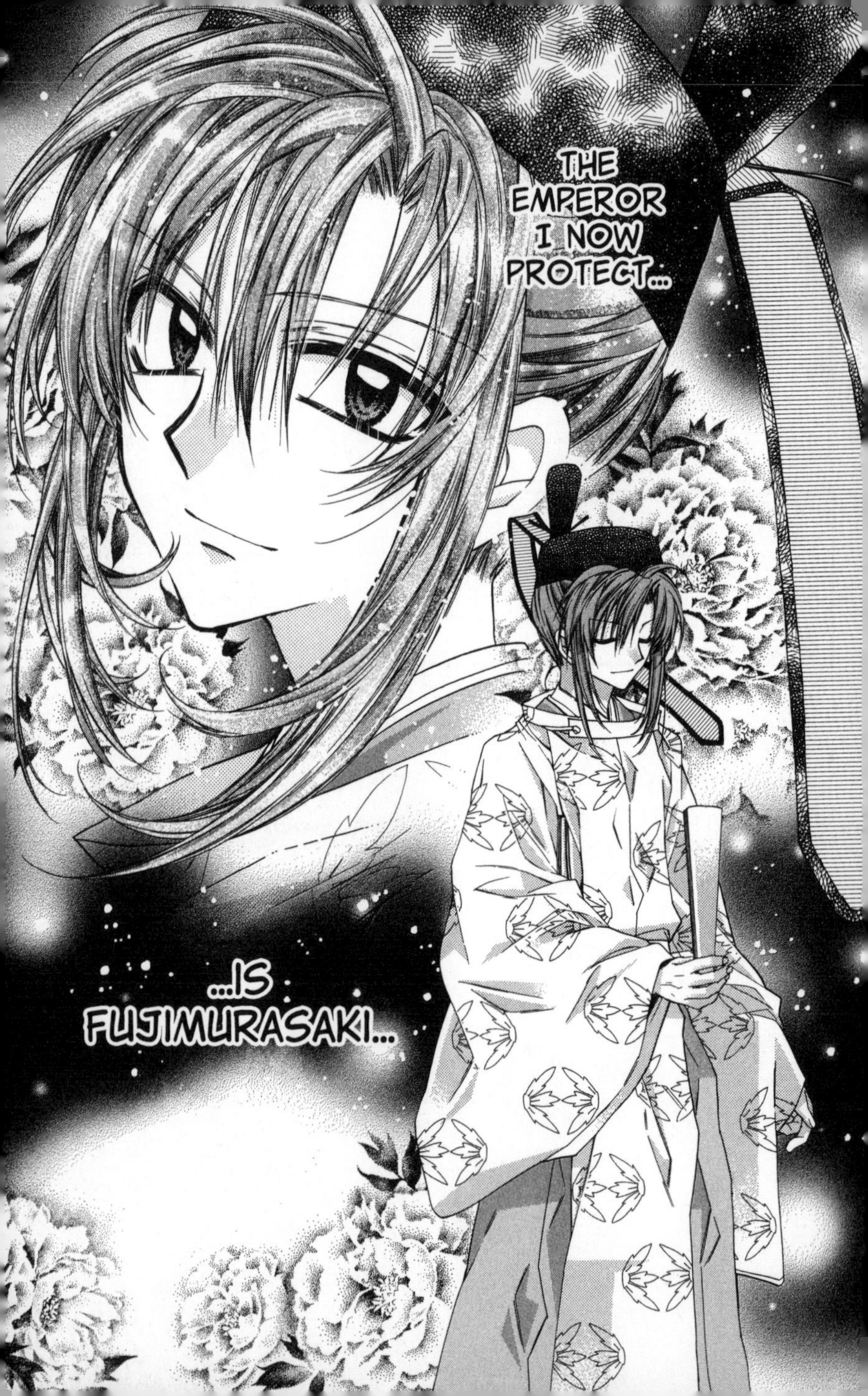
THE EMPEROR I NOW PROTECT...
...IS FUJIMURASAKI...

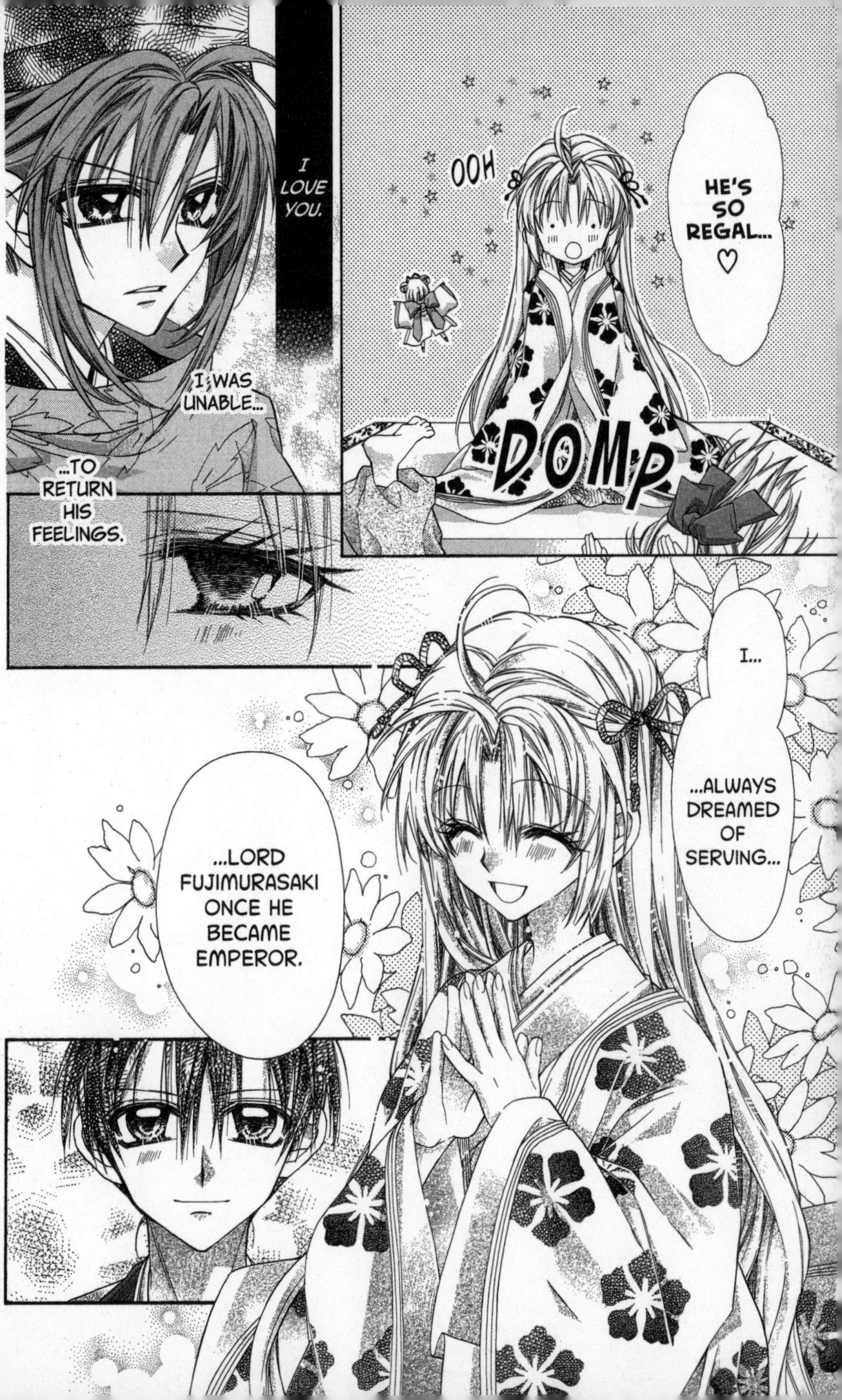
HE'S SO REGAL... ♡
OOH
DOMP
I LOVE YOU.
I WAS UNABLE...
...TO RETURN HIS FEELINGS.
I...
...ALWAYS DREAMED OF SERVING...
...LORD FUJIMURASAKI ONCE HE BECAME EMPEROR.

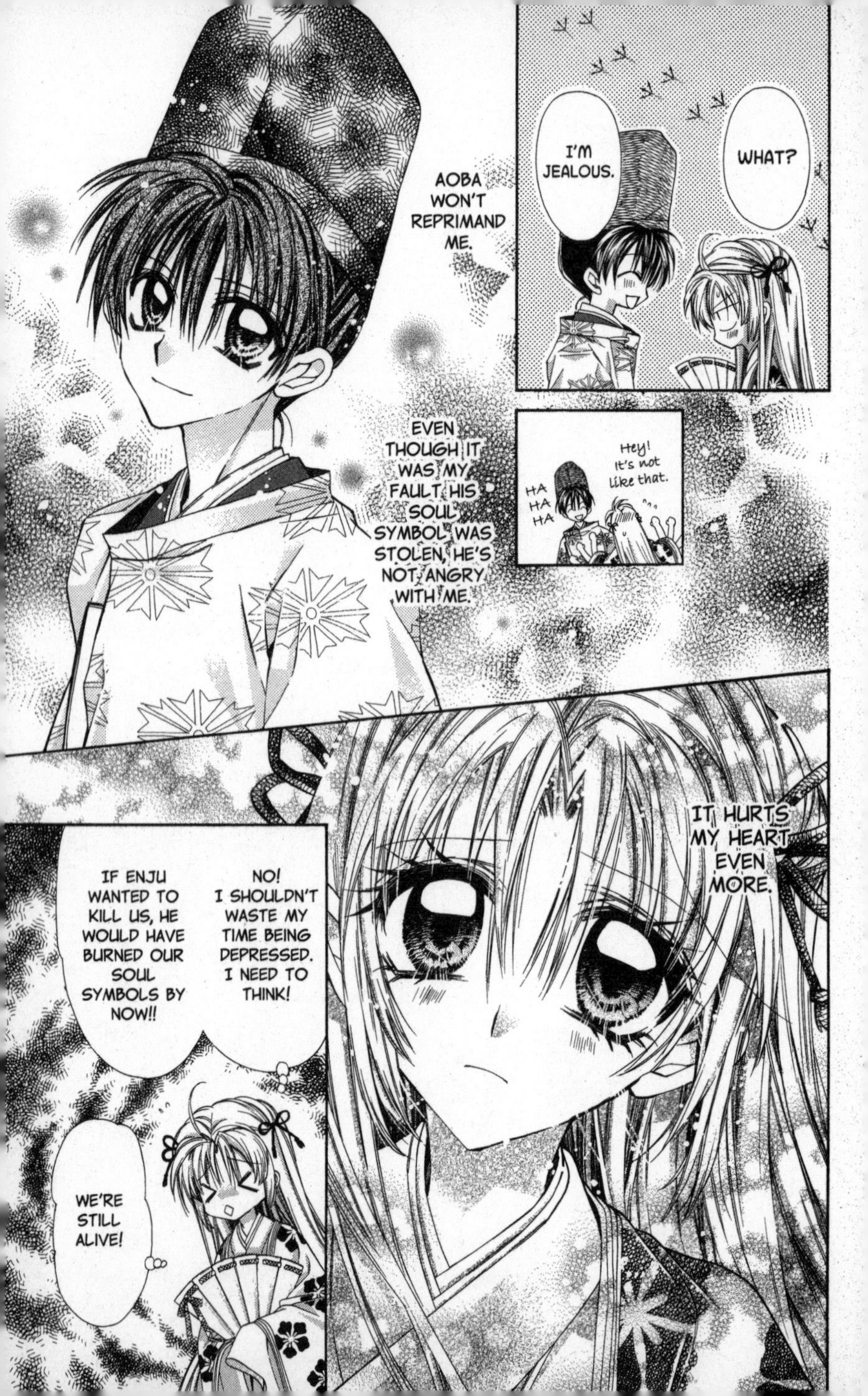
WHAT?
I'M JEALOUS.
Hey! It's not like that.
HA HA HA
AOBA WON'T REPRIMAND ME.
EVEN THOUGH IT WAS MY FAULT HIS SOUL SYMBOL WAS STOLEN, HE'S NOT ANGRY WITH ME.
IT HURTS MY HEART EVEN MORE.
NO! I SHOULDN'T WASTE MY TIME BEING DEPRESSED. I NEED TO THINK!
IF ENJU WANTED TO KILL US, HE WOULD HAVE BURNED OUR SOUL SYMBOLS BY NOW!!
WE'RE STILL ALIVE!

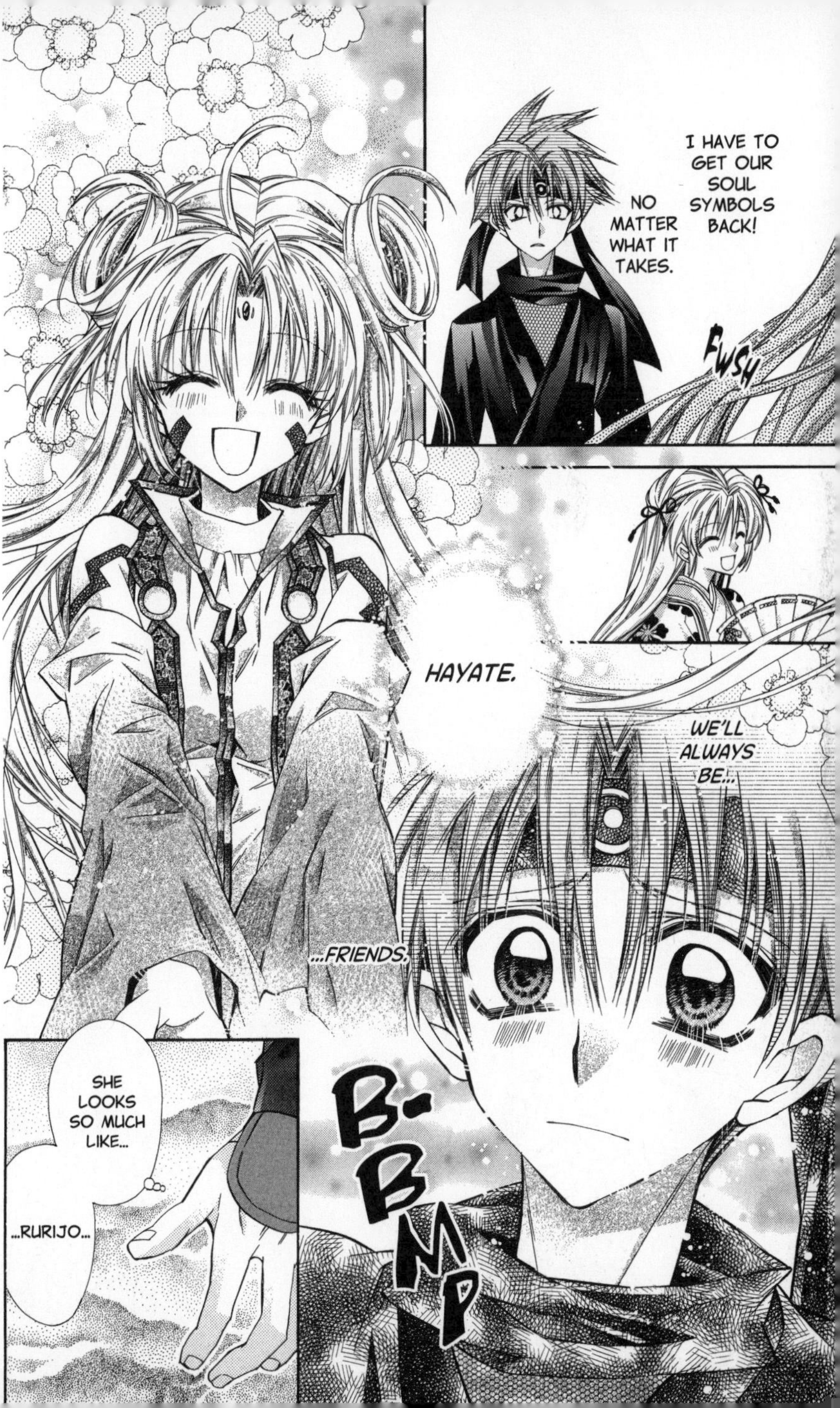
I HAVE TO GET OUR SOUL SYMBOLS BACK!
NO MATTER WHAT IT TAKES.
FWSH
HAYATE.
WE'LL ALWAYS BE...
...FRIENDS.
B-BMP
SHE LOOKS SO MUCH LIKE...
...RURIJO...

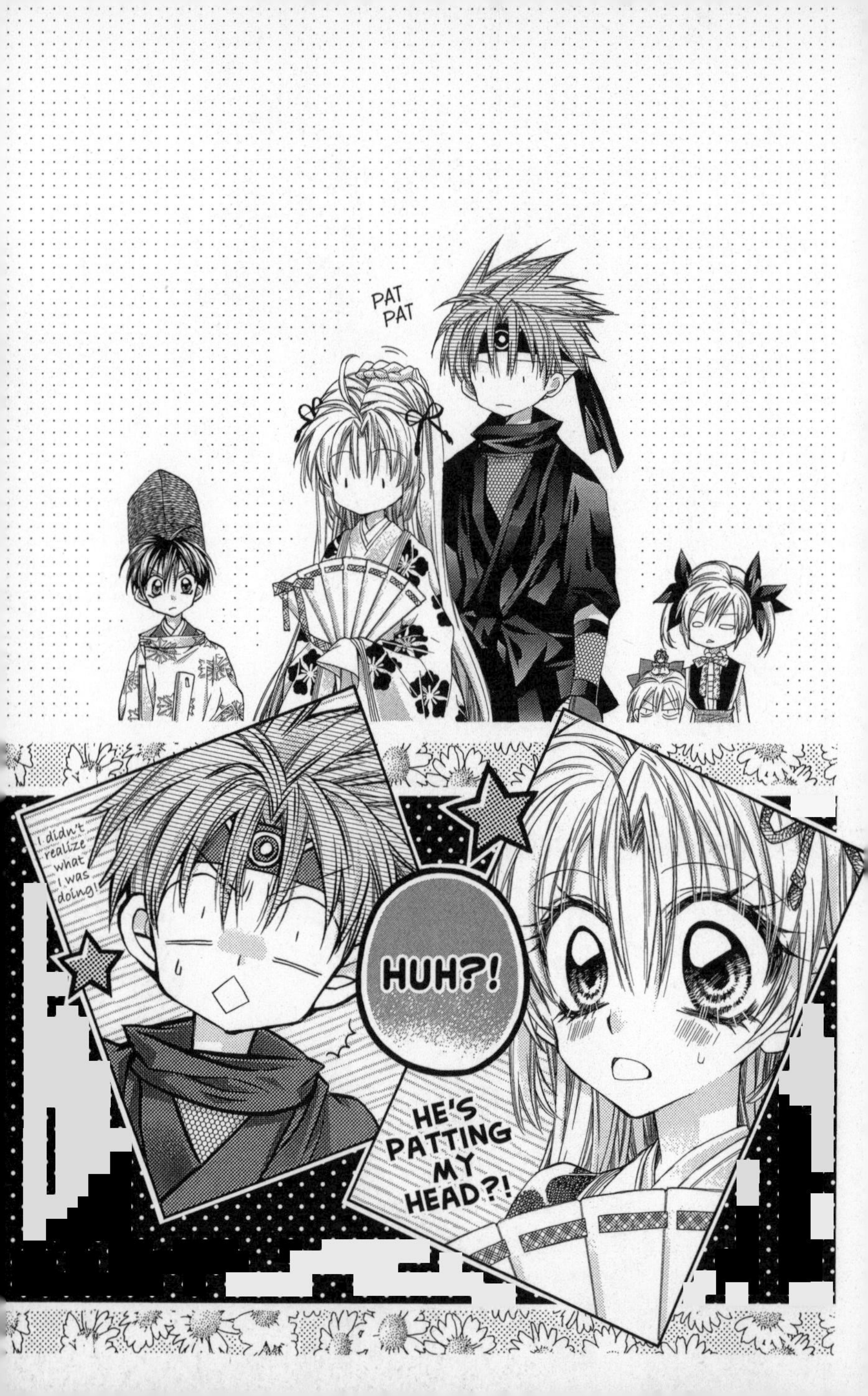
PAT PAT
HUH?!
HE'S PATTING MY HEAD?!
I didn't realize what I was doing!

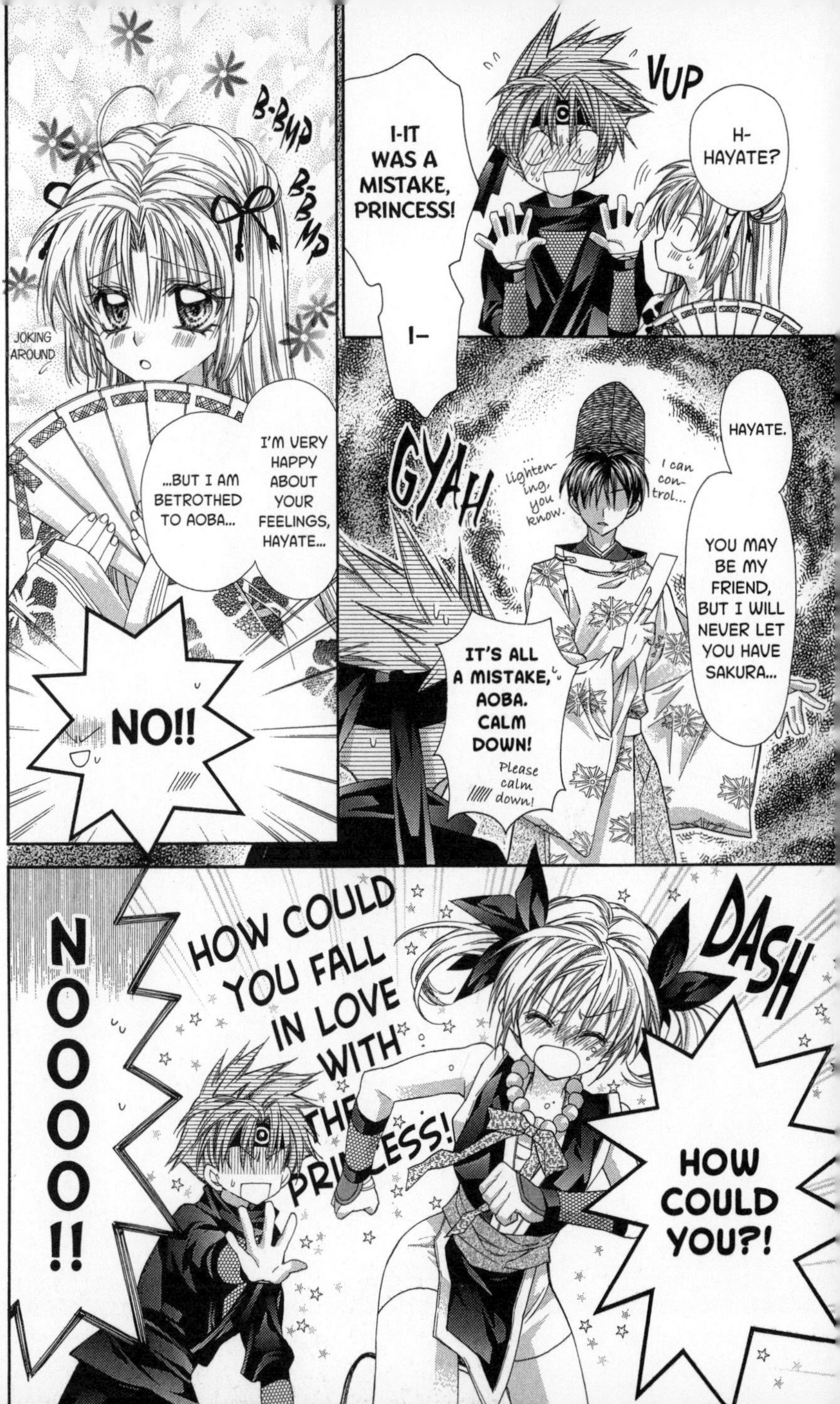
VUP
H- HAYATE?
I-IT WAS A MISTAKE, PRINCESS!
I–
HAYATE.
I can control...
...lightening, you know.
YOU MAY BE MY FRIEND, BUT I WILL NEVER LET YOU HAVE SAKURA...
GYAH
IT'S ALL A MISTAKE, AOBA. CALM DOWN!
Please calm down!
B-BMP
B-BMP
I'M VERY HAPPY ABOUT YOUR FEELINGS, HAYATE...
...BUT I AM BETROTHED TO AOBA...
JOKING AROUND
NO!!
DASH
HOW COULD YOU?!
HOW COULD YOU FALL IN LOVE WITH THE PRINCESS!
NOOOOO!!

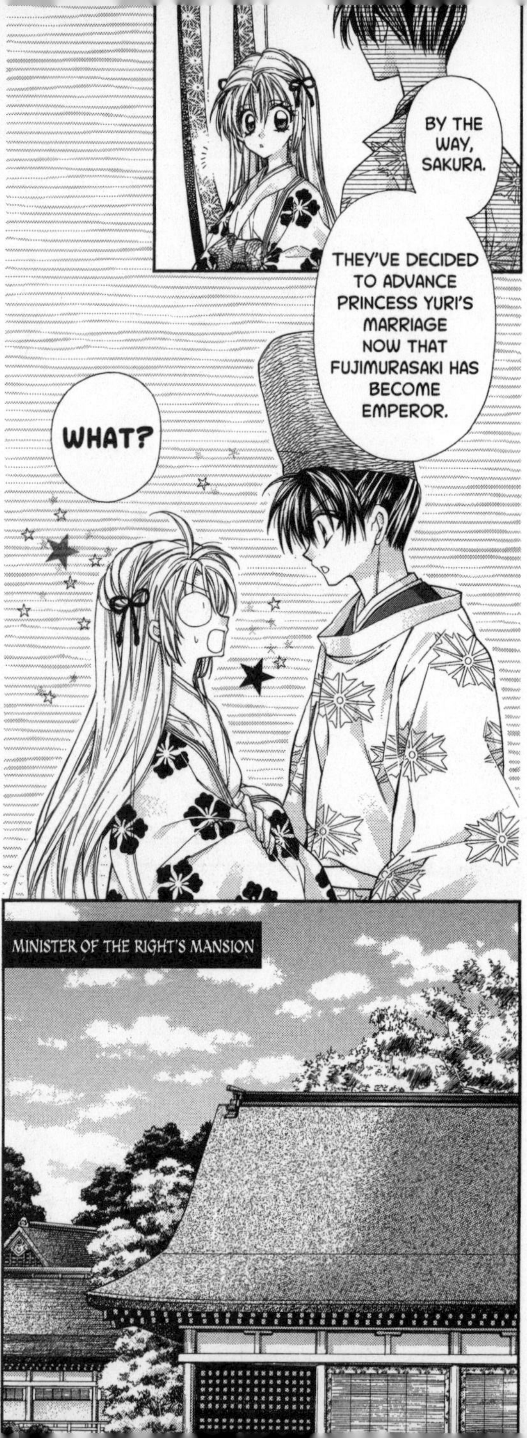
BY THE WAY, SAKURA.
THEY'VE DECIDED TO ADVANCE PRINCESS YURI'S MARRIAGE NOW THAT FUJIMURASAKI HAS BECOME EMPEROR.
WHAT?
MINISTER OF THE RIGHT'S MANSION

Hokkaido continued →

We arrived at Windsor Hotel at Toya! It's a three-star Michelin hotel where they held the G8 summit. I have always wanted to go there!

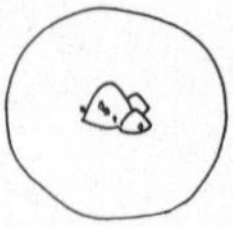

Lake Toya is very interesting. There's an island in the very middle.

We went at the end of November, but it was already snowing. It was very beautiful.
We got to choose between a lake view room and an ocean view room, and we stayed in a lake view room.
They had a pool, a spa, and the like. How do I put it? It was very luxurious. I've uploaded photos of our dinner, etc., to my blog, so please take a look.

"Arina Diary" ↓
http://rikukai.arina.lolipop.jp/

The next day we took a car → train and headed for Asahiyama Zoo, the place we've always wanted to go! But to our horror, they were operating under winter hours. Closing time is 3:30! We had been taking our time eating ramen at Daidaiya and arrived at the zoo at 1:30. (laugh) Will we be able to look around the zoo?! Will the penguins fly?!

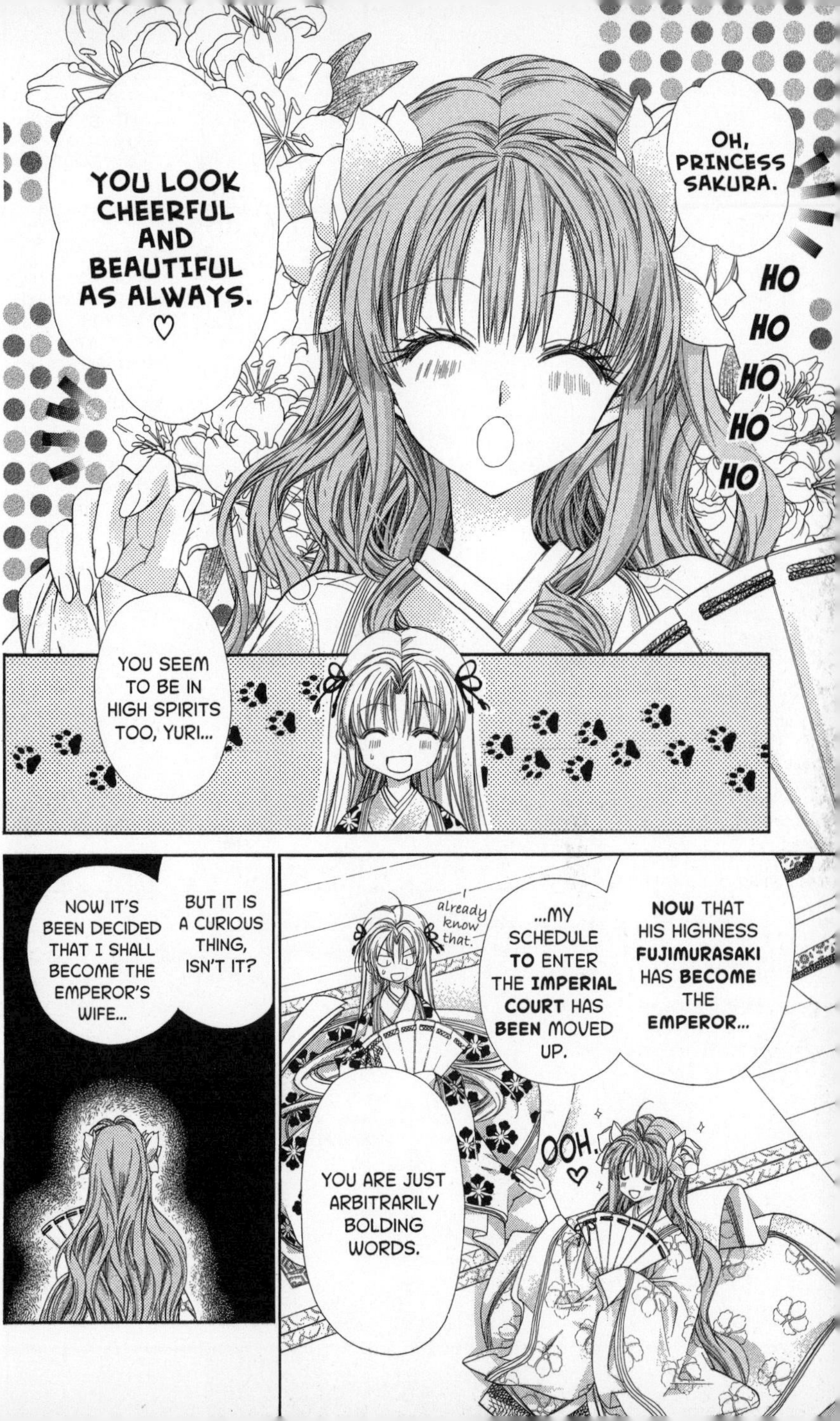
OH, PRINCESS SAKURA.
HO HO HO HO HO
YOU LOOK CHEERFUL AND BEAUTIFUL AS ALWAYS. ♡
YOU SEEM TO BE IN HIGH SPIRITS TOO, YURI...
NOW THAT HIS HIGHNESS FUJIMURASAKI HAS BECOME THE EMPEROR...
...MY SCHEDULE TO ENTER THE IMPERIAL COURT HAS BEEN MOVED UP.
OOH. ♡
I already know that.
YOU ARE JUST ARBITRARILY BOLDING WORDS.
BUT IT IS A CURIOUS THING, ISN'T IT?
NOW IT'S BEEN DECIDED THAT I SHALL BECOME THE EMPEROR'S WIFE...

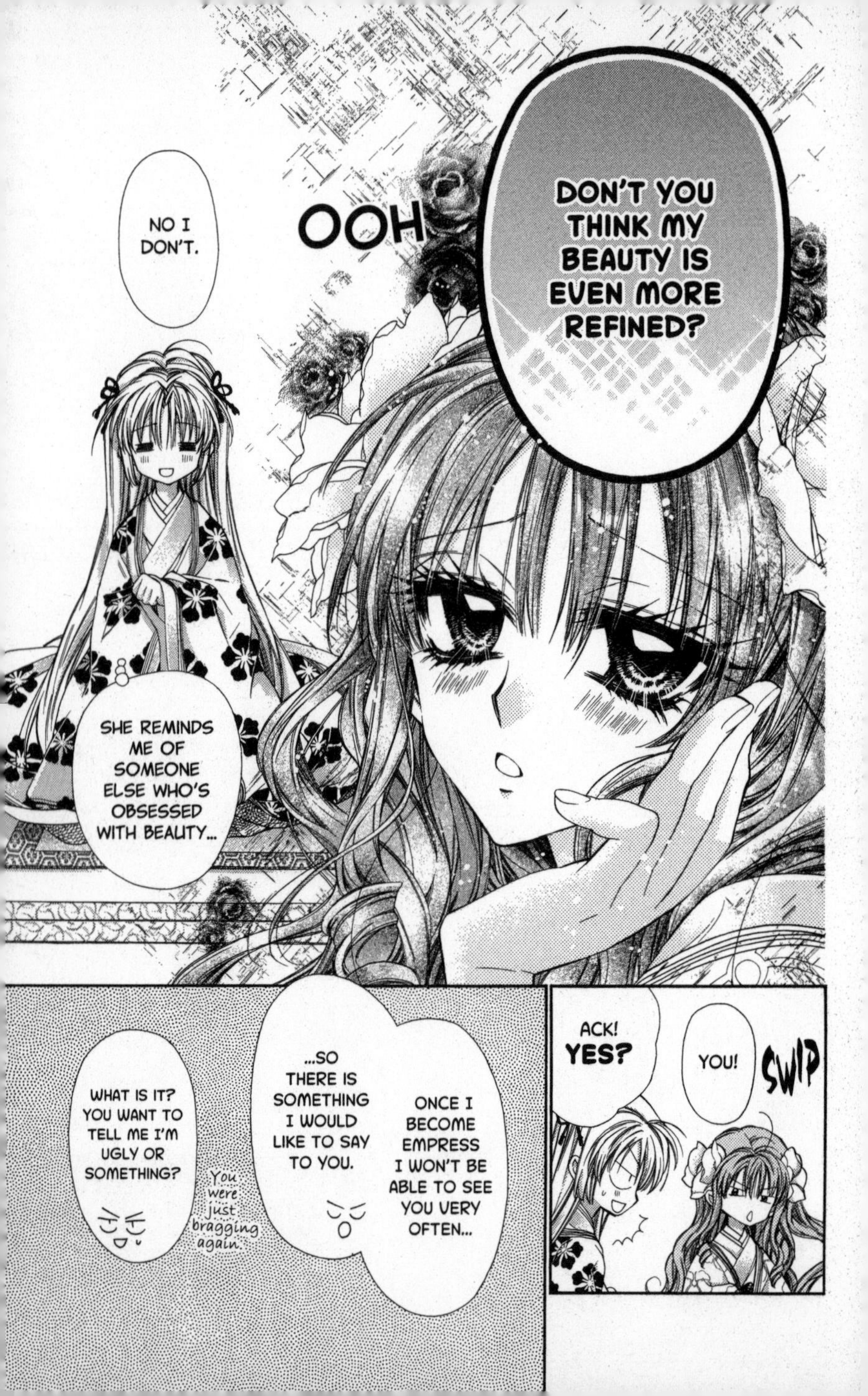
DON'T YOU THINK MY BEAUTY IS EVEN MORE REFINED?
OOH
NO I DON'T.
SHE REMINDS ME OF SOMEONE ELSE WHO'S OBSESSED WITH BEAUTY...
SWIP
YOU!
ACK! YES?
ONCE I BECOME EMPRESS I WON'T BE ABLE TO SEE YOU VERY OFTEN...
...SO THERE IS SOMETHING I WOULD LIKE TO SAY TO YOU.
WHAT IS IT? YOU WANT TO TELL ME I'M UGLY OR SOMETHING?
You were just bragging again.

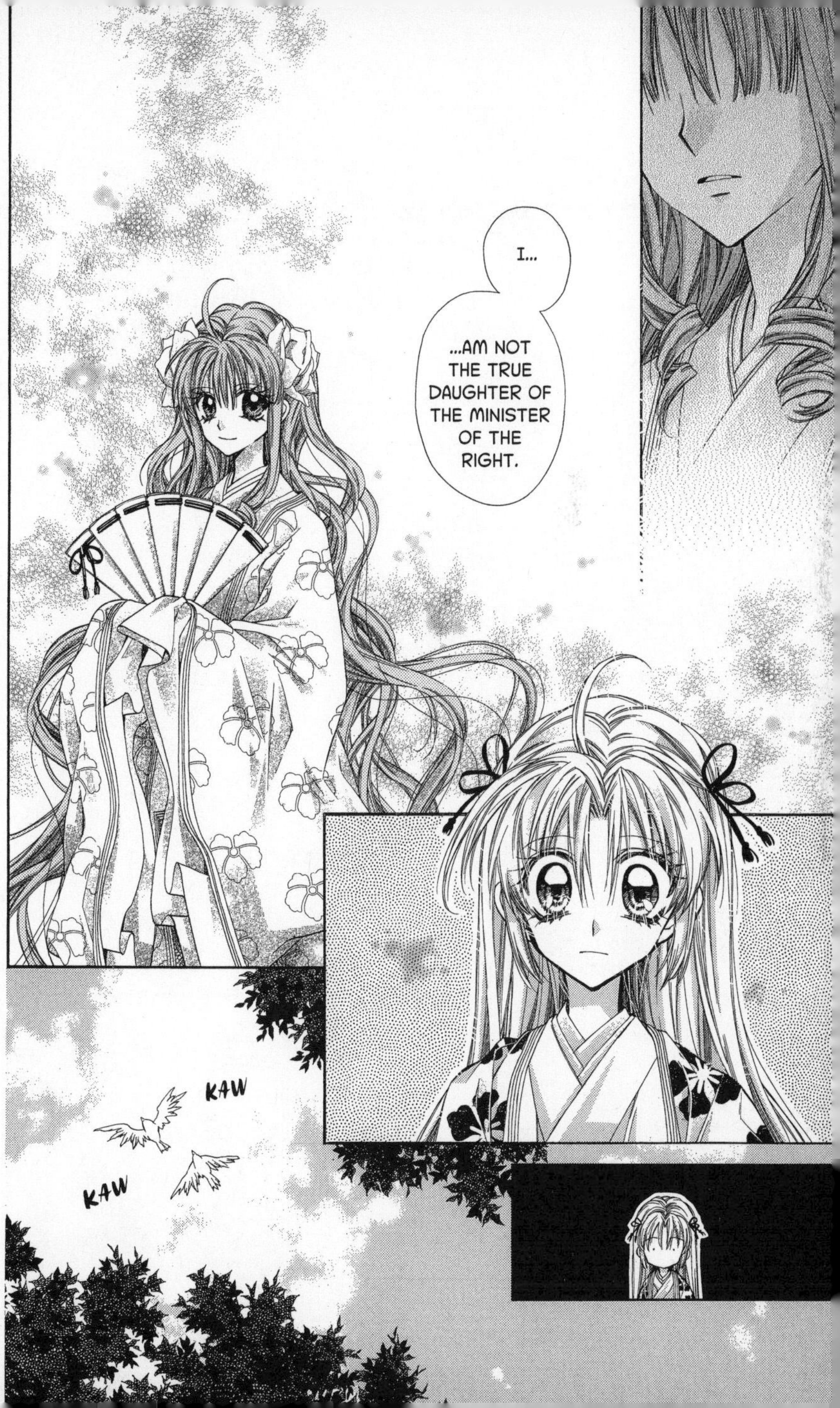
I...
...AM NOT THE TRUE DAUGHTER OF THE MINISTER OF THE RIGHT.
KAW
KAW

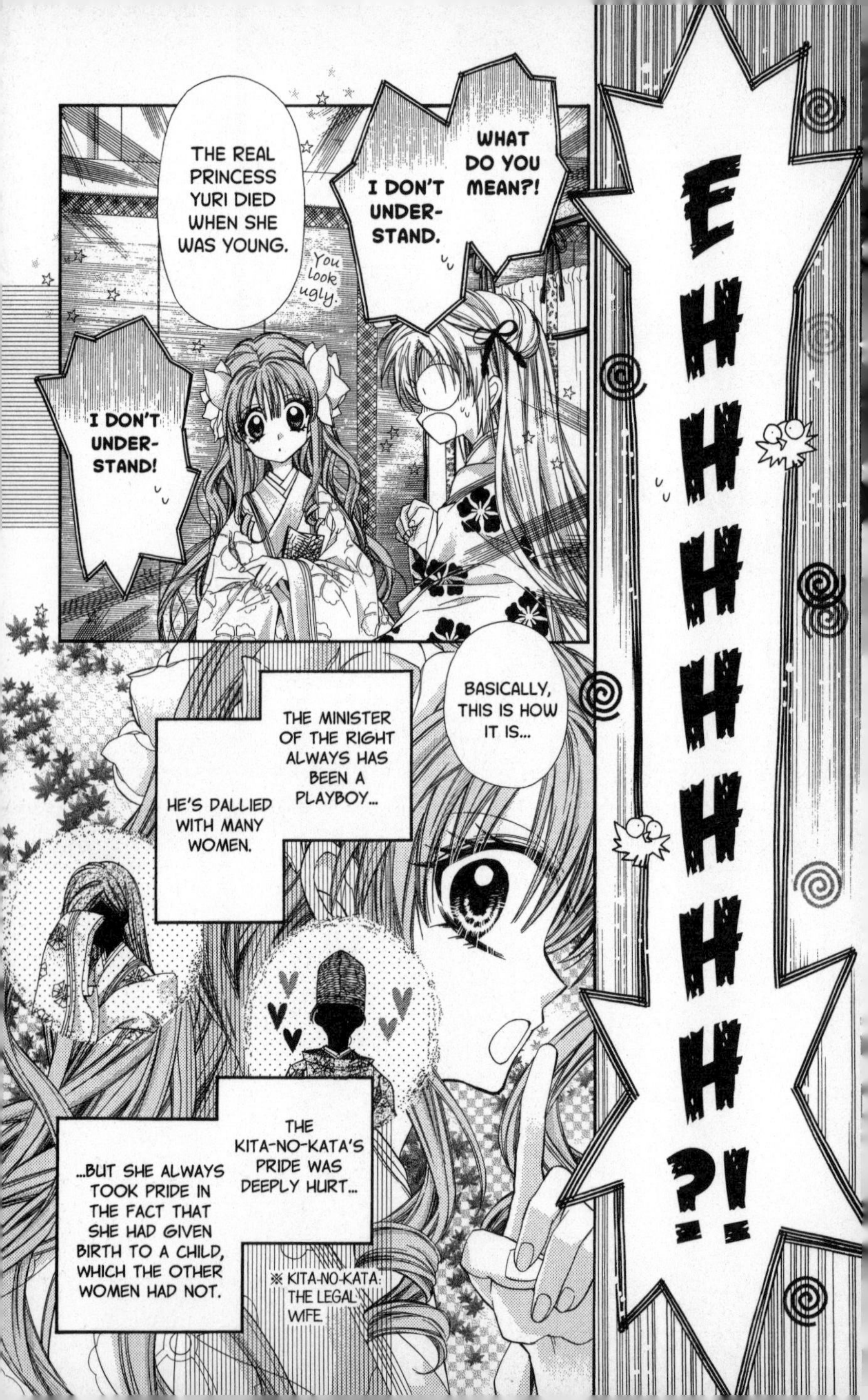
EHHHHHHH?!
WHAT DO YOU MEAN?!
I DON'T UNDERSTAND.
THE REAL PRINCESS YURI DIED WHEN SHE WAS YOUNG.
You look ugly.
I DON'T UNDERSTAND!
BASICALLY, THIS IS HOW IT IS...
THE MINISTER OF THE RIGHT ALWAYS HAS BEEN A PLAYBOY...
HE'S DALLIED WITH MANY WOMEN.
THE KITA-NO-KATA'S PRIDE WAS DEEPLY HURT...
...BUT SHE ALWAYS TOOK PRIDE IN THE FACT THAT SHE HAD GIVEN BIRTH TO A CHILD, WHICH THE OTHER WOMEN HAD NOT.
※ KITA-NO-KATA: THE LEGAL WIFE

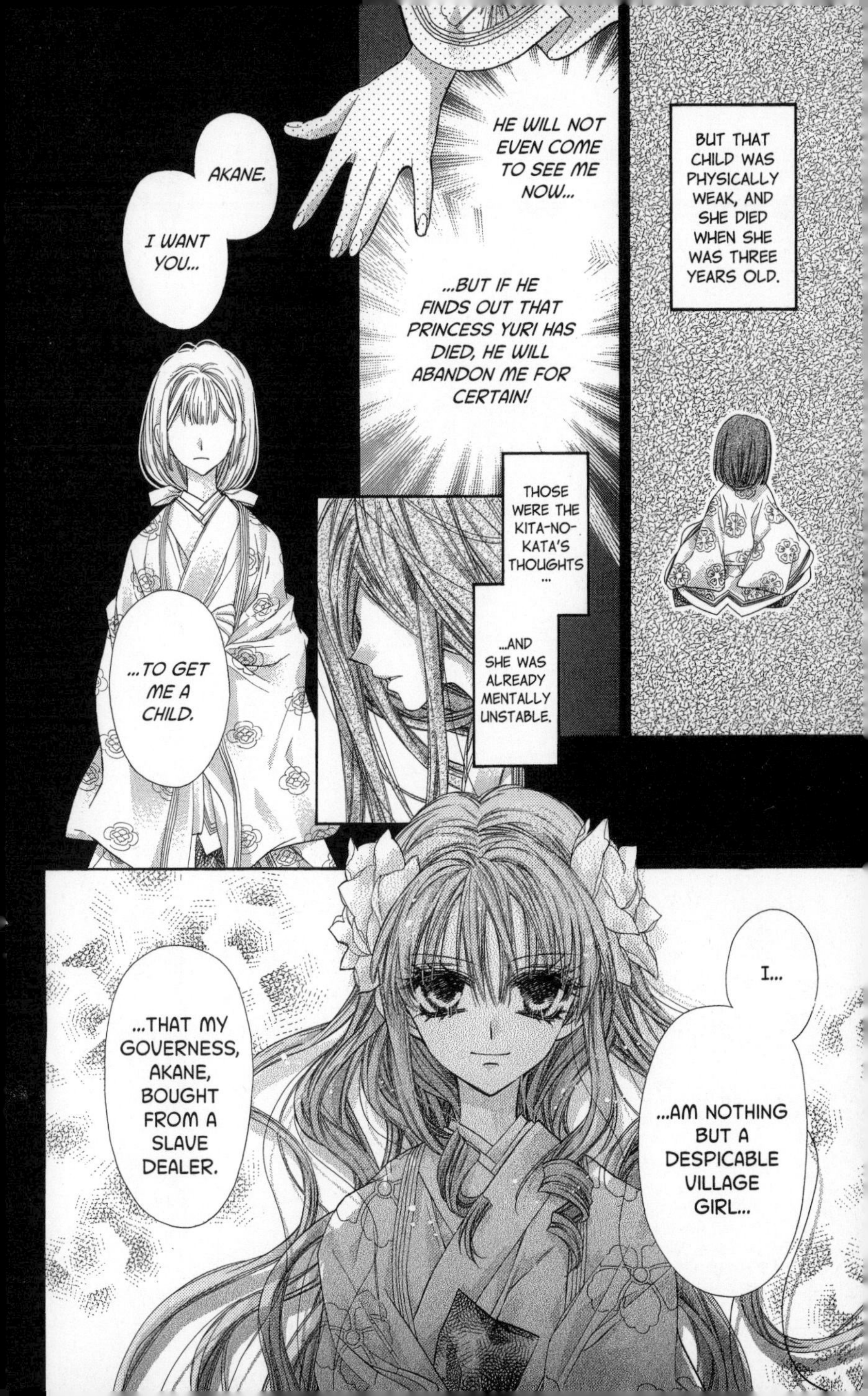

BUT THAT CHILD WAS PHYSICALLY WEAK, AND SHE DIED WHEN SHE WAS THREE YEARS OLD.
HE WILL NOT EVEN COME TO SEE ME NOW...
...BUT IF HE FINDS OUT THAT PRINCESS YURI HAS DIED, HE WILL ABANDON ME FOR CERTAIN!
THOSE WERE THE KITA-NO-KATA'S THOUGHTS...
...AND SHE WAS ALREADY MENTALLY UNSTABLE.
AKANE.
I WANT YOU...
...TO GET ME A CHILD.
I...
...AM NOTHING BUT A DESPICABLE VILLAGE GIRL...
...THAT MY GOVERNESS, AKANE, BOUGHT FROM A SLAVE DEALER.

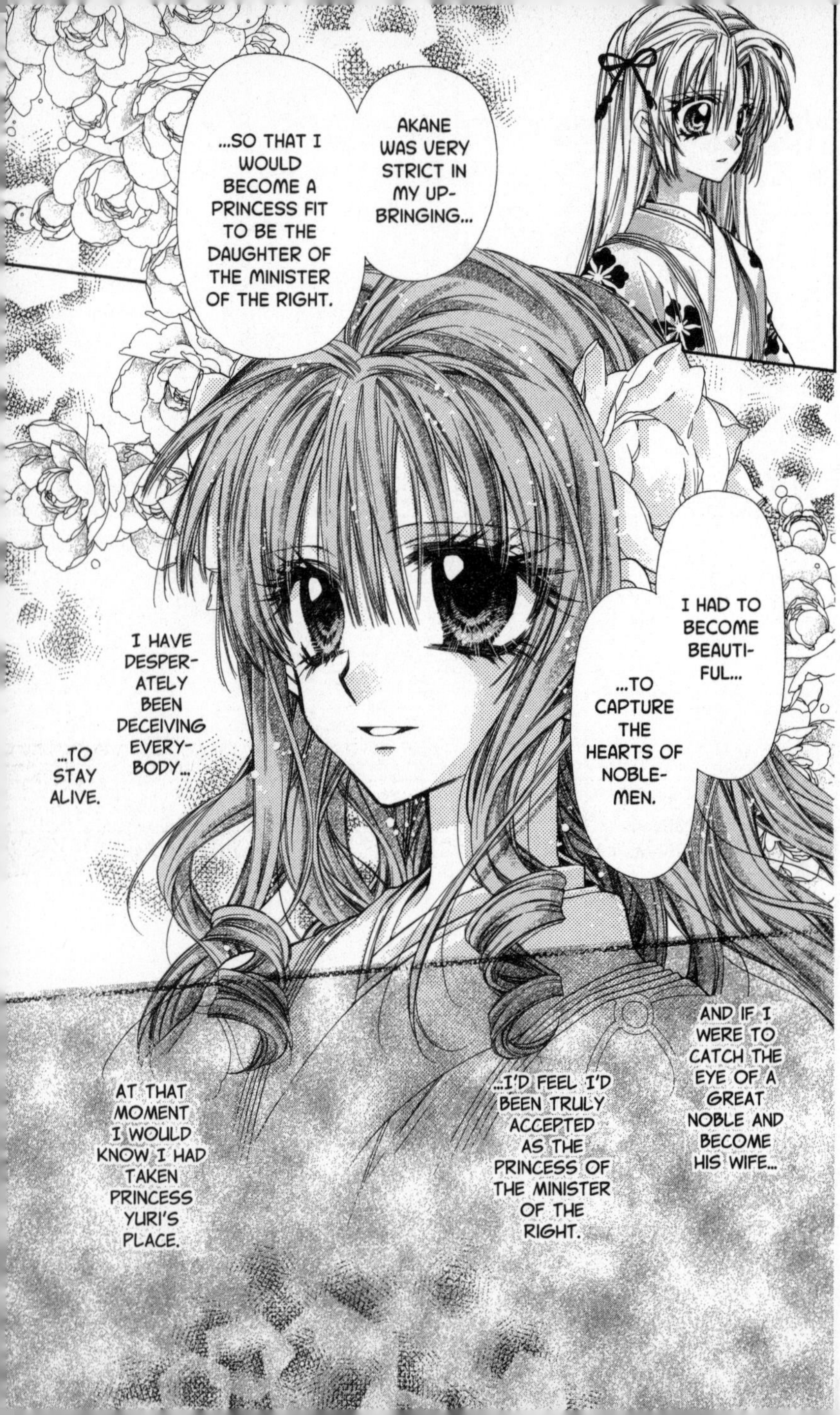
AKANE WAS VERY STRICT IN MY UP-BRINGING...
...SO THAT I WOULD BECOME A PRINCESS FIT TO BE THE DAUGHTER OF THE MINISTER OF THE RIGHT.
I HAD TO BECOME BEAUTI-FUL...
...TO CAPTURE THE HEARTS OF NOBLE-MEN.
I HAVE DESPER-ATELY BEEN DECEIVING EVERY-BODY...
...TO STAY ALIVE.
AND IF I WERE TO CATCH THE EYE OF A GREAT NOBLE AND BECOME HIS WIFE...
...I'D FEEL I'D BEEN TRULY ACCEPTED AS THE PRINCESS OF THE MINISTER OF THE RIGHT.
AT THAT MOMENT I WOULD KNOW I HAD TAKEN PRINCESS YURI'S PLACE.

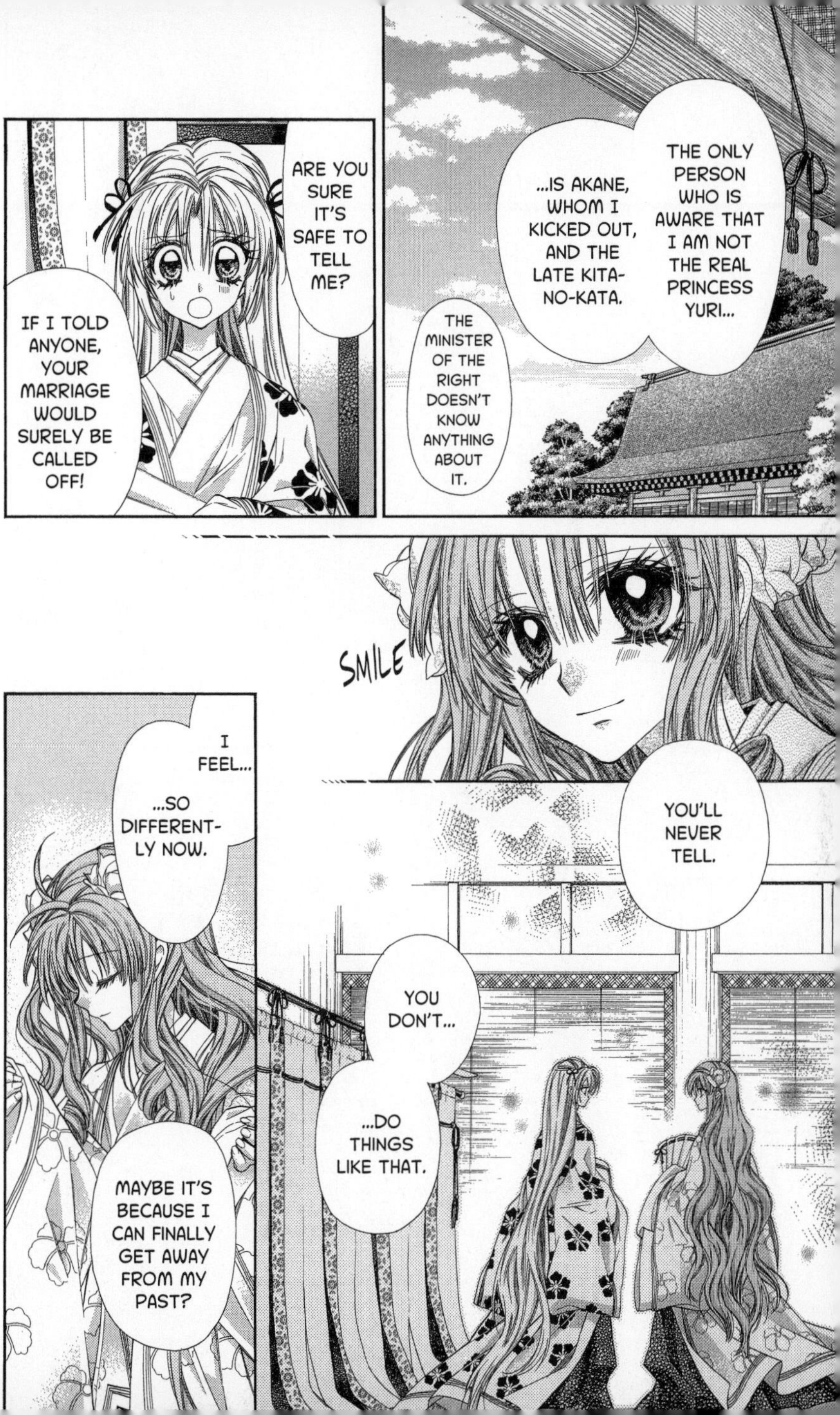
THE ONLY PERSON WHO IS AWARE THAT I AM NOT THE REAL PRINCESS YURI...
...IS AKANE, WHOM I KICKED OUT, AND THE LATE KITA-NO-KATA.
THE MINISTER OF THE RIGHT DOESN'T KNOW ANYTHING ABOUT IT.
ARE YOU SURE IT'S SAFE TO TELL ME?
IF I TOLD ANYONE, YOUR MARRIAGE WOULD SURELY BE CALLED OFF!
SMILE
YOU'LL NEVER TELL.
YOU DON'T...
...DO THINGS LIKE THAT.
I FEEL...
...SO DIFFERENT-LY NOW.
MAYBE IT'S BECAUSE I CAN FINALLY GET AWAY FROM MY PAST?

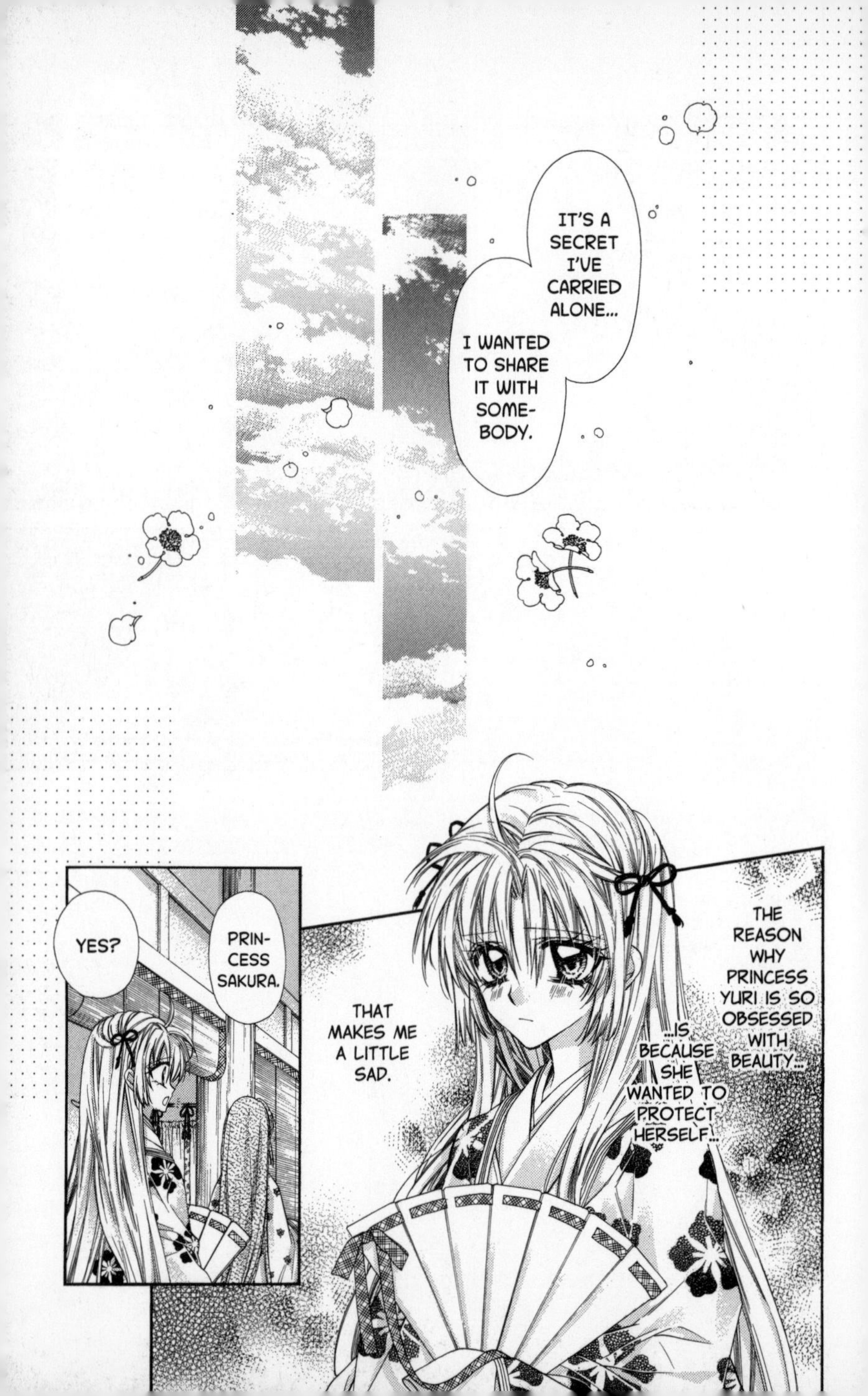
IT'S A SECRET I'VE CARRIED ALONE...
I WANTED TO SHARE IT WITH SOME-BODY.
THE REASON WHY PRINCESS YURI IS SO OBSESSED WITH BEAUTY...
...IS BECAUSE SHE WANTED TO PROTECT HERSELF...
THAT MAKES ME A LITTLE SAD.
PRIN-CESS SAKURA.
YES?

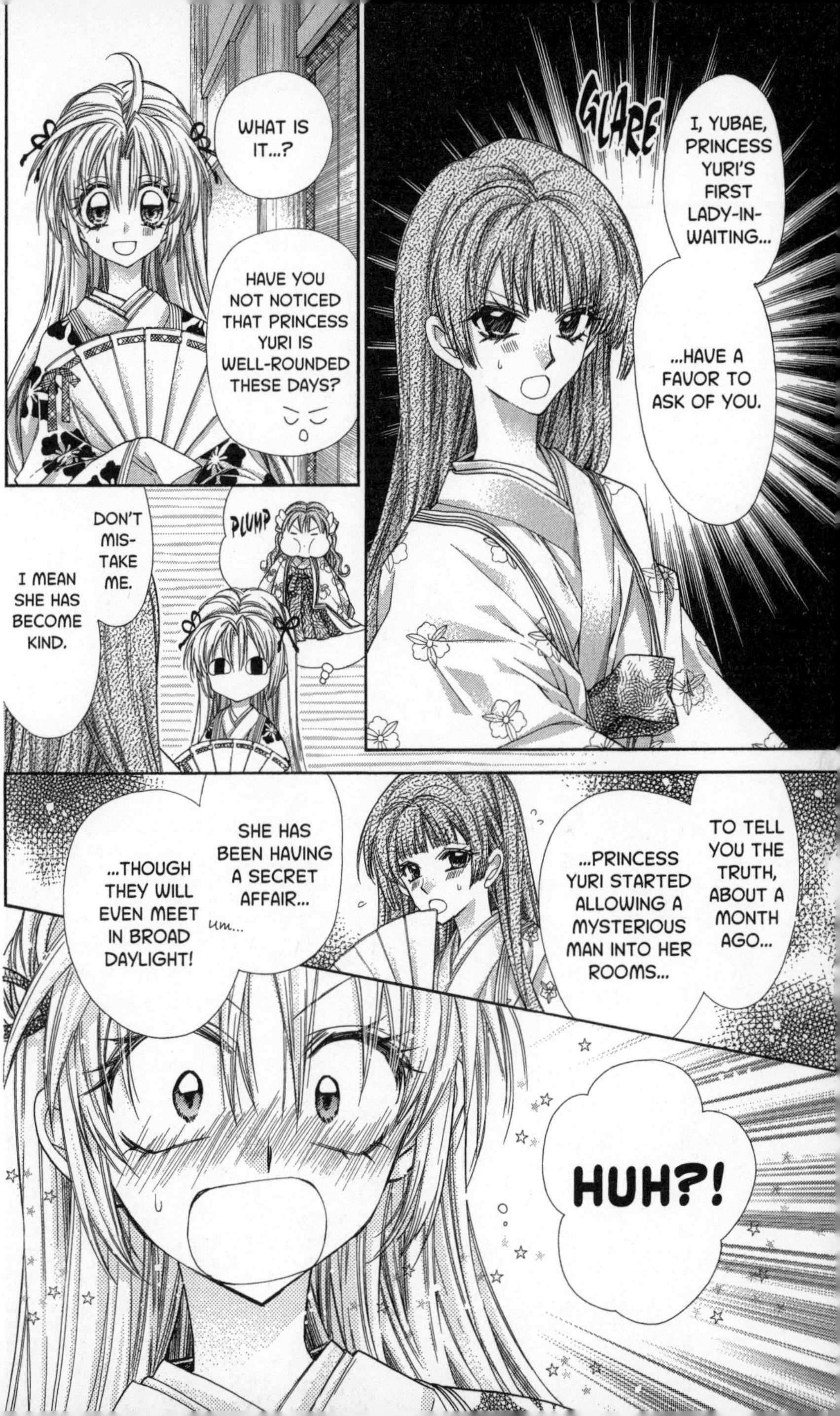
GLARE
I, YUBAE, PRINCESS YURI'S FIRST LADY-IN-WAITING...
...HAVE A FAVOR TO ASK OF YOU.
WHAT IS IT...?
HAVE YOU NOT NOTICED THAT PRINCESS YURI IS WELL-ROUNDED THESE DAYS?
PLUMP
DON'T MIS-TAKE ME.
I MEAN SHE HAS BECOME KIND.
TO TELL YOU THE TRUTH, ABOUT A MONTH AGO...
...PRINCESS YURI STARTED ALLOWING A MYSTERIOUS MAN INTO HER ROOMS...
SHE HAS BEEN HAVING A SECRET AFFAIR...
um...
...THOUGH THEY WILL EVEN MEET IN BROAD DAYLIGHT!
HUH?!

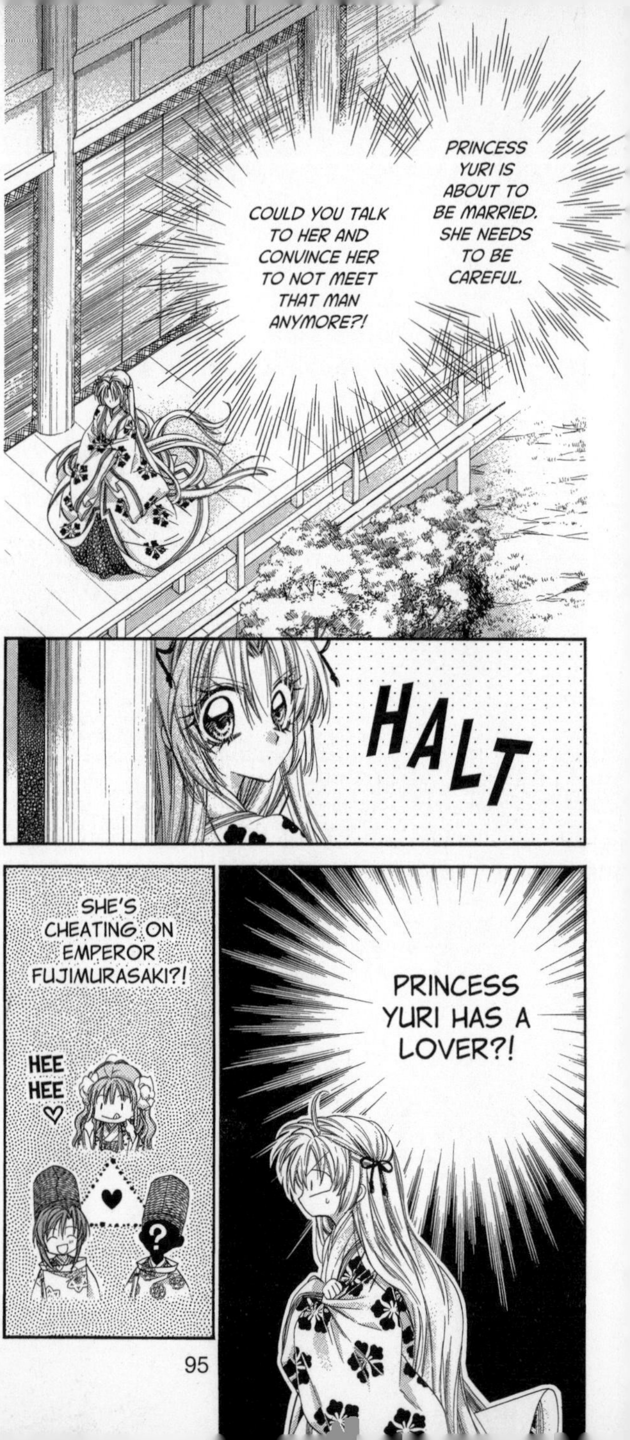
PRINCESS YURI IS ABOUT TO BE MARRIED. SHE NEEDS TO BE CAREFUL.
COULD YOU TALK TO HER AND CONVINCE HER TO NOT MEET THAT MAN ANYMORE?!
HALT
PRINCESS YURI HAS A LOVER?!
SHE'S CHEATING ON EMPEROR FUJIMURASAKI?!
HEE HEE

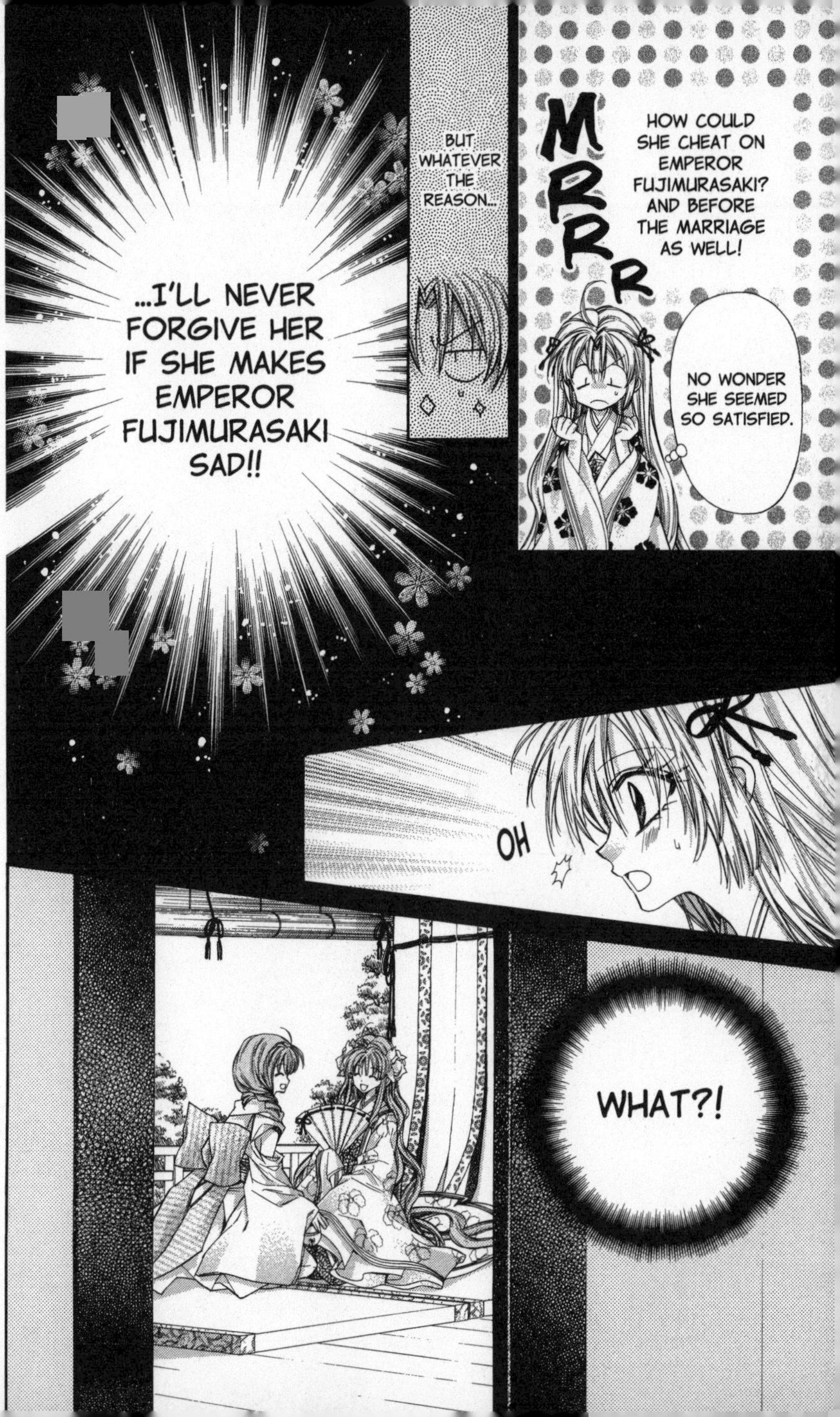

HOW COULD SHE CHEAT ON EMPEROR FUJIMURASAKI? AND BEFORE THE MARRIAGE AS WELL!
MRRR
NO WONDER SHE SEEMED SO SATISFIED.
BUT WHATEVER THE REASON...
...I'LL NEVER FORGIVE HER IF SHE MAKES EMPEROR FUJIMURASAKI SAD!!
OH
WHAT?!

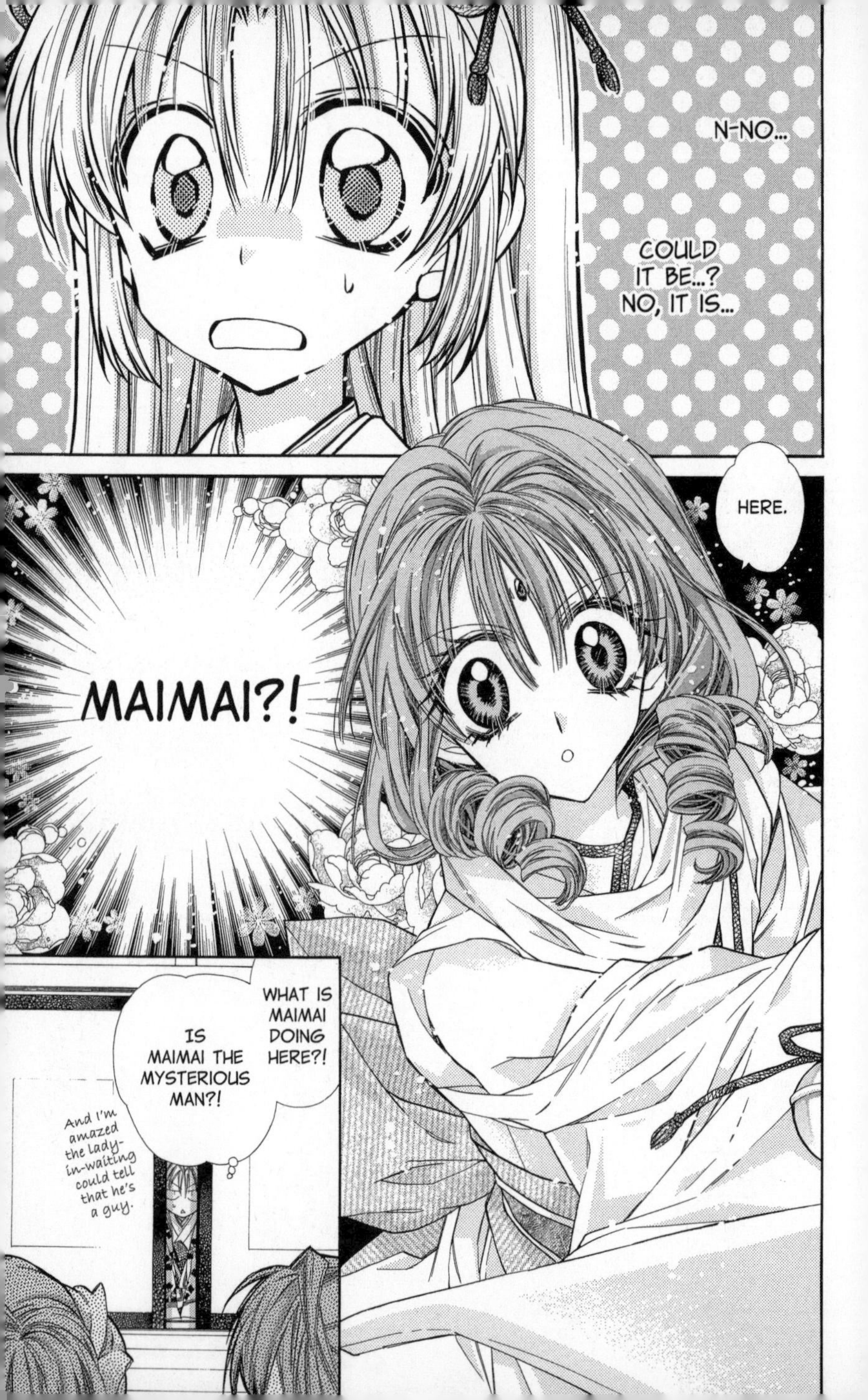
N-NO...
COULD IT BE...? NO, IT IS...
HERE.
MAIMAI?!
WHAT IS MAIMAI DOING HERE?!
IS MAIMAI THE MYSTERIOUS MAN?!
And I'm amazed the lady-in-waiting could tell that he's a guy.

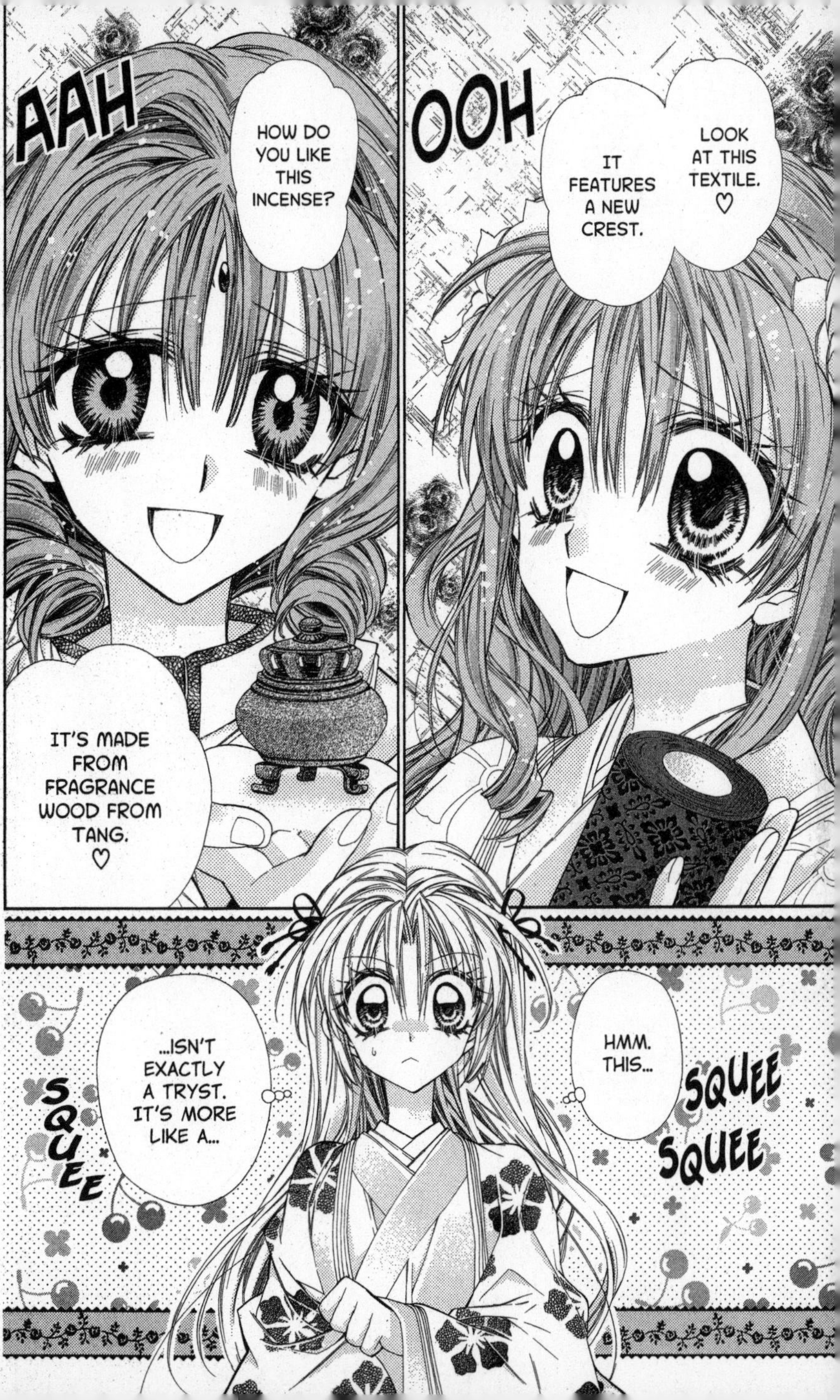
OOH
LOOK AT THIS TEXTILE. ♡
IT FEATURES A NEW CREST.
AAH
HOW DO YOU LIKE THIS INCENSE?
IT'S MADE FROM FRAGRANCE WOOD FROM TANG. ♡
SQUEE SQUEE
HMM. THIS...
...ISN'T EXACTLY A TRYST. IT'S MORE LIKE A...
SQUEE

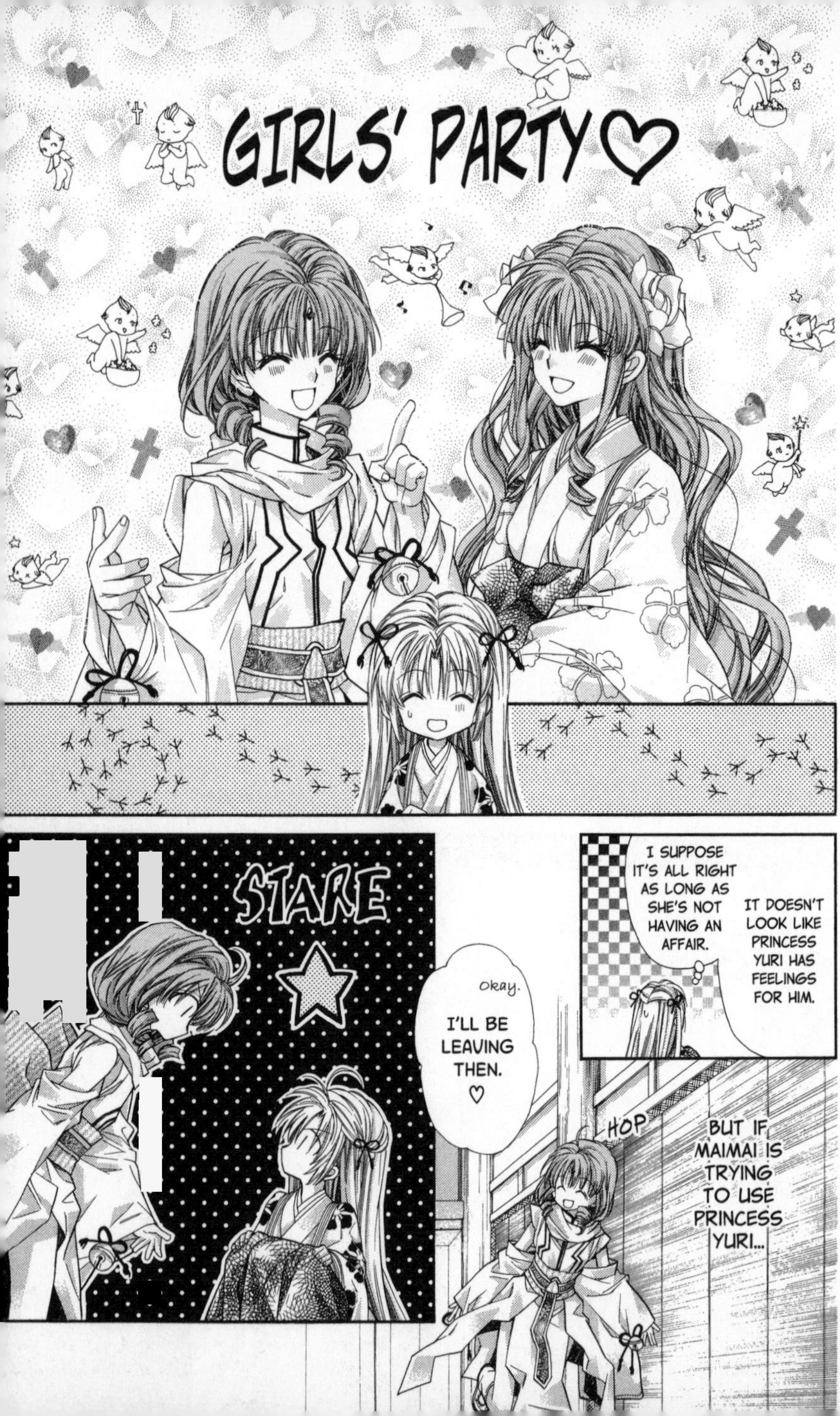
GIRLS' PARTY♡
IT DOESN'T LOOK LIKE PRINCESS YURI HAS FEELINGS FOR HIM.
I SUPPOSE IT'S ALL RIGHT AS LONG AS SHE'S NOT HAVING AN AFFAIR.
Okay.
I'LL BE LEAVING THEN. ♡
HOP
BUT IF MAIMAI IS TRYING TO USE PRINCESS YURI...
STARE

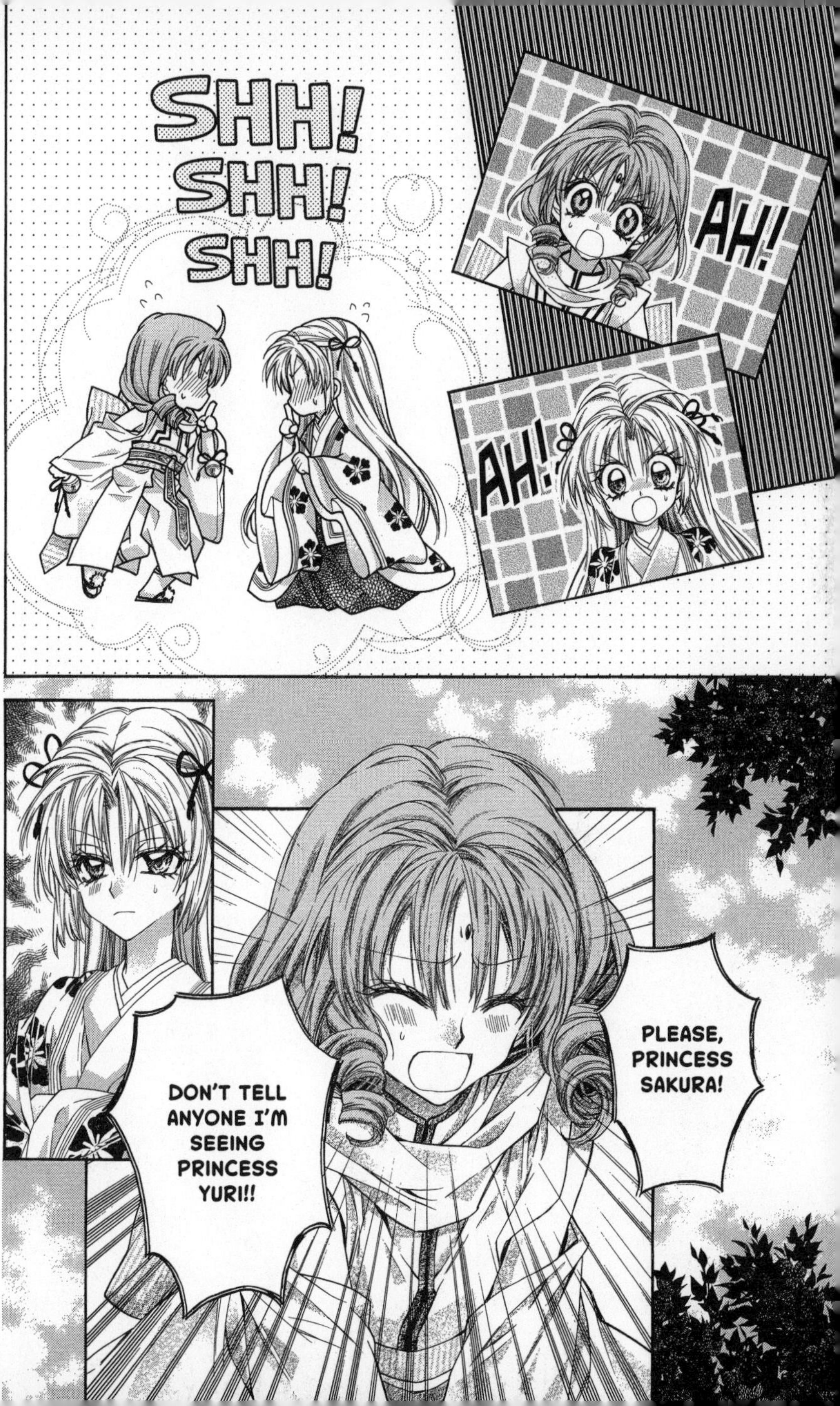
AH!
AH!
SHH! SHH! SHH!
PLEASE, PRINCESS SAKURA!
DON'T TELL ANYONE I'M SEEING PRINCESS YURI!!

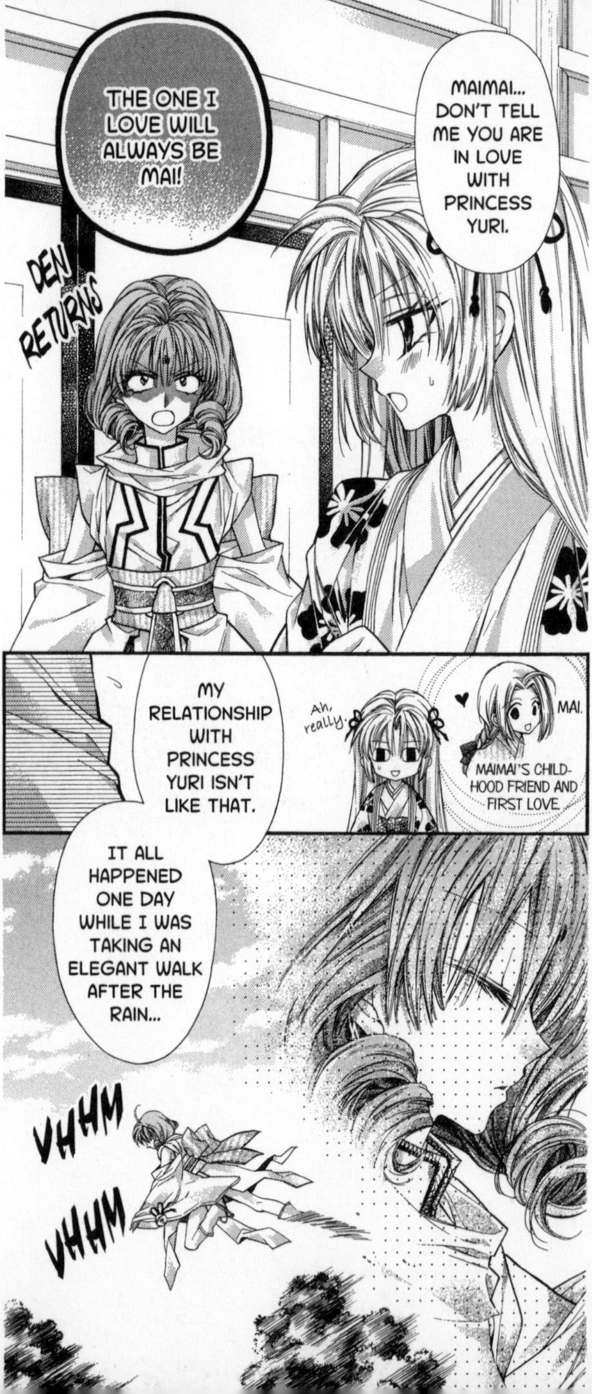
MAIMAI... DON'T TELL ME YOU ARE IN LOVE WITH PRINCESS YURI.
THE ONE I LOVE WILL ALWAYS BE MAI!
DEN RETURNS
MAI.
MAIMAI'S CHILDHOOD FRIEND AND FIRST LOVE.
Ah, really.
MY RELATIONSHIP WITH PRINCESS YURI ISN'T LIKE THAT.
IT ALL HAPPENED ONE DAY WHILE I WAS TAKING AN ELEGANT WALK AFTER THE RAIN...
VHHM
VHHM

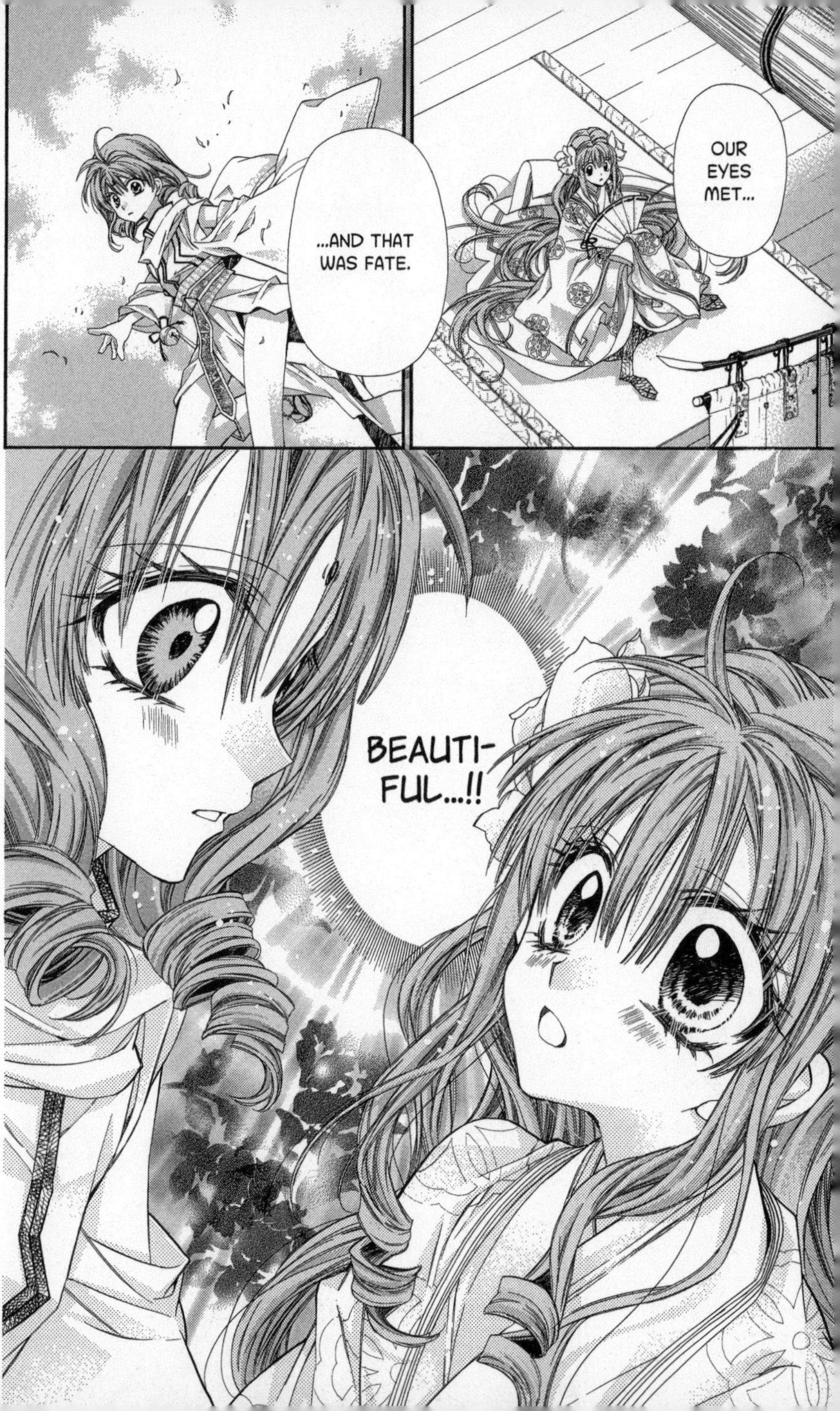
OUR EYES MET...
...AND THAT WAS FATE.
BEAUTIFUL...!!

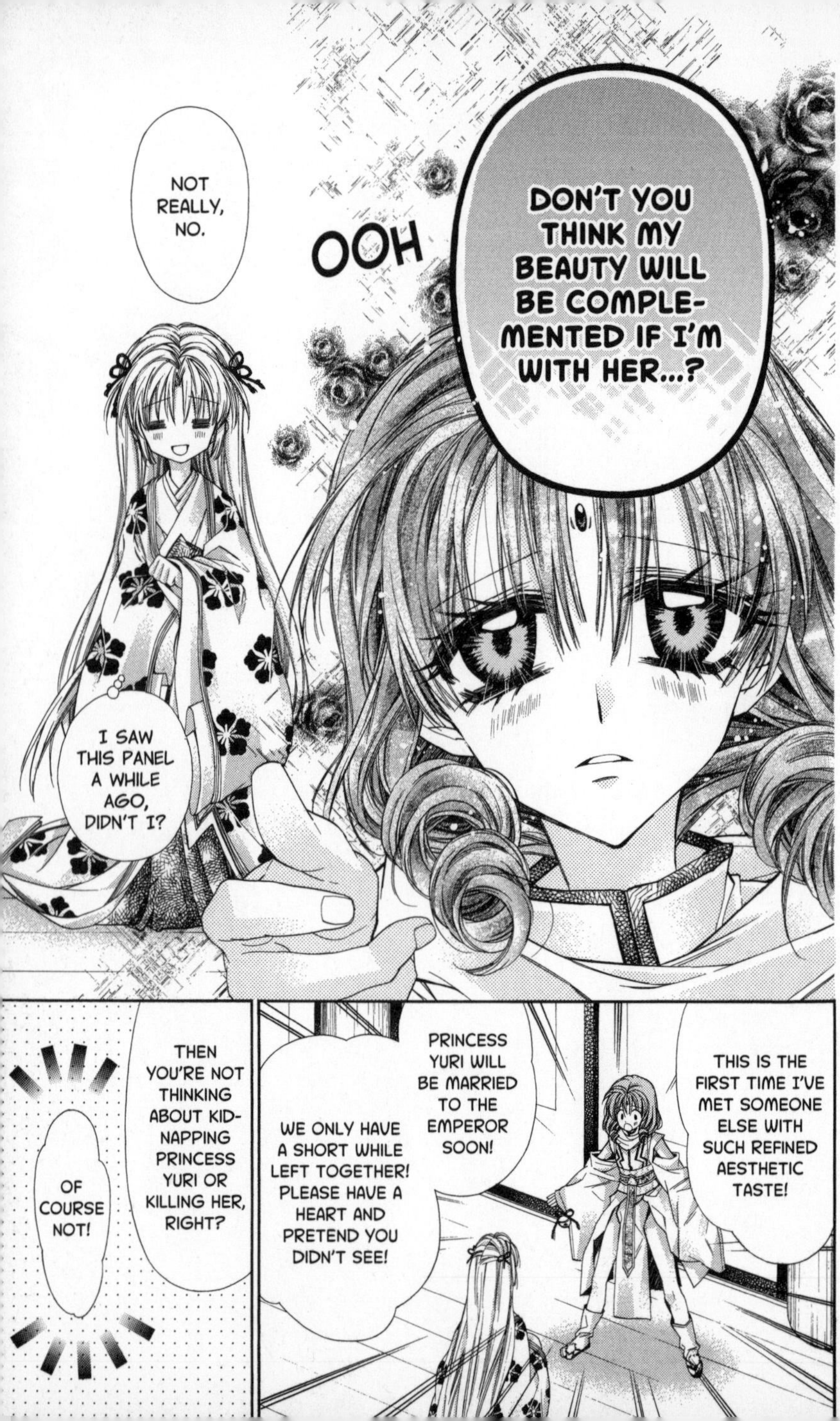
DON'T YOU THINK MY BEAUTY WILL BE COMPLE-MENTED IF I'M WITH HER...?
OOH
NOT REALLY, NO.
I SAW THIS PANEL A WHILE AGO, DIDN'T I?
THIS IS THE FIRST TIME I'VE MET SOMEONE ELSE WITH SUCH REFINED AESTHETIC TASTE!
PRINCESS YURI WILL BE MARRIED TO THE EMPEROR SOON!
WE ONLY HAVE A SHORT WHILE LEFT TOGETHER! PLEASE HAVE A HEART AND PRETEND YOU DIDN'T SEE!
THEN YOU'RE NOT THINKING ABOUT KID-NAPPING PRINCESS YURI OR KILLING HER, RIGHT?
OF COURSE NOT!

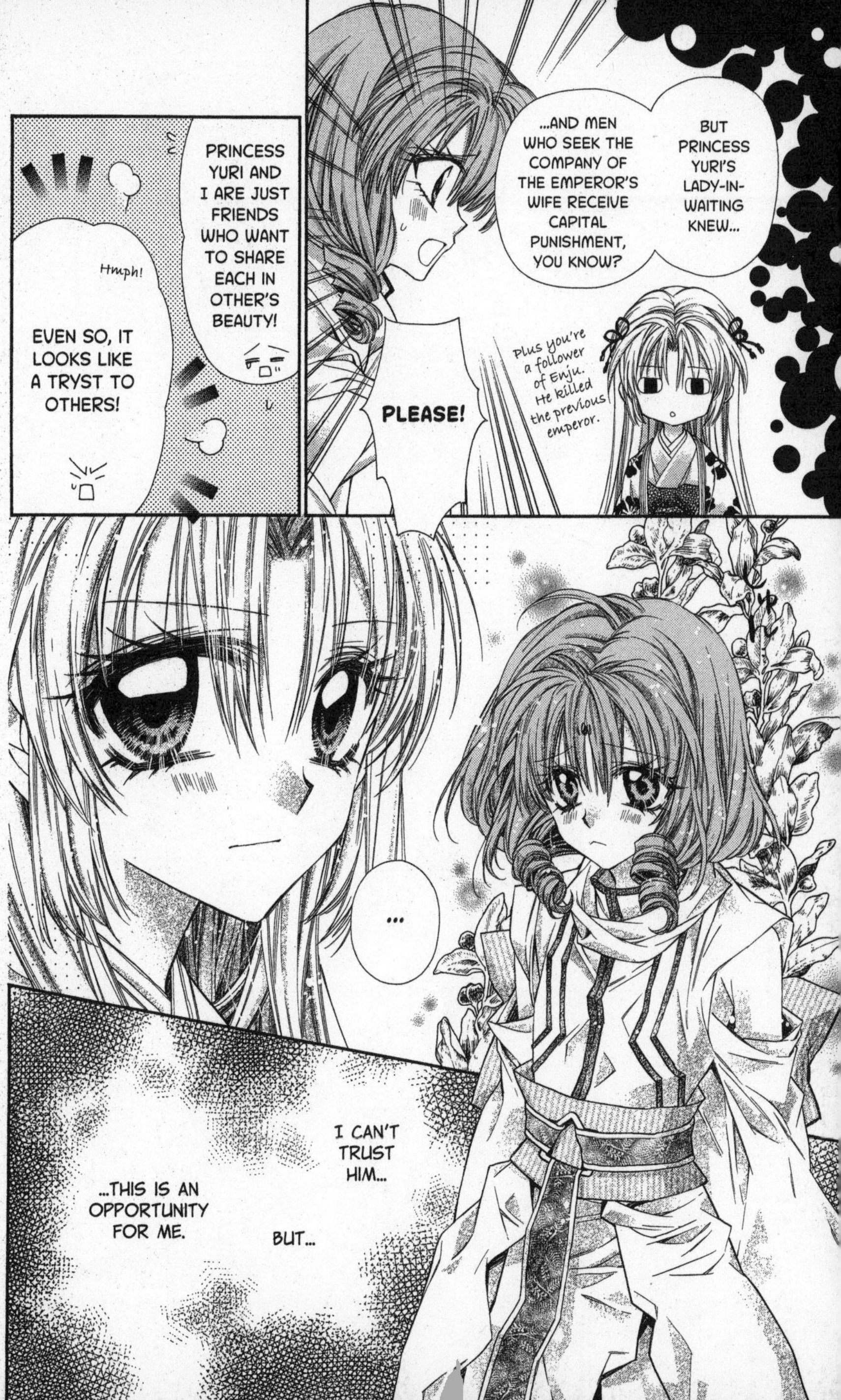
BUT PRINCESS YURI'S LADY-IN-WAITING KNEW...
...AND MEN WHO SEEK THE COMPANY OF THE EMPEROR'S WIFE RECEIVE CAPITAL PUNISHMENT, YOU KNOW?
Plus you're a follower of Enju. He killed the previous emperor.
PLEASE!
PRINCESS YURI AND I ARE JUST FRIENDS WHO WANT TO SHARE EACH IN OTHER'S BEAUTY!
Hmph!
EVEN SO, IT LOOKS LIKE A TRYST TO OTHERS!
...
I CAN'T TRUST HIM...
BUT...
...THIS IS AN OPPORTUNITY FOR ME.

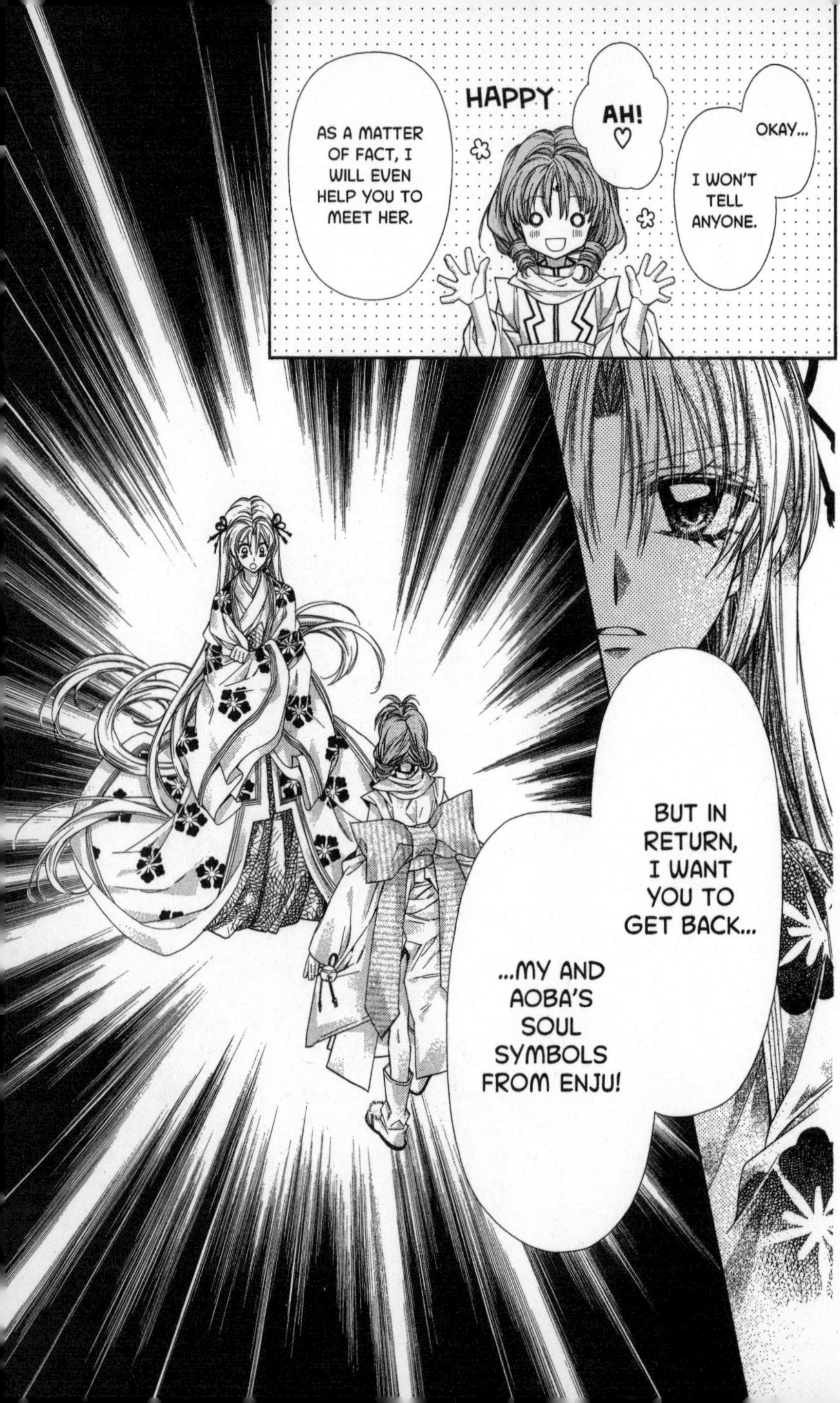
OKAY...
I WON'T TELL ANYONE.
AH! ♡
HAPPY
AS A MATTER OF FACT, I WILL EVEN HELP YOU TO MEET HER.
BUT IN RETURN, I WANT YOU TO GET BACK...
...MY AND AOBA'S SOUL SYMBOLS FROM ENJU!

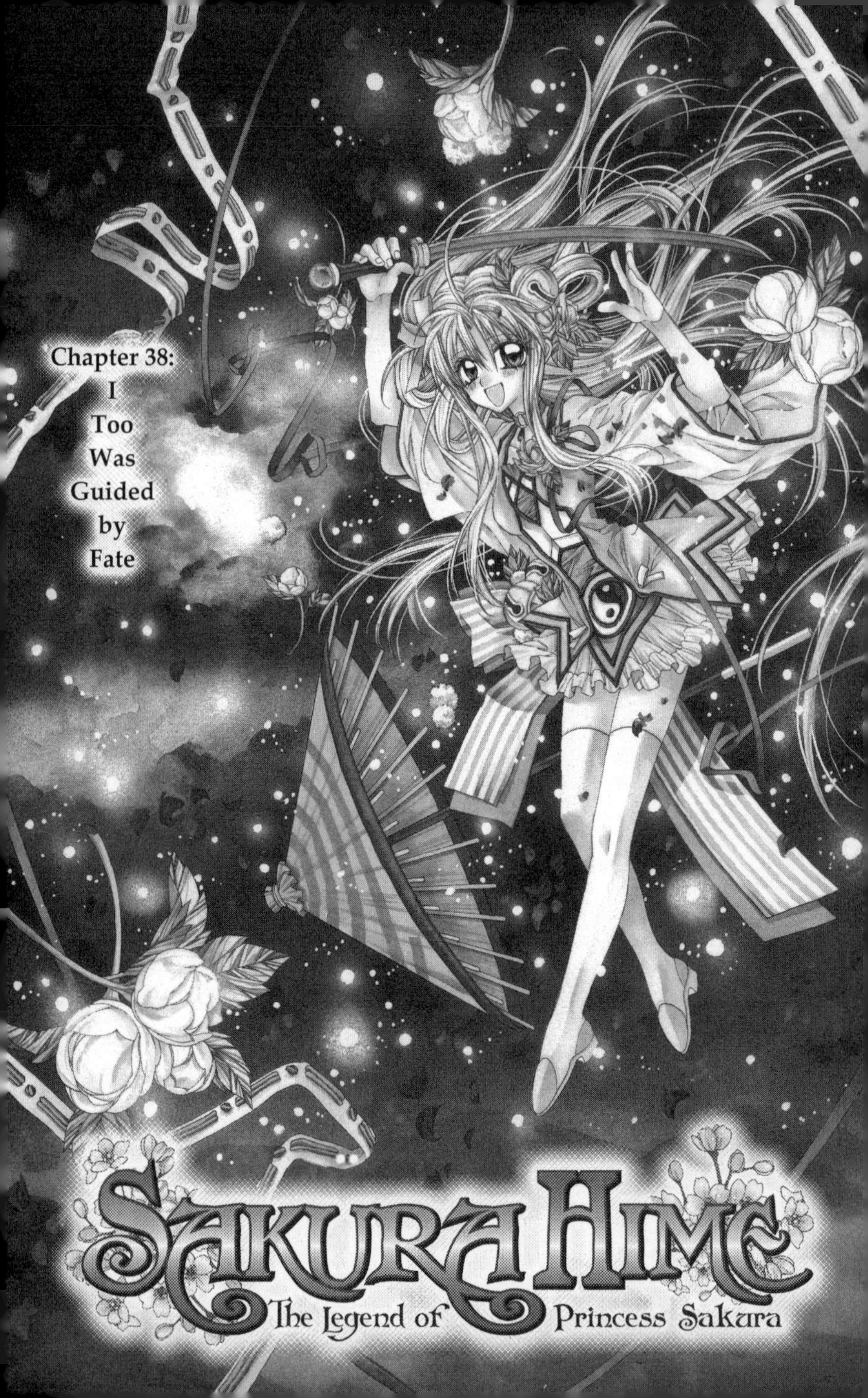
Chapter 38: I Too Was Guided by Fate
Sakura Hime
The Legend of Princess Sakura

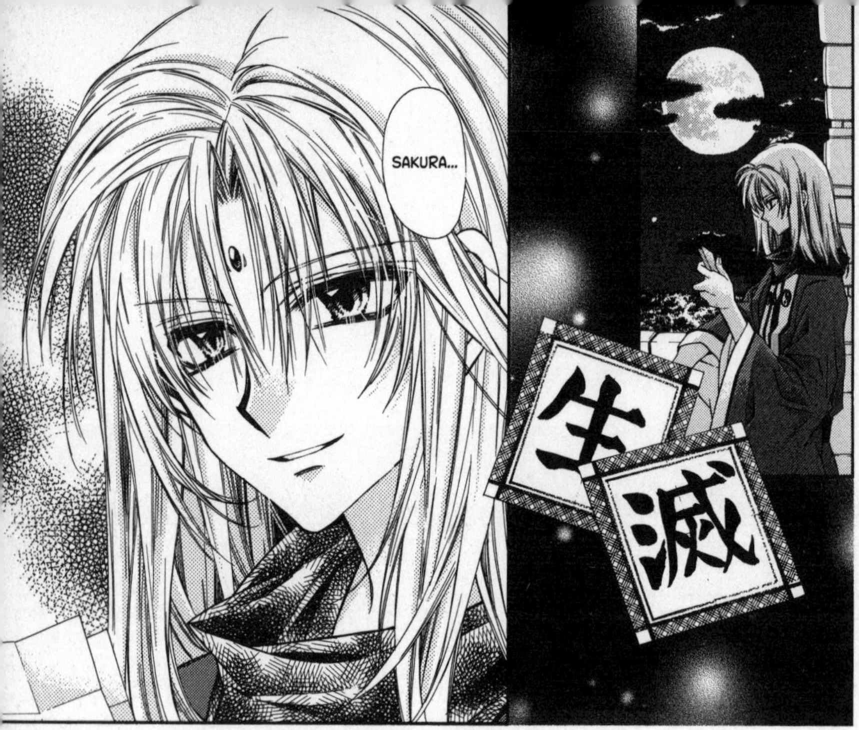
SAKURA...
生
滅

Chapter 38: I Too Was Guided by Fate

※I'm giving away the story.

The illustration for the chapter title page is one of a pair with the illustration for chapter 34 in volume 9. I took a very long time drawing Princess Yuri and Maimai's hair. My assistant did the screentones for their hair, so she seemed to be having a hard time too. (To tell you the truth, their screentones are slightly different). I drew Princess Yuri and Maimai as if they were twins, so I really enjoyed drawing how similar they were. I like the scene where Sakura gives them the pressed flowers. Sakura tells them that Aoba gave them to her, so even though that scene doesn't appear in the actual manga, you can tell that Sakura and Aoba are still lovey-dovey... I couldn't help smiling about it. I was very happy to hear that the "beauty pageant" between Princess Yuri and Maimai was extremely popular with the readers. I wonder which of these two is more popular... I can't wait to see the results of the reader poll. I had decided from the start that the soul symbol for these two had to be this! They get along so well, don't they? (laugh)

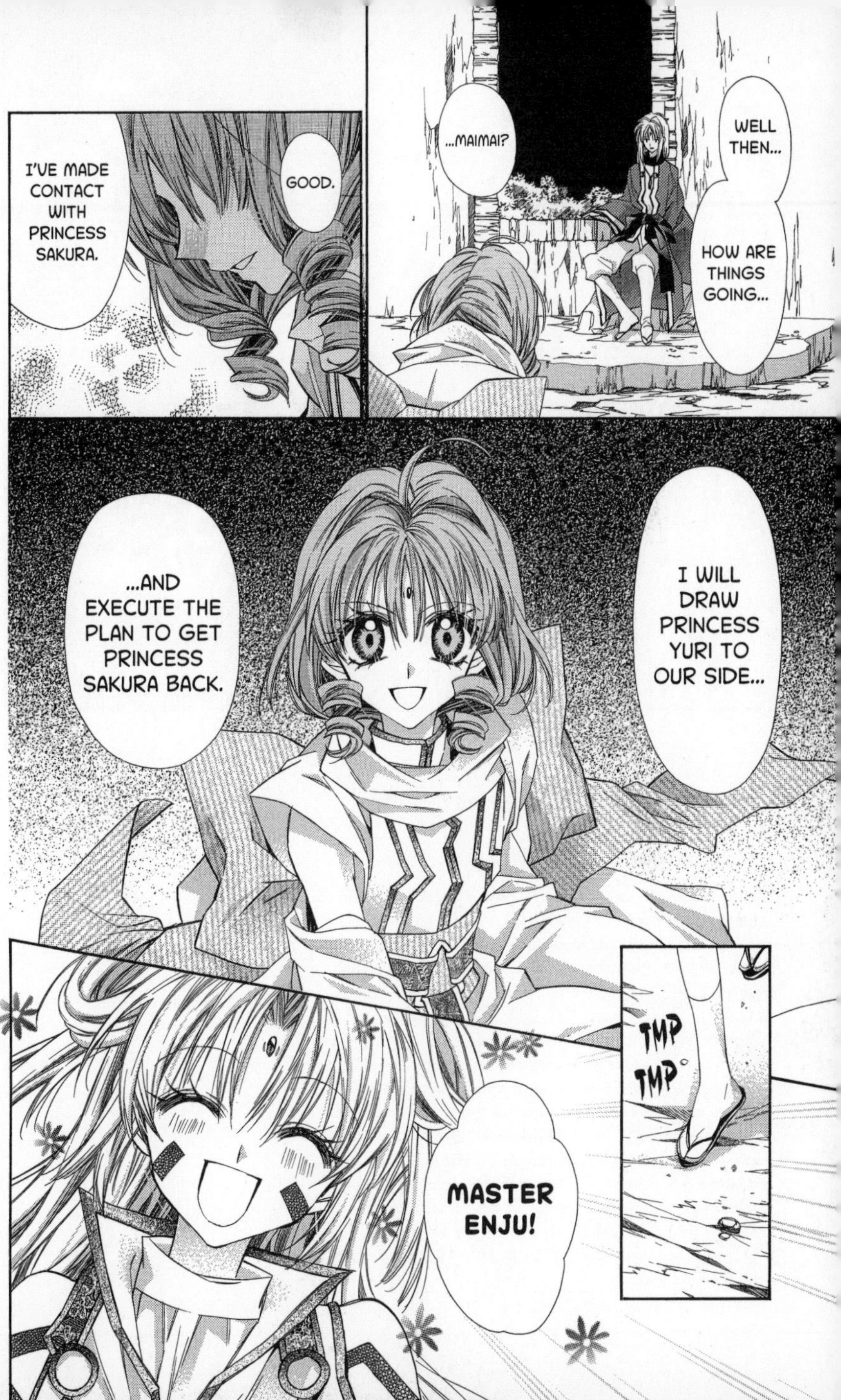
WELL THEN...
...MAIMAI?
HOW ARE THINGS GOING...
GOOD.
I'VE MADE CONTACT WITH PRINCESS SAKURA.
I WILL DRAW PRINCESS YURI TO OUR SIDE...
...AND EXECUTE THE PLAN TO GET PRINCESS SAKURA BACK.
TMP TMP
MASTER ENJU!

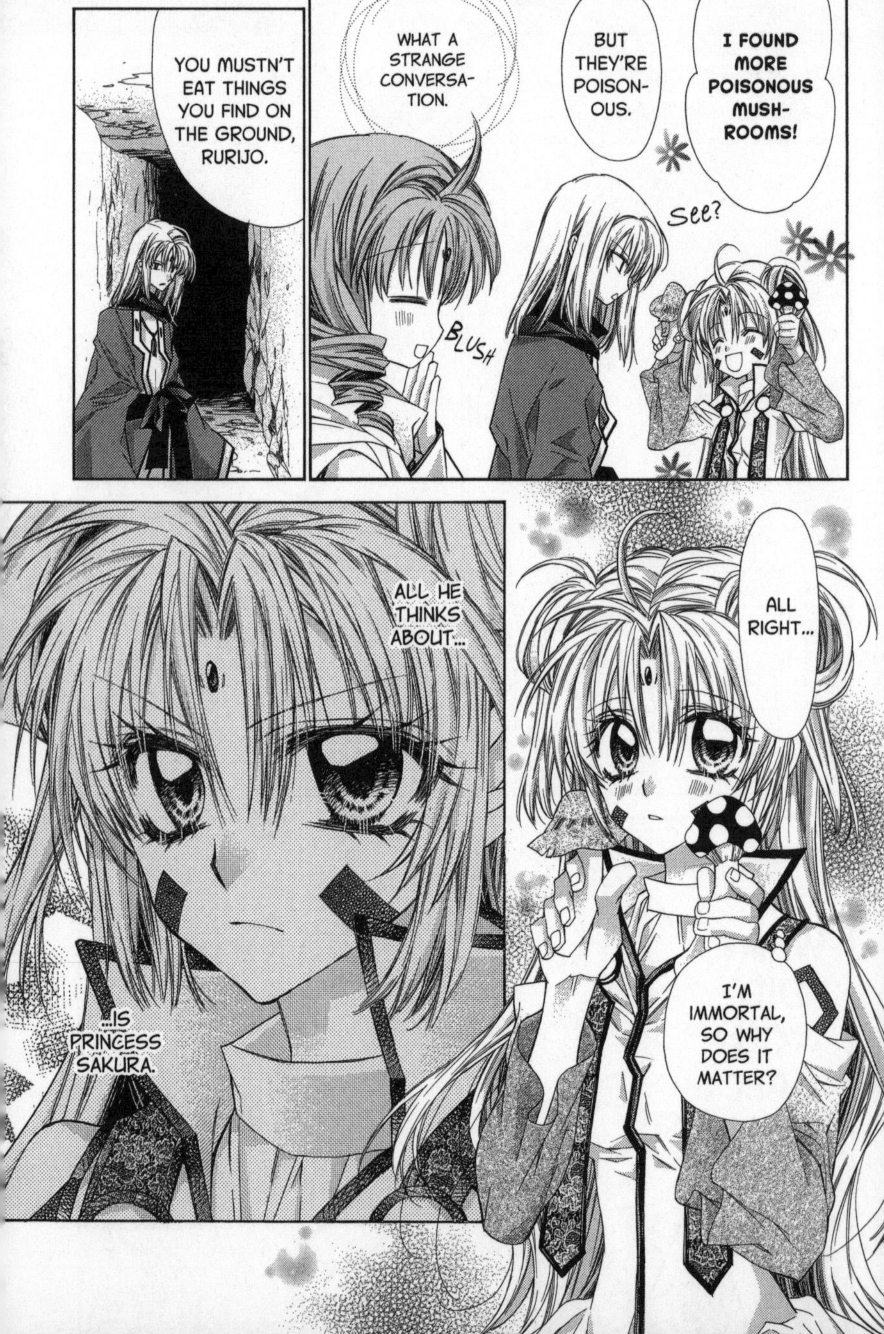
I FOUND MORE POISONOUS MUSH-ROOMS!
See?
BUT THEY'RE POISON-OUS.
WHAT A STRANGE CONVERSA-TION.
BLUSH
YOU MUSTN'T EAT THINGS YOU FIND ON THE GROUND, RURIJO.
ALL RIGHT...
I'M IMMORTAL, SO WHY DOES IT MATTER?
ALL HE THINKS ABOUT...
...IS PRINCESS SAKURA.

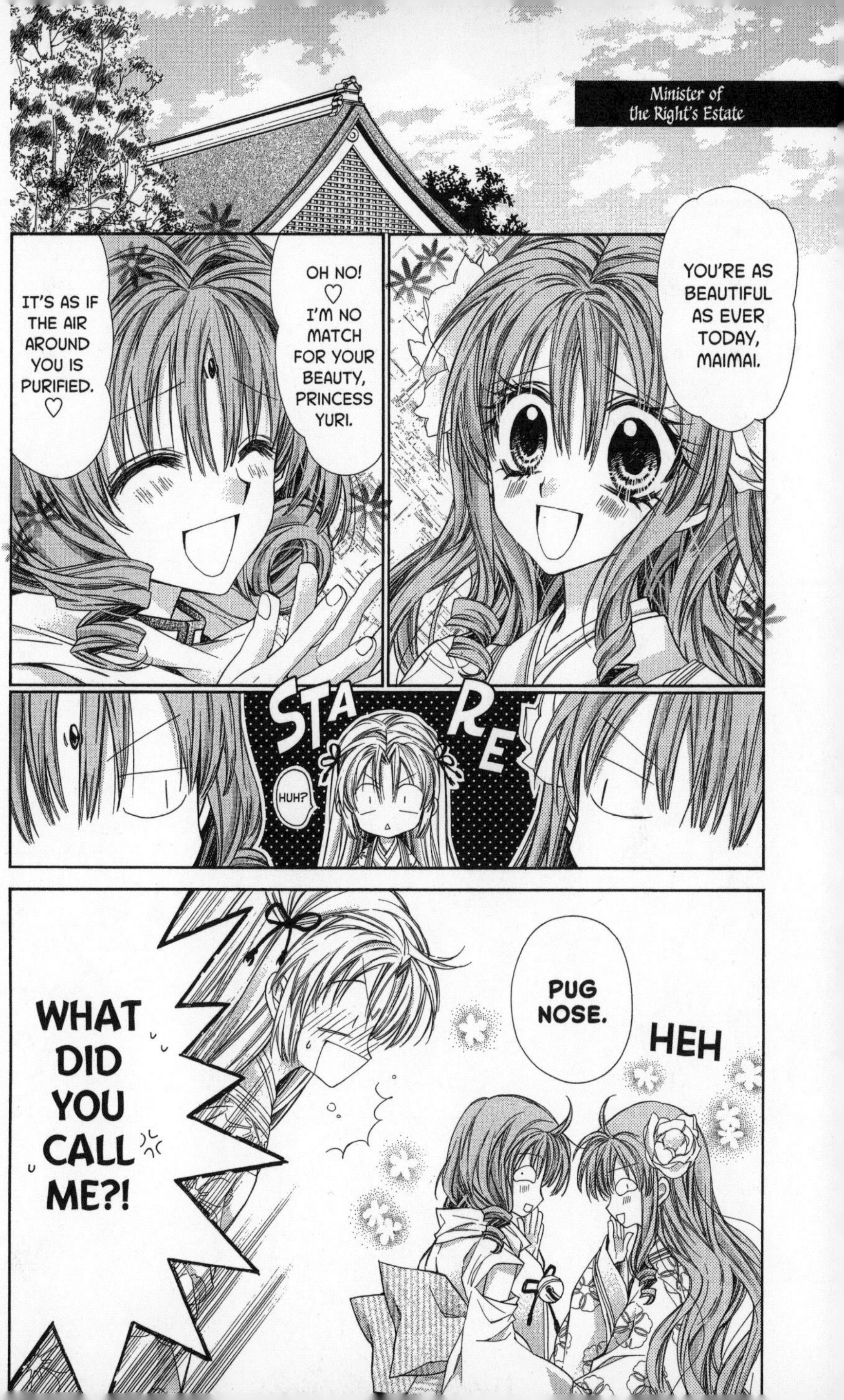
Minister of the Right's Estate
YOU'RE AS BEAUTIFUL AS EVER TODAY, MAIMAI.
OH NO! ♡ I'M NO MATCH FOR YOUR BEAUTY, PRINCESS YURI.
IT'S AS IF THE AIR AROUND YOU IS PURIFIED. ♡
STARE
HUH?
PUG NOSE.
HEH
WHAT DID YOU CALL ME?!

Hokkaido continued →

We went to Asahiyama Zoo, the place of our dreams, and it was just ✧**fabulous**✧! The animals were so close to us! And they're huge!! The location of the zoo is perfect too!! (The zoo was built on a mountain, so the rugged rocks give it a nice atmosphere.)
To be honest, I thought all those TV shows were exaggerating when they introduced the zoo, but it was as exciting as they said!
The best and cutest part were the seals!! There is a tube from the floor to the ceiling that the seals continuously swim through. They had such a dreamy expression on their faces!

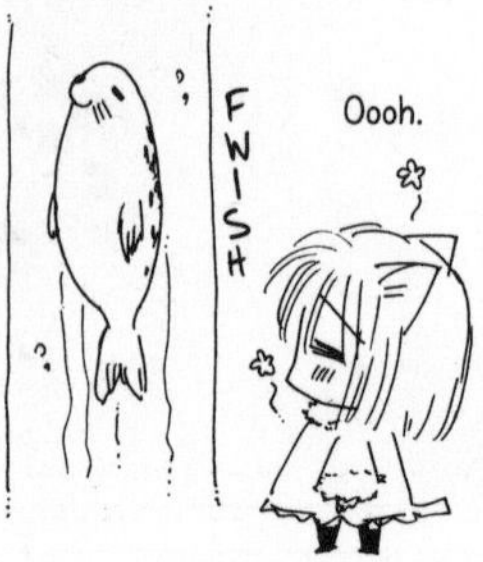
FWISH
Oooh.

Also, I have a thing for owls, and there are many types of owls at the zoo. It was very nice. ♥
There are also animals like a white Ezo red fox. The zoo has many animals from the northern lands that add to the "one and only" atmosphere. I would love to go there again!!

I had a lovely time on my trip to Hokkaido. ♪

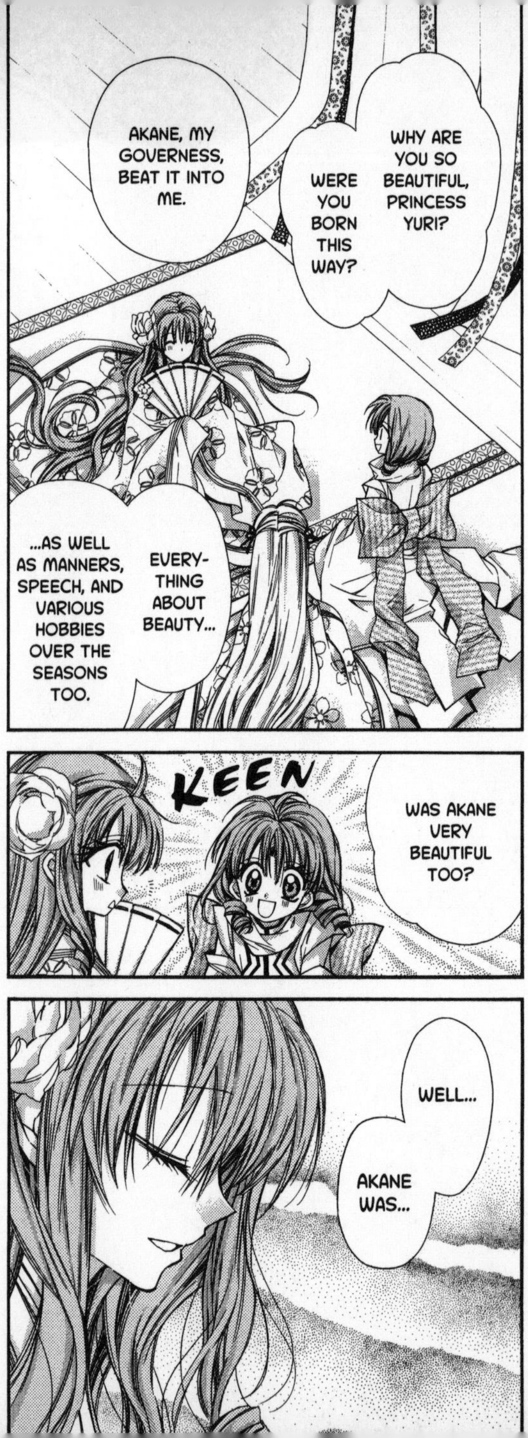
WHY ARE YOU SO BEAUTIFUL, PRINCESS YURI?
WERE YOU BORN THIS WAY?
AKANE, MY GOVERNESS, BEAT IT INTO ME.
EVERYTHING ABOUT BEAUTY...
...AS WELL AS MANNERS, SPEECH, AND VARIOUS HOBBIES OVER THE SEASONS TOO.
WAS AKANE VERY BEAUTIFUL TOO?
KEEN
WELL...
AKANE WAS...

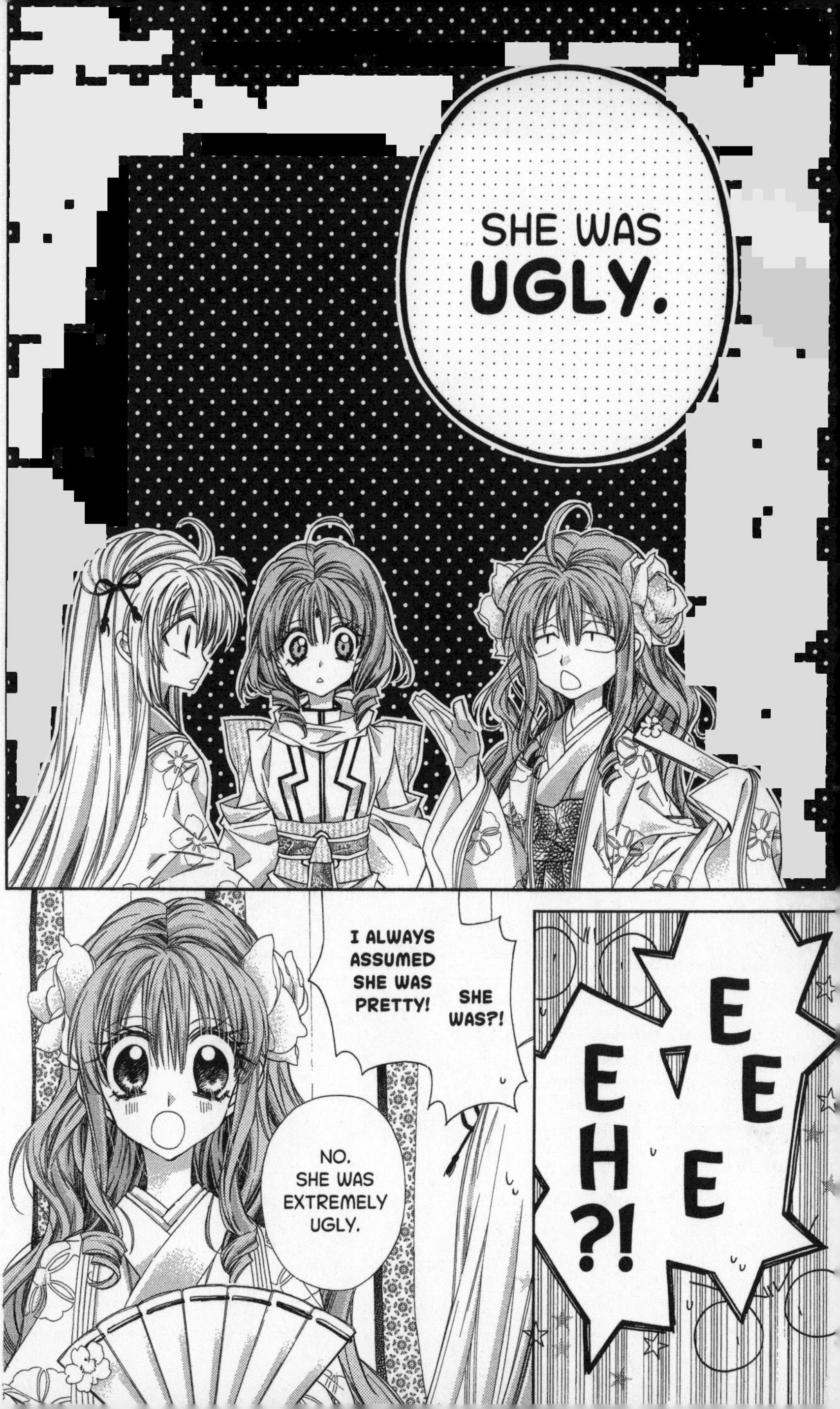
SHE WAS UGLY.
EEEEH?!
SHE WAS?!
I ALWAYS ASSUMED SHE WAS PRETTY!
NO. SHE WAS EXTREMELY UGLY.

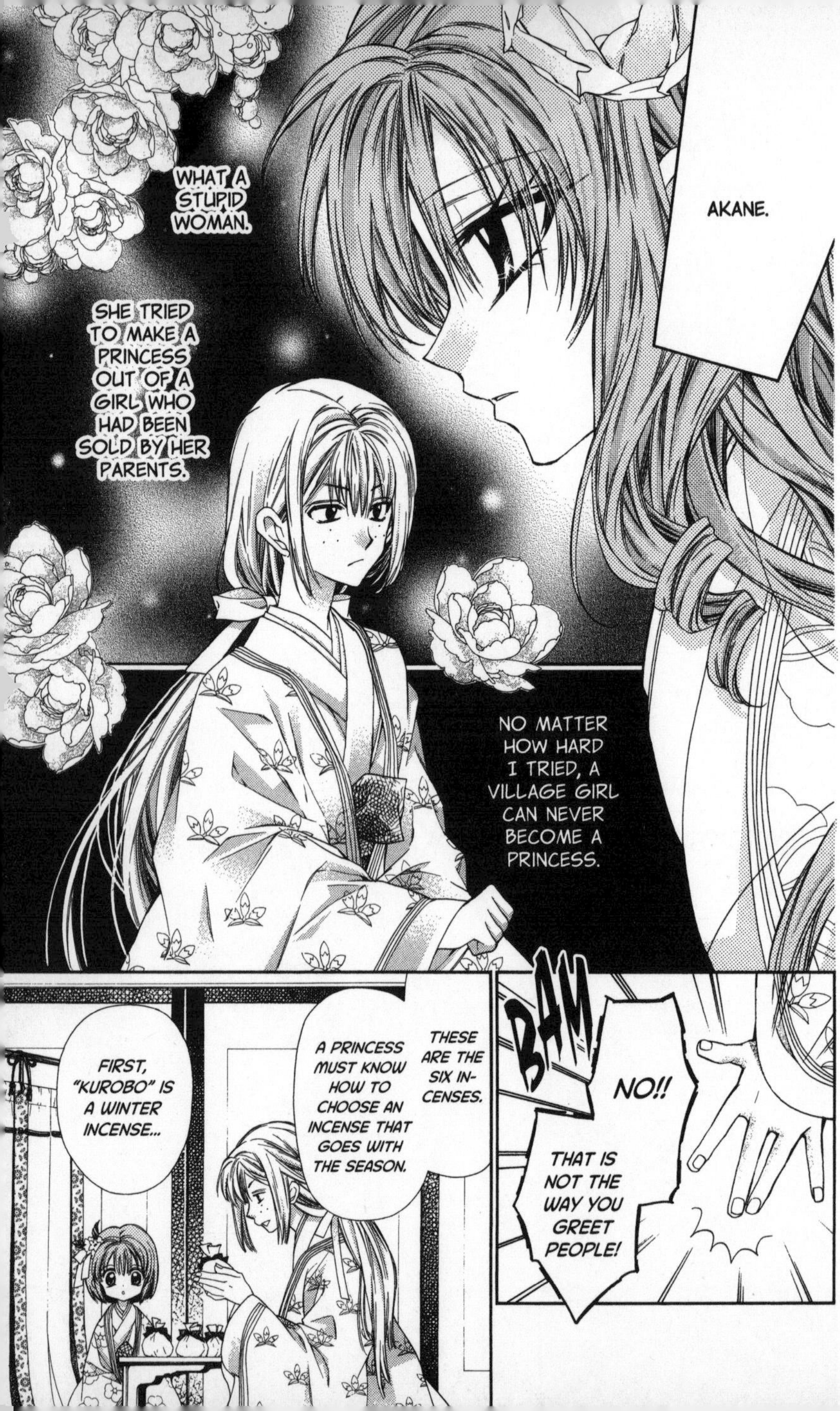
AKANE.
WHAT A STUPID WOMAN.
SHE TRIED TO MAKE A PRINCESS OUT OF A GIRL WHO HAD BEEN SOLD BY HER PARENTS.
NO MATTER HOW HARD I TRIED, A VILLAGE GIRL CAN NEVER BECOME A PRINCESS.
BAM
NO!!
THAT IS NOT THE WAY YOU GREET PEOPLE!
THESE ARE THE SIX IN-CENSES.
A PRINCESS MUST KNOW HOW TO CHOOSE AN INCENSE THAT GOES WITH THE SEASON.
FIRST, "KUROBO" IS A WINTER INCENSE...

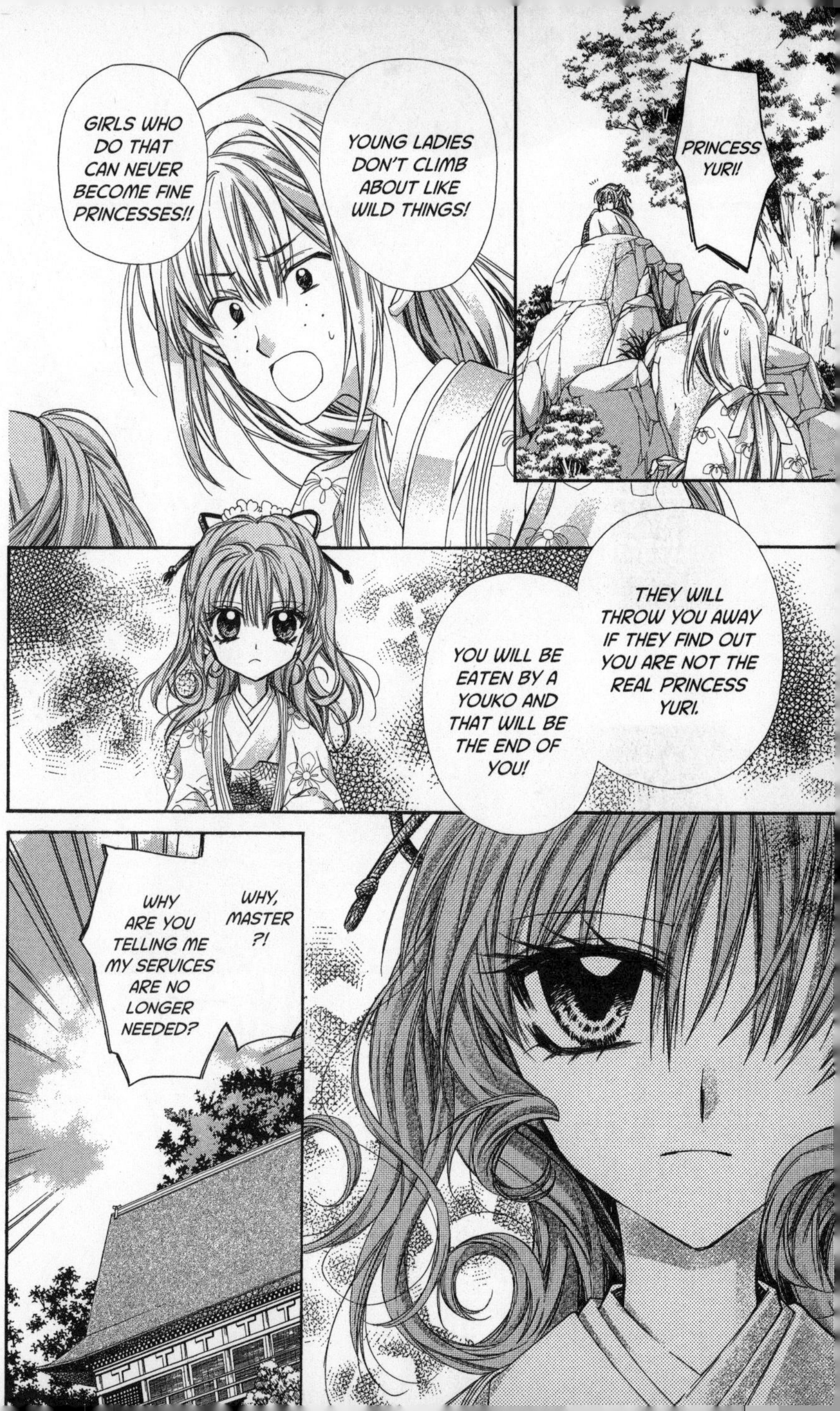
PRINCESS YURI!
YOUNG LADIES DON'T CLIMB ABOUT LIKE WILD THINGS!
GIRLS WHO DO THAT CAN NEVER BECOME FINE PRINCESSES!!
THEY WILL THROW YOU AWAY IF THEY FIND OUT YOU ARE NOT THE REAL PRINCESS YURI.
YOU WILL BE EATEN BY A YOUKO AND THAT WILL BE THE END OF YOU!
WHY, MASTER?!
WHY ARE YOU TELLING ME MY SERVICES ARE NO LONGER NEEDED?

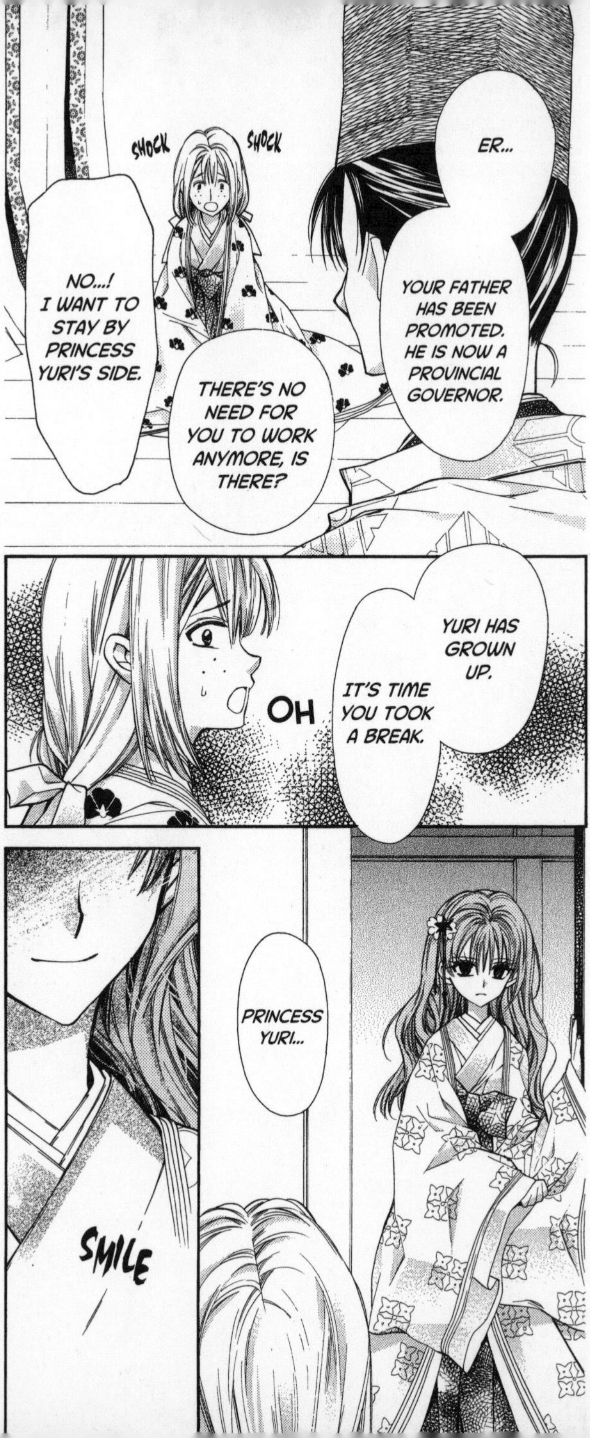
ER...
YOUR FATHER HAS BEEN PROMOTED. HE IS NOW A PROVINCIAL GOVERNOR.
THERE'S NO NEED FOR YOU TO WORK ANYMORE, IS THERE?
SHOCK SHOCK
NO...! I WANT TO STAY BY PRINCESS YURI'S SIDE.
YURI HAS GROWN UP.
IT'S TIME YOU TOOK A BREAK.
OH
PRINCESS YURI...
SMILE

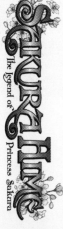

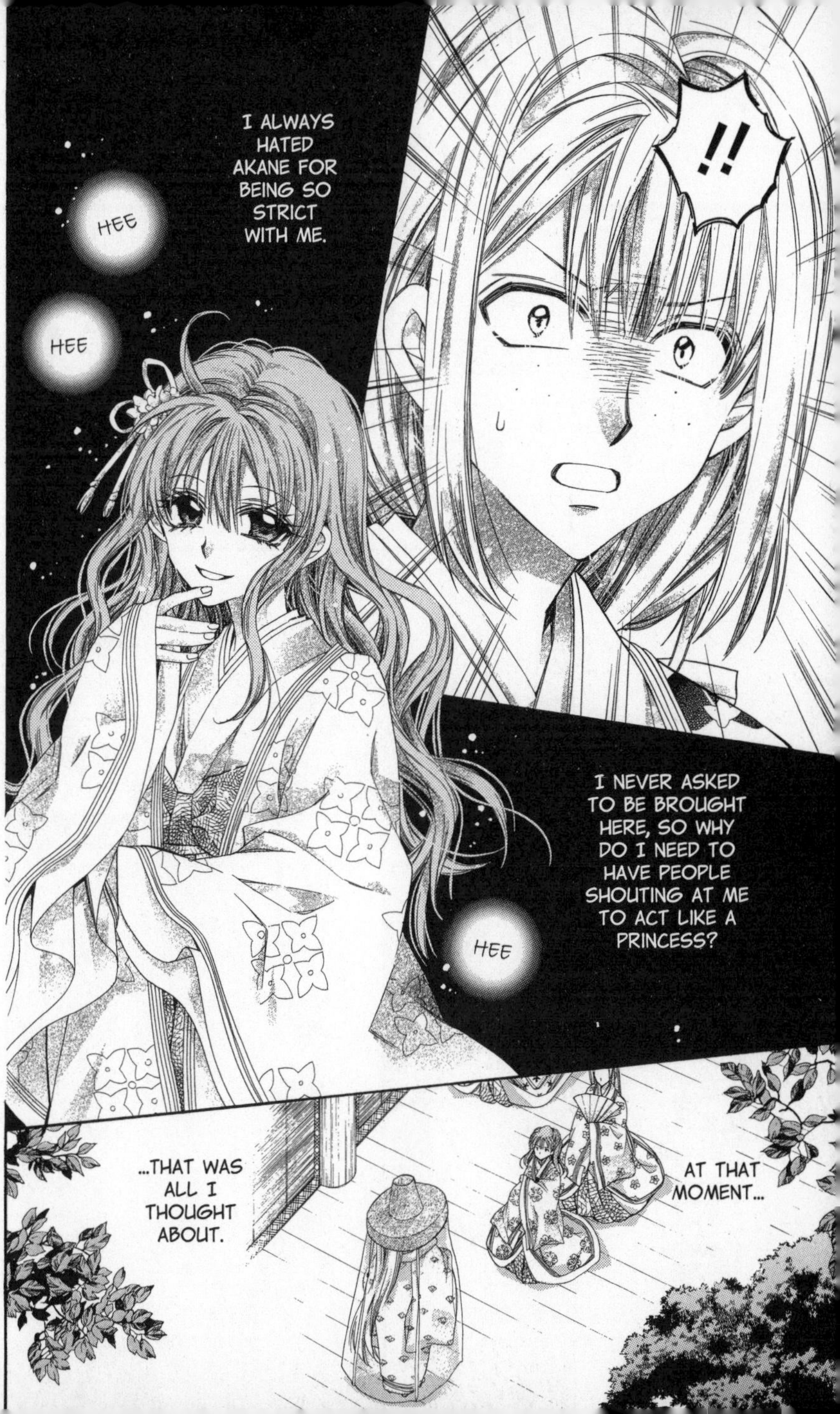
!!
I ALWAYS HATED AKANE FOR BEING SO STRICT WITH ME.
HEE
HEE
I NEVER ASKED TO BE BROUGHT HERE, SO WHY DO I NEED TO HAVE PEOPLE SHOUTING AT ME TO ACT LIKE A PRINCESS?
HEE
AT THAT MOMENT...
...THAT WAS ALL I THOUGHT ABOUT.

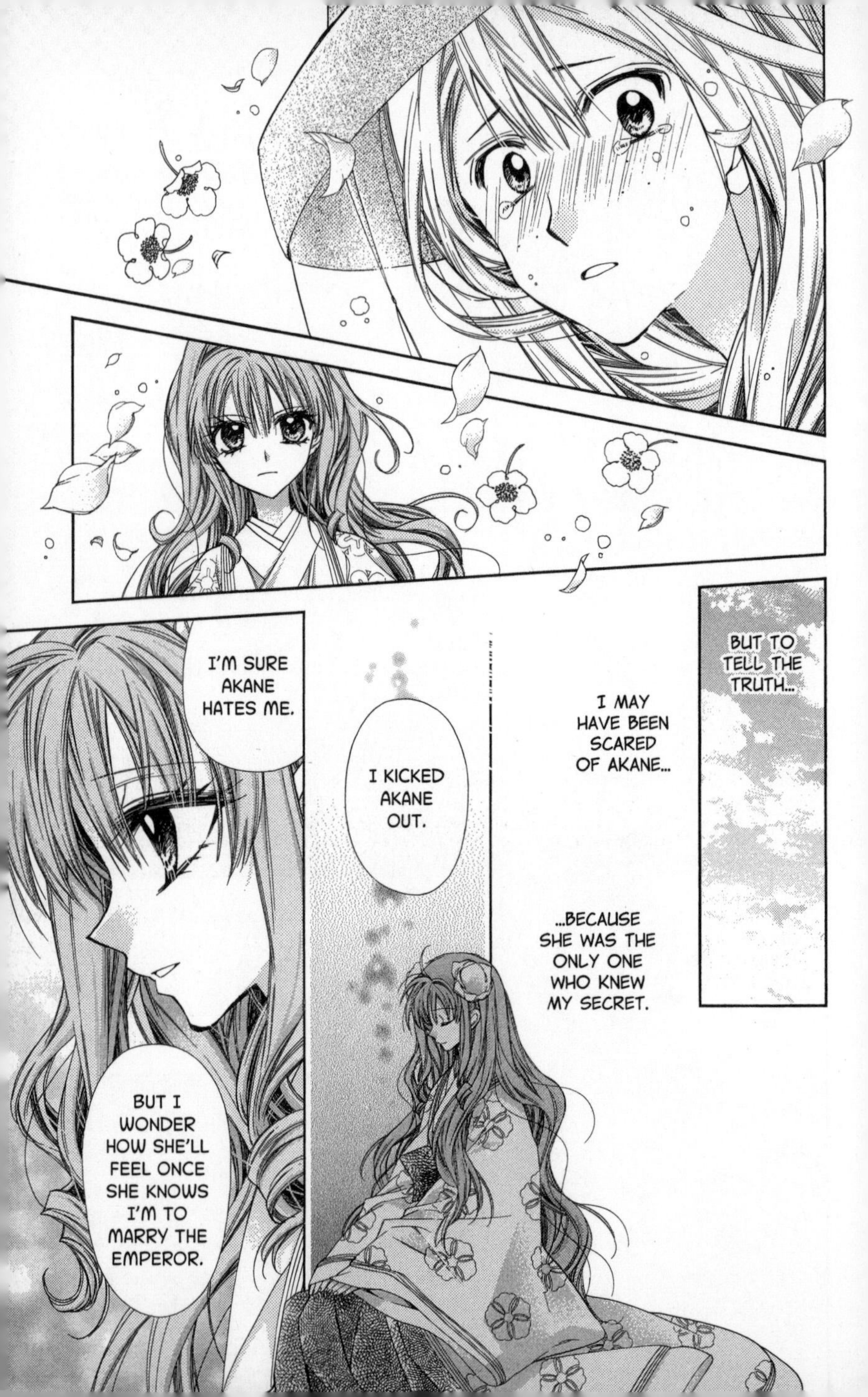
BUT TO TELL THE TRUTH...
I MAY HAVE BEEN SCARED OF AKANE...
...BECAUSE SHE WAS THE ONLY ONE WHO KNEW MY SECRET.
I KICKED AKANE OUT.
I'M SURE AKANE HATES ME.
BUT I WONDER HOW SHE'LL FEEL ONCE SHE KNOWS I'M TO MARRY THE EMPEROR.

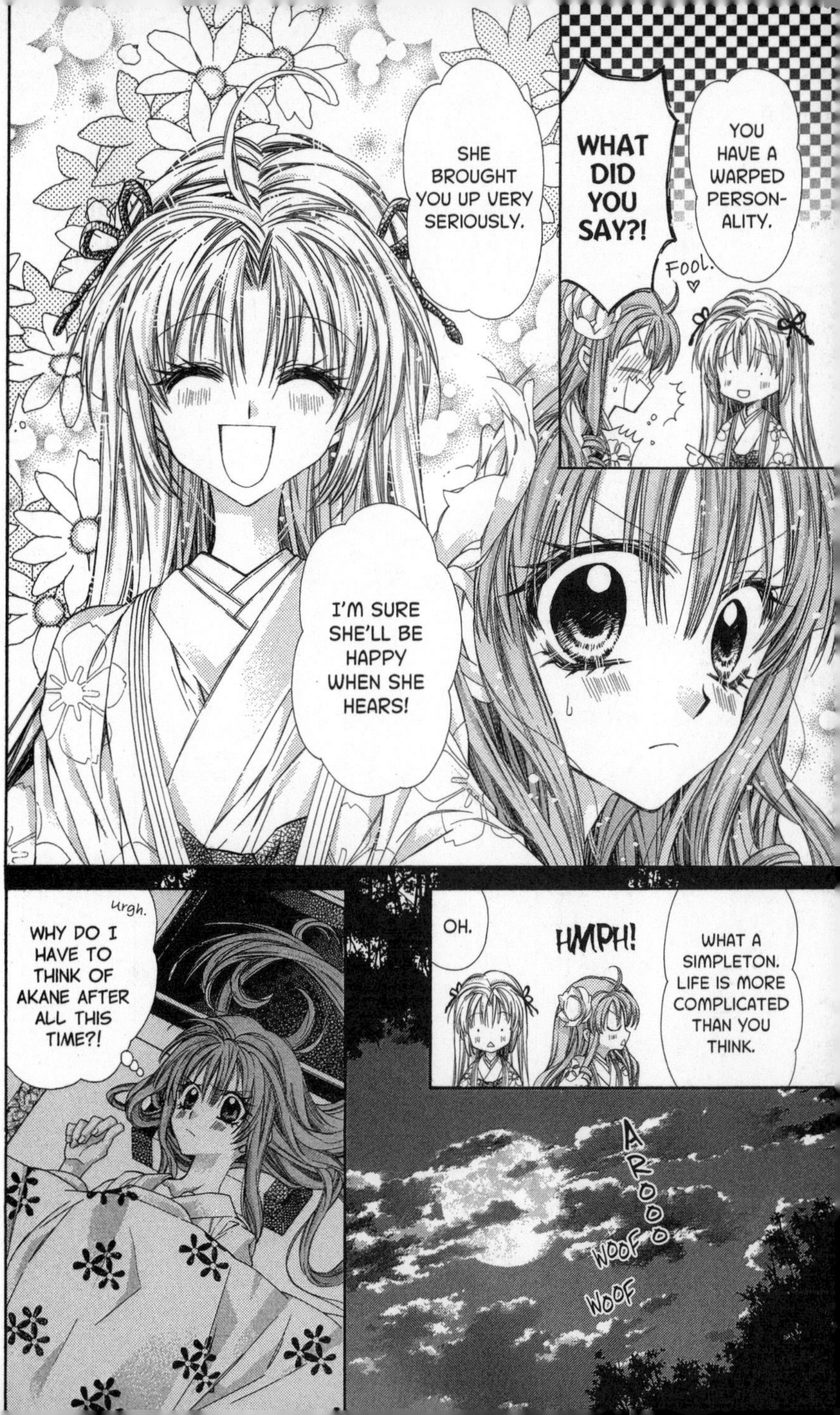
YOU HAVE A WARPED PERSON-ALITY.
WHAT DID YOU SAY?!
Fool. ♥
SHE BROUGHT YOU UP VERY SERIOUSLY.
I'M SURE SHE'LL BE HAPPY WHEN SHE HEARS!
WHAT A SIMPLETON. LIFE IS MORE COMPLICATED THAN YOU THINK.
HMPH!
OH.
AROOO
WOOF
WOOF
urgh.
WHY DO I HAVE TO THINK OF AKANE AFTER ALL THIS TIME?!

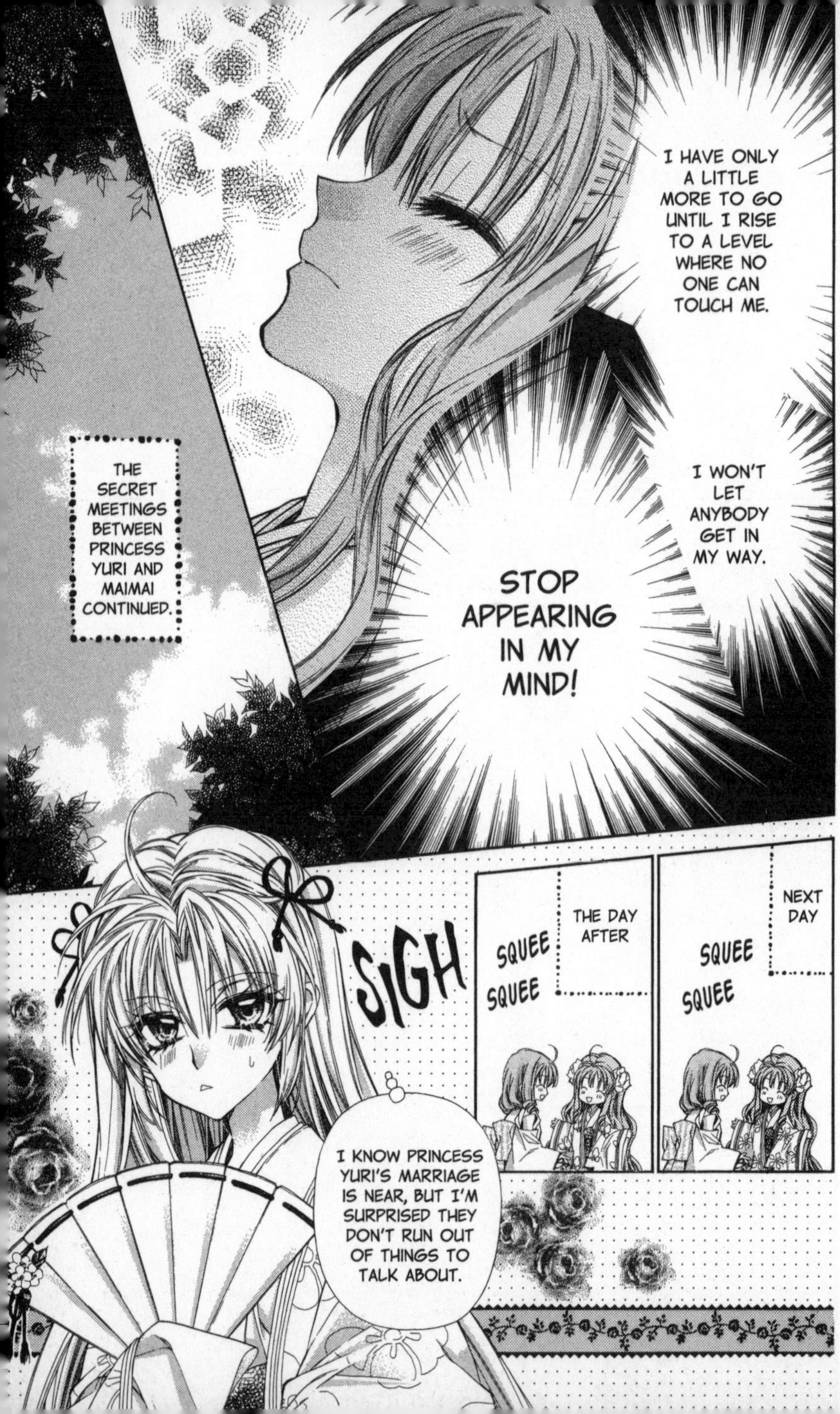
I HAVE ONLY A LITTLE MORE TO GO UNTIL I RISE TO A LEVEL WHERE NO ONE CAN TOUCH ME.
I WON'T LET ANYBODY GET IN MY WAY.
STOP APPEARING IN MY MIND!
THE SECRET MEETINGS BETWEEN PRINCESS YURI AND MAIMAI CONTINUED.
NEXT DAY
SQUEE
SQUEE
THE DAY AFTER
SQUEE
SQUEE
SIGH
I KNOW PRINCESS YURI'S MARRIAGE IS NEAR, BUT I'M SURPRISED THEY DON'T RUN OUT OF THINGS TO TALK ABOUT.

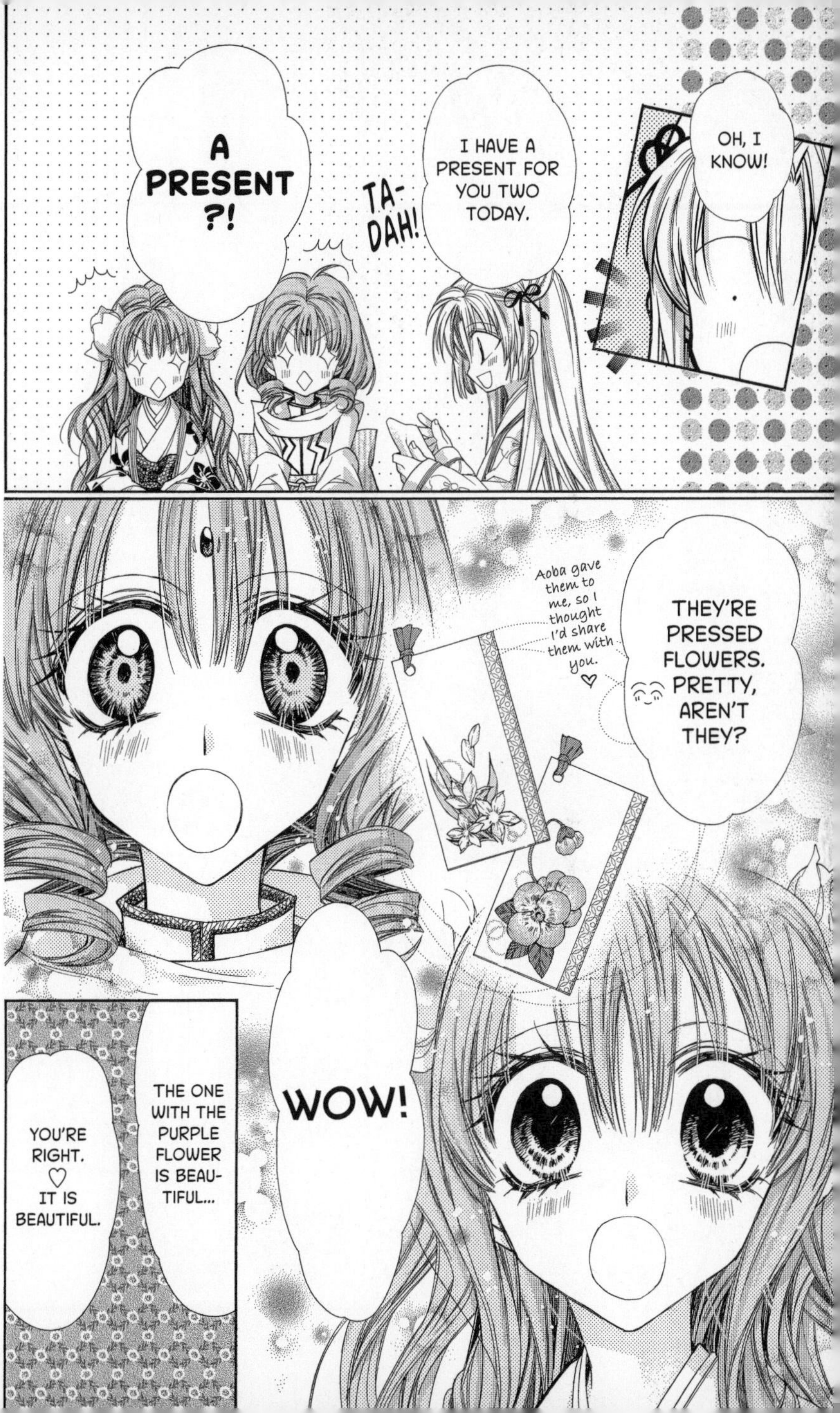
OH, I KNOW!
I HAVE A PRESENT FOR YOU TWO TODAY.
TA-DAH!
A PRESENT?!
THEY'RE PRESSED FLOWERS. PRETTY, AREN'T THEY?
Aoba gave them to me, so I thought I'd share them with you. ♡
WOW!
THE ONE WITH THE PURPLE FLOWER IS BEAU-TIFUL...
YOU'RE RIGHT. ♡ IT IS BEAUTIFUL.

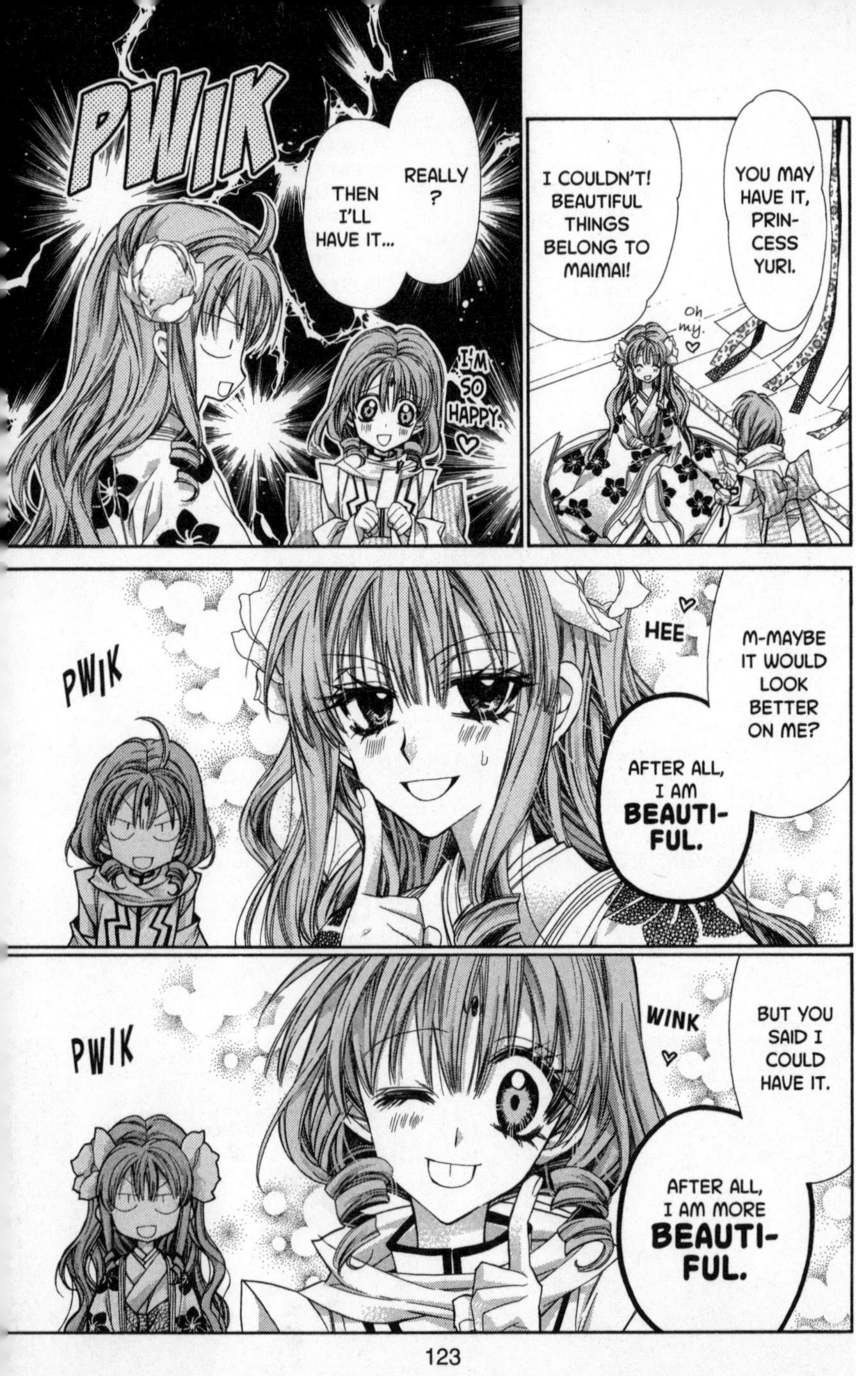
YOU MAY HAVE IT, PRIN-CESS YURI.
I COULDN'T! BEAUTIFUL THINGS BELONG TO MAIMAI!
Oh my.
PWIK
REALLY?
THEN I'LL HAVE IT...
I'M SO HAPPY.
M-MAYBE IT WOULD LOOK BETTER ON ME?
AFTER ALL, I AM **BEAUTI-FUL.**
HEE
PWIK
BUT YOU SAID I COULD HAVE IT.
AFTER ALL, I AM MORE **BEAUTI-FUL.**
WINK
PWIK

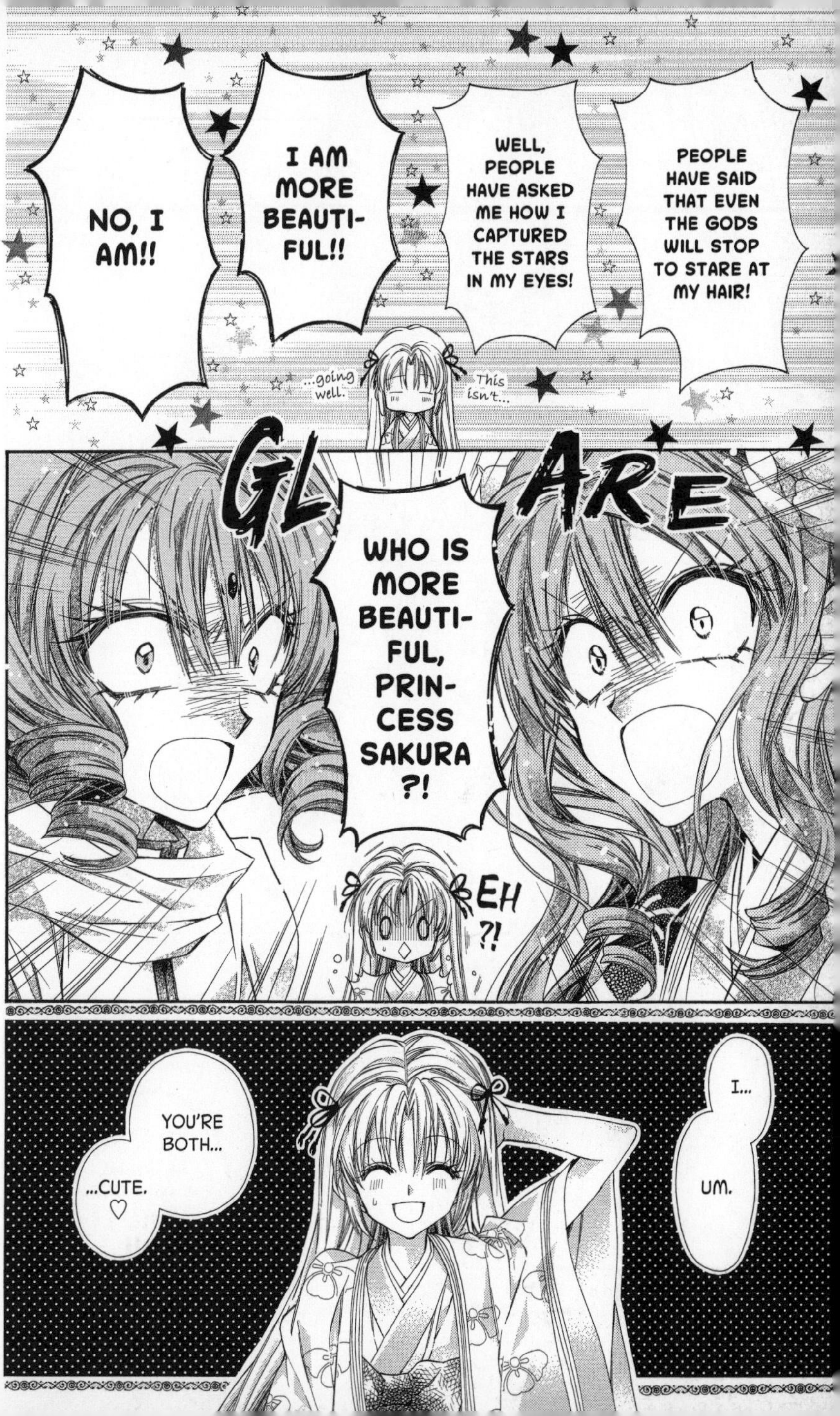
PEOPLE HAVE SAID THAT EVEN THE GODS WILL STOP TO STARE AT MY HAIR!
WELL, PEOPLE HAVE ASKED ME HOW I CAPTURED THE STARS IN MY EYES!
I AM MORE BEAUTI-FUL!!
NO, I AM!!
This isn't...
...going well.
GLARE
WHO IS MORE BEAUTI-FUL, PRIN-CESS SAKURA?!
EH?!
I... UM.
YOU'RE BOTH...
...CUTE. ♡

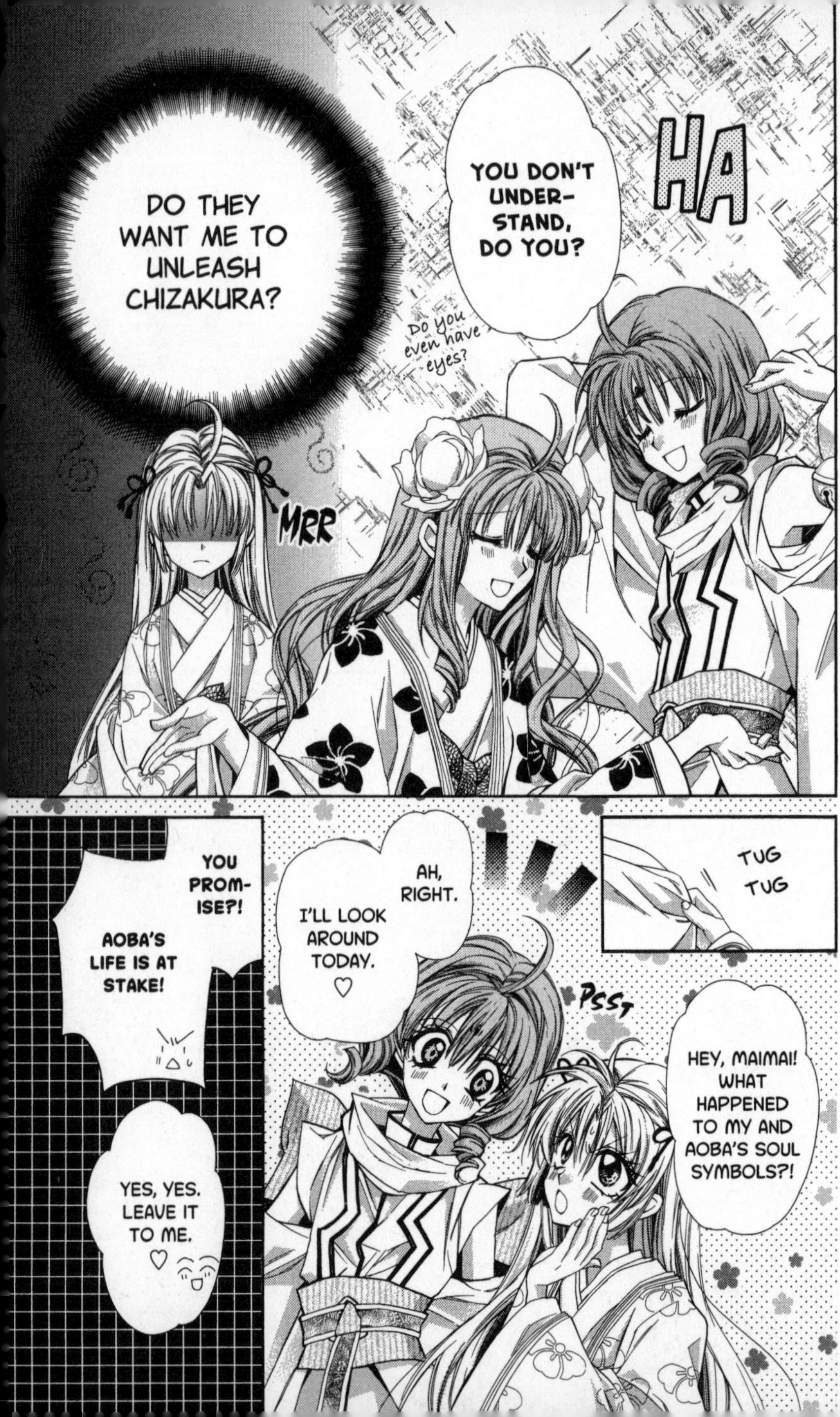
HA
YOU DON'T UNDER-STAND, DO YOU?
Do you even have eyes?
DO THEY WANT ME TO UNLEASH CHIZAKURA?
MRR
TUG TUG
HEY, MAIMAI! WHAT HAPPENED TO MY AND AOBA'S SOUL SYMBOLS?!
PSST
AH, RIGHT.
I'LL LOOK AROUND TODAY. ♡
YOU PROM-ISE?!
AOBA'S LIFE IS AT STAKE!
YES, YES. LEAVE IT TO ME. ♡

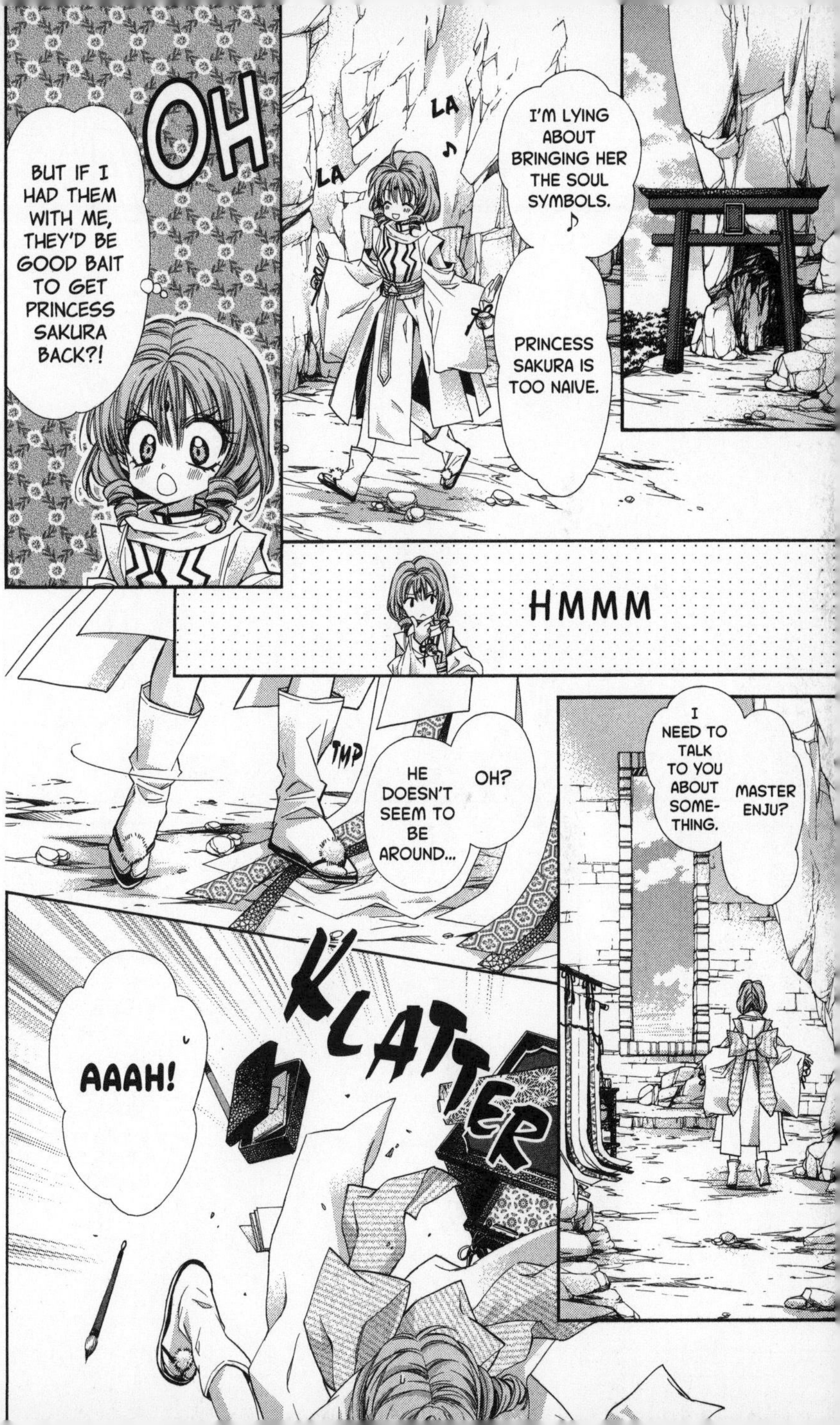
I'M LYING ABOUT BRINGING HER THE SOUL SYMBOLS. ♪
PRINCESS SAKURA IS TOO NAIVE.
LA
♪
LA
OH
BUT IF I HAD THEM WITH ME, THEY'D BE GOOD BAIT TO GET PRINCESS SAKURA BACK?!
HMMM
MASTER ENJU?
I NEED TO TALK TO YOU ABOUT SOME-THING.
OH?
HE DOESN'T SEEM TO BE AROUND...
TMP
KLATTER
AAAH!

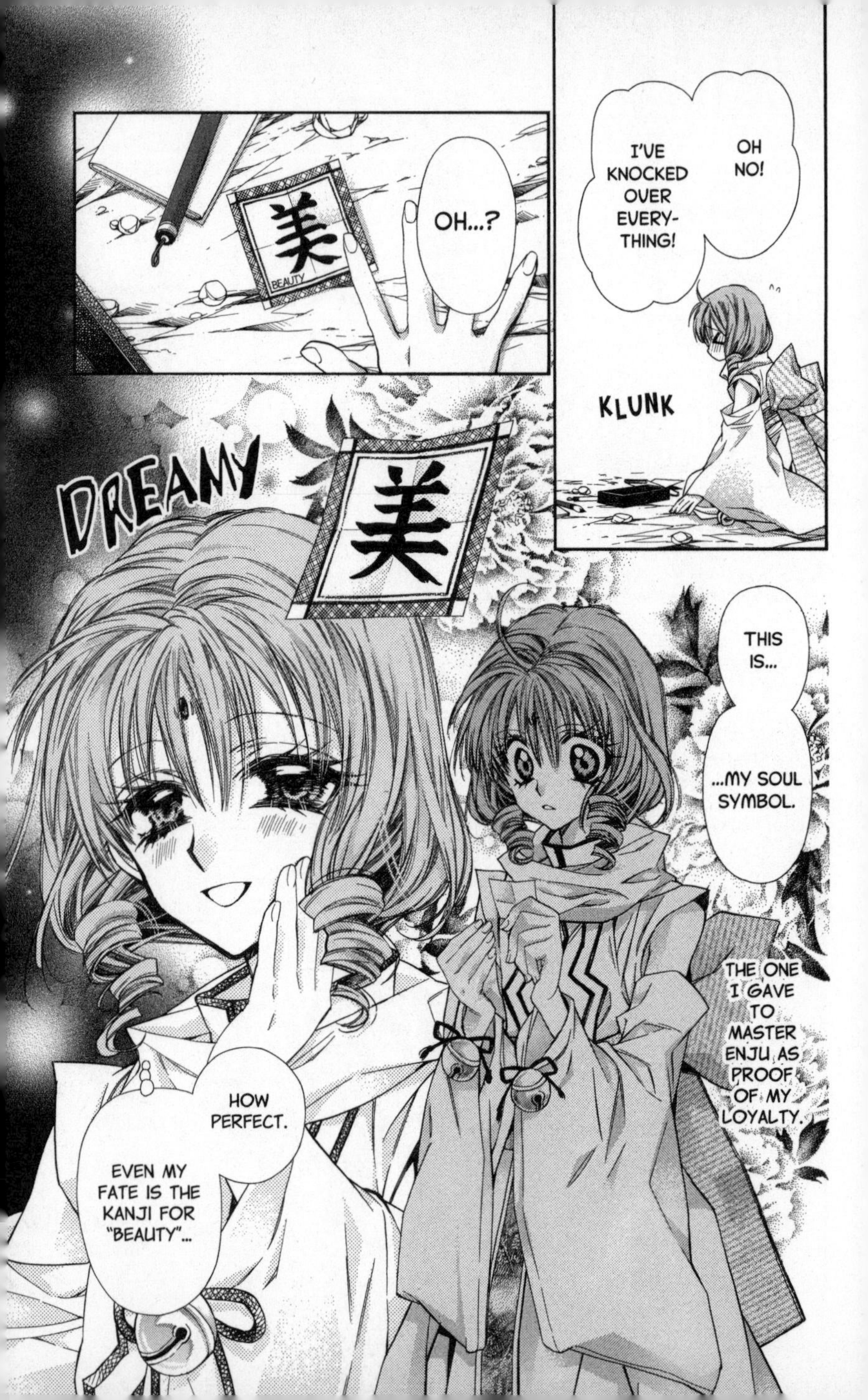
OH NO!
I'VE KNOCKED OVER EVERY-THING!
KLUNK
美
BEAUTY
OH...?
DREAMY
美
THIS IS...
...MY SOUL SYMBOL.
THE ONE I GAVE TO MASTER ENJU AS PROOF OF MY LOYALTY.
HOW PERFECT.
EVEN MY FATE IS THE KANJI FOR "BEAUTY"...

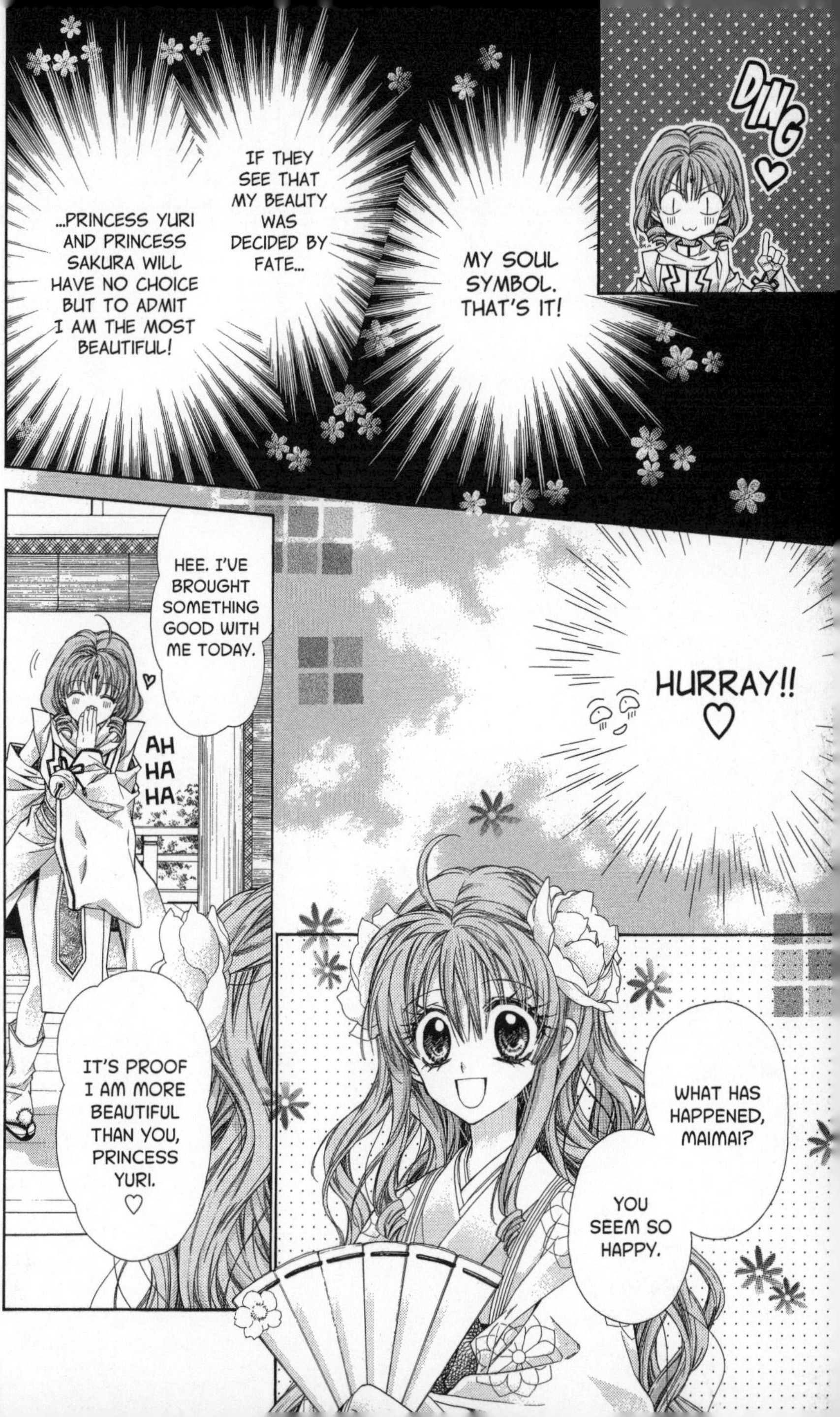
DING
MY SOUL SYMBOL. THAT'S IT!
IF THEY SEE THAT MY BEAUTY WAS DECIDED BY FATE...
...PRINCESS YURI AND PRINCESS SAKURA WILL HAVE NO CHOICE BUT TO ADMIT I AM THE MOST BEAUTIFUL!
HURRAY!! ♡
WHAT HAS HAPPENED, MAIMAI?
YOU SEEM SO HAPPY.
HEE. I'VE BROUGHT SOMETHING GOOD WITH ME TODAY.
AH HA HA HA
IT'S PROOF I AM MORE BEAUTIFUL THAN YOU, PRINCESS YURI. ♡

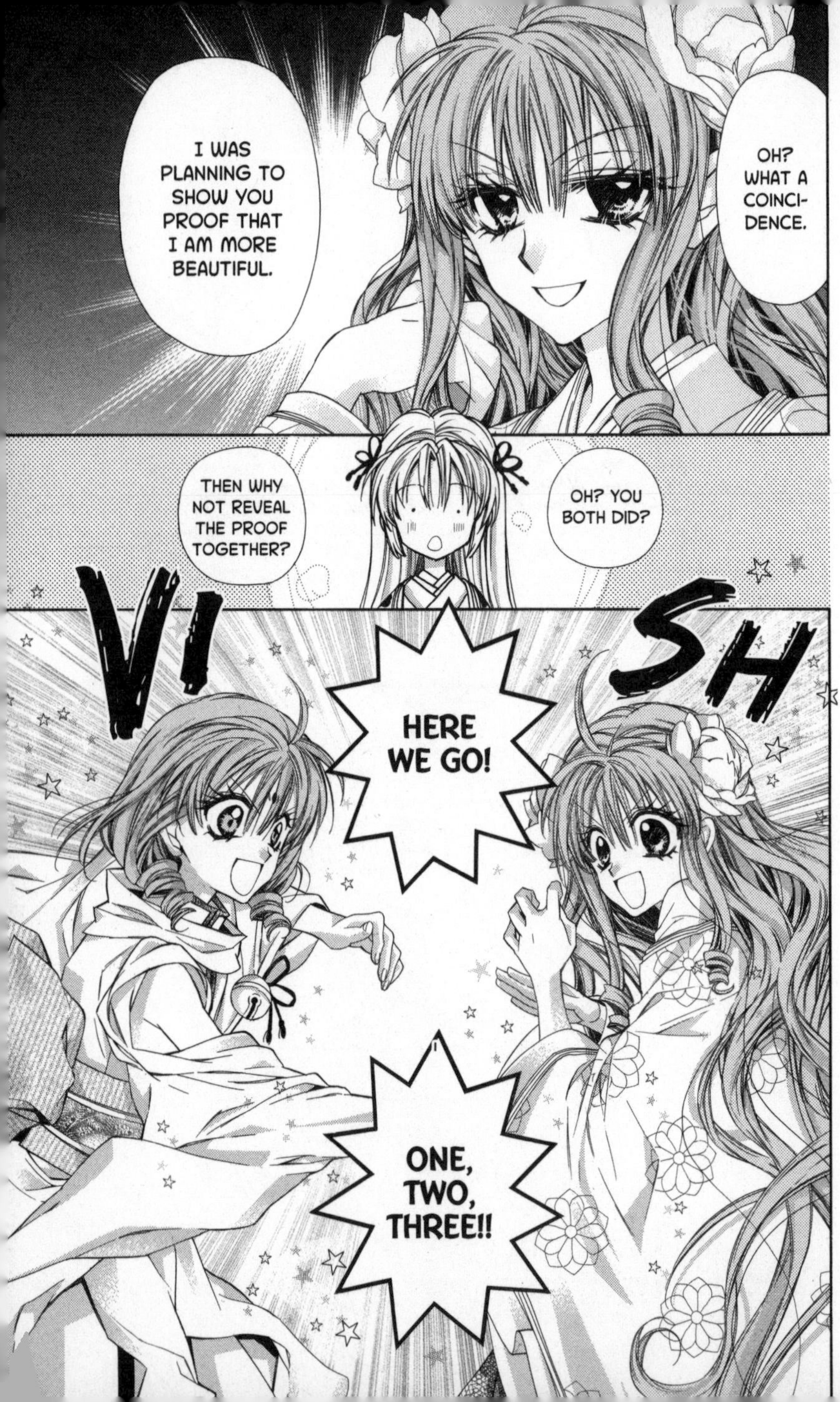
OH? WHAT A COINCIDENCE.
I WAS PLANNING TO SHOW YOU PROOF THAT I AM MORE BEAUTIFUL.
OH? YOU BOTH DID?
THEN WHY NOT REVEAL THE PROOF TOGETHER?
VISH
HERE WE GO!
ONE, TWO, THREE!!

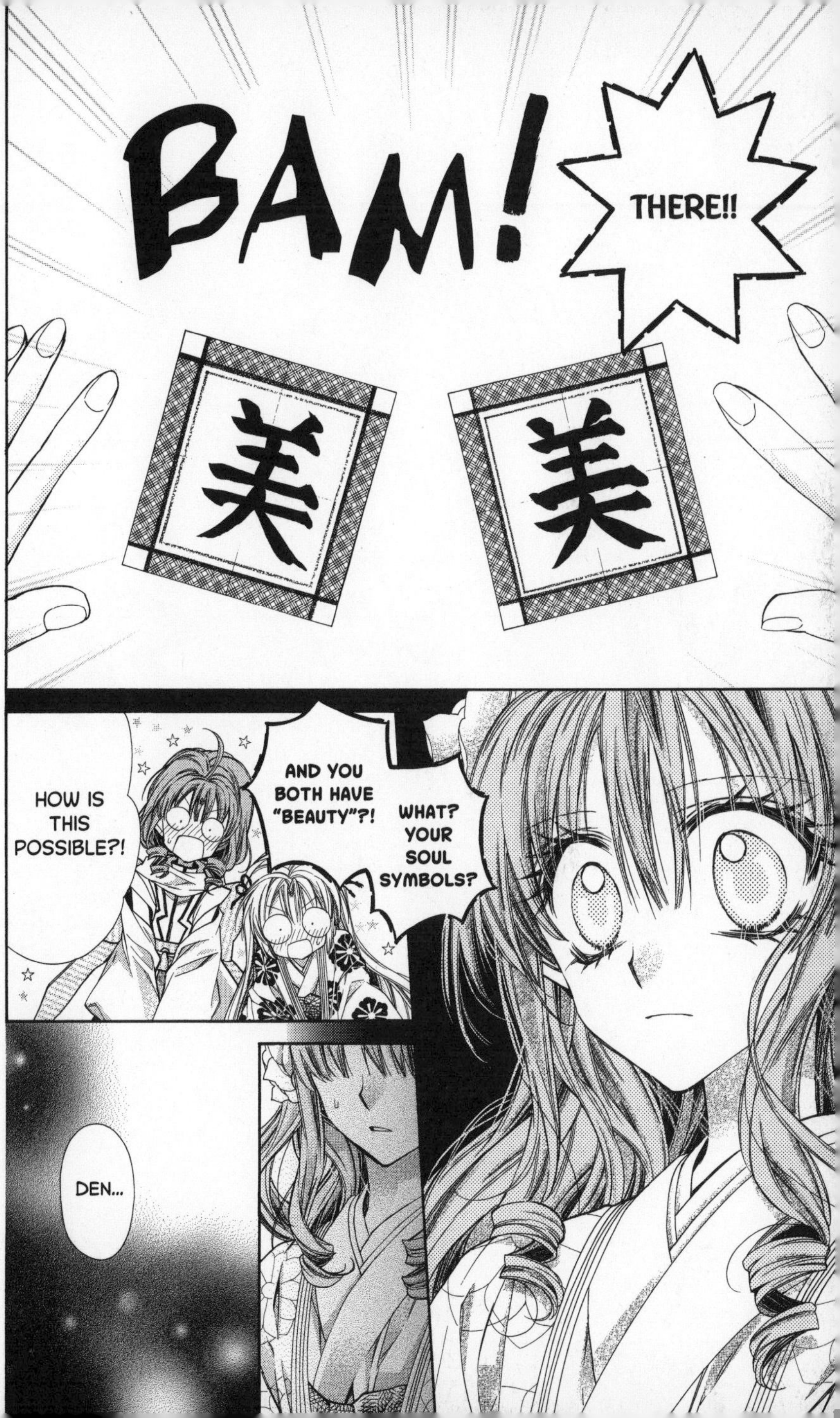
BAM!
THERE!!
美
美
WHAT? YOUR SOUL SYMBOLS?
AND YOU BOTH HAVE "BEAUTY"?!
HOW IS THIS POSSIBLE?!
DEN...

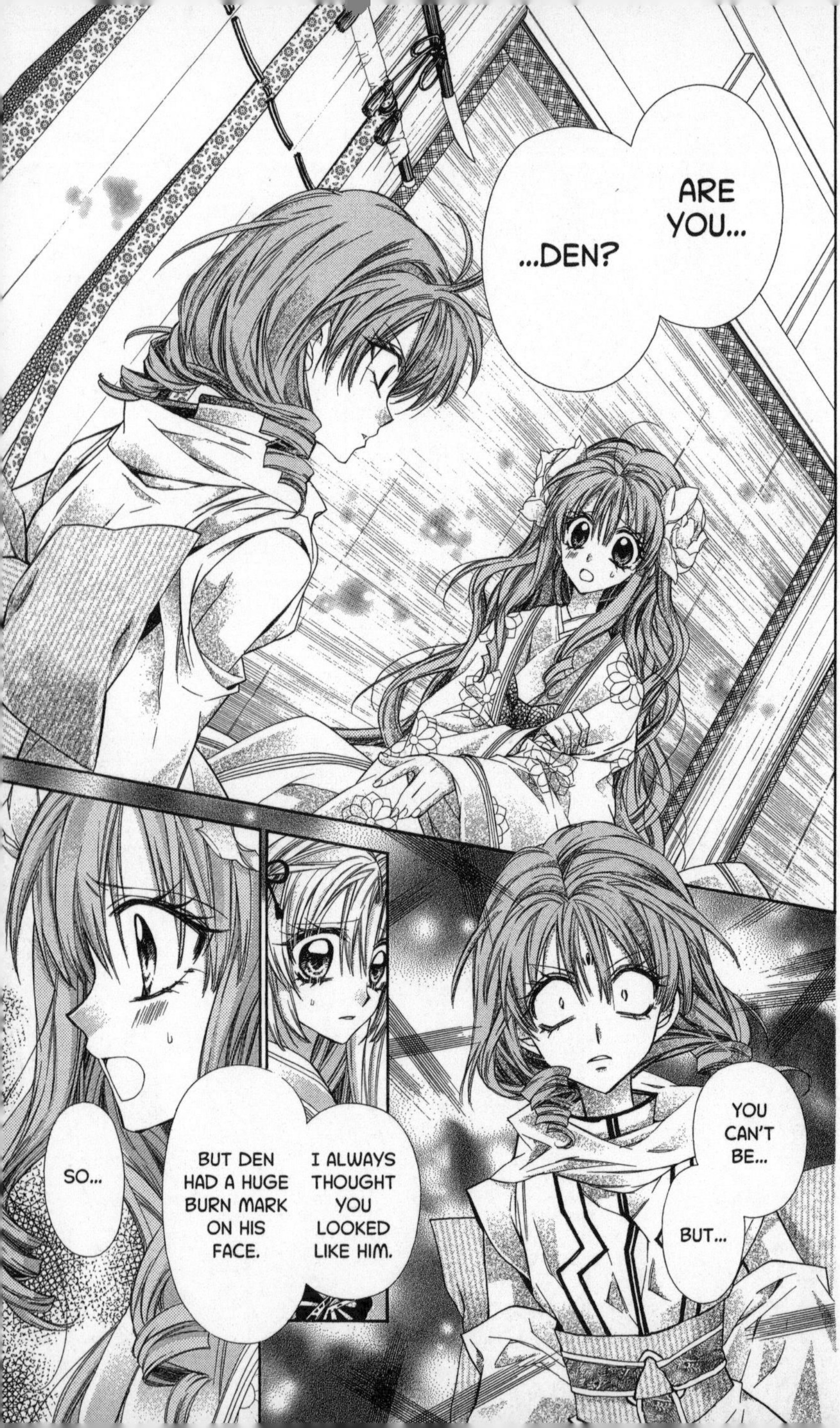
ARE YOU...
...DEN?
YOU CAN'T BE...
BUT...
I ALWAYS THOUGHT YOU LOOKED LIKE HIM.
BUT DEN HAD A HUGE BURN MARK ON HIS FACE.
SO...

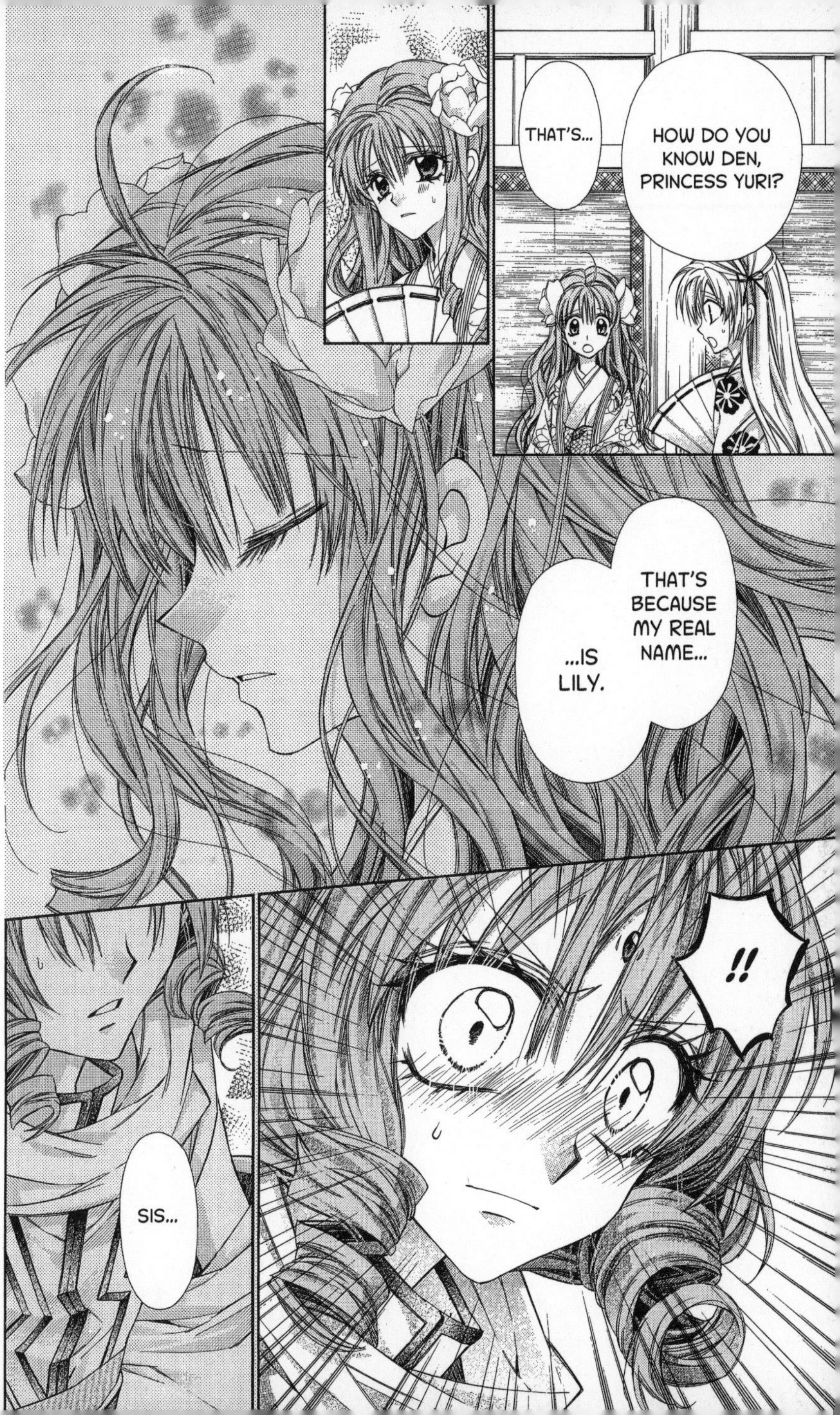
HOW DO YOU KNOW DEN, PRINCESS YURI?
THAT'S...
THAT'S BECAUSE MY REAL NAME...
...IS LILY.
!!
SIS...

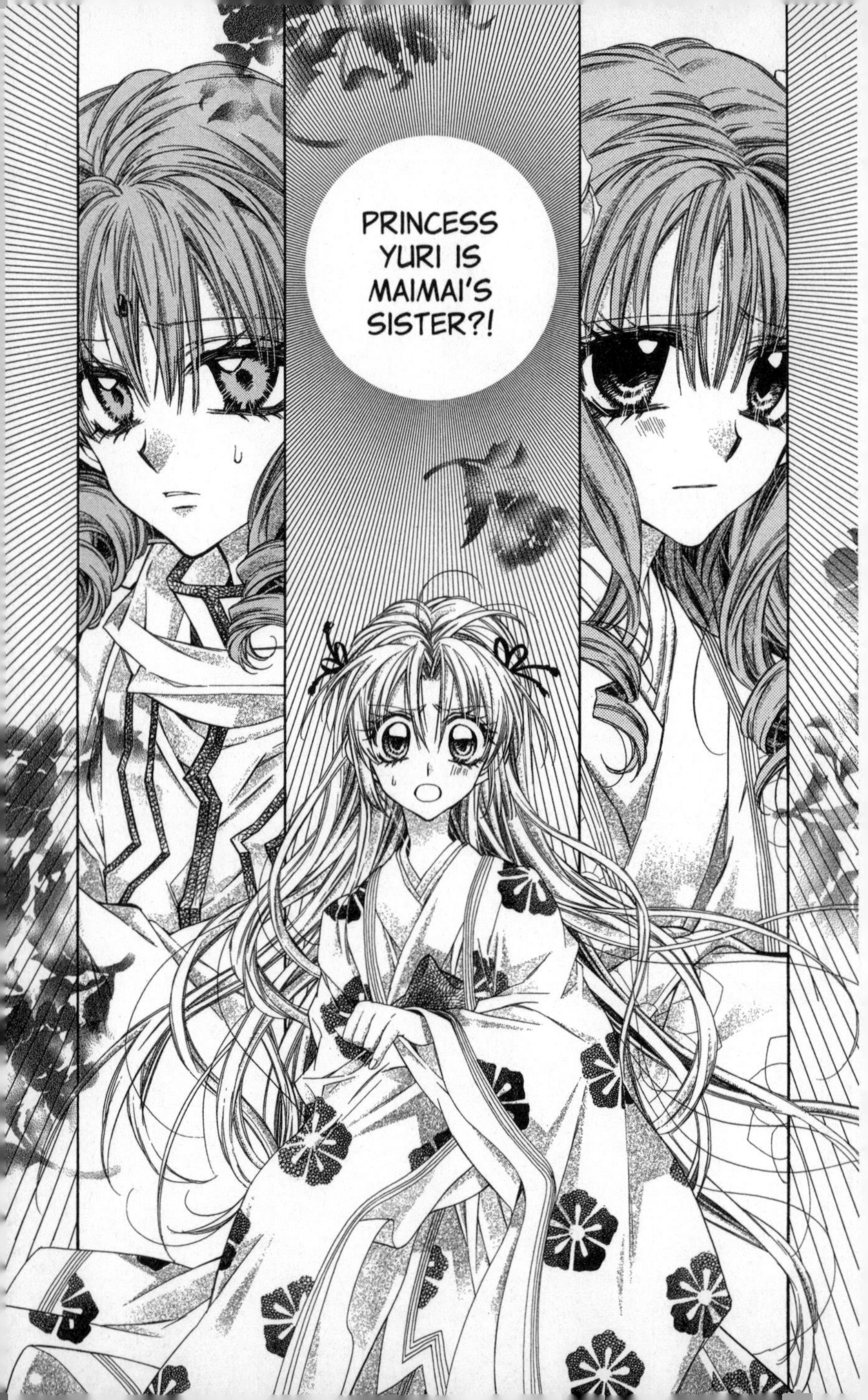
PRINCESS YURI IS MAIMAI'S SISTER?!

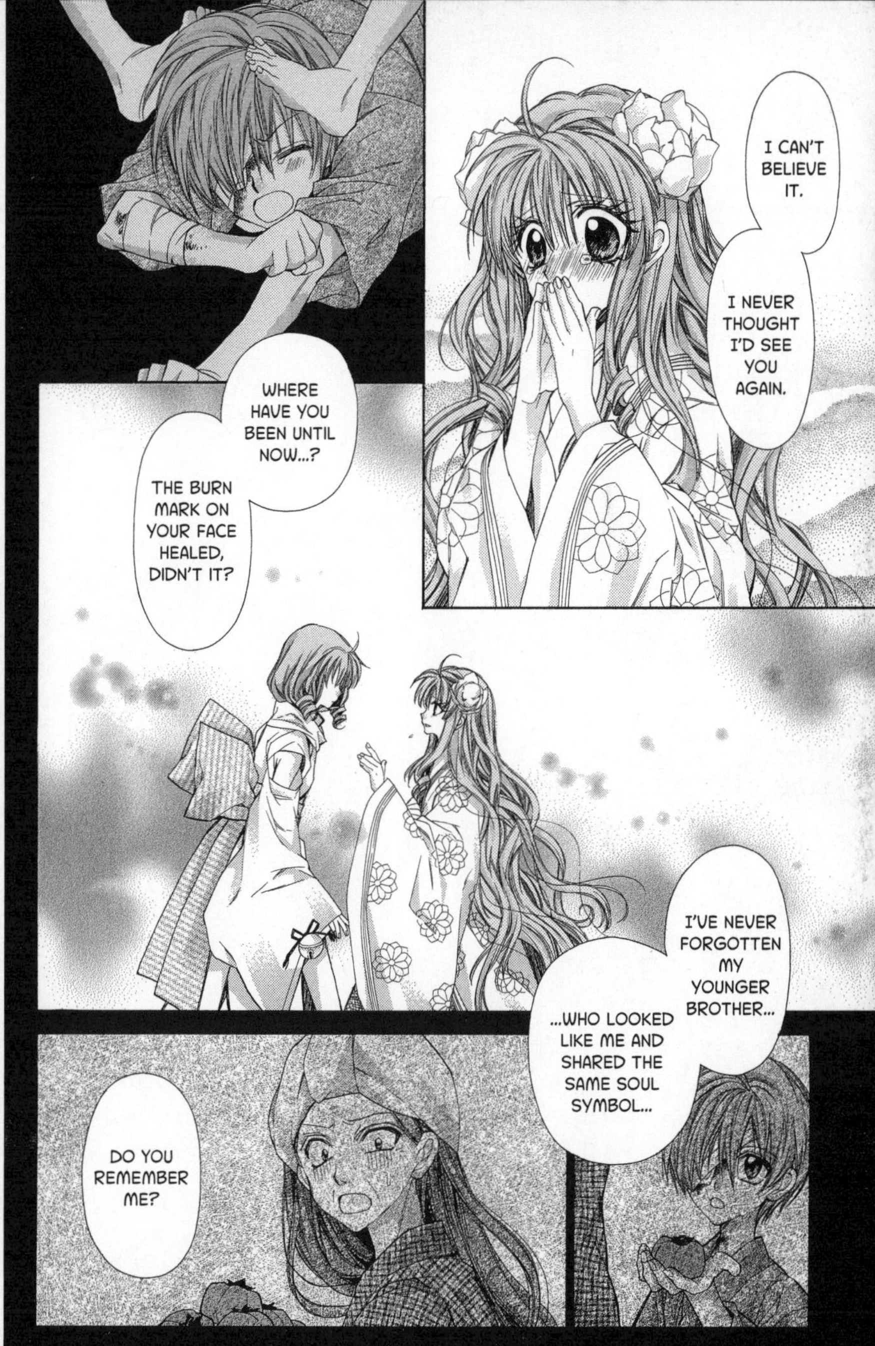
I CAN'T BELIEVE IT.
I NEVER THOUGHT I'D SEE YOU AGAIN.
WHERE HAVE YOU BEEN UNTIL NOW...?
THE BURN MARK ON YOUR FACE HEALED, DIDN'T IT?
I'VE NEVER FORGOTTEN MY YOUNGER BROTHER...
...WHO LOOKED LIKE ME AND SHARED THE SAME SOUL SYMBOL...
DO YOU REMEMBER ME?

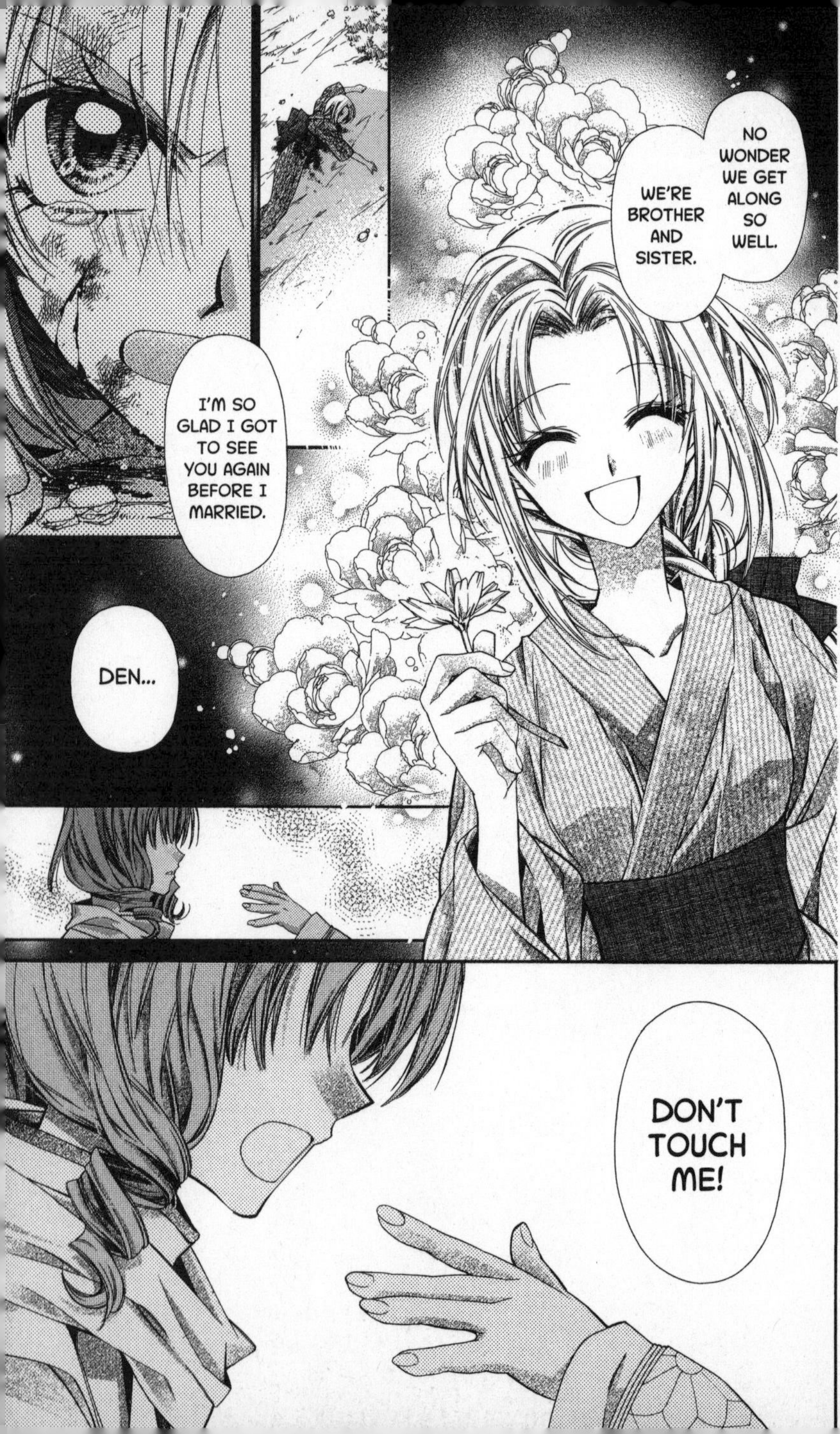
NO WONDER WE GET ALONG SO WELL.
WE'RE BROTHER AND SISTER.
I'M SO GLAD I GOT TO SEE YOU AGAIN BEFORE I MARRIED.
DEN...
DON'T TOUCH ME!

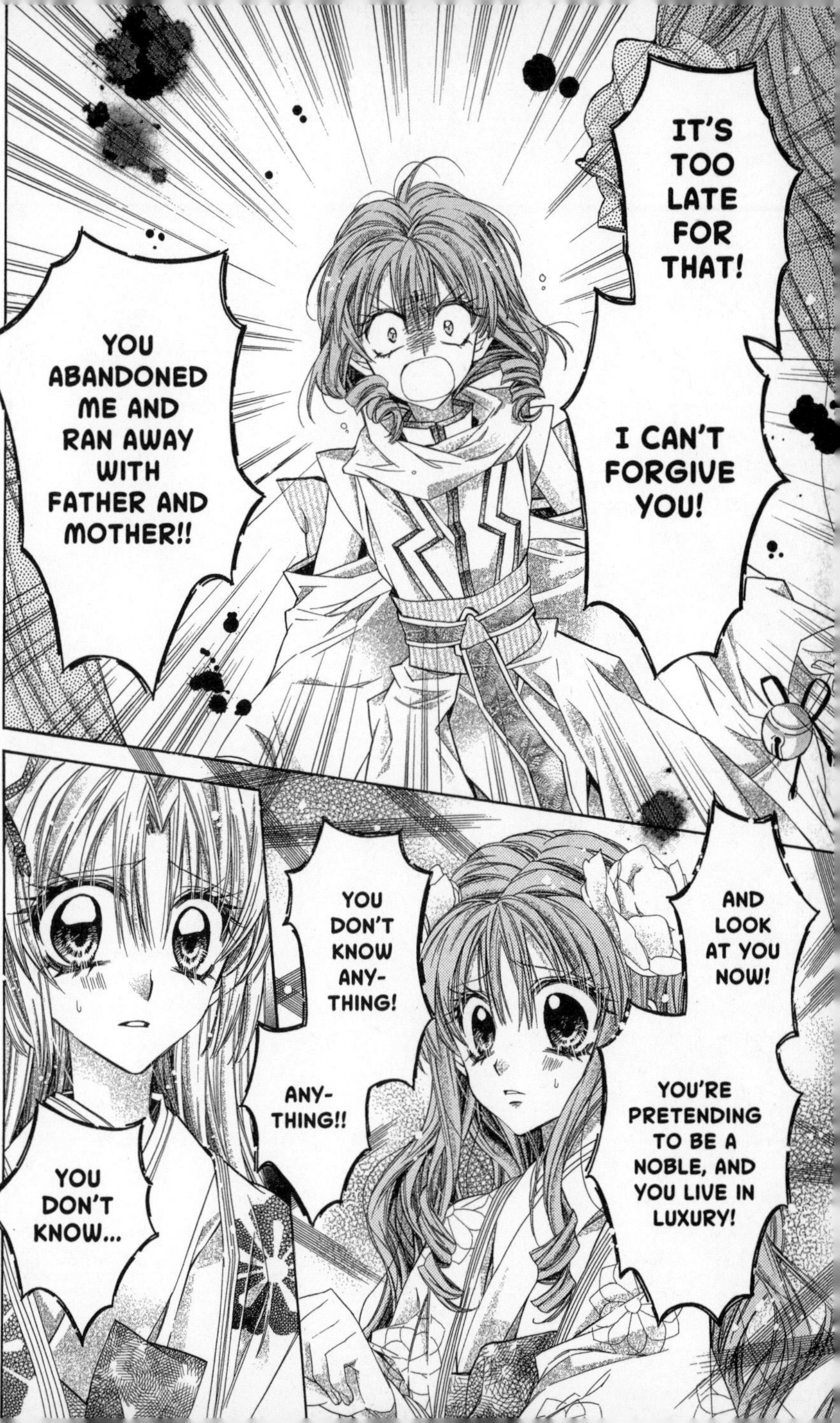
IT'S TOO LATE FOR THAT!
I CAN'T FORGIVE YOU!
YOU ABANDONED ME AND RAN AWAY WITH FATHER AND MOTHER!!
AND LOOK AT YOU NOW!
YOU'RE PRETENDING TO BE A NOBLE, AND YOU LIVE IN LUXURY!
YOU DON'T KNOW ANY-THING!
ANY-THING!!
YOU DON'T KNOW...

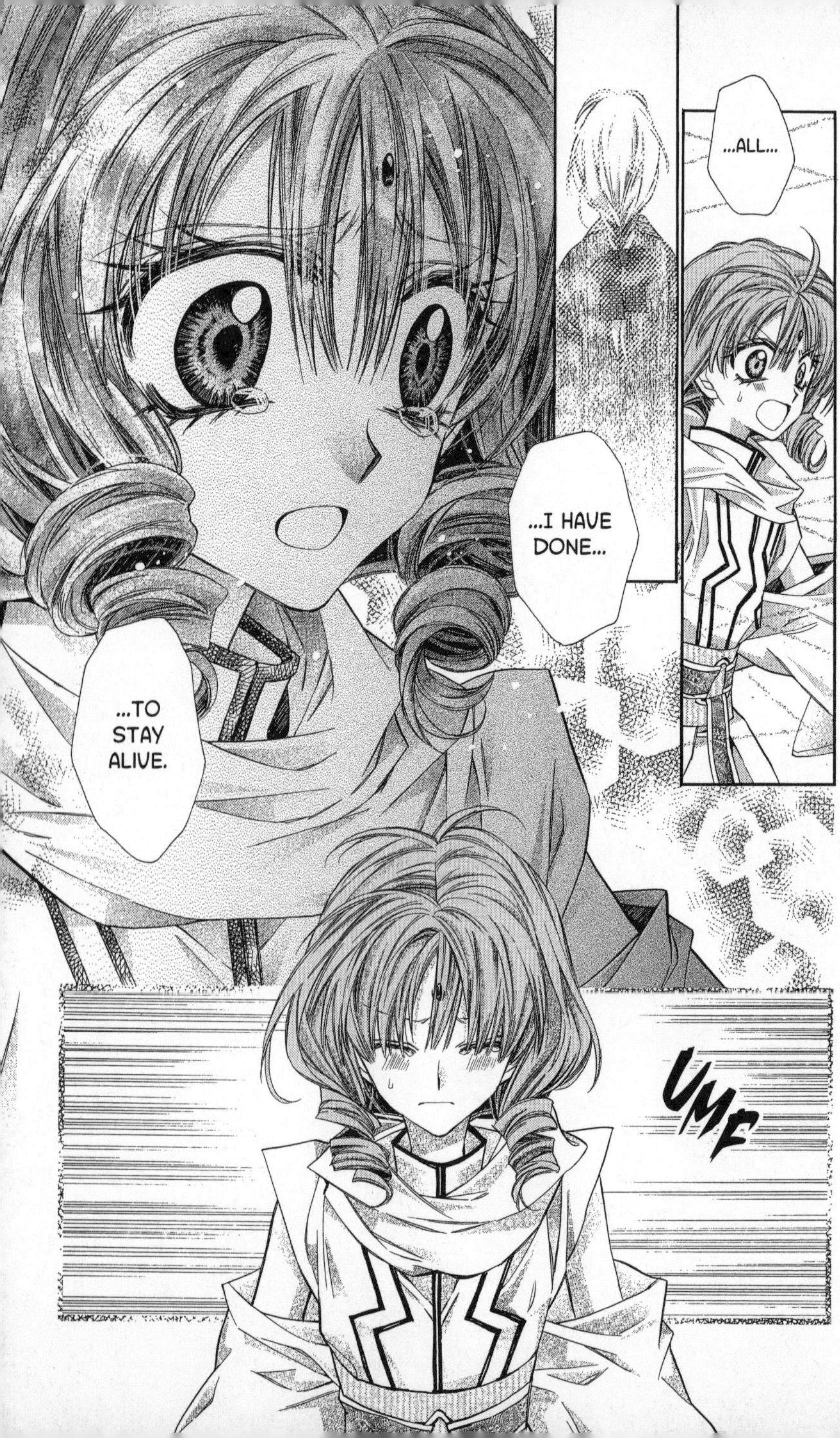
...ALL...
...I HAVE DONE...
...TO STAY ALIVE.
UMF

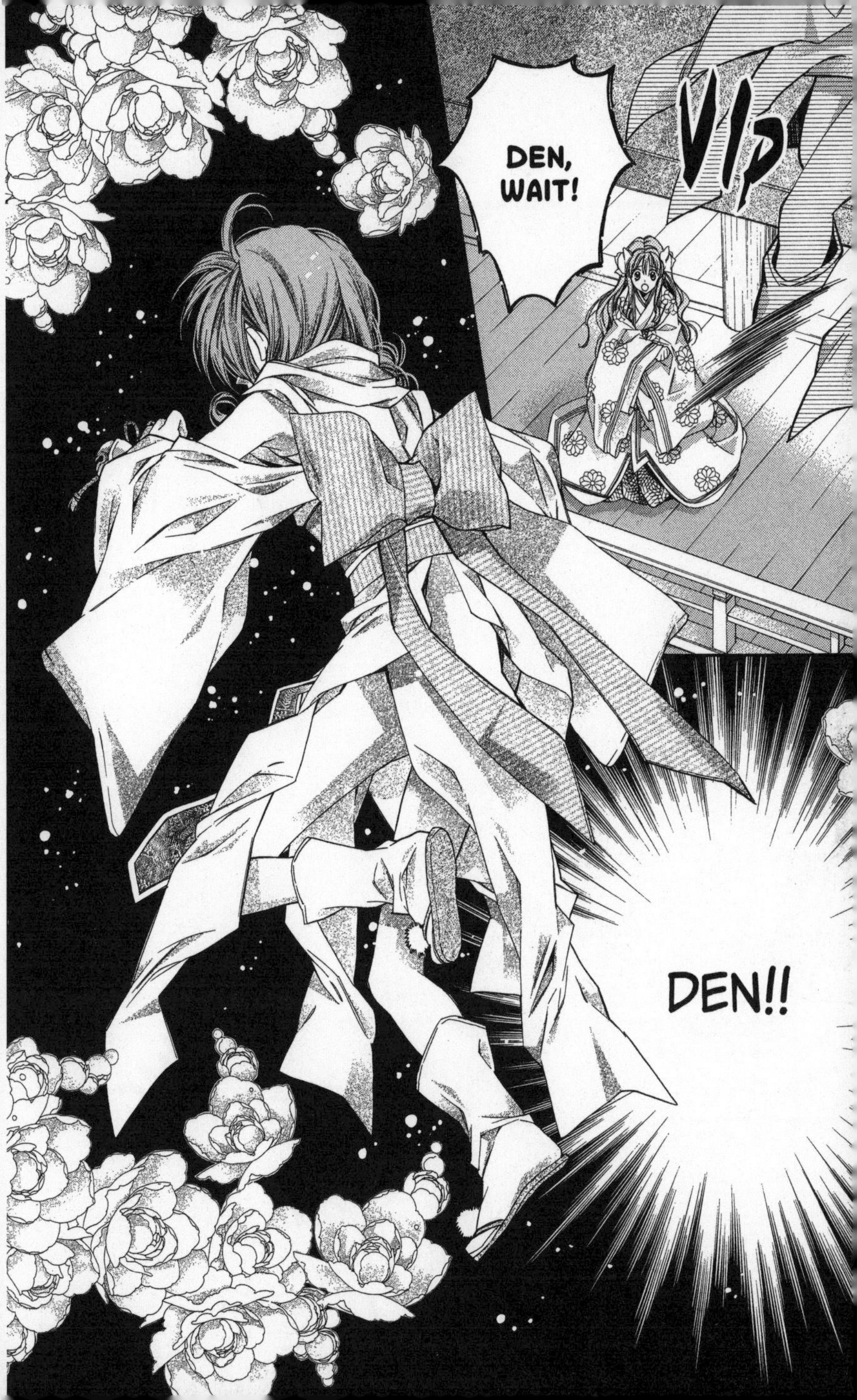
VIP
DEN, WAIT!
DEN!!

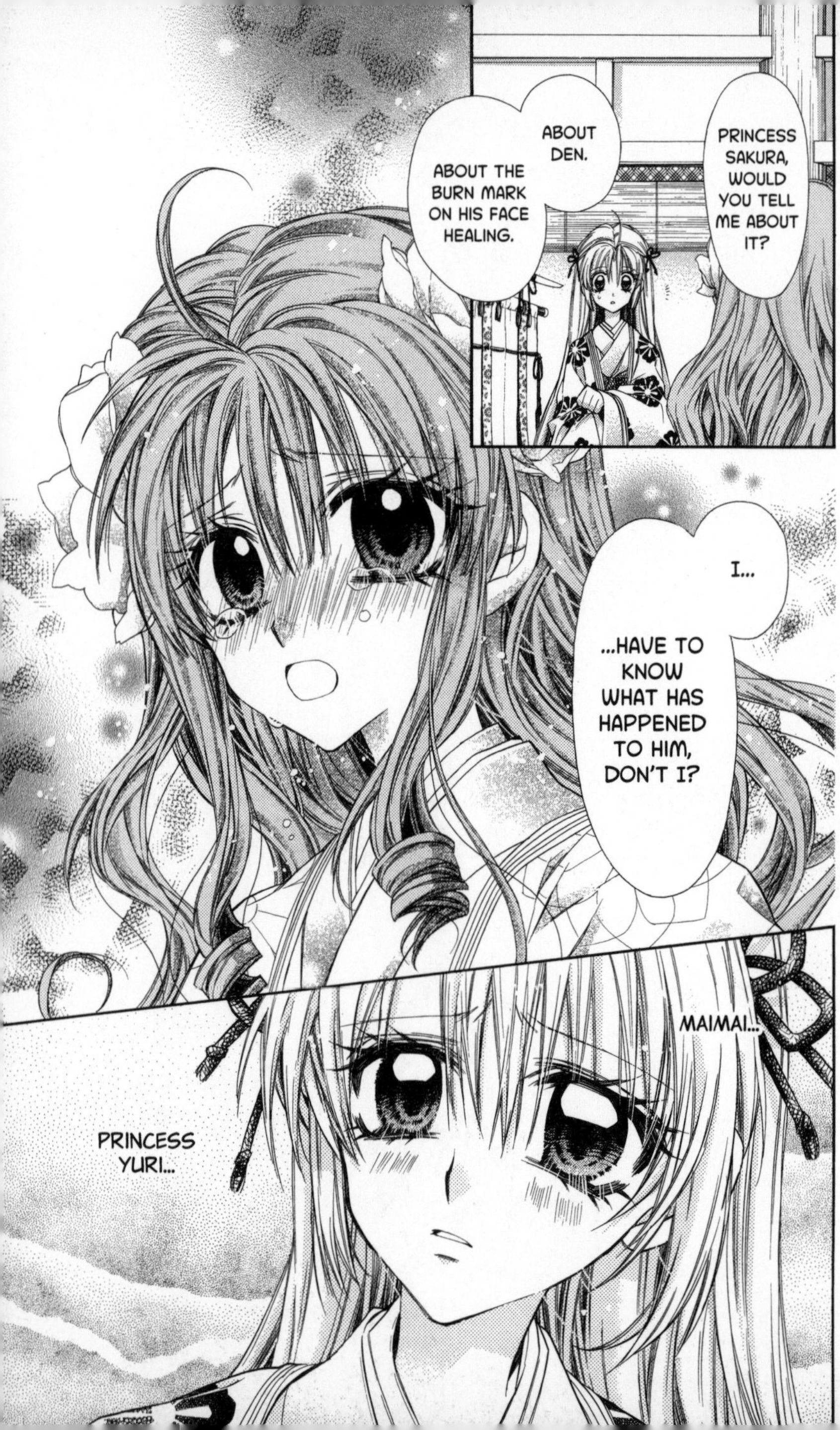
PRINCESS SAKURA, WOULD YOU TELL ME ABOUT IT?
ABOUT DEN.
ABOUT THE BURN MARK ON HIS FACE HEALING.
I...
...HAVE TO KNOW WHAT HAS HAPPENED TO HIM, DON'T I?
MAIMAI...
PRINCESS YURI...

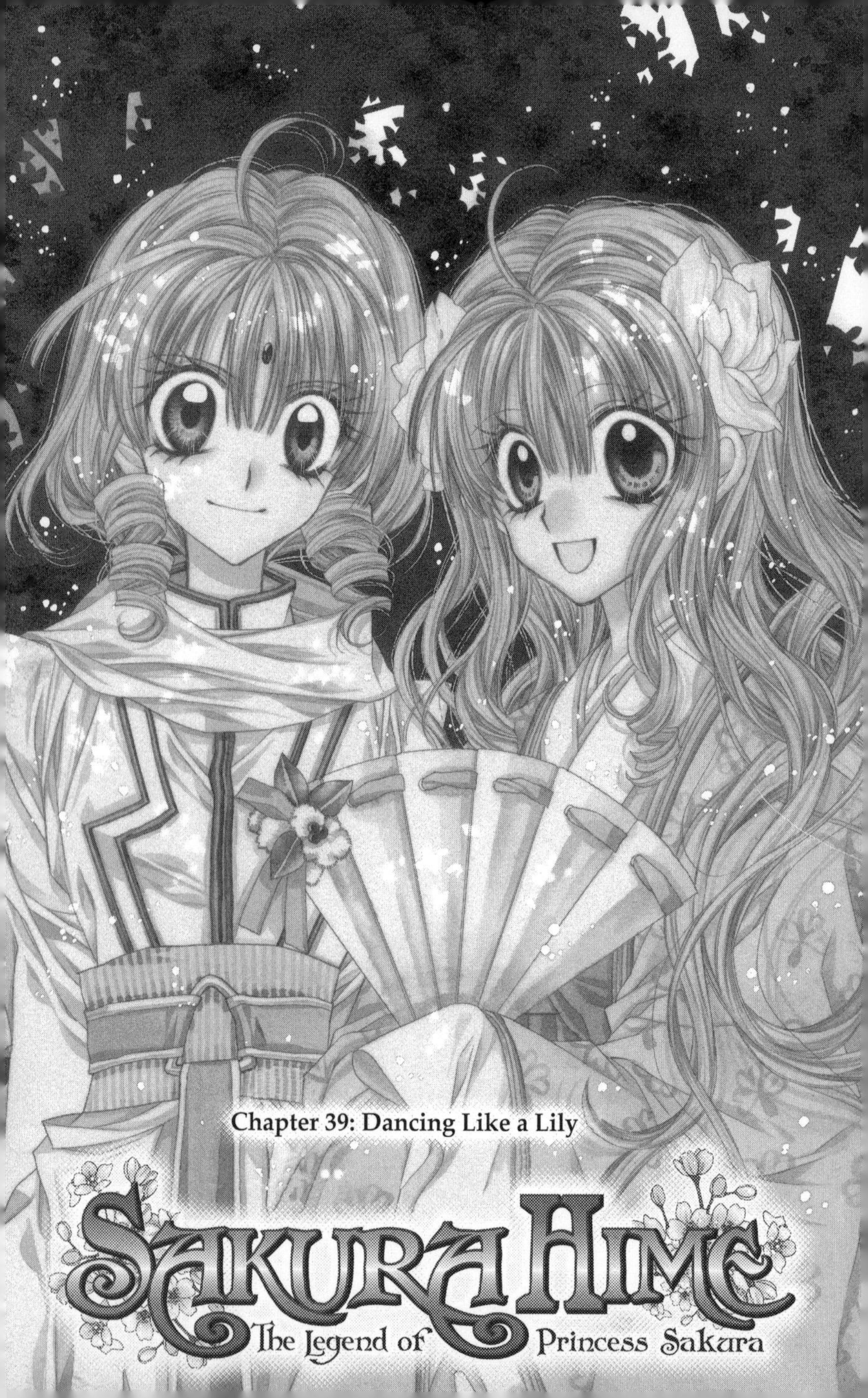
Chapter 39: Dancing Like a Lily
SAKURA HIME
The Legend of Princess Sakura

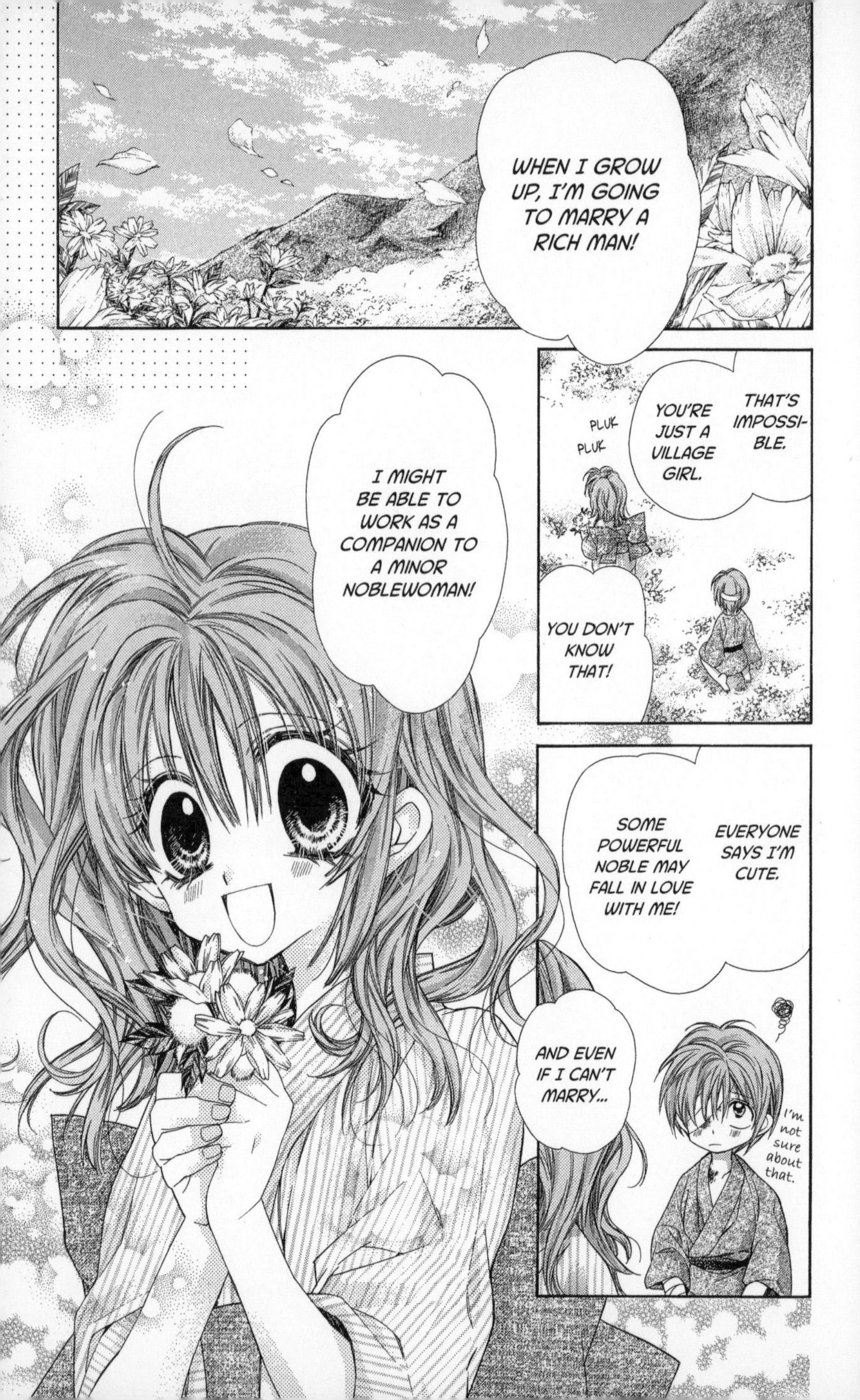
WHEN I GROW UP, I'M GOING TO MARRY A RICH MAN!
THAT'S IMPOSSI-BLE.
YOU'RE JUST A VILLAGE GIRL.
PLUK
PLUK
YOU DON'T KNOW THAT!
EVERYONE SAYS I'M CUTE.
SOME POWERFUL NOBLE MAY FALL IN LOVE WITH ME!
I'm not sure about that.
AND EVEN IF I CAN'T MARRY...
I MIGHT BE ABLE TO WORK AS A COMPANION TO A MINOR NOBLEWOMAN!

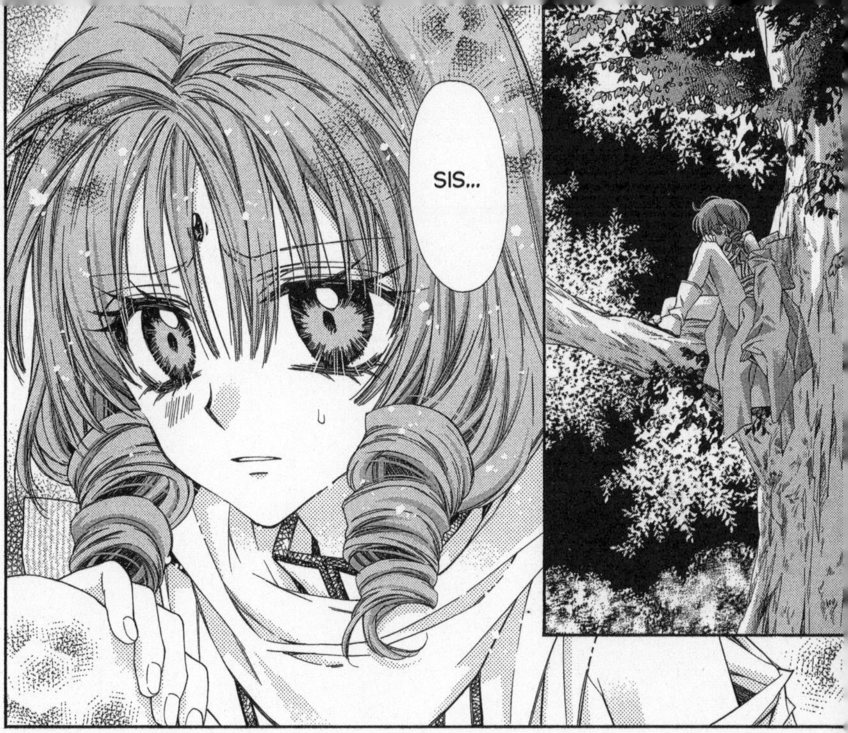
SIS...

Chapter 39: Dancing Like a Lily

I'm giving away the story.

The chapter title page illustration is meant to be like... "The Two Back Then" PLIP

By the way, I wrote in one of the previous volumes that Maimai was 18 years old, but that was a mistake. (I'm sorry.) To be exact, Maimai → 15 years old, Princess Yuri → 14 years old (Lily → 16 years old). Lily was bought when she was 5 years old and took the place of a girl who was 3 years old. Phew. I'm sorry it's so complex.

I had decided on the conclusion for these two from the start, but I was touched by Princess Yuri's decision when I started to work on it. A caring sister and brother, how nice...

Like Princess Yuri (Lily) was saying at the beginning of this chapter, maybe she is to become the companion to a minor noble (Akane)? (Although I'm not really sure if Princess Yuri can handle working under someone.) I just hope they live a peaceful life together without being discovered by the Minister of the Right.

Well then, Enju is gradually starting to lose his followers, Sakura has lost the Soul Symbols, and the emperor has been killed. The story is going the speed up from here on. Please hold on tightly!

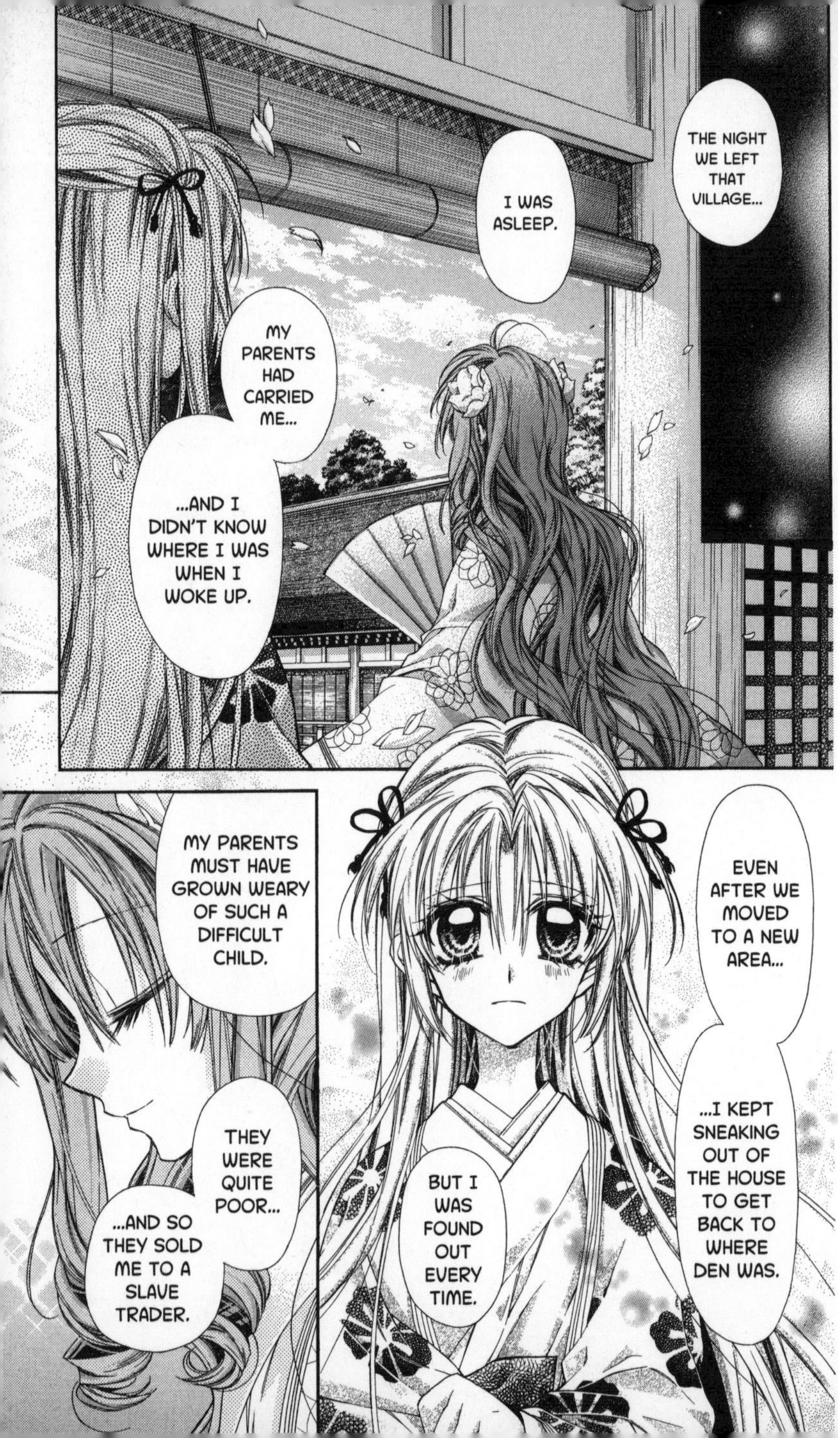
THE NIGHT WE LEFT THAT VILLAGE...
I WAS ASLEEP.
MY PARENTS HAD CARRIED ME...
...AND I DIDN'T KNOW WHERE I WAS WHEN I WOKE UP.
EVEN AFTER WE MOVED TO A NEW AREA...
...I KEPT SNEAKING OUT OF THE HOUSE TO GET BACK TO WHERE DEN WAS.
BUT I WAS FOUND OUT EVERY TIME.
MY PARENTS MUST HAVE GROWN WEARY OF SUCH A DIFFICULT CHILD.
THEY WERE QUITE POOR...
...AND SO THEY SOLD ME TO A SLAVE TRADER.

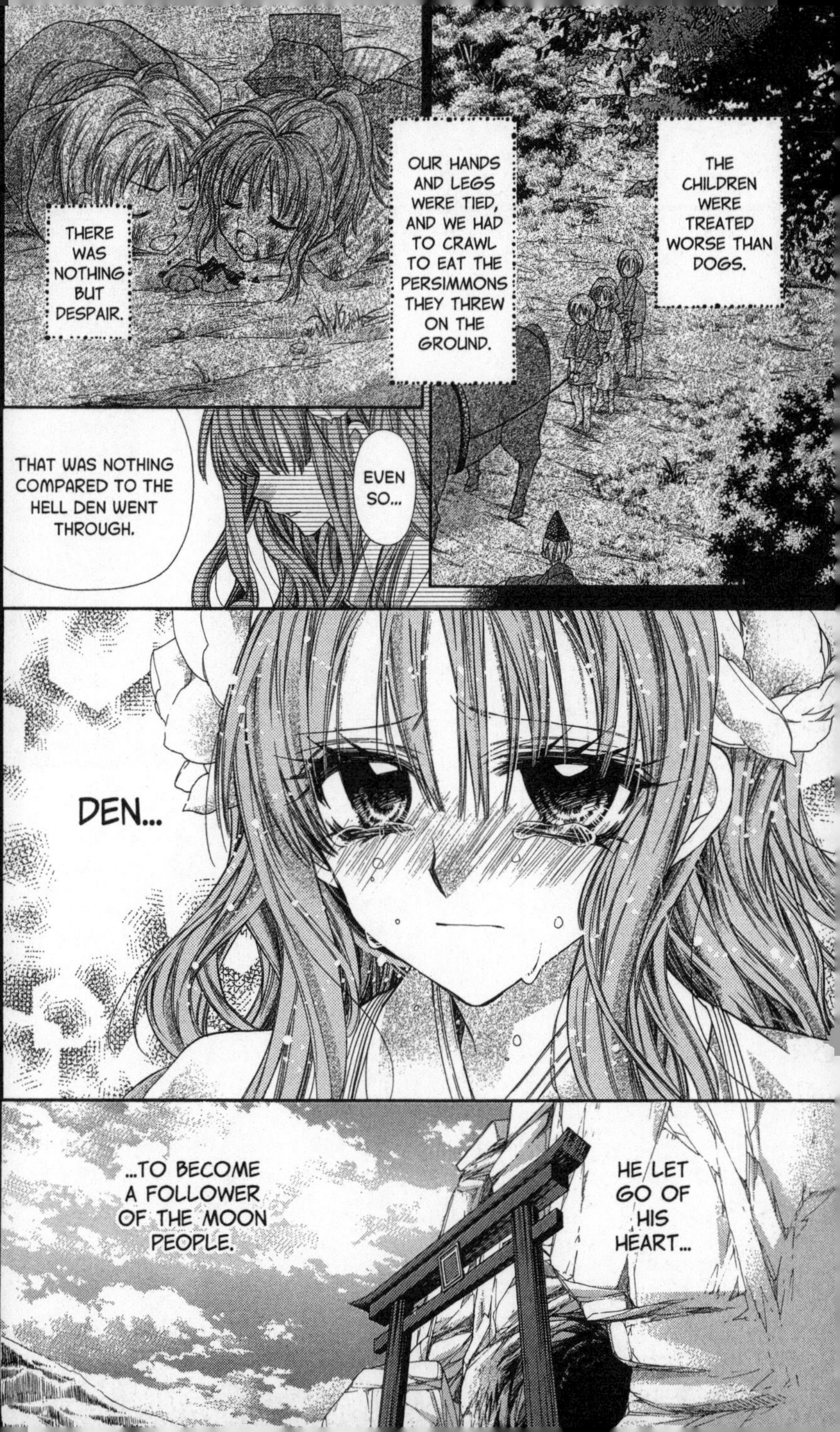
THE CHILDREN WERE TREATED WORSE THAN DOGS.
OUR HANDS AND LEGS WERE TIED, AND WE HAD TO CRAWL TO EAT THE PERSIMMONS THEY THREW ON THE GROUND.
THERE WAS NOTHING BUT DESPAIR.
EVEN SO...
THAT WAS NOTHING COMPARED TO THE HELL DEN WENT THROUGH.
DEN...
HE LET GO OF HIS HEART...
...TO BECOME A FOLLOWER OF THE MOON PEOPLE.

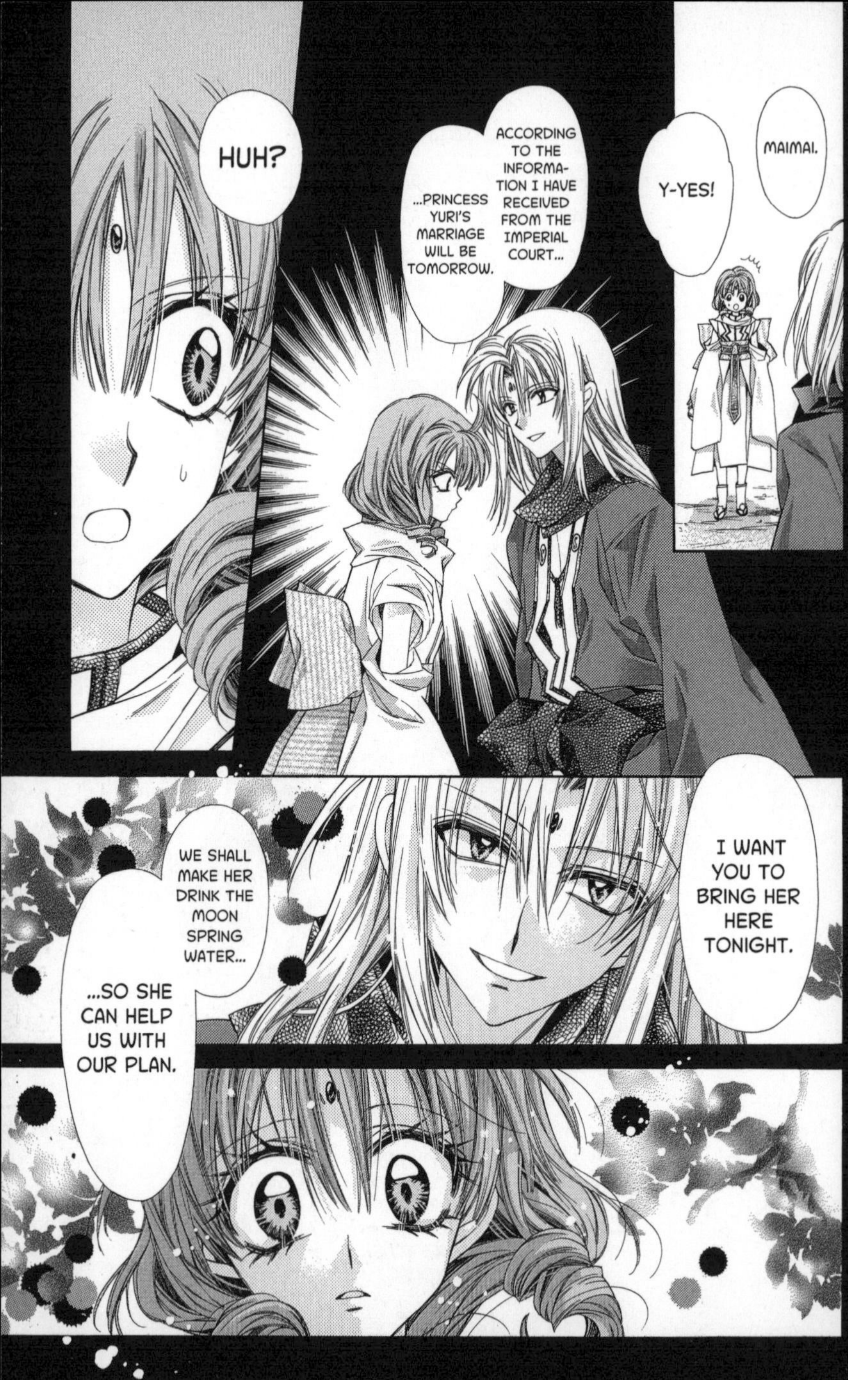
MAIMAI.
Y-YES!
ACCORDING TO THE INFORMATION I HAVE RECEIVED FROM THE IMPERIAL COURT...
...PRINCESS YURI'S MARRIAGE WILL BE TOMORROW.
HUH?
I WANT YOU TO BRING HER HERE TONIGHT.
WE SHALL MAKE HER DRINK THE MOON SPRING WATER...
...SO SHE CAN HELP US WITH OUR PLAN.

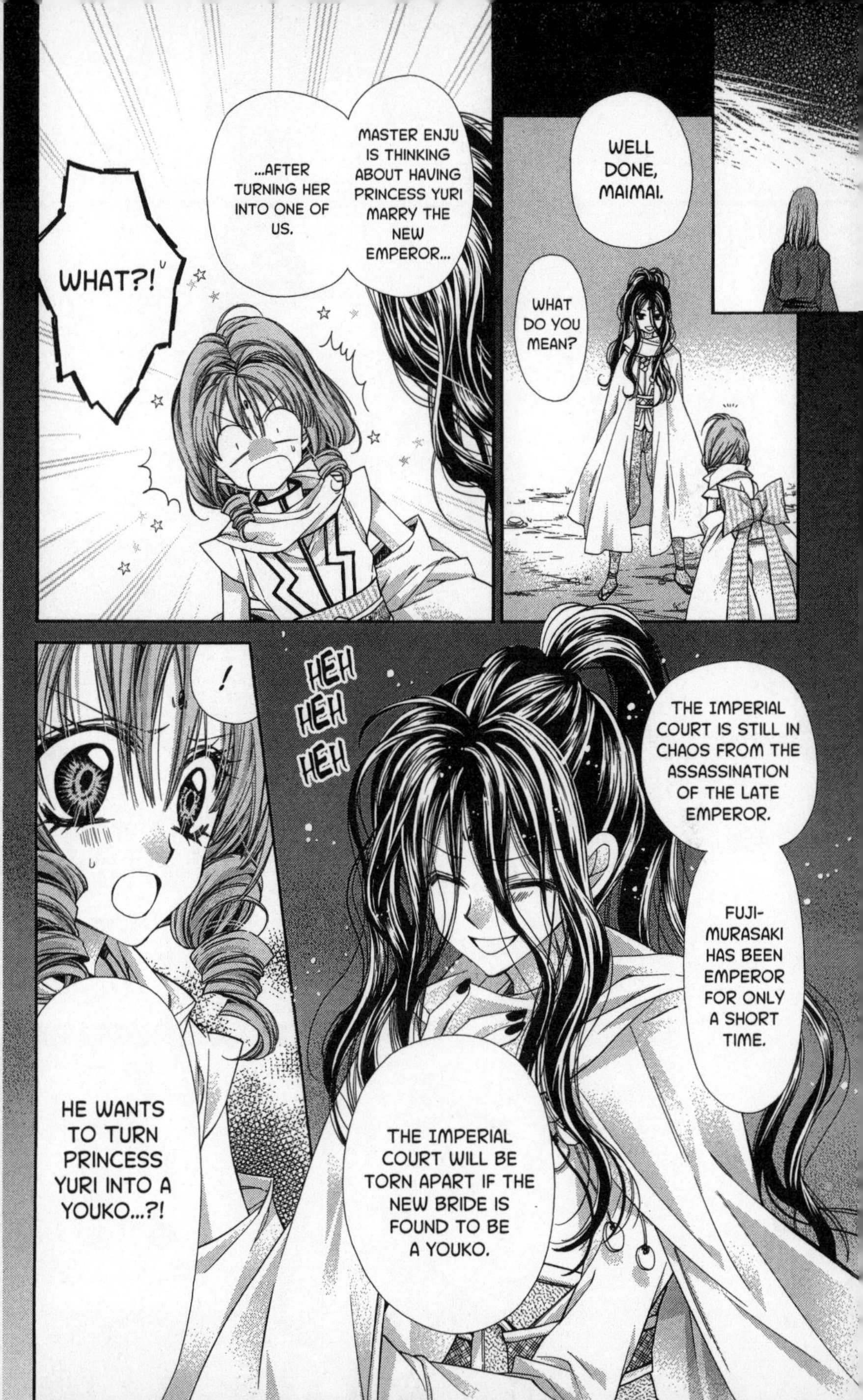
WELL DONE, MAIMAI.
WHAT DO YOU MEAN?
MASTER ENJU IS THINKING ABOUT HAVING PRINCESS YURI MARRY THE NEW EMPEROR...
...AFTER TURNING HER INTO ONE OF US.
WHAT?!
HEH HEH HEH
THE IMPERIAL COURT IS STILL IN CHAOS FROM THE ASSASSINATION OF THE LATE EMPEROR.
FUJI-MURASAKI HAS BEEN EMPEROR FOR ONLY A SHORT TIME.
THE IMPERIAL COURT WILL BE TORN APART IF THE NEW BRIDE IS FOUND TO BE A YOUKO.
!
HE WANTS TO TURN PRINCESS YURI INTO A YOUKO...?!

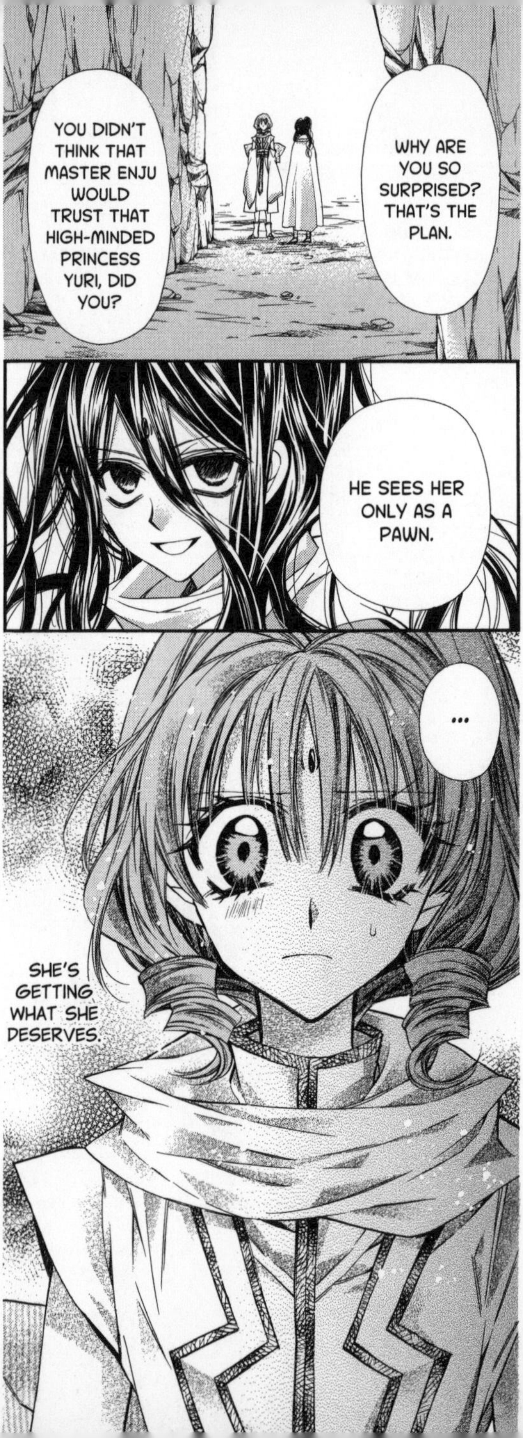
WHY ARE YOU SO SURPRISED? THAT'S THE PLAN.
YOU DIDN'T THINK THAT MASTER ENJU WOULD TRUST THAT HIGH-MINDED PRINCESS YURI, DID YOU?
HE SEES HER ONLY AS A PAWN.
...
SHE'S GETTING WHAT SHE DESERVES.

Greetings.

How did you like volume 10 of *Sakura Hime*? I am going to put all my effort this year into steering the story toward its conclusion, so please look forward to it. ♥

Special Thanks

Nakame
Momo-chan
Matsun

Sakakura-san
Yogurt-chan
Icchi
Hii-chan
Ikurun
Momiji-san
Mari
Rena-san
Acchan
Miichi
Mikami-chan
Konako

Shueisha
Ribon Editorial Department
Ammonite, Inc.

Kawatani Design
Kawatani-san

Riku & Kai

And you...

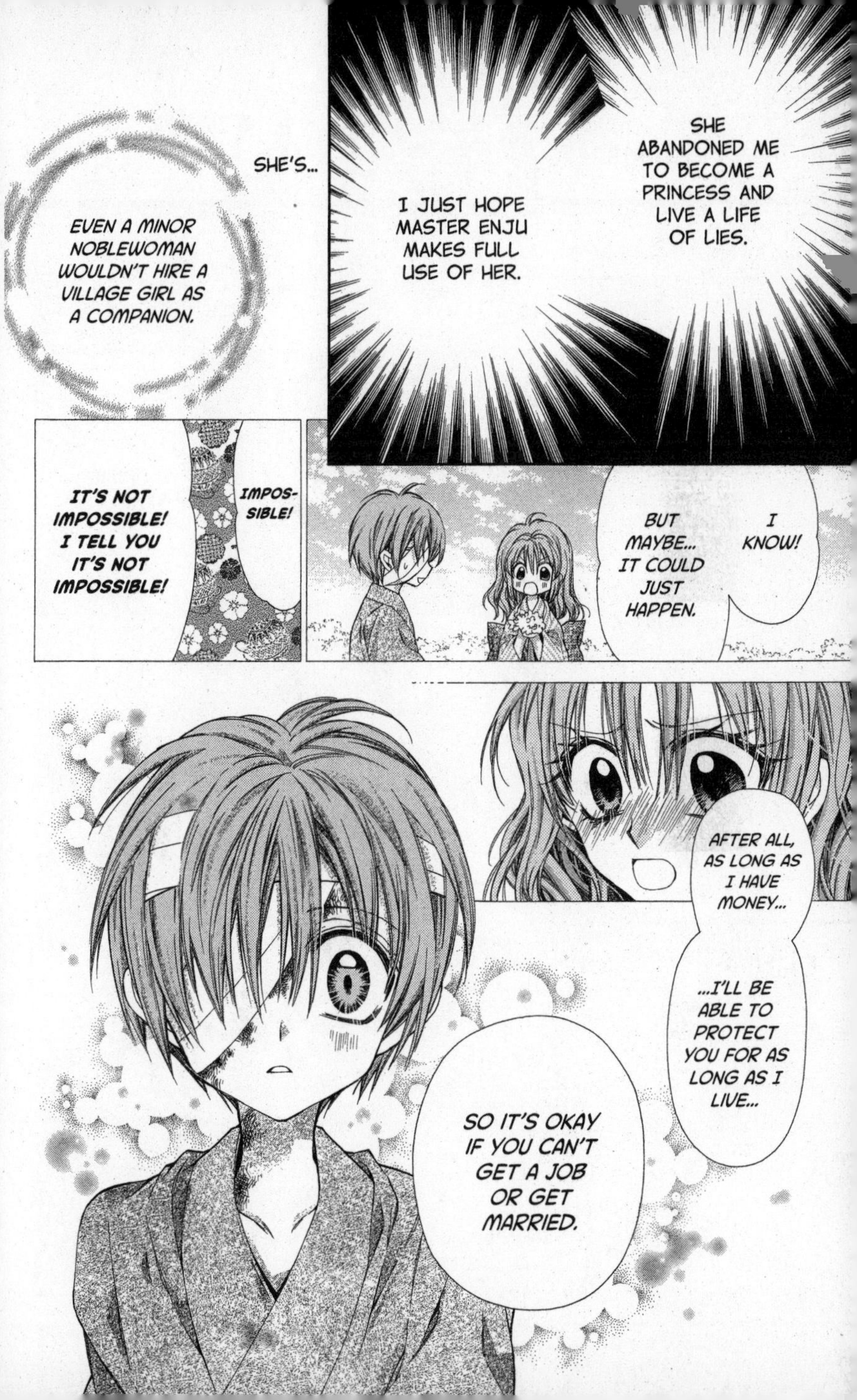
SHE ABANDONED ME TO BECOME A PRINCESS AND LIVE A LIFE OF LIES.
I JUST HOPE MASTER ENJU MAKES FULL USE OF HER.
SHE'S...
EVEN A MINOR NOBLEWOMAN WOULDN'T HIRE A VILLAGE GIRL AS A COMPANION.
I KNOW!
BUT MAYBE... IT COULD JUST HAPPEN.
IMPOSSIBLE!
IT'S NOT IMPOSSIBLE! I TELL YOU IT'S NOT IMPOSSIBLE!
AFTER ALL, AS LONG AS I HAVE MONEY...
...I'LL BE ABLE TO PROTECT YOU FOR AS LONG AS I LIVE...
SO IT'S OKAY IF YOU CAN'T GET A JOB OR GET MARRIED.

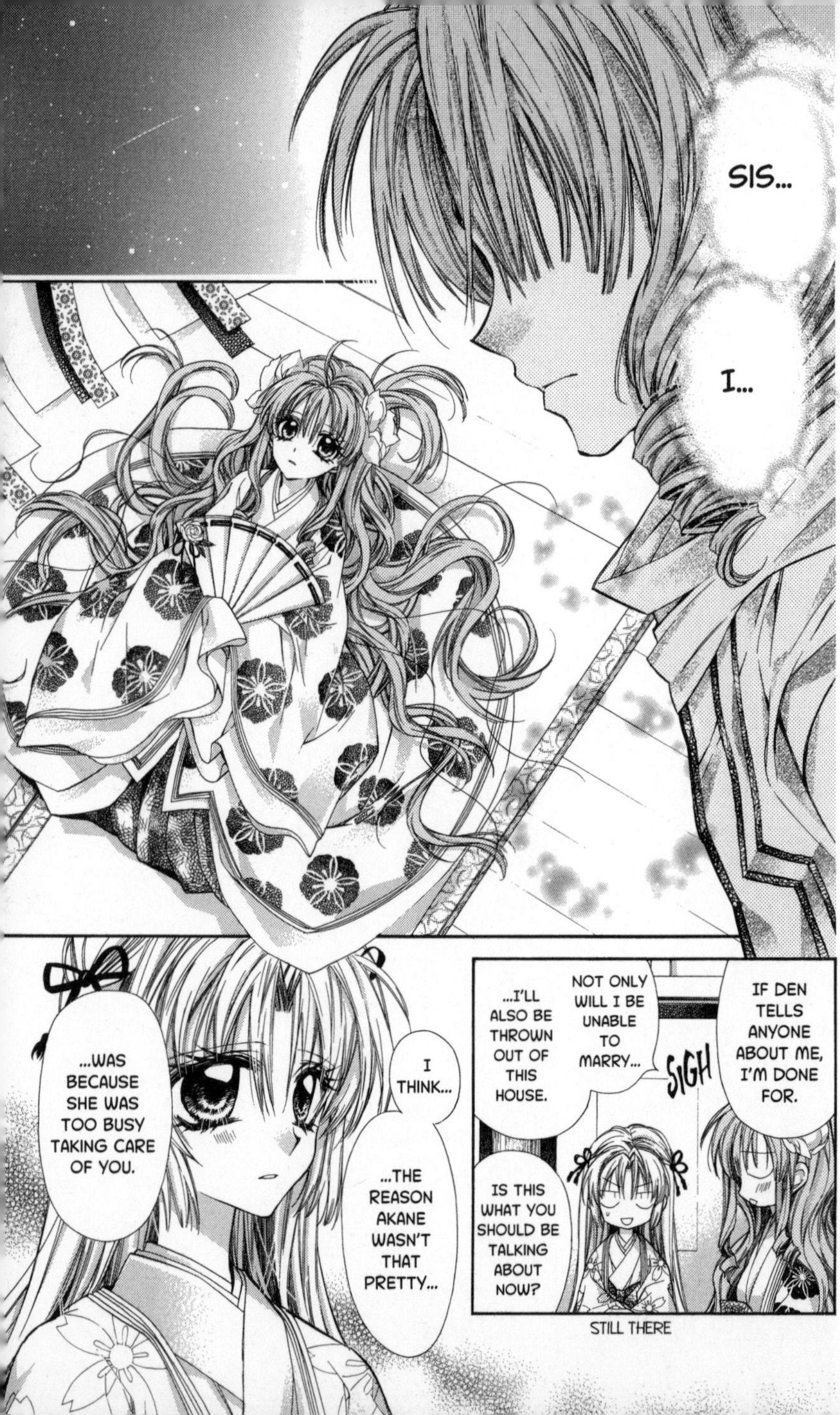
SIS...
I...
IF DEN TELLS ANYONE ABOUT ME, I'M DONE FOR.
NOT ONLY WILL I BE UNABLE TO MARRY...
...I'LL ALSO BE THROWN OUT OF THIS HOUSE.
SIGH
IS THIS WHAT YOU SHOULD BE TALKING ABOUT NOW?
STILL THERE
I THINK...
...THE REASON AKANE WASN'T THAT PRETTY...
...WAS BECAUSE SHE WAS TOO BUSY TAKING CARE OF YOU.

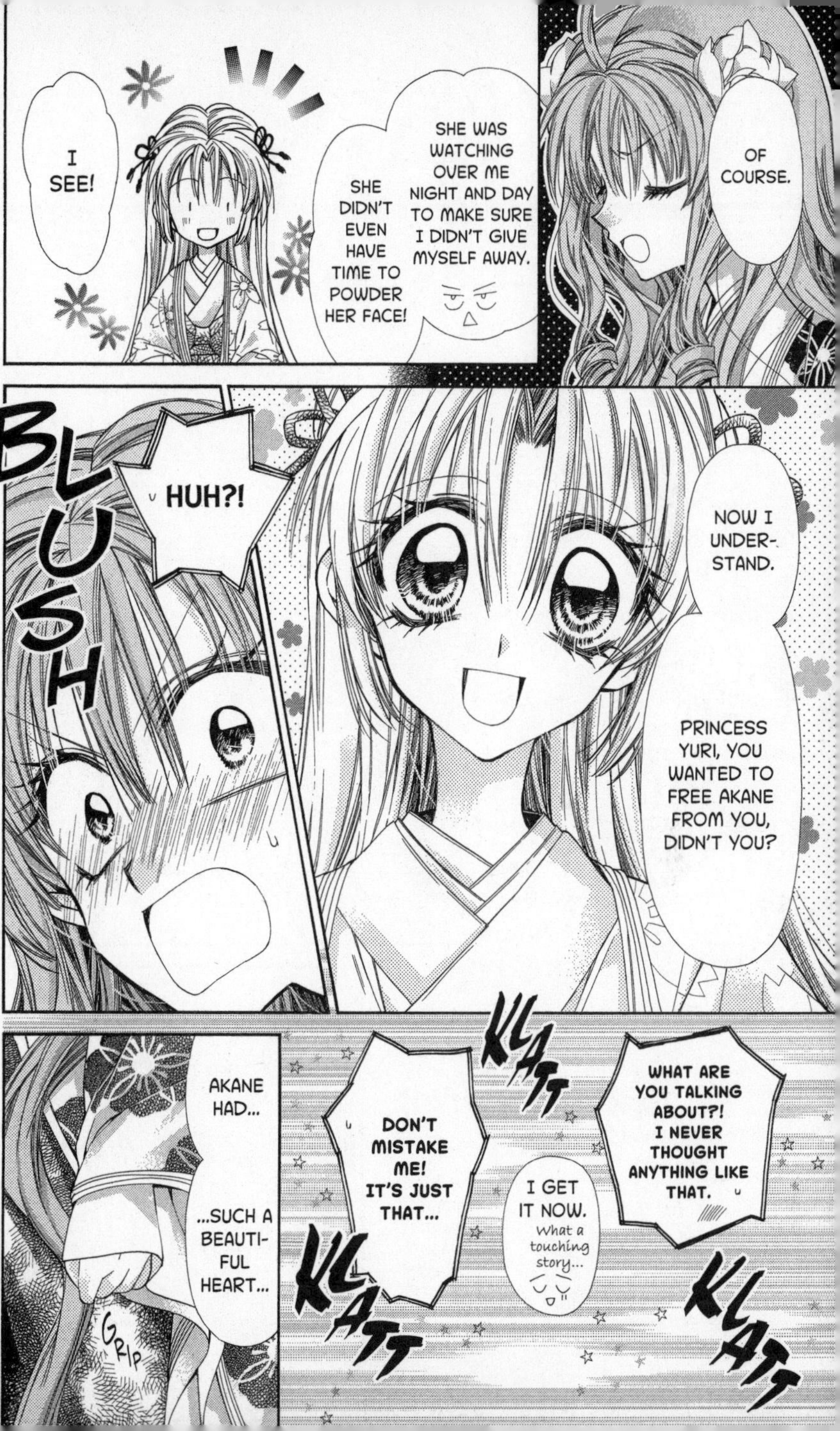
OF COURSE.
SHE WAS WATCHING OVER ME NIGHT AND DAY TO MAKE SURE I DIDN'T GIVE MYSELF AWAY.
SHE DIDN'T EVEN HAVE TIME TO POWDER HER FACE!
I SEE!
NOW I UNDER-STAND.
PRINCESS YURI, YOU WANTED TO FREE AKANE FROM YOU, DIDN'T YOU?
HUH?!
BLUSH
WHAT ARE YOU TALKING ABOUT?! I NEVER THOUGHT ANYTHING LIKE THAT.
KLATT
I GET IT NOW.
What a touching story...
DON'T MISTAKE ME! IT'S JUST THAT...
KLATT
KLATT
KLATT
AKANE HAD...
...SUCH A BEAUTI-FUL HEART...
GRIP

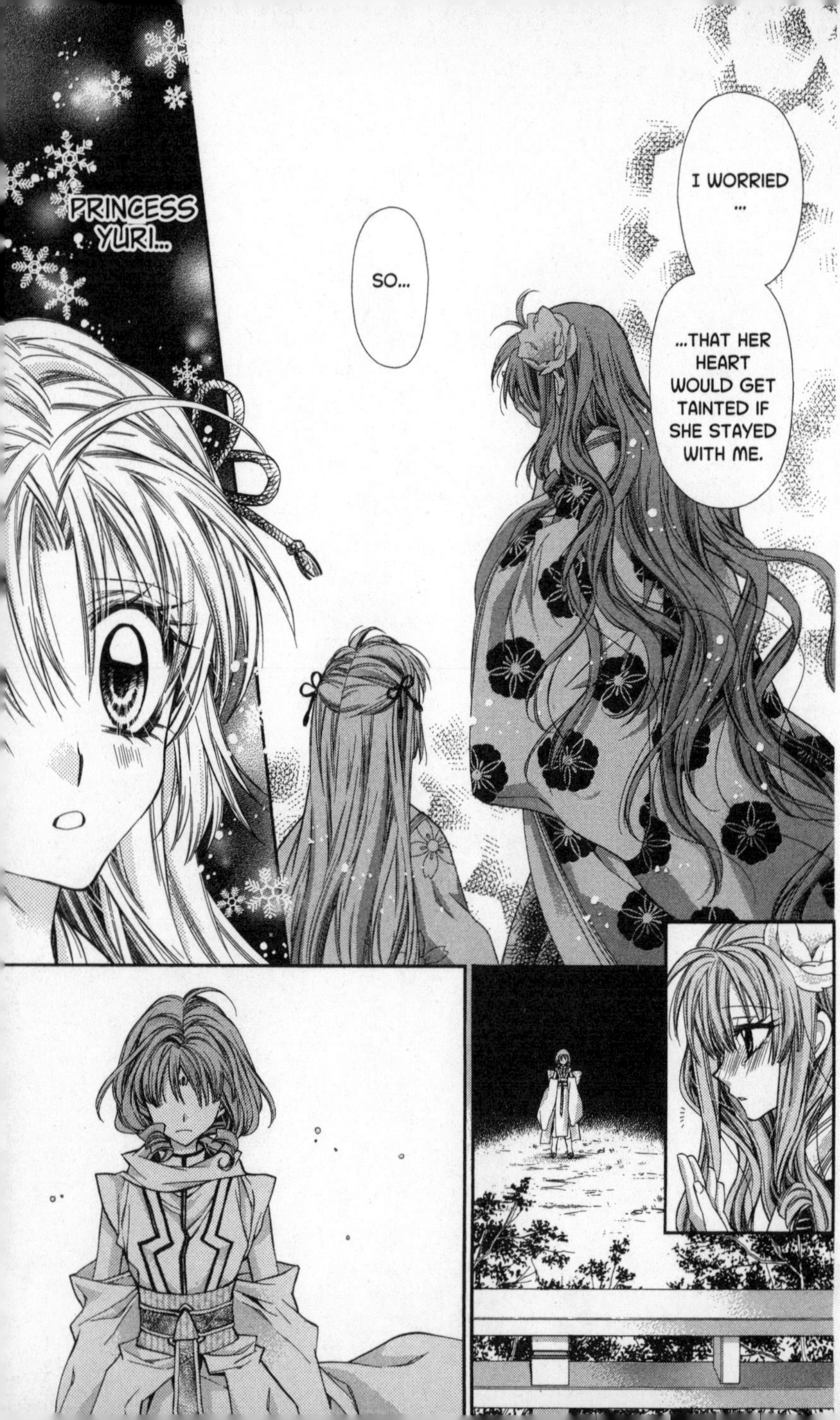
I WORRIED ...
...THAT HER HEART WOULD GET TAINTED IF SHE STAYED WITH ME.
SO...
PRINCESS YURI...

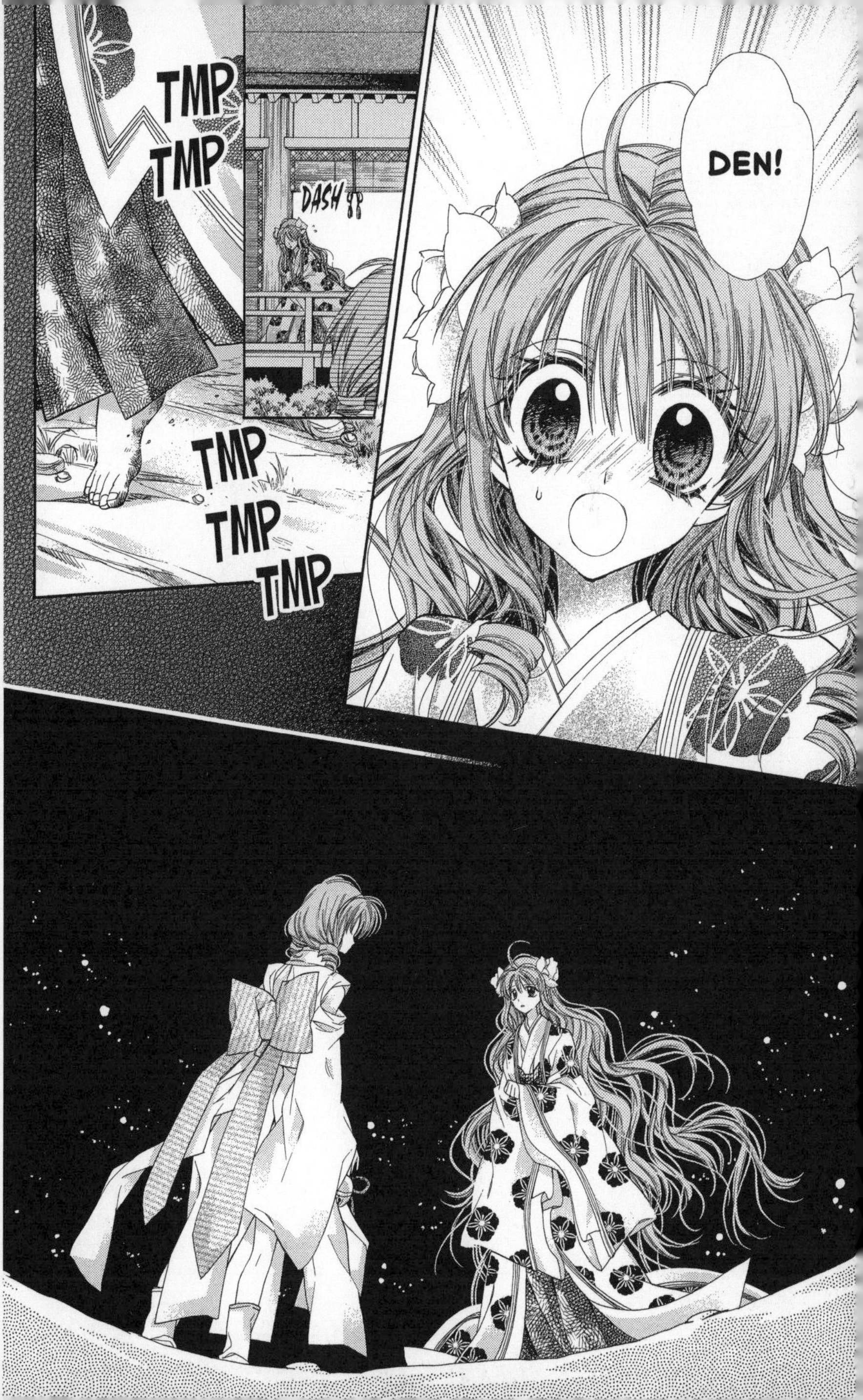
DEN!
DASH
TMP TMP
TMP TMP TMP

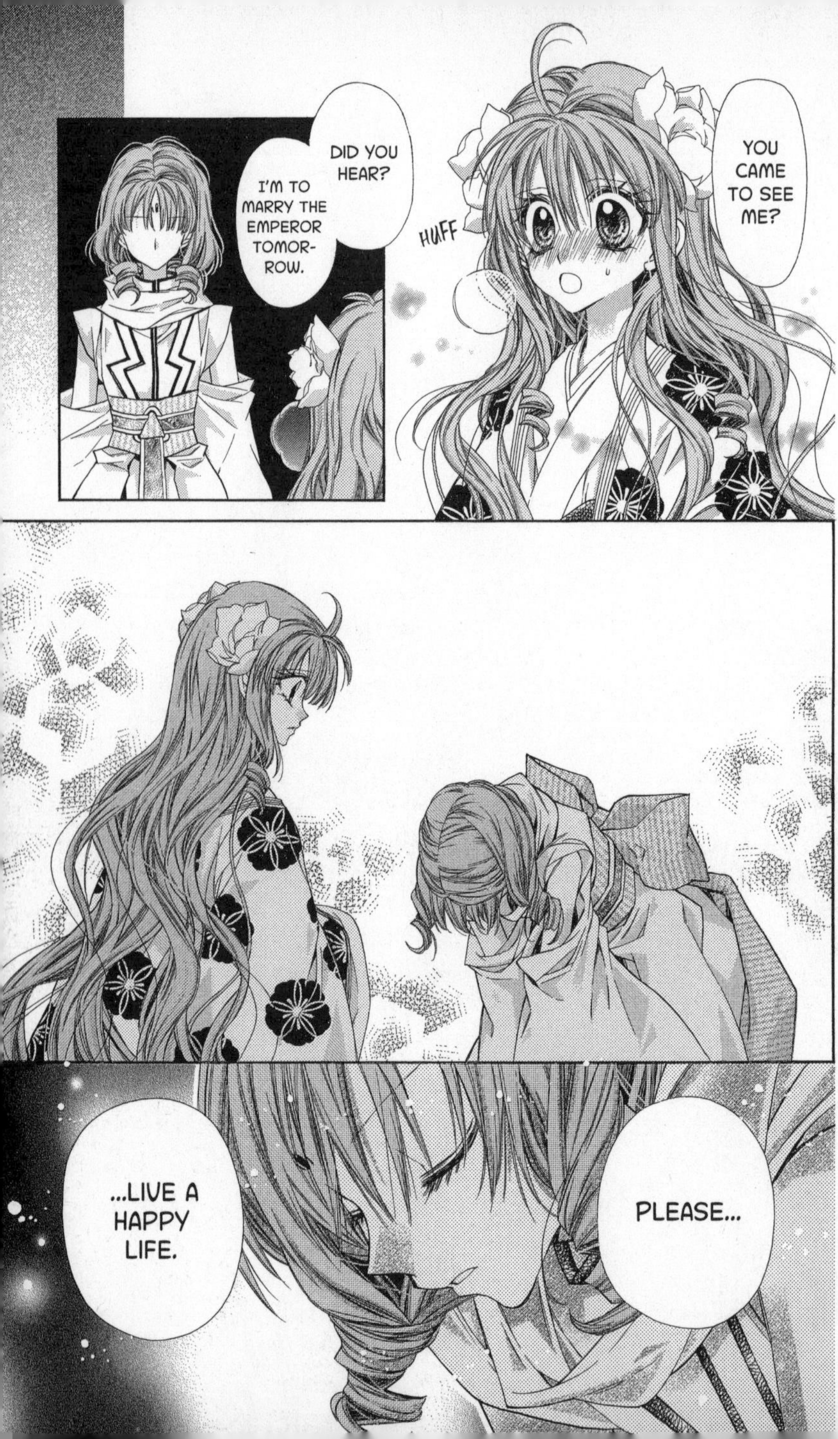
YOU CAME TO SEE ME?
HUFF
DID YOU HEAR?
I'M TO MARRY THE EMPEROR TOMOR-ROW.
PLEASE...
...LIVE A HAPPY LIFE.

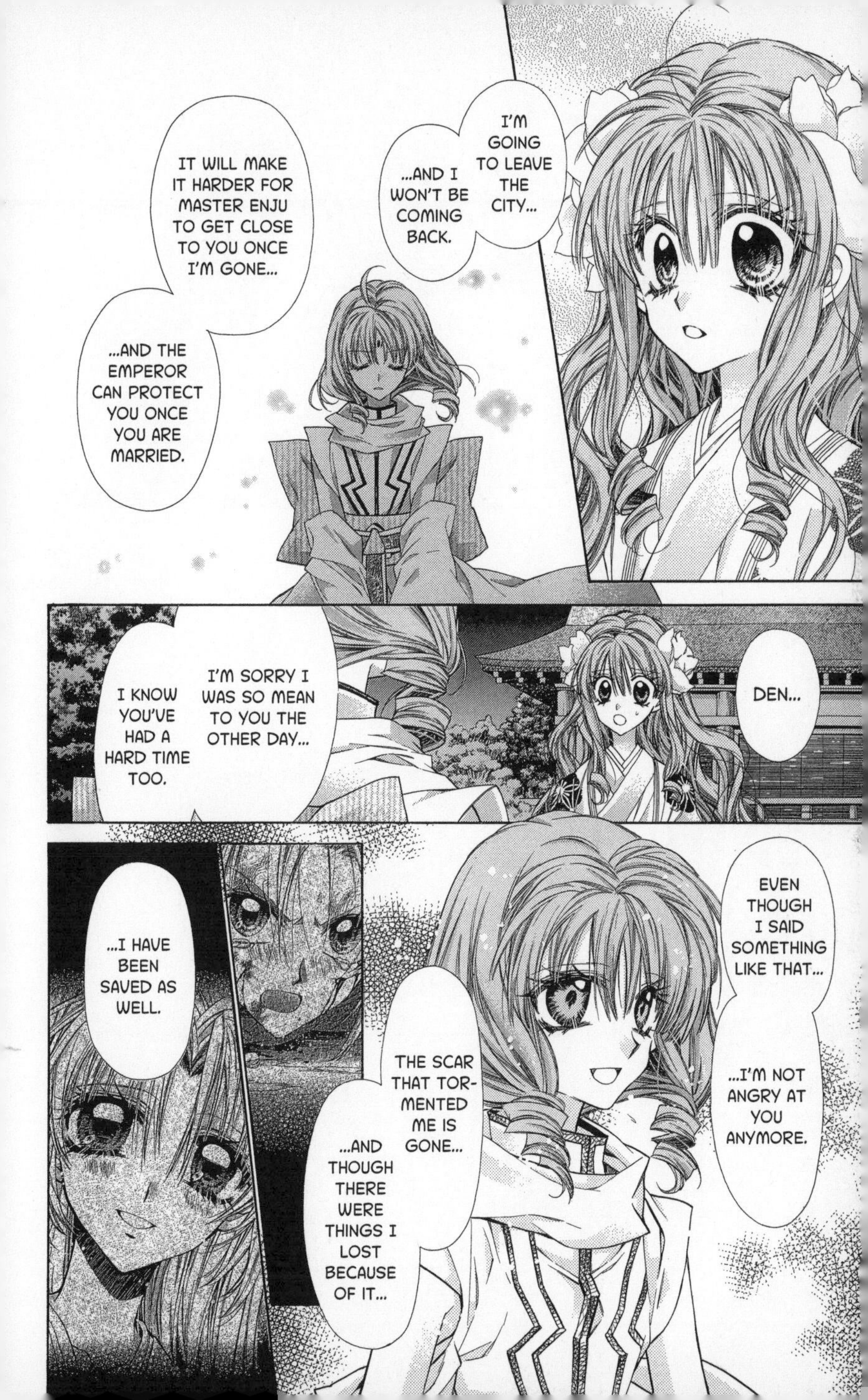
I'M GOING TO LEAVE THE CITY...
...AND I WON'T BE COMING BACK.
IT WILL MAKE IT HARDER FOR MASTER ENJU TO GET CLOSE TO YOU ONCE I'M GONE...
...AND THE EMPEROR CAN PROTECT YOU ONCE YOU ARE MARRIED.
DEN...
I'M SORRY I WAS SO MEAN TO YOU THE OTHER DAY...
I KNOW YOU'VE HAD A HARD TIME TOO.
EVEN THOUGH I SAID SOMETHING LIKE THAT...
...I'M NOT ANGRY AT YOU ANYMORE.
THE SCAR THAT TOR-MENTED ME IS GONE...
...AND THOUGH THERE WERE THINGS I LOST BECAUSE OF IT...
...I HAVE BEEN SAVED AS WELL.

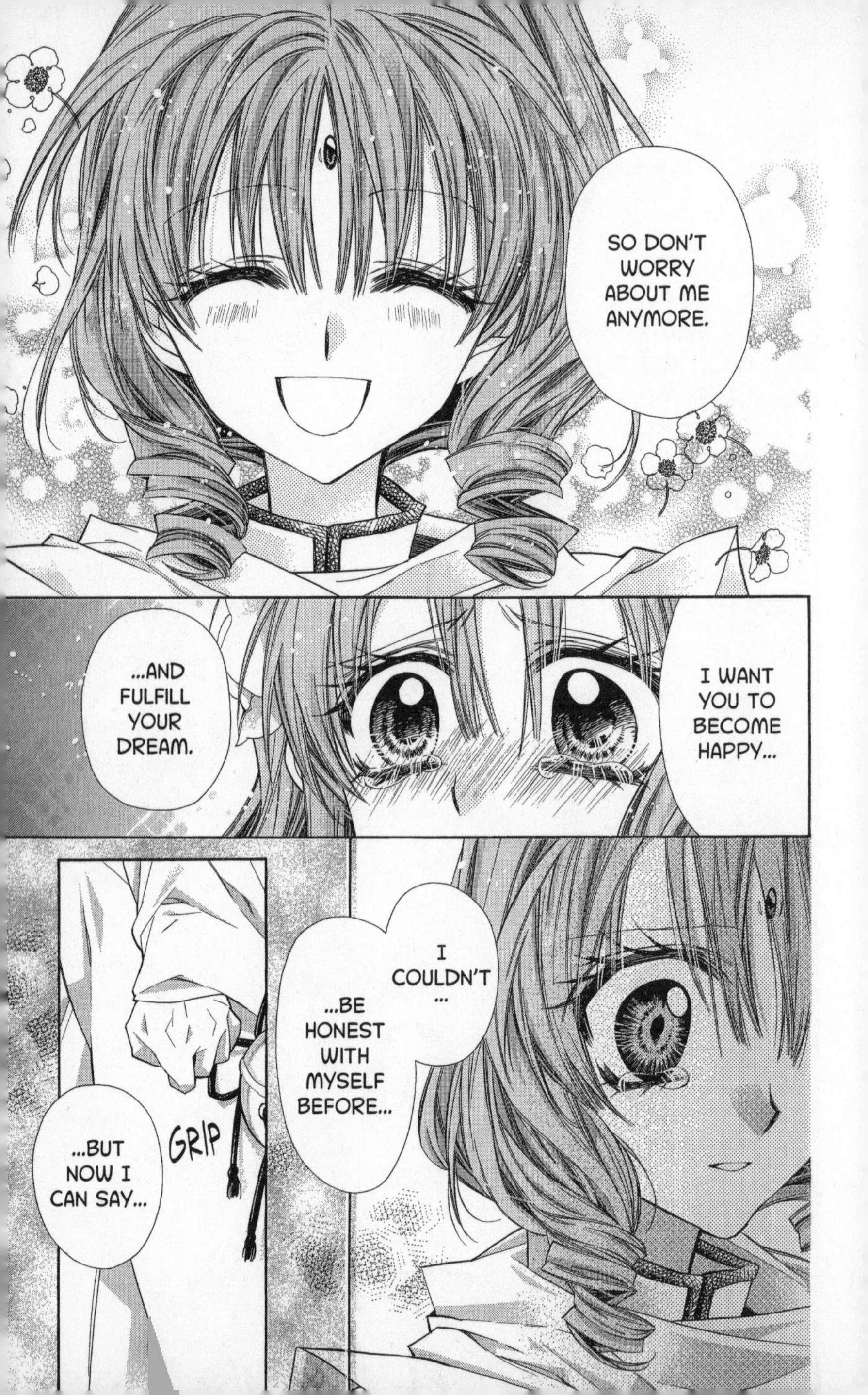
SO DON'T WORRY ABOUT ME ANYMORE.
I WANT YOU TO BECOME HAPPY...
...AND FULFILL YOUR DREAM.
I COULDN'T ...
...BE HONEST WITH MYSELF BEFORE...
GRIP
...BUT NOW I CAN SAY...

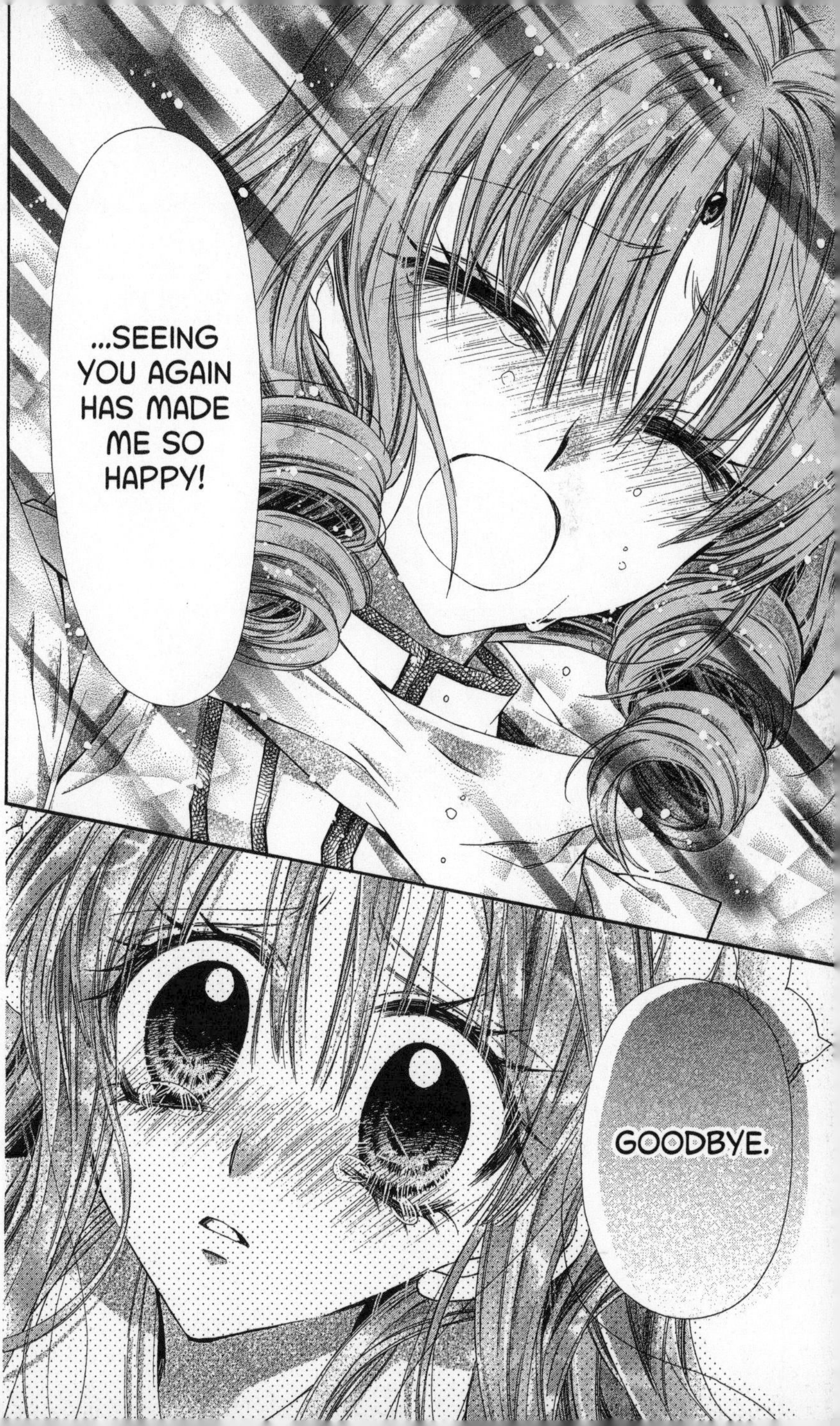
...SEEING YOU AGAIN HAS MADE ME SO HAPPY!
GOODBYE.

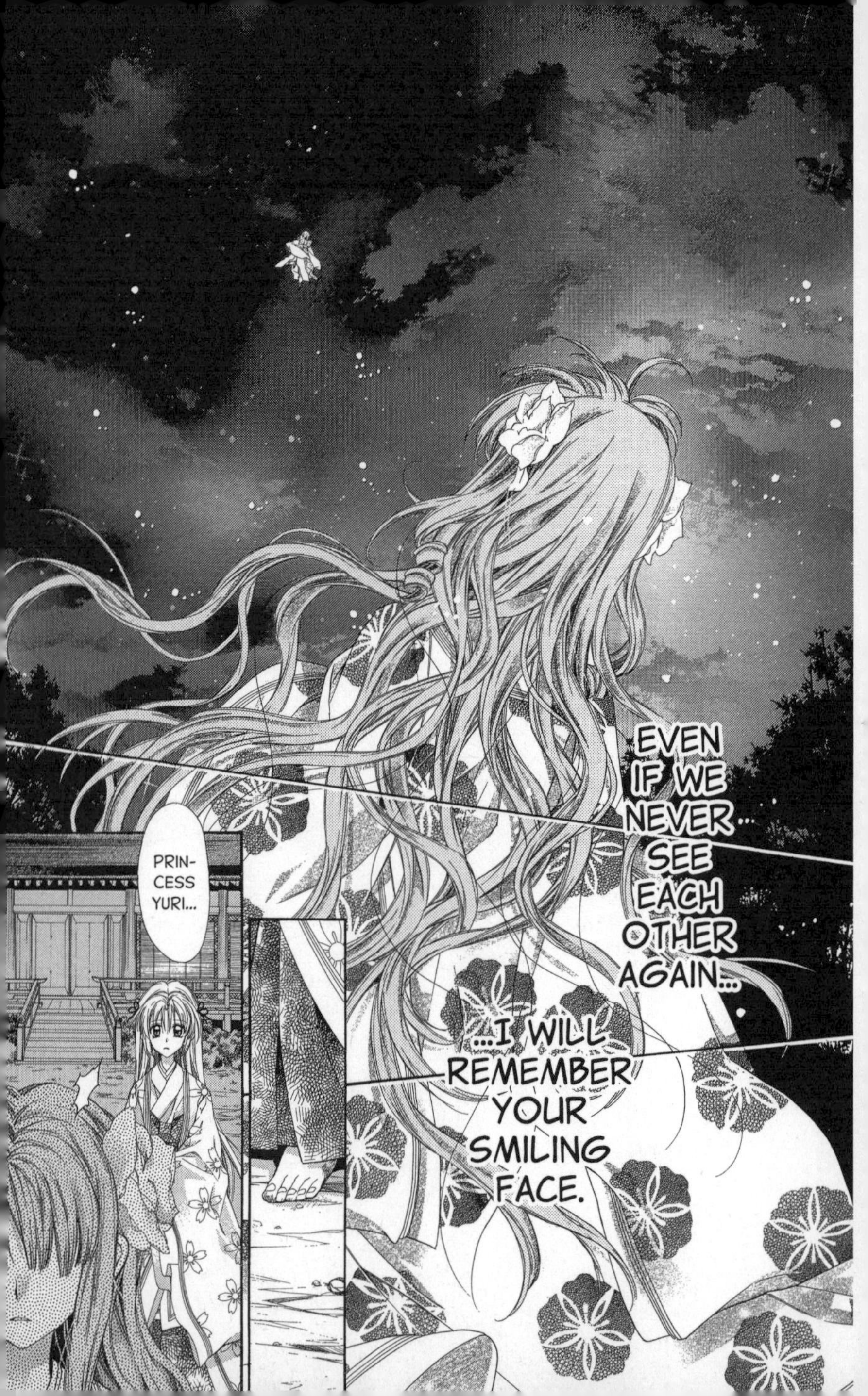
EVEN IF WE NEVER SEE EACH OTHER AGAIN...
...I WILL REMEMBER YOUR SMILING FACE.
PRIN-CESS YURI...

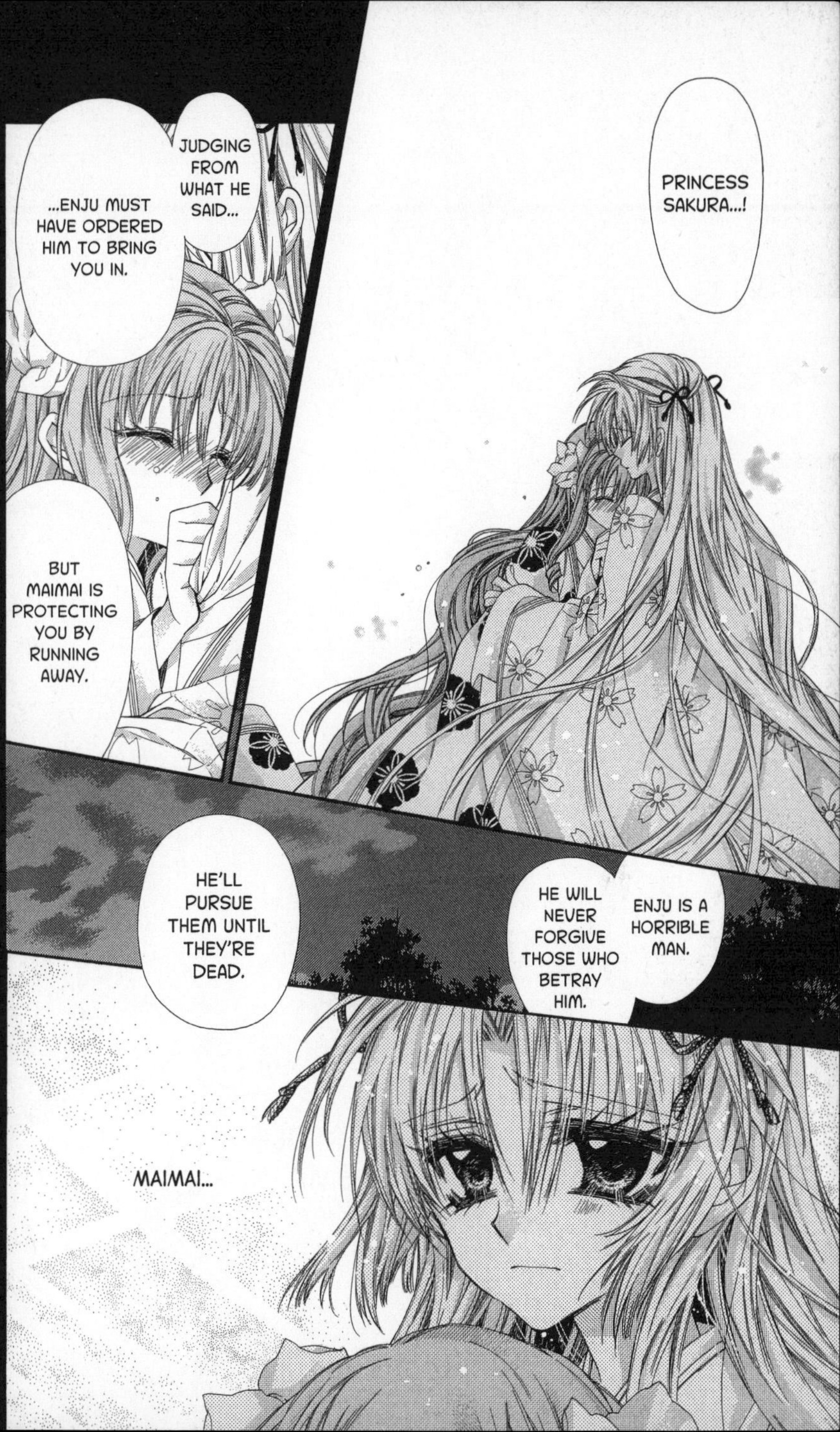
PRINCESS SAKURA...!
JUDGING FROM WHAT HE SAID...
...ENJU MUST HAVE ORDERED HIM TO BRING YOU IN.
BUT MAIMAI IS PROTECTING YOU BY RUNNING AWAY.
ENJU IS A HORRIBLE MAN.
HE WILL NEVER FORGIVE THOSE WHO BETRAY HIM.
HE'LL PURSUE THEM UNTIL THEY'RE DEAD.
MAIMAI...

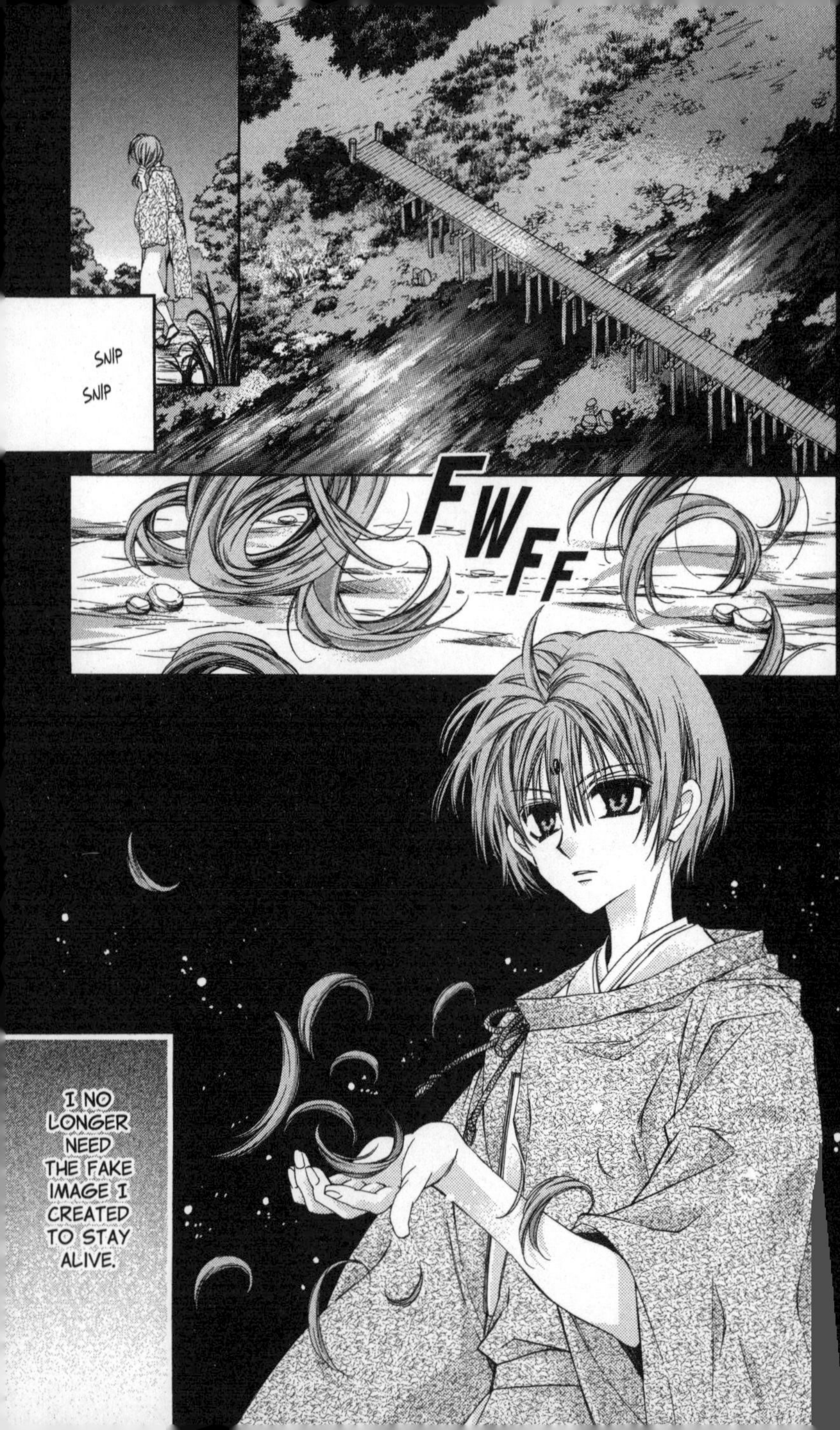
SNIP
SNIP
FWFF
I NO LONGER NEED THE FAKE IMAGE I CREATED TO STAY ALIVE.

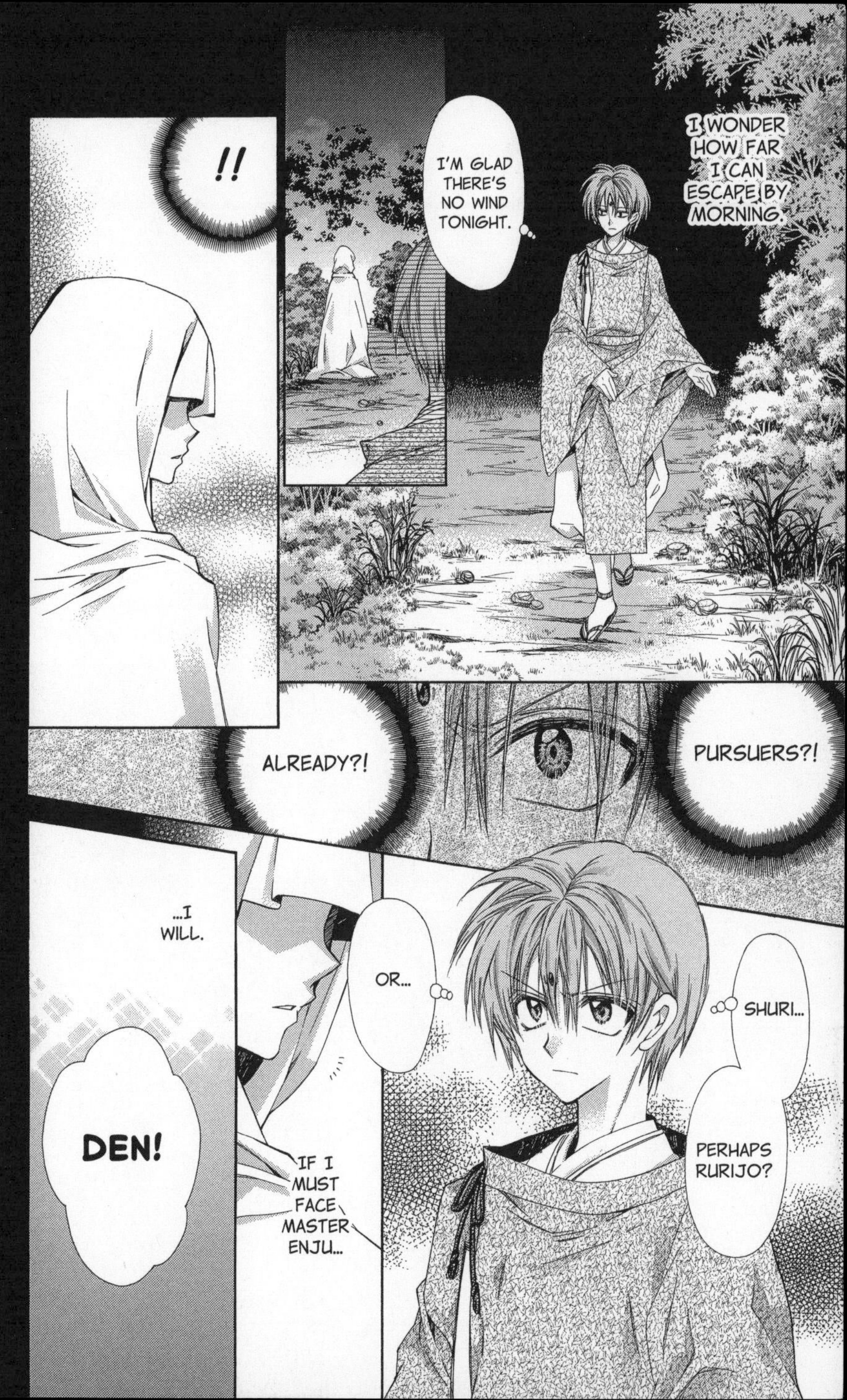
I WONDER HOW FAR I CAN ESCAPE BY MORNING.
I'M GLAD THERE'S NO WIND TONIGHT.
!!
PURSUERS?!
ALREADY?!
SHURI...
PERHAPS RURIJO?
OR...
IF I MUST FACE MASTER ENJU...
...I WILL.
DEN!

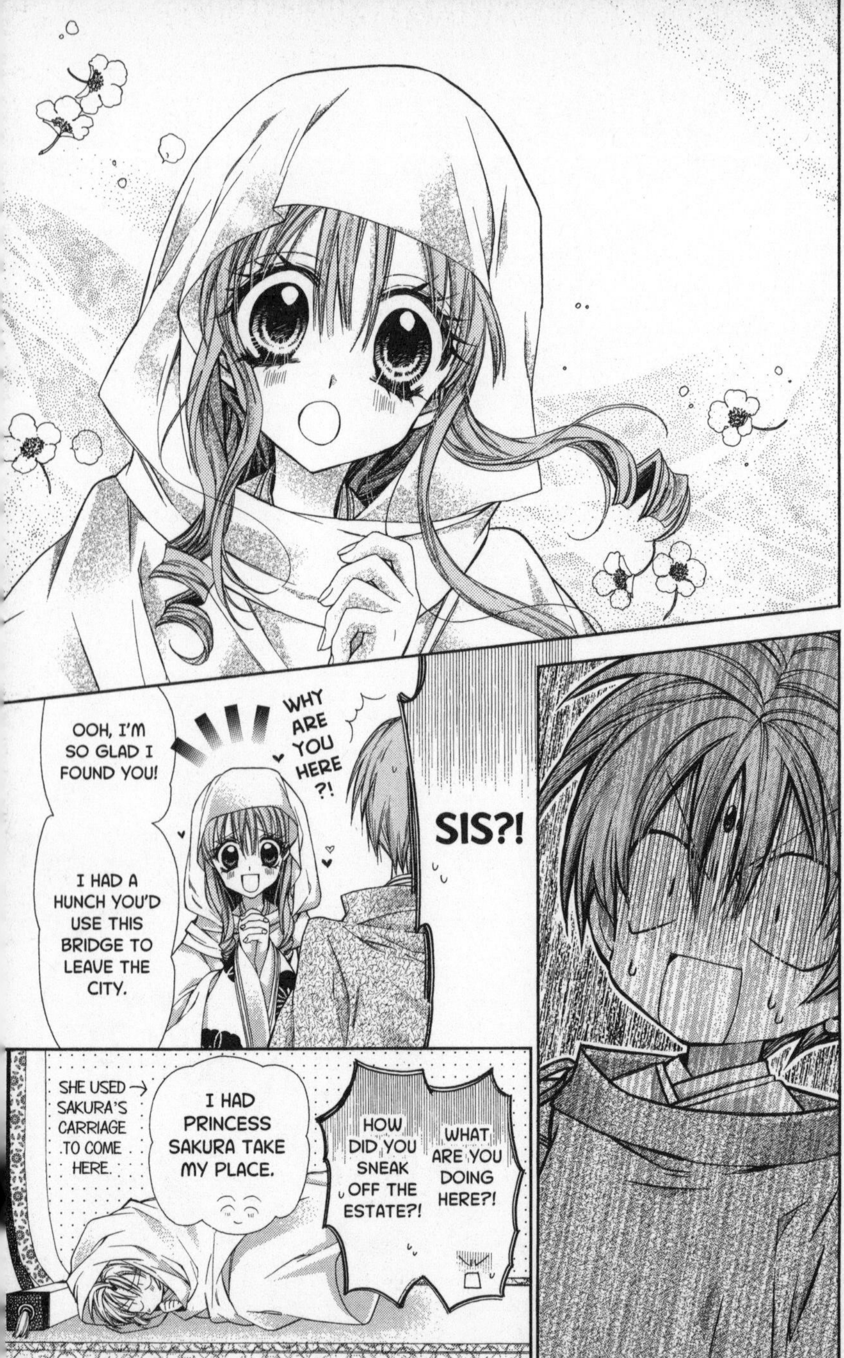
SIS?!
WHY ARE YOU HERE?!
OOH, I'M SO GLAD I FOUND YOU!
I HAD A HUNCH YOU'D USE THIS BRIDGE TO LEAVE THE CITY.
WHAT ARE YOU DOING HERE?!
HOW DID YOU SNEAK OFF THE ESTATE?!
I HAD PRINCESS SAKURA TAKE MY PLACE.
SHE USED SAKURA'S CARRIAGE TO COME HERE.
PRETENDING TO BE ASLEEP

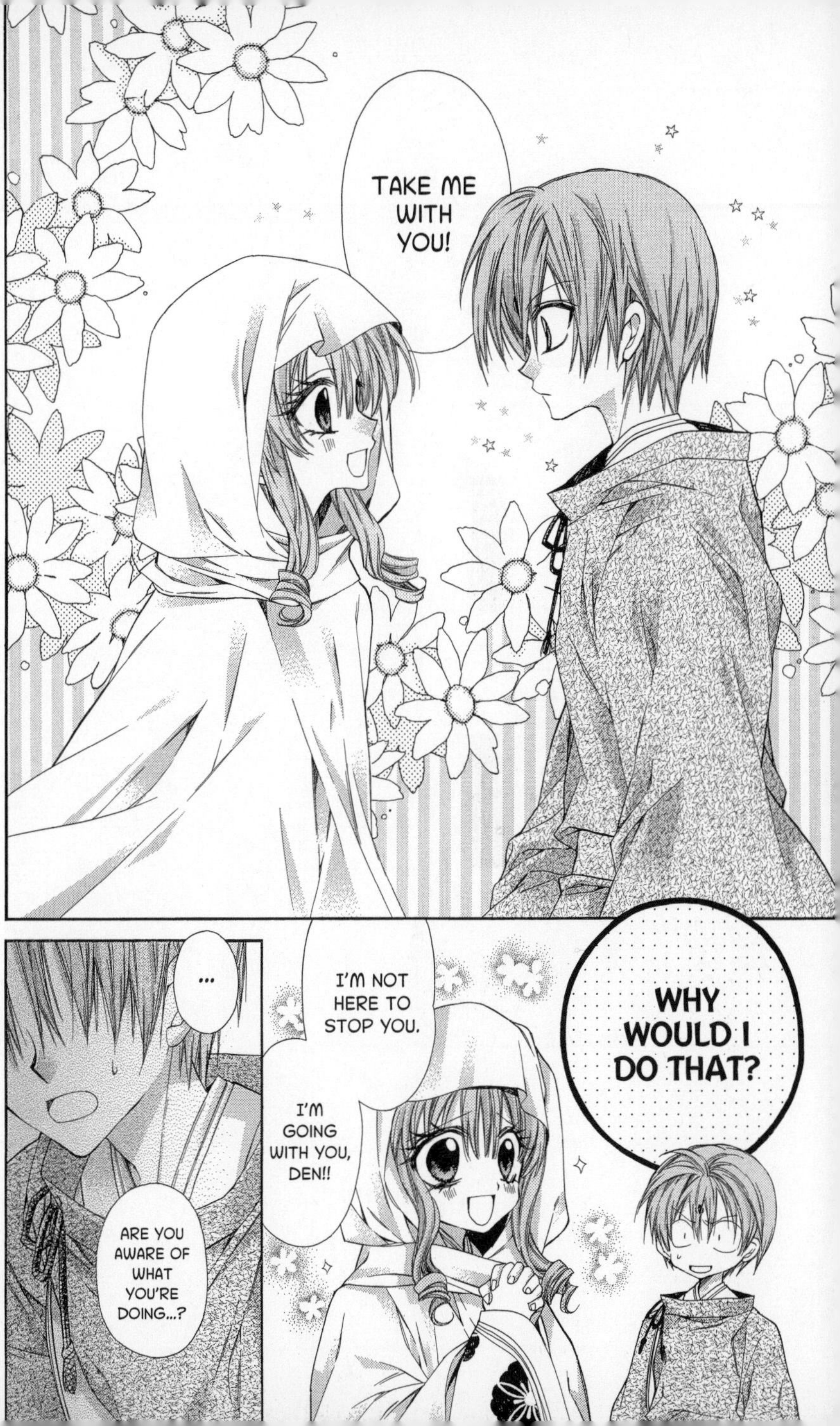
TAKE ME WITH YOU!
WHY WOULD I DO THAT?
I'M NOT HERE TO STOP YOU.
I'M GOING WITH YOU, DEN!!
...
ARE YOU AWARE OF WHAT YOU'RE DOING...?

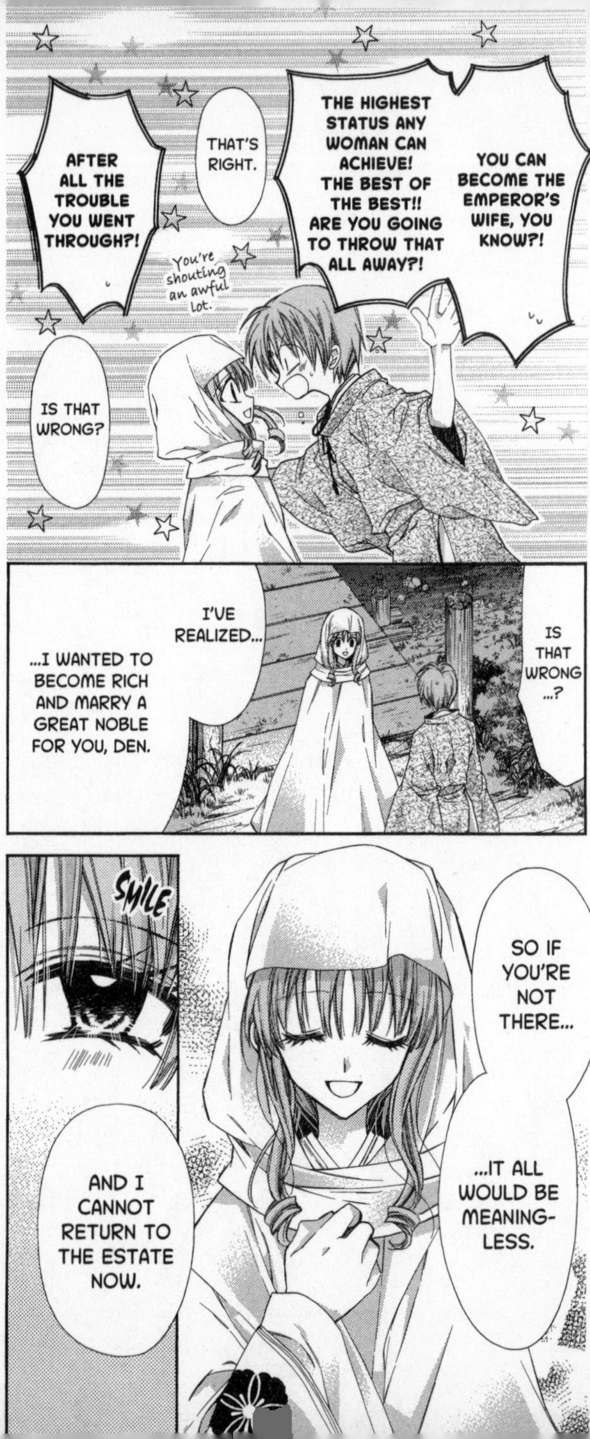
YOU CAN BECOME THE EMPEROR'S WIFE, YOU KNOW?!
THE HIGHEST STATUS ANY WOMAN CAN ACHIEVE! THE BEST OF THE BEST!! ARE YOU GOING TO THROW THAT ALL AWAY?!
THAT'S RIGHT.
AFTER ALL THE TROUBLE YOU WENT THROUGH?!
You're shouting an awful lot.
IS THAT WRONG?
IS THAT WRONG ...?
I'VE REALIZED...
...I WANTED TO BECOME RICH AND MARRY A GREAT NOBLE FOR YOU, DEN.
SO IF YOU'RE NOT THERE...
...IT ALL WOULD BE MEANING-LESS.
AND I CANNOT RETURN TO THE ESTATE NOW.
SMILE

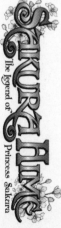

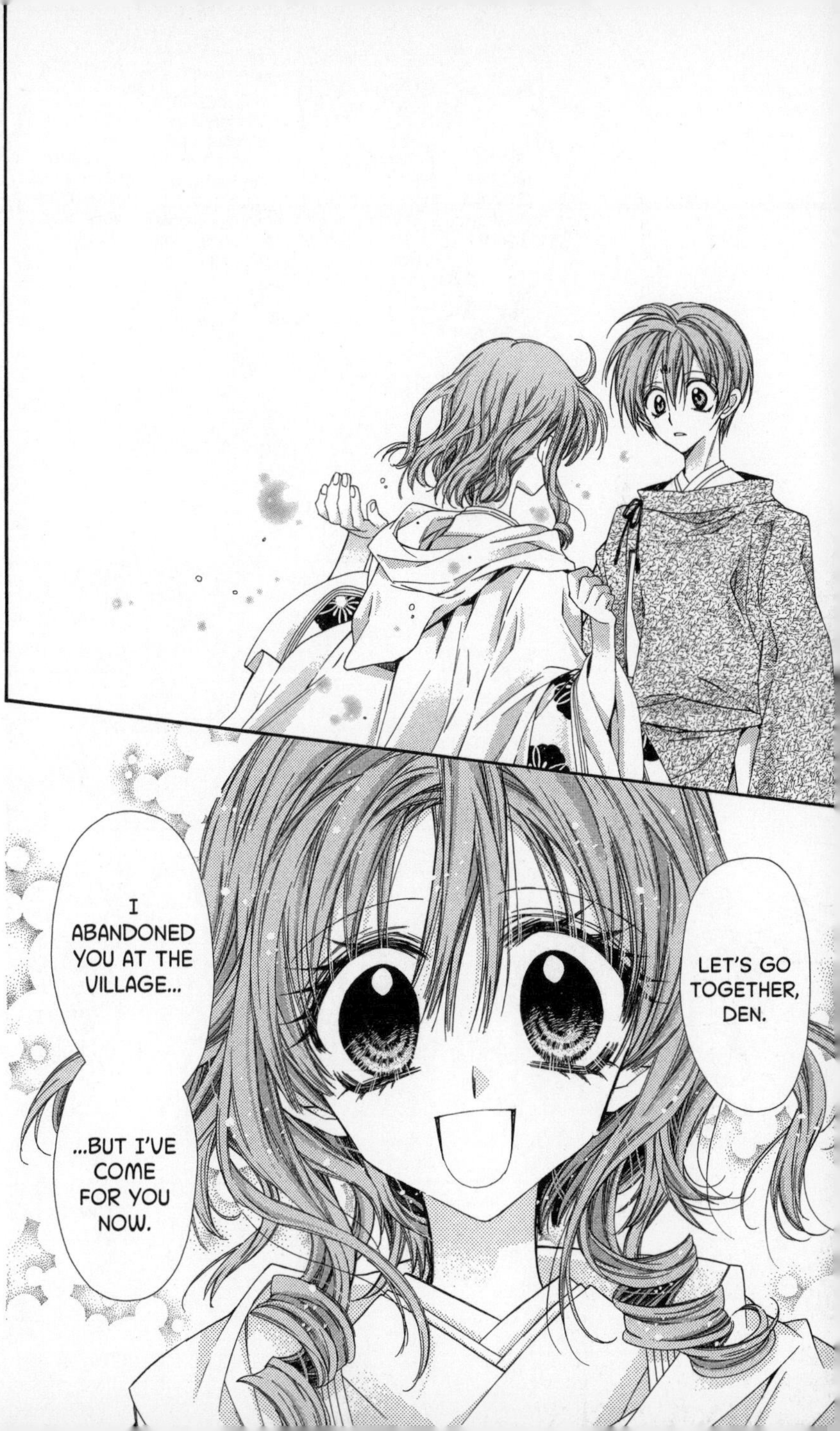
LET'S GO TOGETHER, DEN.
I ABANDONED YOU AT THE VILLAGE...
...BUT I'VE COME FOR YOU NOW.

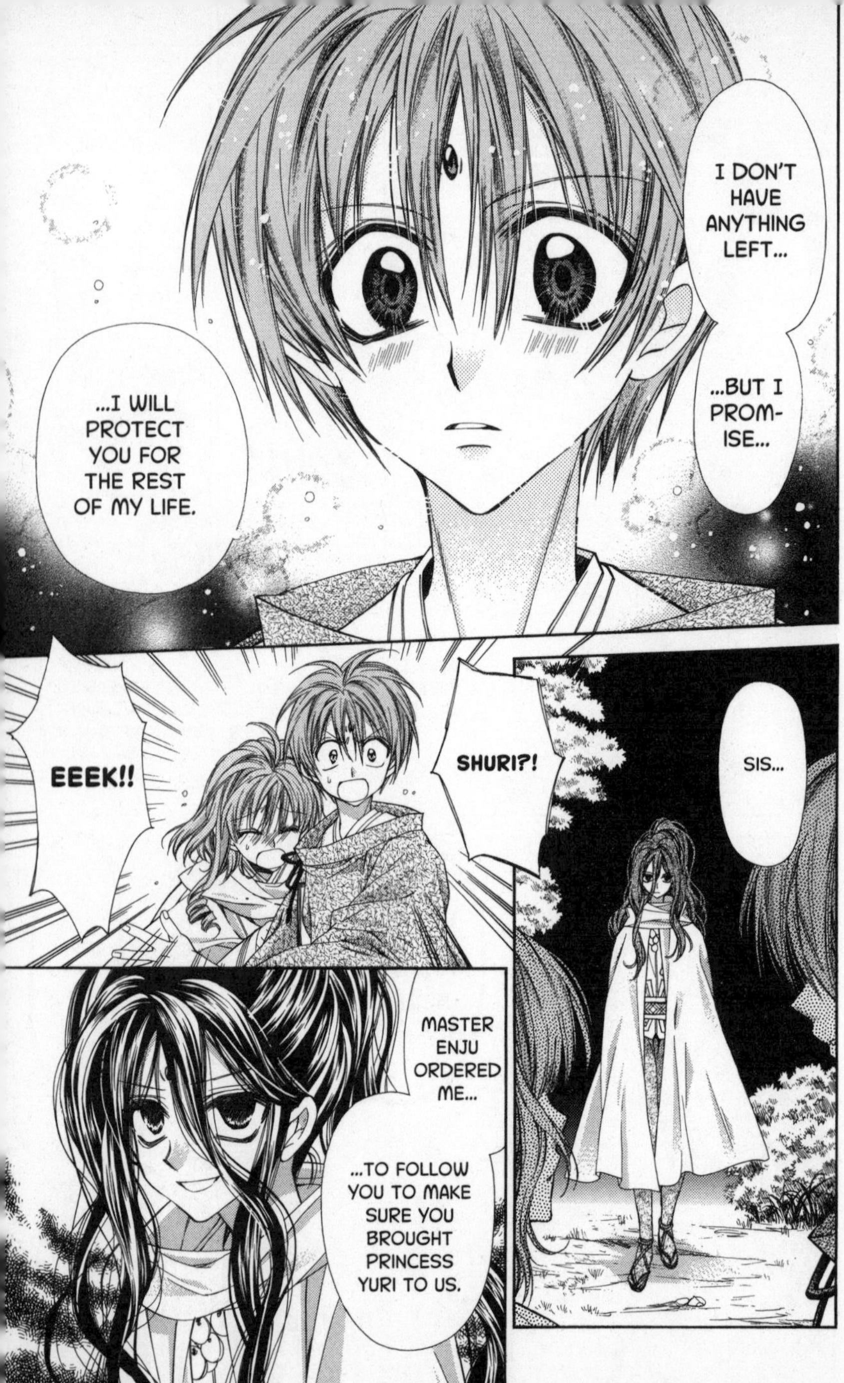
I DON'T HAVE ANYTHING LEFT...
...BUT I PROMISE...
...I WILL PROTECT YOU FOR THE REST OF MY LIFE.
SIS...
SHURI?!
EEEK!!
MASTER ENJU ORDERED ME...
...TO FOLLOW YOU TO MAKE SURE YOU BROUGHT PRINCESS YURI TO US.

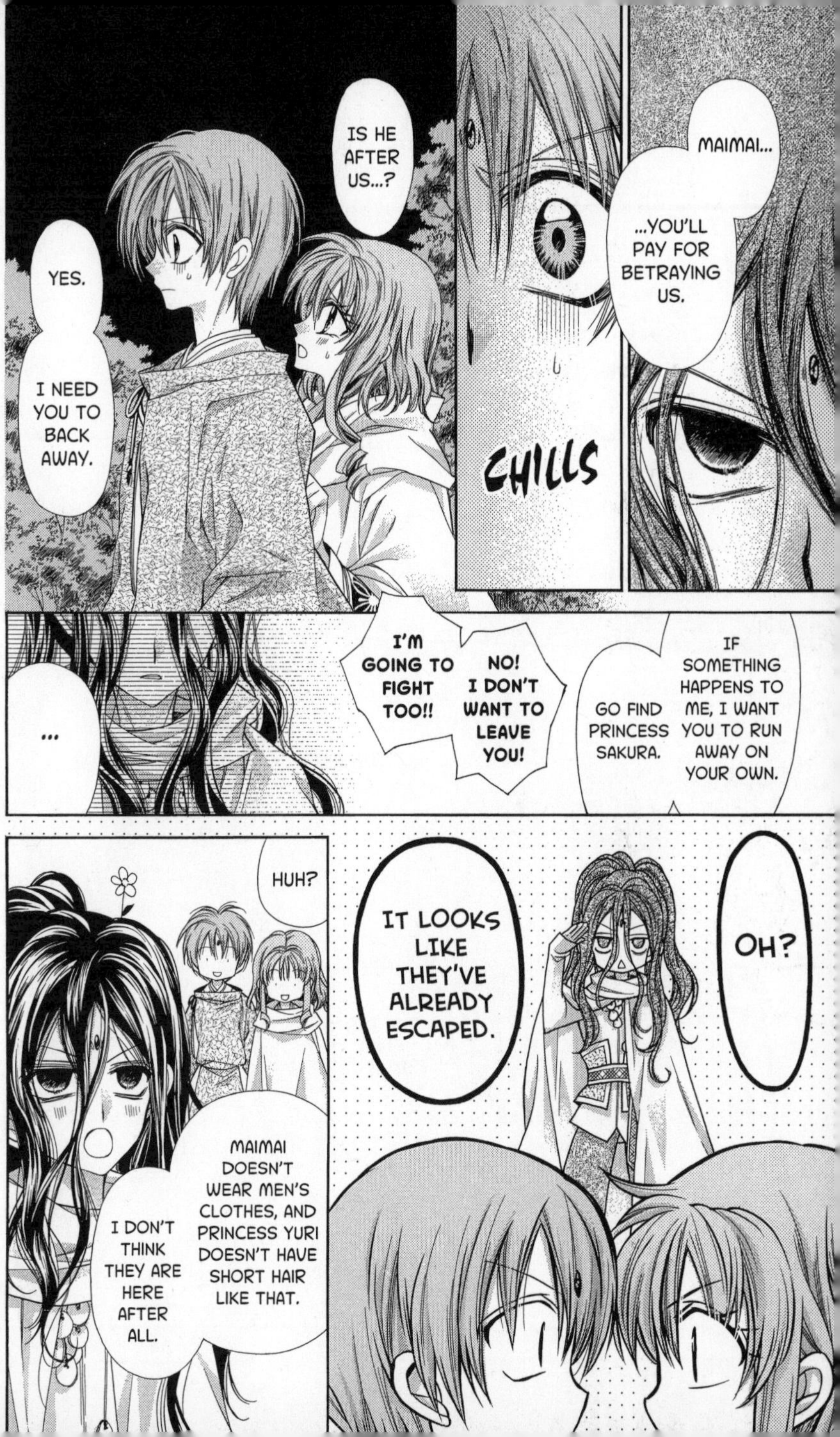
MAIMAI...
...YOU'LL PAY FOR BETRAYING US.
CHILLS
IS HE AFTER US...?
YES.
I NEED YOU TO BACK AWAY.
IF SOMETHING HAPPENS TO ME, I WANT YOU TO RUN AWAY ON YOUR OWN.
GO FIND PRINCESS SAKURA.
NO! I DON'T WANT TO LEAVE YOU!
I'M GOING TO FIGHT TOO!!
...
OH?
IT LOOKS LIKE THEY'VE ALREADY ESCAPED.
HUH?
MAIMAI DOESN'T WEAR MEN'S CLOTHES, AND PRINCESS YURI DOESN'T HAVE SHORT HAIR LIKE THAT.
I DON'T THINK THEY ARE HERE AFTER ALL.

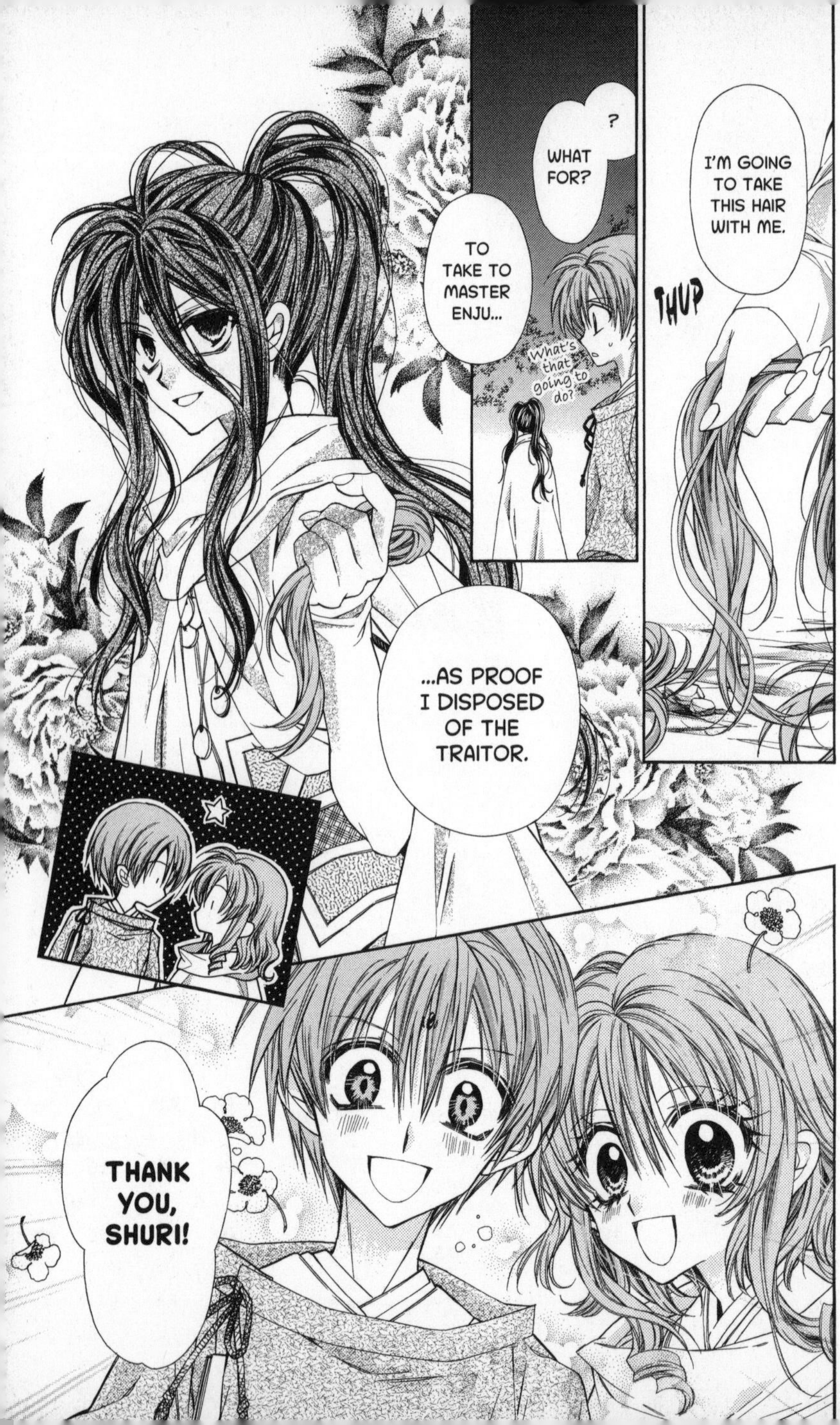
I'M GOING TO TAKE THIS HAIR WITH ME.
THUP
? WHAT FOR?
What's that going to do?
TO TAKE TO MASTER ENJU...
...AS PROOF I DISPOSED OF THE TRAITOR.
THANK YOU, SHURI!

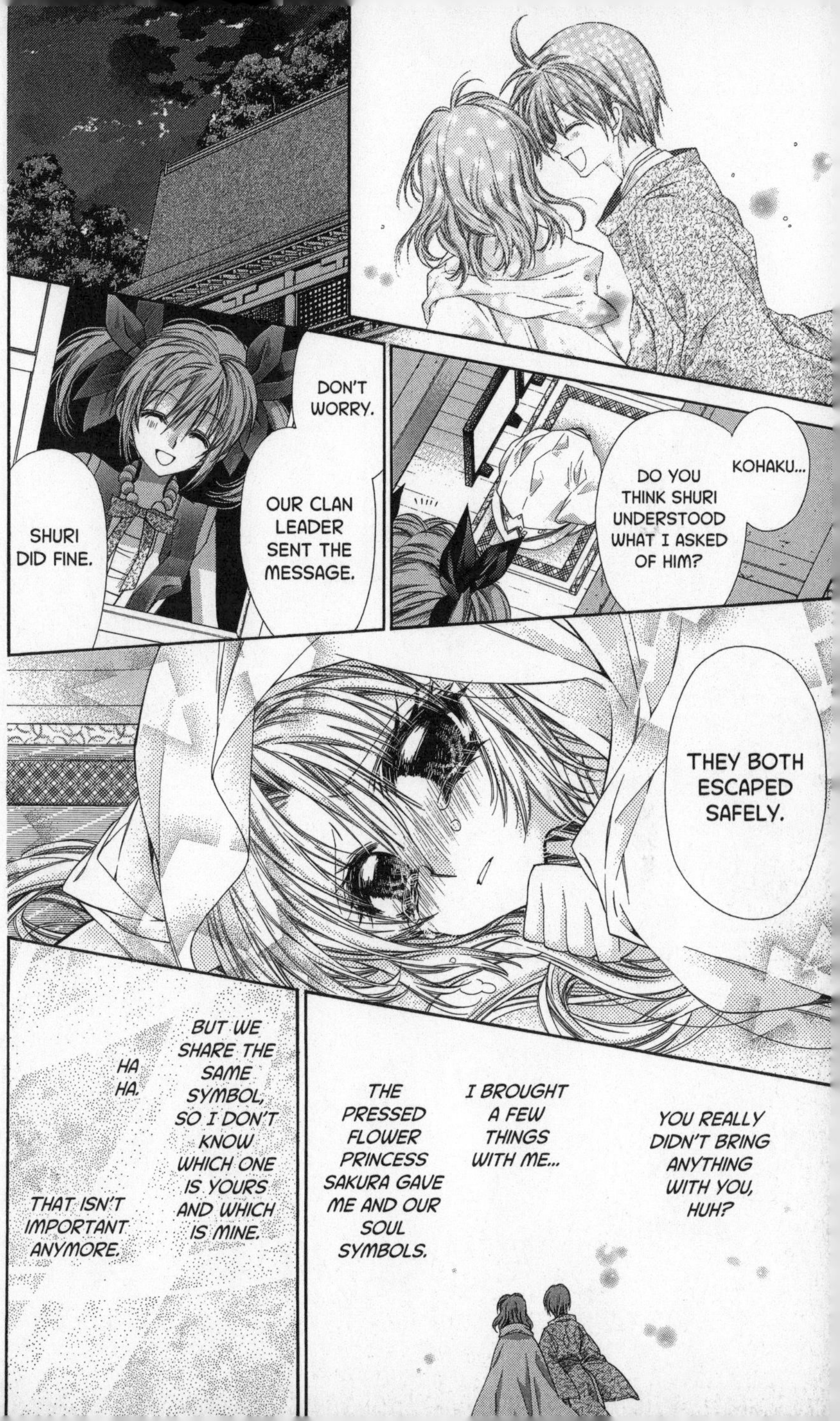
KOHAKU...
DO YOU THINK SHURI UNDERSTOOD WHAT I ASKED OF HIM?
DON'T WORRY.
OUR CLAN LEADER SENT THE MESSAGE.
SHURI DID FINE.
THEY BOTH ESCAPED SAFELY.
YOU REALLY DIDN'T BRING ANYTHING WITH YOU, HUH?
I BROUGHT A FEW THINGS WITH ME...
THE PRESSED FLOWER PRINCESS SAKURA GAVE ME AND OUR SOUL SYMBOLS.
BUT WE SHARE THE SAME SYMBOL, SO I DON'T KNOW WHICH ONE IS YOURS AND WHICH IS MINE.
HA HA.
THAT ISN'T IMPORTANT ANYMORE.

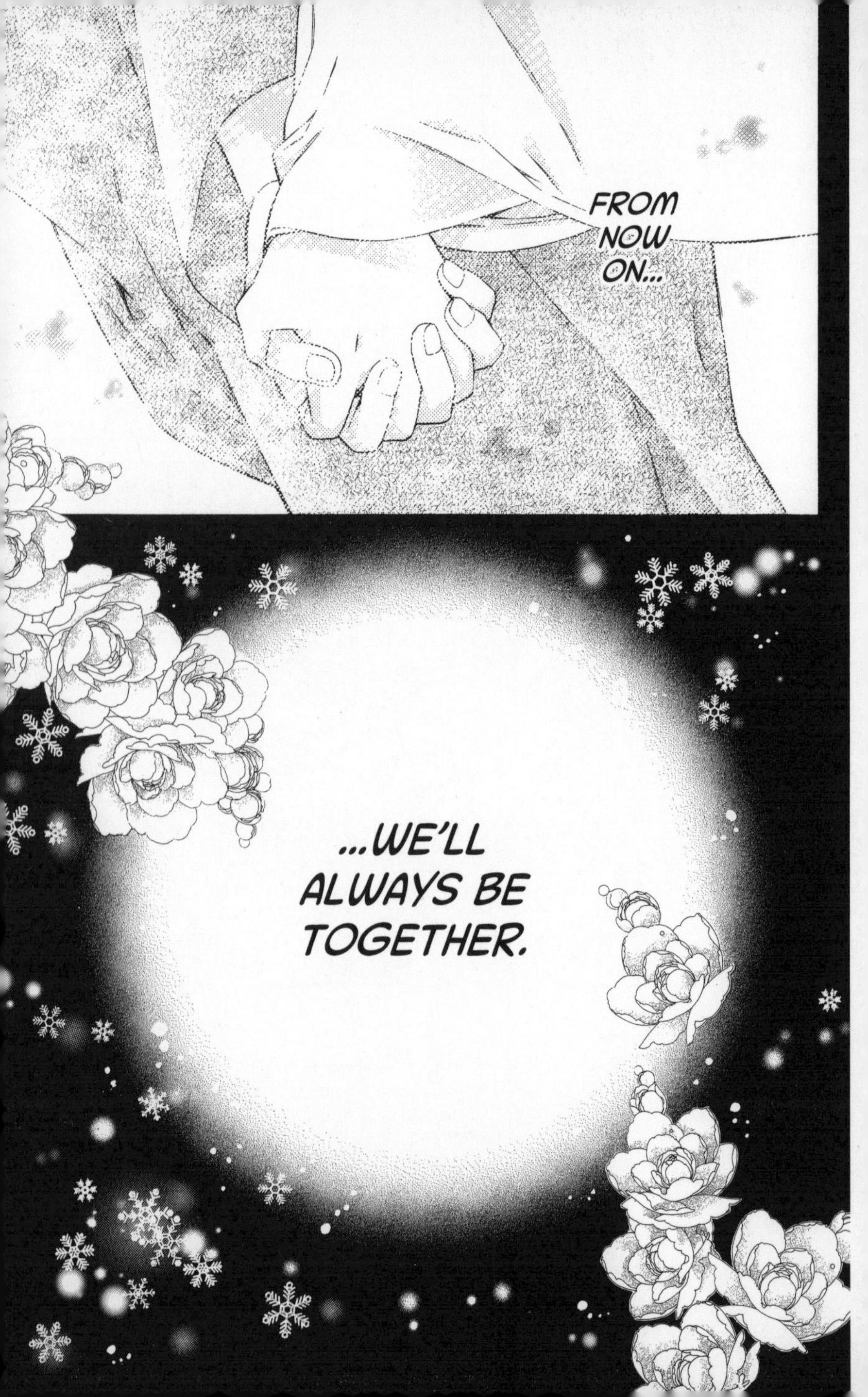
FROM NOW ON...
...WE'LL ALWAYS BE TOGETHER.

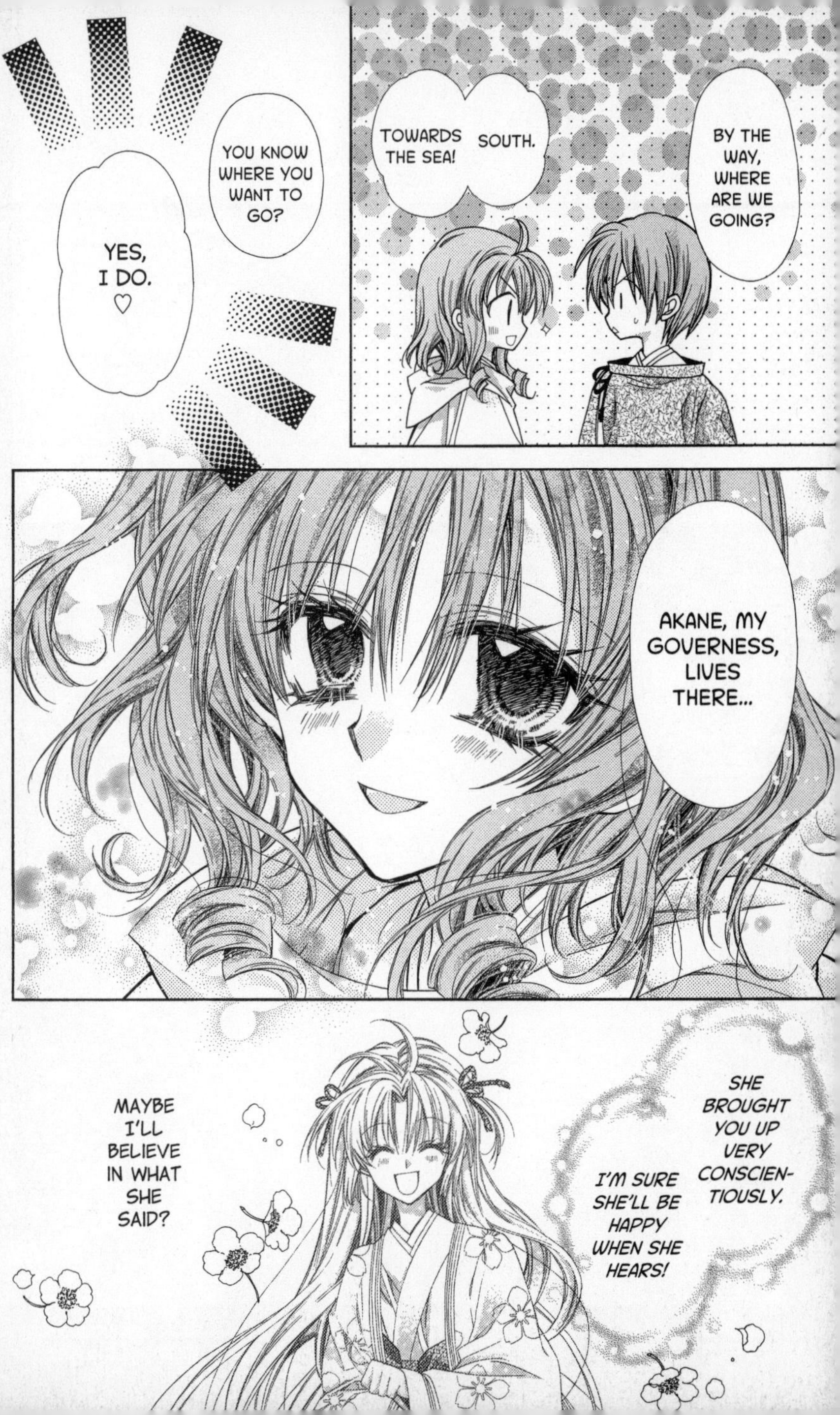
BY THE WAY, WHERE ARE WE GOING?
SOUTH.
TOWARDS THE SEA!
YOU KNOW WHERE YOU WANT TO GO?
YES, I DO. ♡
AKANE, MY GOVERNESS, LIVES THERE...
SHE BROUGHT YOU UP VERY CONSCIEN-TIOUSLY.
I'M SURE SHE'LL BE HAPPY WHEN SHE HEARS!
MAYBE I'LL BELIEVE IN WHAT SHE SAID?

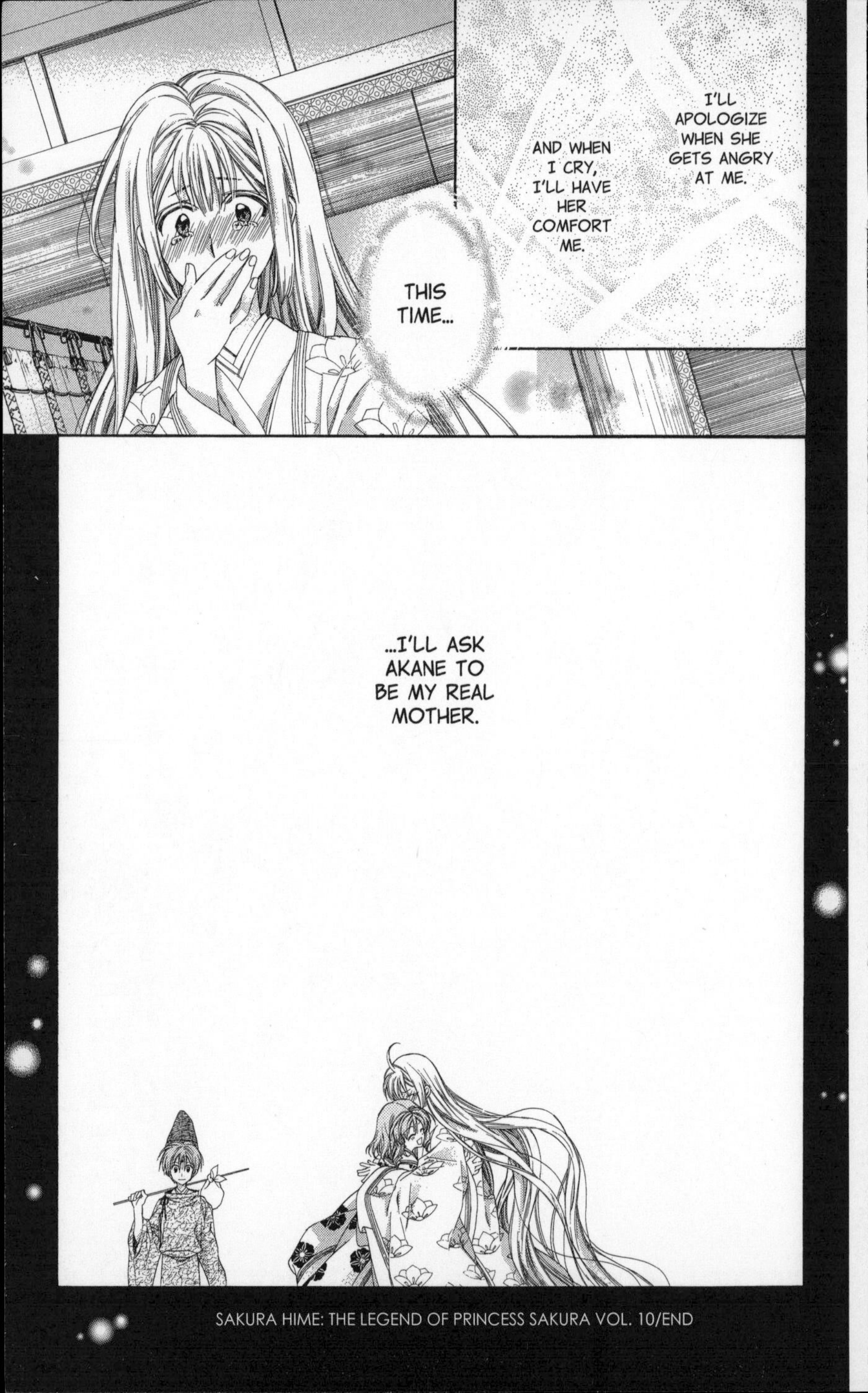
I'LL APOLOGIZE WHEN SHE GETS ANGRY AT ME.
AND WHEN I CRY, I'LL HAVE HER COMFORT ME.
THIS TIME...
...I'LL ASK AKANE TO BE MY REAL MOTHER.

SAKURA HIME: THE LEGEND OF PRINCESS SAKURA VOL. 10/END

Sakura Hime
The Legend of Princess Sakura

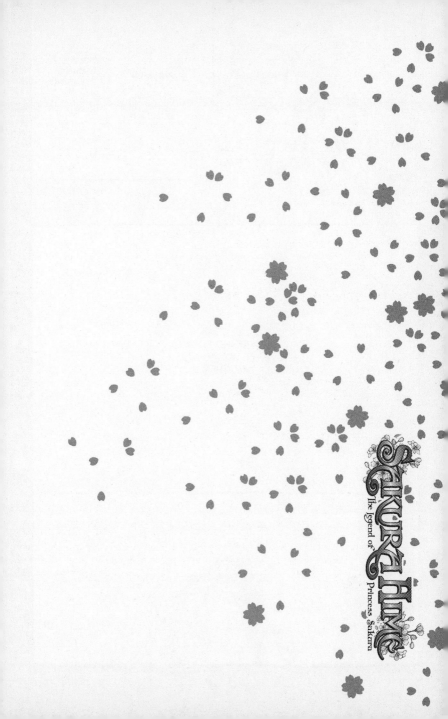

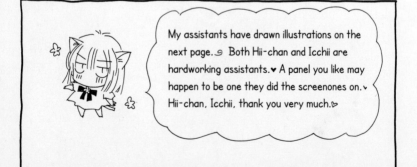

My assistants have drawn illustrations on the next page. ✈ Both Hii-chan and Icchii are hardworking assistants. ♥ A panel you like may happen to be one they did the screenones on. ✓ Hii-chan, Icchii, thank you very much. ✈

Congratulations on the publication of volume 10.

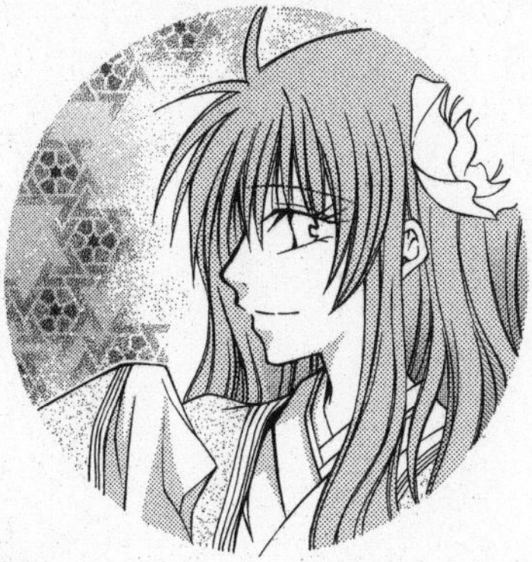

Nice to meet you. I'm the assistant Icchi. I can't wait to see how *Sakura Hime* continues because the series is filled with so many surprises. I'm constantly thinking, "This is going to happen next?!" I really enjoy this series.

Ichi ("Icchii") 2011

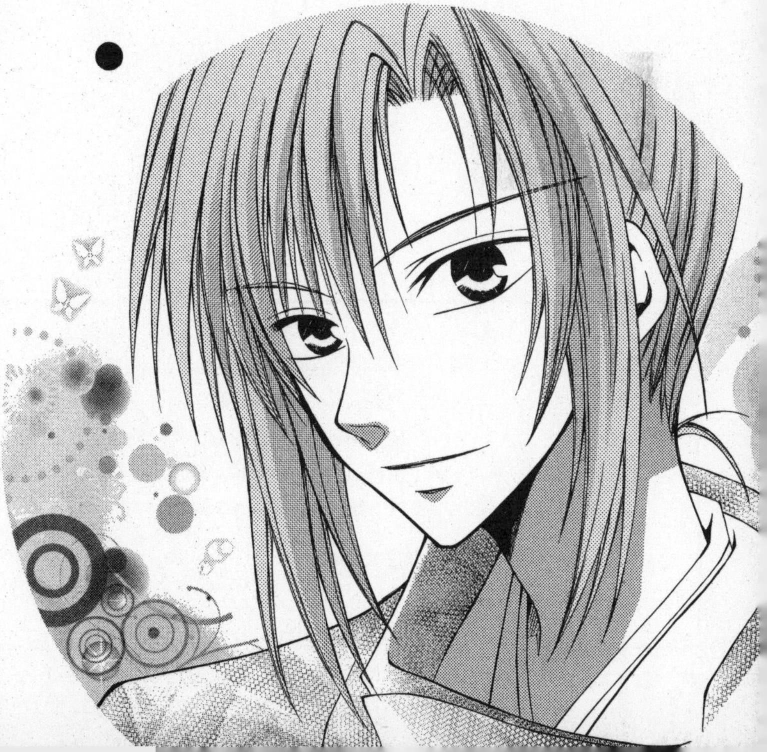

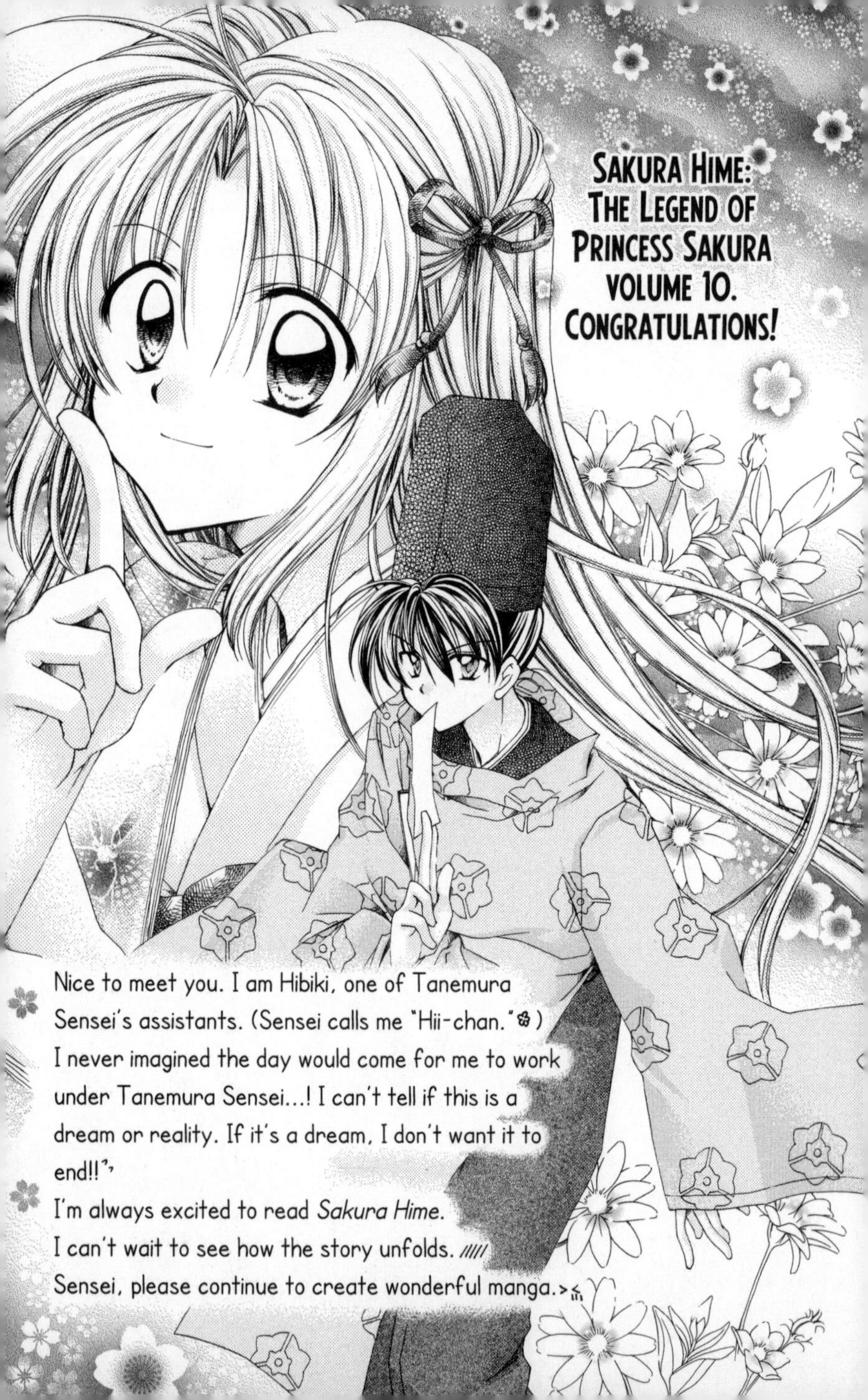
SAKURA HIME: THE LEGEND OF PRINCESS SAKURA VOLUME 10. CONGRATULATIONS!
Nice to meet you. I am Hibiki, one of Tanemura Sensei's assistants. (Sensei calls me "Hii-chan.") I never imagined the day would come for me to work under Tanemura Sensei...! I can't tell if this is a dream or reality. If it's a dream, I don't want it to end!!
I'm always excited to read *Sakura Hime*.
I can't wait to see how the story unfolds. //////
Sensei, please continue to create wonderful manga. >_<

ARINA TANEMURA

I often draw colored illustrations of Rurijo and Hayate because I think they are visually appealing. That goes for Princess Yuri and Maimai too. I draw them a lot because they brighten up the page. Here you will see a lot of interaction between the friends of Princess Sakura and those who follow Enju, but the various incidents involving Sakura will begin to get more chaotic in the next volume. I hope you will continue to watch over the characters.

Arina Tanemura began her manga career in 1996 when her short stories debuted in *Ribon* magazine. She gained fame with the 1997 publication of *I•O•N*, and ever since her debut Tanemura has been a major force in shojo manga with popular series *Kamikaze Kaito Jeanne*, *Time Stranger Kyoko*, *Full Moon*, and *The Gentlemen's Alliance†*. Both *Kamikaze Kaito Jeanne* and *Full Moon* have been adapted into animated TV series.